Curse

of

Kirsan

Adventures in the Chess Underworld

Sarah Hurst

Foreword by
Ken Whyld

2002
Russell Enterprises, Inc.
Milford, CT USA

Curse of Kirsan

ISBN: 1-888690-15-1

Published by:
Russell Enterprises, Inc.
P.O. Box 30
Milford, CT 06460 USA

http://www.chesscafe.com
hwr@chesscafe.com

Cover design by Pamela Terry, Opus 1 Design

Printed in the United States of America

Table of Contents

*This book is dedicated to the memory
of Larisa Yudina, a fearless journalist
who was murdered in the land of chess.*

Foreword

In this book two of Sarah Hurst's shining qualities are displayed. The first is her ability to empathise with those she interviews, to find what makes them tick, and to coax them into revealing themselves. As a result we have here pen-pictures of some of the movers and shakers of the chess world, and a sprinkling of its eccentrics. All is extracted in a subtle but persistent manner, asking the questions that some dare not, or cannot. Despite the warts-and-all approach, she treats her subjects sympathetically. Well, all but one of them.

And that brings us to the second facet of Sarah: her determination to get at the truth, combined with a refusal to back down. There is a proverb to the effect that after a war many heroes emerge. It could also be said that after a villain's fall many accusers emerge. We need only think of British media tycoon Robert Maxwell. Despite being officially branded as unfit to run a public company he survived and prospered, facing few dissenting voices. He put money into our game and we all cheered when he took over the monthly magazine *CHESS*.

When Maxwell died and his villainy was exposed, everyone "always knew" that he was a crook. The few who had said so in his lifetime received no thanks. Sarah attacks one who, away from the chessboard, is the most powerful figure in our special world. The capo of FIDE has brought great wealth to our game, improving the life of many of its professionals. The facts about him that are quoted by Sarah can be verified from public sources. The inferences are plain, but we may be sure that the chess world will not thank her, even if later they will have "always known".

Meanwhile, the chess elite would prefer to be free from the knowledge that perhaps their money is tainted. What touches Sarah especially is the murder of a fellow journalist. An event that most of the chess world considers entirely irrelevant. Bitterness is restricted to a few pages: for the most part the tone is positive. We learn much that is unexpected, such as insights into politicians Janos Kadar and Che Guevara, and also how the prince of chess editors, Jimmy Adams, anticipated rap.

The lasting impression of Sarah is of a fearless and humorous person for whom no challenge is insurmountable.

Ken Whyld
Kirton Lindsey, 2002

Glossary

BCF - British Chess Federation.

Blitz - high-speed chess games, in which players have to make all their moves in a short time - usually a maximum of five minutes on each clock

Candidates matches - in the old-style FIDE World Championship cycles, this series of knockout matches determined who would challenge the world champion.

Elo rating - a four-digit rating system, devised by Professor Arpad Elo and upon which FIDE calculates the ratings of players of, or close to, international standard.

FIDE - Fédération Internationale des Echecs, the world chess governing body. It also organises world and continental championships for all age groups and awards titles and calculates ratings.

GM - grandmaster.

IM - international master (there are also WGM and WIM titles for women only, at a lower level than the gender-neutral GM and IM titles).

IM/GM norm - players achieving a sufficiently high score in an international tournament can obtain a norm for the IM or GM title. Three norms and the possession of a sufficiently high Elo rating, prescribed by FIDE, are usually required to obtain the title.

Interzonal - eliminator to decide the World Championship Candidates.

PCA - Professional Chess Association, the short-lived organisation set up by Garry Kasparov and Nigel Short to run their World Championship match in 1993 after they broke away from FIDE.

Rapidplay/quickplay - chess games with a short time limit, usually around 30 minutes for each player, to make all the moves.

Sacrifice - or "sac" - a deliberate surrender of a piece or pawn in order to obtain some form of advantage, e.g. initiative, material gain, positional superiority or a checkmate.

Simultaneous display - or "simul", an exhibition in which a strong player takes on a number of opponents simultaneously, passing from board to board in a circuit and making and receiving one move at a time.

USCF - United States Chess Federation.

Zonal - regional eliminators serving as qualifiers for the Interzonal tournament.

Introduction

Chess players can be found in nearly every country, yet the world of chess is small and rarely visited or understood by outsiders. I had the pleasure to interview dozens of grandmasters, including past and present world champions. Along with professionals, I also interviewed a number of amateur players. Many of them had intriguing life stories, from Kilkenny's garrulous poet and shoe-store owner Jim Hayes to Rasul Bagirov, a heart surgeon from Azerbaijan whose first posting was to the war in Nagorno-Karabakh, to Jack Moore of London, a nonagenarian aspiring novelist.

Unfortunately, some chess players also conform to the stereotype of being obsessive, or mentally unstable, or both. This is a pattern throughout chess history, with Wilhelm Steinitz, Paul Morphy, Alexander Alekhine and Bobby Fischer all tormented souls.

Hungarian grandmaster Andras Adorjan, whom I interviewed, suffers from manic depression. This give him the creative spark and energy to produce chess games, music and books, but it has also taken him to the ward of a psychiatric hospital. England's first grandmaster, the late Tony Miles, an outspoken and popular figure in the international chess community, had bouts of bizarre behaviour during his prematurely curtailed life.

My historical articles illustrate the way chess players, always somewhat alienated from everyday society, have struggled to cope in turbulent circumstances. The Soviet chess elite had government funding and encouragement that today's players can only dream of, but only so long as they toed the party line. World champions Mikhail Botvinnik and Anatoly Karpov did this happily, and were rewarded for it. Karpov cleverly managed to adapt to the capitalist post-Soviet era, too. Other top players, including Boris Spassky, Viktor Korchnoi and Garry Kasparov, were more troubled by their awkward position, and found their lives did not go so smoothly.

In the West, Alexander Alekhine could never come to terms with his exclusion from the Soviet chess paradise. Desperate to play at the highest level, he ended up colluding with the Nazis. Later, Bobby Fischer was motivated by his hatred of the Soviets (mixed with enormous respect for their chess), to single-handedly wrest the world title from them. The stress got to him, though, and he disappeared from the chess scene at his peak, only to re-appear for an ignominious match with Spassky in war-torn Serbia.

Time and time again, chess players show that they are hopeless at politics. This explains why FIDE President Kirsan Ilyumzhinov has been so successful in the chess world. Firstly, he is an adept politician with years of experience in the murky, dangerous Russian arena. Secondly, he has given professional chess players the money and prestige they crave. He has poured millions of dollars into chess, and few people have bothered to ask where that money comes from. Meanwhile, in his alternate life as president of impoverished Kalmykia, he is a repressive dictator.

This book is not all about Kirsan Ilyumzhinov: only one chapter is devoted to the scandals surrounding his corruption, the murder of a Kalmyk journalist, and my campaign for a boycott of the 33rd Chess Olympiad. But the title *Curse of Kirsan* is appropriate. It is a metaphor for the same dilemmas that chess players face time and time again, in pursuit of their beautiful game.

Since completing Chapter Six, Ignatius Leong and Morten Sand have withdrawn their challenge to Ilyumzhinov's FIDE presidency. Instead of running against him, they agreed to accept vice-presidencies on his ticket. Although Leong initially claimed he could win the election, soon afterwards Sand said that defeat would have been assured. "I can understand the disappointment of those who have been waiting for a change in FIDE and of those who believed we could win," he wrote in a statement. "However, we have to be realistic. There is no way the Leong ticket could have won the election. Not because the ticket and the individuals involved are not hard-working people. Not because the Manifesto for Reform in FIDE addresses the wrong issues, but simply because Kirsan and his ticket will win if he puts in the necessary recourses. And we understood that 'the machinery' was starting to work."

Subsequently Sand told me: "It is a classical conflict: should we stay out of activities we disagree with or should we try to work 'inside'. FIDE consists of 160 federations and the easy way out is to say we do not want to participate. There is a 25-year tradition in FIDE for buying elections and we know that Kirsan easily could (and would) do this if necessary. Ignatius and I want changes in FIDE and to achieve this there is no other way than getting inside. Unless someone tries there will be no change."

Computers are another scourge of chess. Professional players are dependent on them for pre-game preparation and post-game analysis; and computers are now stronger than most players on the planet. Chess will probably not be "solved" as draughts was, but the top players are slaves to theory. However, the Internet has made it possible for millions of people around the world to play chess, watch chess, and read chess articles and history.

The popularity of chess might actually be increasing, although it is no longer a game that requires long hours to be spent in an unheated club room. The most promising new chess country today is China, where the government's enthusiasm for the game resembles the Soviet approach. There will always be something for chess journalists to write about...

I am so grateful to the people who collaborated on this book at long distance. My publisher, Hanon Russell, and his editorial/design team who were patient and meticulous. Chess editors Jimmy Adams and Jon Manley, who voluntarily proofread the manuscript and gave me numerous suggested improvements. Photographers Mark Huba, Lesley Collett and Vladimir Barsky, whose work can be seen on these pages. My intention was to include only photographs that were personal to me, but I had no picture of Ilyumzhinov, so Vladimir Barsky kindly agreed to provide one of the FIDE president with one of the players I interviewed, Ruslan Ponomariov. Thank you also to Ken Whyld for the advice and the words of endorsement that appear here.

Sarah Hurst
Anchorage, October 2002

1. First Moves

There are only a few chess players scattered over the brutal Alaska landscape. Charging up mountains on snow machines and mushing sled dogs across the tundra are the local sports. I could easily find a chess club in my new home town of Anchorage, but I'm taking a break from all that. Chess is an obsession – you play or you don't play, no half-measures. And, like gambling, you keep on playing even when you lose and lose and lose.

At the age of 10 I was Goring Primary School chess champion. That being the pinnacle of my playing career, I did a Bobby Fischer and retired, to make a pitiful comeback a decade later. It was 1993, and I was staying with my friend Amy Spurling at her parents' house in Islington, north London. "I'm going to watch the first move of the World Chess Championship," Amy's dad said, sucking on his pipe thoughtfully. "Yeah, right, boring," was my response.

Minutes later, I was hooked. It was more than mere lust for Garry Kasparov and his Armenian eyebrows. A commentator, Jonathan Speelman or Daniel King, was explaining that Garry's knight was being attacked by a pawn, but in response he could attack Nigel's queen with his bishop. Amazing! It had never crossed my mind that there could be an alternative to retreating your attacked piece to another square. It was an epiphany.

Back at university in Birmingham I followed every move of the Kasparov-Short rout and joined the chess club. A few dozen people turned up to the first meeting, most inspired by the fleeting celebrity of a British player. The tall redhead on the board next to mine was leaning back, legs outstretched, reading a newspaper. He's obviously not as intellectual as me, he won't stick with it, I thought. He was IM Andrew Webster. He could beat the entire club in a blindfold simultaneous display. I had a lot to learn.

It was time to choose a subject for my 12,000-word history dissertation. The idea came to me in the midst of another Kasparov brilliancy. Weren't most of the famous chess players from the Soviet Union? I had a vague feeling they were. There must have been some politics behind it, I assumed. I decided to write about Soviet chess. I'll never forget what one of my tutors asked. "Will there be enough material on it?" "I hope so," I said.

The dissertation was still in the planning stages when I travelled to Minsk for a three-month Russian language course. I ended up staying an extra two months, working for a European Union agricultural project. The trip also resulted in my first chess interview.

A national newspaper had run a chess competition with prizes. I sent in the answer to the problem, got it wrong, but received a complimentary copy of *British Chess Magazine*. It happened to mention that former world champion Mikhail Botvinnik was alive and working in the Moscow Central Chess Club, designing a chess computer. So I went in search of him.

Meeting Mikhail Botvinnik
(*CHESS*, November 1994)

Today's Moscow, city of casinos, high-class nightclubs, stretched limos, pie-selling babushkas and subways lined with beggars, has transformed its image from Soviet dreariness to cosmopolitan, capitalist colour. The communist presence has been relegated to a small patch of grass round the back of the White House (the former Parliament building), where elderly die-hards sit under a tree from which a torn red flag hangs and argue with passers-by about politics. One important feature of the Russian capital has not changed: it is still bizarre.

I arrived at Moscow's Sheremetyevo-2 airport on a snowy afternoon and was to take the train to Minsk the next evening, where I would be studying for a few months. I had no time to pause for breath and absorb the culture shock as I was bundled off to the television studios by some Russian friends who had tickets to a game show.

Along with all the members of the audience of *Million Lottery* I was given a large badge with a number on it and balloons to hold, and I sat through the live show terrified that I might have to answer inane questions in a language that I had hardly spoken for seven months, or run up and down in a hula hoop throwing footballs into plastic buckets.

I came through that experience unscathed, clutching the bottle of Cyprus wine I had been given, but it was into the breach once more the next day. I found myself face to face with Mikhail Botvinnik, chess world champion for 13 years between 1948 and 1963.

Although the average British citizen-on-the-street would be hard-pressed to remember Nigel Short if asked to name a famous chess player, Botvinnik is known to every ordinary Russian, despite the fact that he hasn't played a game for more than 20 years. He was born in 1911 and was already a celebrity in 1933, when the audience at the Bolshoi Theatre rose to applaud him as he took his seat – not for a chess game, but to watch the ballet. Nowadays the doctor of electronic engineering is still working on his chess computer in the Moscow Central Chess Club. I went there hoping to make an appointment with him for an interview and ended up chatting with him about his old acquaintances in Birmingham.

Gogol Boulevard is bisected by a narrow park that forms a tranquil approach to the Central Chess Club, whose inauspicious exterior can easily be overlooked from the dusty pavement it stands directly on. An old man sells chess books and journals inside the doorway; he assured me that he had a huge stockroom full of valuable material, but on the day I was there he regretted that he had temporarily lost the key to it. In a back room on the ground floor, GM Yuri Averbakh has his editorial office of the magazine *Shakhmatny Vestnik (Chess Herald),* which is published in English and Russian.

Inside, the building is grandiose, with high ceilings and gilt trimmings, expropriated by the Chess Federation in order to instil respect for the game, no doubt. Great players are honoured with grainy black-and-white photographs of themselves on the walls. High-backed wooden chairs stand empty behind rows of polished chess tables, on which a few scattered carved figures lie untouched and forlorn.

I found two solitary gentlemen who were planning some kind of boat trip for chess-playing veterans of World War II. They told me all about it and gave me a list of phone numbers in the hope that I would do some publicity for them. Fortunately, they also knew where Botvinnik's office was and showed me upstairs. Did they think he would see me? "He might speak to you for one or two minutes."

It turned out that the veteran of veterans was in no time trouble. All his words and actions are unhurried, thoughtful and calm. This is not just because he is 83 years old; it is the result of a lifetime of self-discipline. Botvinnik was renowned for his meticulous preparation: his regular walks before games were timed to the minute. He played training games in which his friend blew smoke in his face so that he could withstand his opponent's noxious habit.

I expected to see the former champion in a vast computer laboratory, behind a panel of flashing lights and switches, gazing up at an electronic chessboard on the wall, like a real-life Wizard of Oz. Where I met him there was no technology apart from a telephone, and he had an ordinary chess set on the desk in front of him. Botvinnik was slightly bemused to see me at first, as I had walked in so unexpectedly, but when I said I was from Birmingham his face brightened and he began to talk about his visit there in 1967, remembering the people who had shown him around.

Botvinnik was also pleased to hear that I was going to live in Minsk, because his father came from there, and he told me where to find the Minsk Palace of Chess. He had been talking for 20 minutes, and I felt that I had already been enormously privileged to meet him at all, so I decided it was probably time for me to go, although Botvinnik himself seemed happy to continue reminiscing. Yes, I could come back and interview him, but only after reading his memoirs, *Achieving the Aim*, and his *Red Book*, a collection of his articles and essays. I went to Minsk determined to start straight away on the homework I had been set.

Five months later, having found and read the books in Russian, prepared my questions and bought my ticket to Moscow (this is an incredibly complex procedure which has to be done through "contacts" at the railway station because black market dealers buy up all the tickets in advance), I returned to the Central Chess Club and did the interview. This time it was I who waited in the office as Botvinnik came up the stairs, and he was taking so long that his assistant, who had run out of small talk about Minsk, phoned down to find out if he was coming. "Where's the hero?" he asked jokily.

The hero finally shuffled in and sat down. He talked for an hour and a half and was interrupted only once, by the president of the St. Petersburg Chess Federation, who had come to discuss a possible television appearance with Anatoly Karpov. Botvinnik introduced me to the St. Petersburg man, remembering the details I had mentioned at our first meeting, such as where I was studying, then said, "And she's not from a very rich family. They're not rich, are they?" "No, they're average," I assured him, not wishing him to think of me as a class enemy.

In 1936 Botvinnik tied for first place with Capablanca at the Nottingham International Tournament, in which three other world champions played. He sent a letter to Stalin which began, "Dear beloved teacher and leader," and continued, "This was only possible because I sensed behind me... that daily care which you, our great leader, have taken... to rear in us representatives of Soviet youth a healthy and joyful generation in all fields of our socialist construction."

It goes without saying that such letters were obligatory in those days, but how far did these words represent Botvinnik's real feelings? "Mass repression started in 1937. I was very busy in that year with tournaments, and I had my doctoral thesis to write, so I didn't feel the effects of it. Then the war started. Stalin's first speech on the radio in 1941 was very optimistic, and the people united. I never met Stalin personally, but I believed in him for encouraging education, developing science, creating a new generation of engineers, industrialising the country, improving agriculture and making a big army. I stopped believing in him in 1952, because of the doctors' plot." This was when Kremlin doctors, most of them Jewish, were arrested on false charges of having conspired to murder Soviet leaders.

Is Botvinnik still a communist, then? He joined the party in 1940. "I am a true communist," the chess genius says with pride. "Stalin was not a true communist, he was a poor, uneducated person who could only come to power through revolution. I am a communist in the tradition of the first communist on earth, Jesus Christ. I am also an atheist. My parents were atheist. I am Jewish by race but Russian by culture."

This raised the question of whether Mikhail Moiseyevich had ever experienced anti-Semitism. "The first time I felt it was at school. I liked the sister of my friend a lot, but he came up to me and said, 'Misha, she won't kiss you.' 'Why not?' I asked him. 'Because you're a Jew.' Later I knew that anti-Semitism was around, but people weren't outwardly chauvinistic towards me, they were afraid to say anything because of who I was. Such people are idiots, and you should feel sorry for idiots. Anti-Semitism never had a serious effect on me and my work."

Botvinnik repeatedly gave me the impression that he lives for his work and has always done so (although he had "a good wife, we looked after each other"), and if politics didn't interfere with his work, then it didn't bother him. The same goes for people. Asked to name a past acquaintance whom he considered a bad person, he said that in general he tried not to have any business with his enemies, but there was one person who stopped him from working, and that was Boris Weinstein, who died recently.

Weinstein was a senior figure in the Soviet Chess Federation who was instrumental in preventing the organisation of a World Championship match between the champion, Alexander Alekhine, and Botvinnik. Alekhine died in 1946 before the match could be held and Botvinnik became the first Soviet world champion by winning a tournament in which the five top players competed.

In his memoirs, Botvinnik praised Nikolai Krylenko for his work as first chairman of the Soviet Chess Federation. Krylenko also happened to be Commissar for Justice in the 1930s and was shot in 1938. He himself had defended the practice of detention and execution without trial. Perhaps Botvinnik had reconsidered his view of Krylenko? "Krylenko was a wonderful person for chess. A year after he started working in chess, in 1925, he organised the international tournament in Moscow which created a huge interest in the game. He was not independent, of course."

The same can be said for Botvinnik, who was an ideal ambassador for the Soviet Union while he was achieving glorious victories over Western society and culture. He acknowledges that Krylenko participated in show-trials as prosecutor, but says, "I don't think anyone was shot as a result of them. Those people who received prison terms were rehabilitated afterwards." He still portrays Krylenko as a sympathetic person, someone who did mountaineering, went by bike to Kremlin congresses and loved chess. Botvinnik recalls him playing in the team tournament at the 7th Soviet Championships in 1931, sitting at the chessboard like anyone else, without any bodyguards.

Krylenko often helped Botvinnik personally, for instance when he arranged for his wife to accompany him to the 1936 Nottingham Tournament. It was rare enough for a Soviet citizen to be allowed to travel abroad, let alone with his wife as well. Botvinnik remembers this trip and the subsequent triumph in the tournament as one of the best times of his life.

Although Botvinnik was one of the elite, things were not always easy. He was born into a wealthy family: his father earned a lot of money as a dentist before the revolution. Later there were famines in the Soviet Union that Botvinnik did not escape.

"In 1918 and 1919 we lived very modestly in Leningrad – we did not have much to eat. I went hungry again in 1932, during the collectivisation of agriculture, but I went to the countryside for a holiday and they had butter there. In Leningrad they only had bread, so I brought back several kilos of butter to my brother and his wife, so we ate bread *and* butter for a week. During the war we lived in very bad conditions in Perm, where my daughter was born. We had just enough bread, but it was hard currency. My wife would go to the market and exchange it for fruit and vegetables."

Russians usually find enough to drink to console themselves in their eternal misery, but Botvinnik is exceptional in this case as well. He hardly ever drank alcohol, except wine occasionally. A chess master in Minsk who helped me prepare my questions came to my flat with 14 cans of beer and a chess set to play blitz while he drank. He urged me to ask Botvinnik if he had ever been drunk in his life, so, with a little trepidation, I did. Instead of rebuking me for being so impertinent, Botvinnik gave me a straight answer. "I got drunk once on vodka when I first became Soviet champion, in 1931. I didn't feel very well afterwards and didn't do it again. I smoked for two months but gave it up because I realised it was harmful."

Botvinnik's concern for his health has obviously paid off. He has very poor eyesight and wears thick glasses, but otherwise he looks remarkably well and has an alert mind. This he attributes to the Müller system of calisthenics, which he has done every day for 71 years, "and I did it this morning. You should do it, too. It's good for the heart, brain, and for your breathing." Botvinnik's assistant brought me a coffee, but the man himself didn't have one – "I'm too old for cups of coffee."

So how does he find life in Moscow these days? "I didn't like it before and I like it even less now. It seems that there is nothing for people to be happy about at the moment. The programme of Yeltsin's government is not right for Russia. I wrote a short article which was published as a letter to the editor in *Nezavisimaya Gazeta* to explain why I wouldn't be voting in the recent elections." Presumably Russia is suffering from a shortage of genuine communists.

Botvinnik has lived through the entire history of the Soviet Union and has never once wanted to leave the country permanently. "The thought of emigrating never came into my head. My relatives lived here and are buried here, my daughter and grandchildren are here. There is no order in Russia, but it is a good country. It will again play a great role in history."

Finally, I came to the crucial question that would definitely establish whether chess is superior to draughts. Perhaps the person I was asking was a little biased on this issue. *Is* draughts equal only to a rook endgame in chess? "No. The rook endgame is more complicated. Draughts used to be played on an eight-by-eight board, which meant that it always ended in a draw, but even when it was enlarged to ten-by-ten, that still meant that only 50 squares were used, as opposed to 64 in chess. There was one draughts master of my generation, Vasily Sokov, who used to win even on the eight-by-eight board. He died in the war. It is no coincidence that thousands of people are working on chess computers, but only one person has ever tried to create a draughts computer."

That reminded me – how was Botvinnik's work on a chess computer going? "Maybe we'll get somewhere, I don't know." With so many achievements behind him, Botvinnik has nothing left to prove, but, true to character, he shows no signs of resigning.

I sent a copy of the published article to Botvinnik and received a handwritten note back: "Sarah, Vy – molodets. Vash M. Botvinnik. Moskva 23.11.94." *("Sarah, you are very smart. Yours, M. Botvinnik. Moscow 23.11.94.") Botvinnik died on May 5, 1995. I'd caught up with him just in time.*

The interview with Botvinnik was intended for my dissertation, but when I returned to England I thought of trying to sell it to a chess magazine, too. I had been writing for local and national publications on various subjects since I was 15, so I wasn't a novice journalist. *The Writer's Handbook* informed me that there were two major monthly chess magazines in the UK, *British Chess Magazine* and *CHESS*. I called *CHESS* because apparently it had more of an international slant. The magazine was owned by IM Malcolm Pein and based at his London Chess Centre on Euston Road; its editor was Jimmy Adams.

In his relaxed cockney manner Jimmy insisted that he would have to cut my phone call short, because he had to get on with his editing, but the conversation went on and on. Jimmy was not the sort of editor who would say, "One thousand words by next Tuesday, we'll use it if there's space, goodbye." He wanted to hear all about Botvinnik and my future chess writing plans, of which I had none. He invited me to meet him at the Chess Centre to talk more about the article.

After a brief tour of the shop, Jimmy took me to a café down a back street, where we spent at least two hours discussing Botvinnik and Minsk. Jimmy had plenty of titled players willing to analyse their games for the magazine, but few feature writers to fill up the pages with "something you can read on the bus." This was the beginning of a great collaboration. Jimmy's head was full of quirky chess facts and anecdotes; he would supply the background knowledge that I lacked, the punning headlines and the funky fonts. I would bring to chess journalism innocence. I'd ask anyone anything, and I wasn't in awe of the famous players, because I'd never heard of most of them before.

In all the years I wrote for *CHESS*, I was paid £25 (about $40) per printed page, half as much as a titled player. One of the reasons why I wrote such long articles was to pay my electricity and phone bills...

Jimmy inspected my photograph of Botvinnik, with newspapers spread out on the desk in front of him, my coffee mug in the foreground and a calendar hanging behind him on the wall, and said he looked like a used car dealer. Fortunately, Mark "BLOODY HELL!" Huba had an excellent photograph of Botvinnik with a toothy grin on his face. Both pictures appeared with the article.

Mark had no qualms about barging past people to get the picture he wanted. At the Kasparov-Short match, Mark was so engrossed in what he was doing that he was the only photographer who didn't turn away from the main stage to snap Princess Diana when she made a fleeting appearance up in a box. When Mark finally noticed that he was pointing his lens in the wrong direction, Diana saw the momentarily stupefied look on his face and broke into her beautiful smile. Mark eventually got his picture – a little later than everyone else.

Next, Jimmy suggested that I should go to the Hastings International Chess Congress and interview some of the top players there, especially the Russian speakers. He wanted to go with me, but he had the flu, so he gave me a detailed rundown on the phone. Mark Huba was there, and we met for the first time. Hastings is a decaying seaside resort about two hours from London, known for William the Conqueror's invasion in 1066 and the chess congress, which is held at the coldest, windiest time of year (December-January) and has been going since 1895. The headquarters of the British Chess Federation were also there in the 1990s.

Another player whom Jimmy wanted me to talk to was England's No. 1 woman, Susan Lalic. He thought that a woman player would be more likely to open up to a woman interviewer. I am not sure if that was true. On the other hand, many of the men I met quite enjoyed being interviewed by a woman. Anyway, Susan was very approachable. A glutton for punishment, she was with her second grandmaster husband. The first was Keith Arkell.

Immovable Susan
(*CHESS*, March 1995)

Not many women at the top of their profession face competition from a 16-year-old schoolgirl, but, as Luke McShane and David Bronstein have demonstrated, chess recognises no boundaries of age. That is why Susan Lalic, Britain's No. 1 woman chess player, can be magnanimous about the successes of her nearest rival, Harriet Hunt.

Although Susan is now having to divide her time between career and baby, she believes that giving up chess would be unfair to Harriet as it is her duty to be a target for the younger player: "To cop out would be cheating," as she puts it. "I'd rather play chess unsuccessfully than do anything else. I've always wanted to be an IM, but, even though I've got some norms, I'm not sure if I'm going to make it, as now I have my baby to look after."

Susan was battling in the Premier, the top section of the event, and her husband, GM Bogdan Lalic from Croatia, took part in the Challengers. "I feel privileged to be playing in the Premier," she said, "but I'm having a rough time. I wouldn't have qualified for it if there hadn't been a decision to include five women and five men." She added that all the other women in the Premier (two from Georgia, one from Serbia and one from Hungary) had been to chess schools and "have a wealth of experience, so they're good technically. In Britain we rely on the weekend circuit, going through lots of games and asking people the best moves."

At Hastings Susan prepared for three hours every morning before each game, but she is not sure if this was the best course. "It's very tiring. Perhaps it's better to have a good night's sleep, not look at any chess beforehand, then come to a game and fight. I have had some good results using that method."

As chess is so unpopular amongst women, Susan found when she was a girl that she was often invited to travel around the world to tournaments, while her brother, who also played chess, was not. He gave up chess and she remained keen on it, giving up a place on the Mathematics course at Nottingham University to play full time.

Despite her achievements, Susan believes that women are inherently worse at chess than men. "We don't concentrate as hard. We are made differently." There is at least one advantage to being part of a husband-and-wife chess team, though – she understands when Bogdan goes away for a tournament and she has to stay at home with the baby.

From Bogdan's point of view, "It's good when I'm winning, but when I lose, I feel like quitting." Bogdan's background is very different from Susan's. In Yugoslavia chess players used to get a wage from the government, and the amount varied from town to town, so he and other Croatian grandmasters went to Sarajevo to play for Bosnia as there was more money there.

Bogdan becomes animated when he talks about the war. "Serbia has 30 percent of Croatia and I think that the West has the tricky intention of rewarding Serbia for starting the war. I have even seen a map of Europe in a bookshop here which quoted Greater Serbia. I want the old borders back. War would be better than accepting the situation as it is now."

Being a professional chess player has to be one of the most insecure careers in Britain, something like being a jazz musician. It means that Susan and Bogdan have to avoid going for a mortgage or getting into any kind of debt. Susan knows people who wanted to become chess professionals but went into other jobs for lack of money.

Repeatedly apologising for sounding negative, Susan tries to brighten the tone with the rejoinder, "Playing chess is a very good life if you can make a living out of it." However, lots of international masters live with their parents and depend on them for support. As chess is not officially recognised as a sport in this country, it is not eligible for government funding and Susan thinks that it should have a share of the lottery money.

Chess could be boosted by other means than throwing money at it, though. "It should be taught in schools, because it encourages sportsmanship and discipline and it teaches you how to study. It would also be good if the Chess Olympiad is held alongside the Olympics in Sydney, as has been suggested, because then chess would be regarded as a sport."

Bogdan Lalic does not agree with his wife's definition of chess as pure sport. "It used to be considered an art, a science and a sport," he says, "but now it's a science, because computers are better than people, for sure." The couple are both depressed by the sight of chess players carrying computers around in their briefcases; they themselves do not have a computer and think this could be holding them back, although Bogdan has had a string of successes recently.

"There's still a little room for creativity in chess," Bogdan concedes, gesturing just how much with his thumb and forefinger half an inch away from each other. "You can't break through if people just want a draw," says Susan. The idea of generating more excitement with rapidplay chess – 30 minutes for each player – appeals to Bogdan and also Susan, who competed in the women's rapidplay World Championship. "It's really enjoyable, a quick fight, and there's no preparation for it. Blitz is OK, but you can easily make mistakes because of the short time."

Bogdan doubts that chess can be made into a spectator sport, as you can follow it just as easily in the newspapers, and admits that the last time he watched a game was when Korchnoi played Petrosian in a 1980 Candidates match. Susan agrees: "If I had the choice of watching Wimbledon or the World Chess Championship, I'd go to the tennis."

This article shows just how quickly chess changed in the late 1990s. Soon afterwards it was unheard of for strong players to be without a laptop and the latest version of ChessBase, a giant database of games that could be analysed by the super-fast chess computer Fritz. Bogdan referred to following chess in the newspapers; at the time of the interview, I had barely used e-mail and had never seen an Internet website. A few years later, games were broadcast and played live on the Internet, and the FIDE World Championship was a knockout, with rapidplay tiebreaks.

Susan Lalic did obtain the international master title. I chatted with her and Bogdan a few more times at chess events around Britain and Ireland. They were always friendly.

Eastern Influences
(*CHESS*, March 1995)

Moscow and St. Petersburg are not the only Meccas of chess in the former Soviet Union. Georgian women say it's a myth that chess sets are a traditional dowry in their homeland: chess was made popular there by Nona Gaprindashvili and the republic continues to turn out an extraordinarily high number of women grandmasters.

Alma-Ata, the capital of Kazakhstan, is expecting a major earthquake any day now and maybe their chess players are about to shake the world, too. They beat England at the Moscow Chess Olympiad and their top player, Vladislav Tkachiev, has been storming the heights recently in the Intel Grand Prix. Also, Elvira Sakhatova, having just won her women's grandmaster title, played in the Hastings Challengers. There is more to Russia than its two largest cities...

Sunny and Sher

Miron Sher, an affable man with a swashbuckling black moustache and a conspiratorial grin, qualified for his place in the 1994/95 Premier by winning the previous year's Challengers Tournament. He is well acquainted with Hastings, as this was his fifth visit, and for the first time he was accompanied by his wife, who played in the Challengers, and son, who operated a demo board.

"I like it here," Sher says. "There are always a few sunny days and I have lots of friends in Hastings. There are so many amateurs here, it's not just a chess congress but a real festival." Playing women is "not a problem" for Sher, who points out that he has won almost all his games with women grandmasters, but adds, "in this tournament it's difficult because you get no glory from beating a woman and if you lose, it's shameful."

Can a woman ever be world champion? "Judit Polgar can. If not her, then sooner or later women will defeat men." Computers are also taking over chess, and Sher admits that they can analyse better than humans. "They interfere, and the level of chess has fallen a little because of them."

Sher is from Kaliningrad, which was the German city of Konigsberg until it became part of Russia in 1945. It is very similar to Hastings, he says, as it is on the shores of the Baltic Sea, between Poland and Lithuania. Despite the decline and fall of the Soviet Empire, Sher thinks that the position of chess players is still better in Russia than it is in the West. "Two years ago I predicted that chess would be ruined in Russia, but it hasn't happened. Although there are some very strong British players, unfortunately Short didn't give much of a boost to British chess, and it's a pity that there are no good sponsors here."

Living permanently in the West does not appeal to Sher, although his parents have moved to America and he could go there if he wanted to. He describes England as "a slow country." Events are moving more quickly in Russia in a direction that Sher is angry about: "I worked in Grozny for two years as a mathematician and I know people down there, one of whom has just moved to Moscow while his parents are still in Chechnya. What's happening now is terrible."

According to www.chessintheschools.org, Miron Sher now conducts weekly chess lessons at CIS headquarters in New York.

Georgia on My Mind

War has affected Ketevan Arakhamia more than Miron Sher. She is from Abkhazia, the region that has been fighting for independence from Georgia. "The situation is hard there now," she says. "My family are Georgian, not Abkhazian, and they moved to the Russian town of Sochi a year ago. They also have a flat in Tbilisi, but conditions are not very good there, either. My mother is a biology teacher and my father is an agronomist, but since they moved they haven't had jobs."

Arakhamia's father taught her to play chess and when she was 14 she went to study it in Tbilisi. "Now life is more difficult for chess players because there used to be more state support," she says. Advances in theory do not deter her: "You just have to work harder. I used to see chess as an art, but now out of necessity I have to treat it as a sport." Arakhamia considers her victory in a women's Interzonal tournament in Jakarta 1993 her biggest success to date. As for politics, "It's a dirty business and there's no need to touch it."

Ketevan Arakhamia married Scottish chess player Jonathan Grant and moved to Edinburgh. She is featured on a Georgian postage stamp alongside other members of the national women's team.

If I can't be world champion...

The youngest player in the Premier Tournament, 23-year-old Ketino Kachiani-Gersinska, is also from Georgia but now lives with her husband in Germany. He competed in the Challengers but is not a professional chess player – he works for an insurance company – and she says she is only able to play chess full time because of this.

Kachiani-Gersinska is adamant that playing chess should not be the only activity in her life, and so she writes about it as well, for Georgian magazines. She graduated in Tbilisi with a degree in journalism and is also a proficient linguist, which became obvious when she was showing me her game with Arakhamia and lapsed from Russian into German without noticing. "Oh, sorry," she said, "with Georgian, Russian, German and now a little English, it's very confusing."

Having been junior girls' world champion in 1989 and 1990, and also a Women's World Championship candidate, Kachiani-Gersinska's chess career has been impressive so far. She says she is recognised on the streets of Georgia, but she lacks a trainer and considers this a hindrance. She has high hopes for her own future: "I would like to have a very good position amongst women grandmasters, and if I can't be world champion, then even runner-up would be good!"

Ketino Kachiani-Gersinska has not yet achieved her ambition.

Buddhist Elvira

The easygoing attitude of Elvira Sakhatova could hardly contrast more with the ambitions of Arakhamia and Kachiani-Gersinska. Sakhatova, whose philosophy of life is to take things as they come, is always ready to smile and laugh, and does so as she recalls a tournament in Chelyabinsk, where there was no running water, or talks about the grant of $50 a month she receives from the Kazakh Ministry of Sport. "The average wage in Kazakhstan is $45 a month. I stay with my sister in England for three months at a time and then go back home for three months, so it works out OK."

Sakhatova says it was only possible to gain her women's grandmaster title in England, because in Kazakhstan there are no women's tournaments apart from the national championship, and there are only a few men's tournaments. "England has a higher cultural level than Kazakhstan. The men there are – how shall I put it? – ruder." What about Tkachiev? "He's very young. His mother asked me to look after him when he first went abroad to a tournament, and we have been to several together since then."

Tkachiev has announced that he will play chess for another year and then give up, but Elvira does not believe him. "He has lots of plans. He wants to set up an organisation like the PCA. I honestly don't think he'll give up chess." Until recently, Sakhatova and Tkachiev had a sponsor, a businessman and amateur chess player from Kazakhstan, but he went bankrupt, a common fate in the former Soviet Union.

Problems and setbacks do not disturb Sakhatova's feelings of inner harmony and contentment, which stem from or are reinforced by her interest in Buddhism. In her spare time, when she's not reading *Catcher in the Rye* to improve her English, she meditates. "I'm a very calm person. I'm happy whatever happens. A Buddhist monk was once asked what he'd like to be reincarnated as, and he replied, 'a dead dog,' because it is in a state of complete tranquility."

While other chess professionals anxiously pounce on the names of their opponents well in advance of a tournament, Elvira enjoys not knowing who she's going to play until five minutes before the game, and she does no preparation during tournaments. "The best preparation is playing blitz with my sister," she says. "I look through games in magazines, but I have no computer and no trainer."

It was Gulnara Sakhatova who inspired her sister to take up chess when Gulnara was 13 and Elvira was 11. Gulnara read a book about Nona Gaprindashvili and said, "Let's play chess," so they did. Elvira spent three years at university studying journalism, but got fed up with hours of Marxism-Leninism and the history of Kazakhstan, so she stuck with chess, while Gulnara gave up serious play after she married an Englishman.

This year Elvira Sakhatova was at Hastings for the second time, and despite an improved score of 5½ out of 9, she said her result was bad. When I suggested that her will to win cannot be very strong if she is such a peaceful person, she replied with a characteristic smile, "Chess is different."

Vladislav Tkachiev, one of the world's top chess players, lives in France. Elvira Sakhatova married IM Fred Berend from Luxembourg, where she now lives. They are the country's two highest-rated players. The capital of Kazakhstan has been moved to Astana.

The Premier tournament, for invitees only, was held at the comfortable Cinque Ports Hotel. All the other tournaments, including the Challengers (which attracted numerous grandmasters and international masters) and weekend tournaments for all manner of lowly amateurs, took place in a draughty hall at the end of the pier. Hundreds of players sat here day after day, unperturbed by the high winds and creaky floorboards, including myself at one end of the hall, and at the other, David Bronstein, who more often than not could be seen pacing up and down in his coat and woolly hat.

Bronstein happily chatted to me in Russian and invited me to talk to him again at the hotel where he was giving master classes for young players, but he wouldn't go on the record. The legacy of Soviet-era paranoia, perhaps. Bronstein failed to capture the World Championship from Botvinnik in 1951, and there was always a rumour that some kind of KGB pressure had been put on him. Bronstein was keen to perpetuate that rumour.

I was glad to notch up another encounter with a Soviet chess legend, but really he has to be counted as one who got away, because he wouldn't let me do a proper interview with him.

By this time I was finishing my degree and trying to persuade Batsford to publish a book on the history of Soviet chess, *Silent Struggles*. I wrote a synopsis and Graham Burgess, the Batsford chess editor, supported the idea. After leaving university I went to St. Petersburg, planning to research the book there. I'd spent a summer there in 1993 and thought it was the most intriguing city in the world.

Batsford never commissioned *Silent Struggles*: apparently their U.S. partners didn't think it would sell. I got a job as a reporter on the *St. Petersburg Press*, an English-language newspaper later renamed the *St. Petersburg Times*. I didn't pay much attention to chess during my 11 months in St. Petersburg; there were mafia murders and political shenanigans to report. But I had already adapted part of my dissertation to become an article for *CHESS*. It was published while I was in Russia.

Punishments and Privileges
(*CHESS*, October 1995)

In his new book *Selected Games*, Russian GM Mark Taimanov writes, "As is well known, the Soviet and Party bosses of the time took a very dim view of my sensational 0-6 defeat against Bobby Fischer in 1971, and reckoned that the reasons behind this unprecedented result were not so much to do with chess, as with politics, and if this was so, then the 'culprit' had to be taught a lesson and punished very severely, so that others should not do the same. Thus I was simultaneously stripped of the titles awarded for previous services, suspended from taking part in international tournaments, and excluded from the USSR team, which also entailed financial sanctions. This was a genuine 'civil execution.'"

However, he was neither the first nor the last to suffer such a fate...

It is possible to imagine a leisurely game of chess in a café on Nevsky Prospekt, St. Petersburg's main thoroughfare, being rudely disturbed by the cannon fire of the battleship *Aurora* one day in October 1917. Chess was an aristocratic pastime in pre-revolutionary Russia, a game enjoyed by Tolstoy and the characters in Pushkin's poem *Evgeny Onegin*. The *Aurora*'s signal for the Bolsheviks to seize power also heralded a chess explosion, the like of which has not been known in any other country of the world.

Chess happened to be Lenin's favourite game, and this was no small factor in the decision by the new government to organise chess on a mass scale. Chess was too important to be left to the players themselves – they needed a certain amount of friendly encouragement from above.

From the moment it was founded in 1924, the Soviet Chess Section linked chess with politics. Its early philosophy was expressed in these terms: "In the hands of the proletariat chess has to become a weapon which must be used to strengthen the growth of intellectual culture amongst the industrial and peasant masses, bringing them closer to a conscious participation in the political struggle of the proletariat."

It is ironic that "intellectual" would later become a term of abuse in the Soviet Union and that people would speculate that chess was encouraged precisely for the purpose of distracting Soviet citizens from politics. An assertion made to World Championship challenger Viktor Korchnoi by one of his friends, "Footballers and hockey players are necessary so that people drink less vodka, but they show you [chess players] to the nation so that it reads less Solzhenitsyn!" carries some credence.

In the 1920s the spread of literacy was a political aim and it was believed that an interest in chess would cause people to read chess books and journals and then start reading more widely. Healthy competition was also sanctioned by the Communist Party as a way of developing the fully rounded socialist citizen; Lenin wanted workers to compete with each other to increase production.

The subtext to this, of course, is that the isolated Soviet Union had to find a way of bringing itself to the centre of the world stage and to prove that its communist system could achieve greater successes than the supposedly decaying capitalist nations. Winning at sport was an obvious way of doing this.

In 1925, for the first time, the Soviet government funded an international tournament in Moscow, spending 30,000 rubles on it. The Cuban world champion, José Capablanca, and 10 other foreign masters competed in the tournament alongside 10 Soviet players. Efim Bogolyubov triumphantly won the tournament for the Soviet Union, but he had already emigrated to the West and gave up his Soviet citizenship a year later. The title of Soviet champion, which he had also won in 1925, was taken away from him by the chess organisation.

This was one of the first of numerous punishments meted out throughout the Soviet period to chess players who in one way or another did not adequately represent the system that had nurtured them. Alexander Alekhine, who emigrated to France after the Civil War, and subsequently became world champion, was never allowed back into the Soviet Union.

If Bogolyubov was the first player to "betray" the Soviet system, Mikhail Botvinnik was the first hero of it. He was lauded with ecstatic praise by *Pravda* after his victory at Nottingham in 1936: "Botvinnik progressed calmly and confidently from the beginning of the tournament, showing great skill, endurance, determination and will to win and demonstrating the strength given by a combination of theoretical knowledge and complete technical mastery... The USSR is becoming the classical land of chess. The famous masters of Western Europe and America watch the growth of our chess culture with envy. There is nothing like it in their countries."

With the outbreak of World War II, it seemed that the Soviet Union's march towards world chess supremacy would halt. Many chess players were sent to the front. Boris Weinstein, a colonel in the NKVD (forerunner to the KGB), lamented this fact, and in an interview given to *Shakhmatny Vestnik* in 1993, just before his death, related the steps he took to revive Soviet chess.

"In January 1942, as the head of the planning section of the NKVD, I telephoned Rosalia Zemlyachka, the deputy chairwoman of the Council of Ministers. I informed her that the country's Chess Section had ceased to exist, but even so chess could now be of great value. She said that she didn't understand what use it could be at a time of war. I... pointed out that in the first place, chess could help in the hospitals – amongst the wounded there were many enthusiasts of the game."

As a result of his ideas, Weinstein became chairman of the resurrected Chess Section. During the war it produced tournament bulletins and organized congresses in various towns of the Soviet Union. Weinstein remarks that unlike other areas of culture, which were devastated by losses in the war, chess managed to preserve its ranks, with only four masters killed and one seriously wounded. Another, the Latvian Vladimir Petrov, was sent to a camp in Siberia, where he died. Weinstein admitted that he knew of Petrov's arrest immediately, but presumably made no protest.

The Estonian Paul Keres was another player who was in great danger during the war. Weinstein was in Estonia in 1944 to investigate the possibility of building a naval base there, and he was greeted by the head of the Estonian NKVD, who asked if Keres could be allowed to play in the Soviet Championships, as chess was his only source of income.

Weinstein says, "He proposed that I should meet Keres, but I refused, explaining that in any case I couldn't take such a decision myself: there was a general rule – those who lived in occupied territory during the war could not enter the first post-war championships. But with Keres the situation was even more complicated. 'I personally have great sympathy for him,' I said, 'both as a chess player, and as a person, although I have never met him. But according to the law, for his collaboration with the Germans he should get 25 years, and you know this as well as I do. He played in their tournaments, consorted with Alekhine…' At this we said no more."

Fortunately, the brilliance of Keres was important enough to the Soviet authorities for him to be forgiven. In 1945 he wrote a letter to Foreign Minister Molotov asking to "again become a full member of the Soviet chess family," and in 1947 he became Soviet champion.

Soviet grandmasters were essentially actors in a political drama, and the chess organisation monitored not only their match results but also their personal behaviour at home and abroad to ensure that it followed the Party line. Players who won when they had to – and drew when they were asked to – and at the same time exemplified model Soviet citizens, were lavished with praise and rewarded materially. Conversely, lapses such as a politically incorrect remark, a marital infidelity or a too-friendly attitude towards foreigners could incur heavy punishments. Poor chess form could result in the withdrawal of the allowance which was secretly paid by the Sports Committee to the so-called "amateur" chess players.

Permission to travel abroad was granted to very few grandmasters, and then only a maximum of twice a year, with KGB surveillance, but a larger number of masters and grandmasters received a range of other benefits. Before his match with Czechoslovakia's Salo Flohr in 1933, the Chess Section arranged for Botvinnik to have a month's leave from his scientific work to prepare for it.

Then, after winning the 1935 Moscow International Tournament and becoming the first Soviet grandmaster, Botvinnik was sent this message from Politburo member Sergo Ordzhonikidze: "By order of the Minister of Heavy Industry: M. Botvinnik… for successfully combining his technical studies with achievement in chess, is awarded an automobile."

In relation to Botvinnik, the words of *Pravda* were as rich as the presents he received. When he became world champion for the first time in 1948, chess was elevated to yet new planes of significance by the newspaper: "Botvinnik was not simply playing chess, he was defending the honour of his country, the honour of his socialist motherland. Botvinnik's brilliant victory is not only a testimony to his own heroic powers, it is a victory of our socialist culture, an integral part of which is chess."

It thus stood to reason that defeats in chess brought shame and dishonour to the Soviet Union and had to be responded to accordingly. This verbal reprimand of 1961 in *Shakhmaty v SSSR* (*Chess in the USSR*) was relatively mild: "Leading Soviet players are well known for their modesty and openness. Unfortunately, this cannot be said of Grandmaster E. Geller… a disdainful attitude towards his comrades and an unwillingness to consider their opinions. Braggarts and boasters are not popular with us."

Korchnoi was slammed by former world champion Tigran Petrosian in *Sovietsky Sport* in 1974 with an article entitled "Unsporting, Grandmaster!" merely for having had the audacity to agree with Bobby Fischer's suggestion that draws should not be counted in World Championship Candidates matches. Fischer's idea was interpreted by the chess authorities as a criticism of Anatoly Karpov (which it was) for the way he had dragged out his match with Korchnoi that year.

A more concrete punishment than the rhetoric of chess magazines, however, was the withdrawal of permission to travel abroad. In his memoirs, Korchnoi noted that even as the Soviet team for the 1968 Olympiad in Switzerland, of which he was a member, was about to leave for the airport with their packed suitcases, former world champion Mikhail Tal was told by the deputy chairman of the Sports Committee to "go back to Riga. You see, Smyslov is already in Lugano, he will replace you."

Korchnoi says that from 1968 to 1972 Tal was not permitted to travel because of "frequent marital transgressions," and that Boris Spassky received the same punishment after his World Championship match with Fischer for "incautious political pronouncements." Between 1962 and 1965 Korchnoi himself was forced to stay in the Soviet Union for various misdemeanours committed in the West, including placing a bet in a casino and inviting a German woman to the cinema.

In his time Korchnoi had received a large flat from the Sports Committee as a reward for becoming Soviet champion in 1960, so he was aware of both sides of the Chess Section's carrot and stick policy.

After Bobby Fischer won the World Championship for the United States in 1972, the Soviet Union demanded a new chess hero. When Karpov became the next challenger for the title and was subsequently awarded it because of Fischer's refusal to play, he was exalted as the favourite of the Soviet chess organisation in a way that no one had been since Botvinnik. Sycophantic interviews with Karpov raised him to the status of a demi-god whose personal morals and lifestyle were an example to all Soviet people.

Chess editor Alexander Roshal wrote in 1977, "Anatoly Karpov is conversant with the life of many countries, their customs and traditions. He's met many noted public figures and talked to heads of state. Yet his main interest lies in meeting common people... He is also a member of the Komsomol [Communist Party youth organisation] Central Committee and twice winner of the badge for Active Komsomol Work."

Korchnoi says that as early as 1974, when he and Karpov were contending for the right to challenge Fischer, Karpov had extraordinary backing. "By the efforts of the All-Union Chess Federation, a powerful staff was set up to help Karpov. Apart from the main trainers, there were Petrosian, Averbakh, Tal and Botvinnik... I was told a story of how once Tal and Vaganian arrived back from the Yugoslavia-USSR match. A car from the Komsomol Central Committee was awaiting them by the airport entrance. 'We're going straight to Karpov,' said the official, 'he's having trouble against the French Defence.'"

There was no particular movement against Korchnoi in the Soviet chess world at this time; the press assessed him as a contender for the World Championship in the same way as they did Karpov, but Karpov had made valuable contacts and it was paying off. After Korchnoi defected, when he was playing Karpov in 1978, Korchnoi's family was still in the Soviet Union, and the intense psychological pressure on Korchnoi was exacerbated by the knowledge that his opponent's influence was capable of getting them permission to join him in the West.

The force of the Soviet Chess Federation's bias towards Karpov was again demonstrated blatantly when Kasparov succeeded Korchnoi as challenger. Kasparov was told by Nikolai Krogius, in charge of the chess department of the Sports Committee, "We've got one world champion, we don't need another." Kasparov believes that he would not have been able to become world champion without his own patron in the Politburo, Heydar Aliev.

Chess administrators were fully prepared to send Kasparov to obscure tournaments where he would never achieve the public successes he needed. Nevertheless, when Kasparov actually reached the World Championship match with Karpov in 1985, the Chess Federation resorted to desperate measures once it became clear that towards the end of a long match there was a possibility that the champion might lose. The match was stopped because the Chess Federation was "concerned over the state of the players' health."

Kasparov had no idea that there was anything wrong with his state of health. This extraordinary action could do no more than postpone the inevitable. Kasparov was just as much a protégé of Botvinnik's chess school as Karpov, and this early training was indispensable; the chess system was not designed to produce just one world champion…

* * *

In St. Petersburg I did write about one tournament, where I briefly met two more great players of the past, Mark Taimanov and Andor Lilienthal. The article was published shortly after I got back to England.

The Chigorin Memorial
(*CHESS*, July 1996)

So inspiring was the atmosphere at the first Chigorin Memorial Congress in 1909 that one of the participants wrote a 20-line poem in its honour. From 1963, international tournaments dedicated to 19th-century GM Mikhail Chigorin were held annually at the Black Sea resort of Sochi, and their prestige was hardly less than when chess giants Lasker and Alekhine were victorious in 1909.

Since the collapse of the USSR in 1991, however, times have been tougher. The tournament has taken place in St. Petersburg for the last three years, but has only managed to cling on to the label "international" because the republics of the former Soviet Union are now independent countries.

This year 77 of the 78 players were from the Commonwealth of Independent States and the Baltics. Switzerland was the only Western European country represented. The winner was a graduate of one of St. Petersburg's engineering institutes, Vladimir Burmakin, whose passion for the game has obviously not been chilled by his recent move even further north to a city within the Arctic Circle.

Burmakin finished with 7/9 ahead of Sakayev, Bezgodov and Chernayev on 6½. St. Petersburg's strongest young player, Russian champion Peter Svidler, was away at another tournament, but 21-year-old Konstantin Sakayev is another of the city's finest, a bronze medallist at the Moscow Olympiad in 1994 and winner of the best game at the Chigorin tournament.

Russia is still turning out chess prodigies, one of whom is 12-year-old Dmitri Yakovenko, who scored four points in the tournament. While grandmasters racked their brains over the tasks he set them, Dmitri entertained himself and some of the spectators by watching his wind-up plastic bear toddle up and down the table. So young, and already so adept at psychological warfare.

That's not so surprising when you find out that Dmitri takes lessons from Alexander Nikitin, who used to train a certain Garik Kasparov, as the little boy from Azerbaijan was known. The only problem is that Nikitin is based in Moscow and Dmitri lives 3,000 kilometres away in the Siberian town of Nizhny Vartovsk. Their discussions on the latest advances in opening theory take place by telephone.

Dmitri is men's champion of the town, which has a population of 250,000, and he hopes to become an international master "in a year or two." He assured me that he fits in some time for schoolwork around his travel schedule, which has so far taken him to Germany, Hungary, Slovakia and Malta.

Going abroad may be nothing special for Dmitri Yakovenko, but for Mark Taimanov it is a freedom that was denied him for decades. "I'm playing more chess now than I did in my best years, because before I played where I was told to play," he said. This increased activity has twice been rewarded by the title of senior world champion, perhaps some compensation for the crushing of Taimanov's World Championship dreams by Bobby Fischer in 1971.

Taimanov said he was confident that a very good chess tradition had been preserved in St. Petersburg, which would survive the withdrawal of state support. The St. Petersburg team won the CIS Championship last May and the Chigorin tournament's establishment in the city is another sign that Taimanov's judgment is as sound as ever.

Judgments on aesthetic excellence in the Chigorin Memorial were made by 85-year-old Andor Lilienthal, after Miguel Najdorf and Arthur Dake the world's third-oldest grandmaster, who still has the energy to divide his time between Budapest and Moscow and make guest appearances in St. Petersburg.

"Russia is the El Dorado of chess," said the grand old man who trained world champions Smyslov and Petrosian. Lilienthal grew up in Hungary, but in 1935 decided to stay in the Soviet Union after the 2nd Moscow International Tournament "because of the beautiful women." He has been married three times, always to Russian women, and he boasts that his present wife is 30 years younger than him.

Lilienthal not only claims to have been the first grandmaster to play on a collective farm – he got there on a horse in 1939 and gave a simultaneous display on 30 boards – but also remembers playing past women's world champions Vera Menchik and Olga Rubtsova. Asked how they compared to Hungary's modern-day chess phenomenon, he was in no doubt: "They were nowhere near as good as Judit Polgar. History has never known a woman chess player like her, she is a genius."

In his best playing days Lilienthal defeated, amongst others, world champions Lasker, Euwe, Botvinnik – and Capablanca in only 26 moves and with a queen sacrifice! In the last few years he has renewed his friendship with another world champion, the exiled Bobby Fischer, who visits him regularly at his home in Budapest. It was Lilienthal who hosted the recent meeting between Fischer and the new FIDE president, Kirsan Ilyumzhinov.

Dmitri Yakovenko is now an international master. Mark Taimanov continues to play. Andor Lilienthal, who is now the world's oldest grandmaster, celebrated his 90th birthday in 2001. My interview with him in Budapest appears later in these pages.

2. Developing My Pieces

After leaving my job at the *St. Petersburg Press* I wanted to set myself up as a freelance writer, but the stress and the poverty got to me first. I returned to England and moved from my parents' house to my uncle's to my grandfather's while writing a book about my experiences in Russia, *A Shrimp Learnt to Whistle*. I thought of calling Jimmy, but I knew that if I did, chess would take over, so I hesitated. Anyway, he called me, to ask for help with his translation of the book of the Moscow 1935 International Tournament.

Jimmy had taught himself to read Russian, and had no problem translating the annotated games from the tournament. The long introduction to the book was more difficult for him, so I translated that and wrote a foreword for a portion of the payment Jimmy got from the American publisher, Dale Brandreth. At the same time I was publishing *Shrimp* myself, thanks to a bank loan, as I had run out of money for photocopying the manuscript and sending it to publishers, who would reply with a misspelled rejection letter six months later.

While I was staying with my grandfather, Jimmy told me that Kasparov was coming to the London Chess Centre. I couldn't resist an eyeball-to-eyeball experience with the world champion.

Desperately Seeking Gazza
(*CHESS*, December 1996)

One wonders why Garry Kasparov bothers pulverising his opponents at the chessboard, when a single glare from the 33-year-old world champion does the trick just as effectively, in a fraction of the time. On his flying visit to London in October, a stopover between New York and Moscow, Kasparov turned journalists and grandmasters to jelly as he swept through a hectic day of public appearances. His first victim was Scottish chess journalist John Henderson, who came out weak-kneed from a 15-minute audience (sorry, interview) with He Who Must Be Obeyed in the department store Selfridges.

Kasparov was there to promote the chess computers that have his name emblazoned on them, but he was stony-faced and moody – "jet-lagged", according to his publicists – and not inclined to answer many of Henderson's questions in more than a monosyllable. "I'd rather go three rounds with Mike Tyson," said Henderson afterwards. Surely Kasparov couldn't still have been upset about losing to Israeli politician Natan Sharansky in a simultaneous display a few weeks previously?

Later in the afternoon Kasparov was greeted by a huge crowd of fans at the Chess & Bridge Centre in Euston Road. Before they were let loose with their autograph books, IM Malcolm Pein took the champ into a back room to show him some games that Judit Polgar had lost recently. Kasparov cheered up considerably at this and discussed chess enthusiastically with him for several minutes.

Garry Kasparov signs autographs at the London Chess Centre
while I sit behind him nervously. Photo: Lesley Collett

I thought this might be the right time to introduce myself, so I stepped up to Kasparov and said, "Hello, I'm Sarah Hurst from *CHESS* magazine, I'm hoping to ask you some questions about your business interests." Kasparov's black expression returned instantly. Without turning his head to acknowledge me he said, "No. Only chess." "OK," I said meekly, and backed out of the room like a medieval eunuch.

Kasparov's rapport with the children who queued up to meet their hero was of the silent variety. He signed whatever they put in front of him, and then placed his hand on the left side of the desk to indicate where they should stand to have a photograph taken. Reckoning his mental capabilities were powerful enough to concentrate on this task and talk to me at the same time, I pulled up a chair next to him and asked him whether he'd enjoyed chess more as a child or as an adult. Again, he continued to stare straight ahead, and after a while it seemed that he was going to ignore me for having the audacity to speak without being spoken to. Eventually he muttered, "Hard to say." "Well, do you enjoy chess now?" I continued. "Still most of the time, yes," he said.

There was another pause as I considered what to try next. John Henderson and the other people who have met Kasparov have all said that he is unstoppable once he gets onto a subject that he is interested in. So I changed tack. What did he think the future of chess in Russia was now that state support had collapsed? "The potential in Russia is still strong enough to override tendencies caused by economical disaster," he recited, Brezhnev-style. "You had a chess magazine in Russia, didn't you, *Shakhmatny Vestnik*?" I persisted. "No." "Oh." "You mean *Shakhmaty v Rossii*? I helped them at the beginning, but I don't any more."

I asked Kasparov if he planned to continue playing competitive chess for the rest of his life. "The rest of my life is a long time…" he mused, bringing smiles to the faces of his audience at last. "I don't like to make predictions." "Do you have any unfulfilled ambitions left?" I prompted. "Yes, many. I am studying some business opportunities." This was the subject I wasn't allowed to talk about, so I stopped. Kasparov completed the signing session and Malcolm Pein took him on a tour of the chess centre, which brought him to life.

While Kasparov was looking at computers and giving advice on problem solving, I chatted to a young Russian businessman and chess player, Vladimir Meshersky, who was videotaping the event. "Would Kasparov make a good Russian president?" I asked him. "He wouldn't be the worst president, certainly. He is still young, and maybe he needs more experience, but he has achieved a lot in life through his own efforts. In fact, he would have been one of the best presidential candidates amongst those who contested the election last June. It was a shame he didn't stand." Kasparov formed a political party in the early '90s and has been an advocate of market reforms since the Gorbachev era.

Kasparov sat down again at the end of his tour and Malcolm Pein engaged him in a lively discussion about his forthcoming World Championship PCA-FIDE reunification match with Anatoly Karpov. No date or venue for the match has been set, but negotiations are in progress. "We have to agree on the rules," said Kasparov. "The most important thing is who is going to run the match, as there is no umbrella organisation. There are some outstanding items on the agenda, issues of rights. But if Karpov's ready to play, we'll play. I don't think he has any choice: he can't delay any more because people will doubt his right to play the match. Is he stronger than Anand? I doubt it. In a match he is probably better than Kramnik. In a few months, especially if he plays at Las Palmas and comes second or third, he loses his legitimacy. We have to play early next year."

Kasparov was confident that a sponsor for the match could be found outside of Russia. "I would estimate the value of the match on the market to be £2.5 million," he said. "There is a public perception that this match is needed. The public wants this kind of fun. I am not sure that from a chess point of view the match is fully justified, but we shouldn't run another competition. Cycles are dead – who's going to pay for them? If you go to a big company and ask them to sponsor a Candidates cycle, they'll say, who are the top six players? So you choose the six best and two others with the best ratings. Why do you need 100 players if at the end of the day one of those six will play the world champion anyway? With eight players it's commercially, financially viable."

The future of FIDE is bleak, according to Kasparov. "The old system is dead. The organisation is dead. [FIDE President Kirsan] Ilyumzhinov walks away and they have to close the office because they can't pay the wages." It was no surprise that FIDE proposed Baghdad as a venue for the Karpov-Kamsky match: "They were looking for some international publicity FIDE had no internal moral protection. Expectations were too high, they expected someone to come up with a huge sum of money and they looked for any dubious source. Ilyumzhinov had already paid a lot of money, all the debts of the small federations. It is important to recognise the fact that FIDE is not a commercial organisation. In 1995 and 1996 FIDE ran the World Championship with no money. FIDE never raised any money for the World Championship."

Kasparov is determined that the prizes for the World Championship should be high, but I asked him if more money should be distributed amongst lesser-ranking players so that they could at least earn a living from chess. He insisted that the top players must be paid first. "Many talented kids have to choose a profession other than chess because there is no professional circuit they can join like in tennis or golf. We should forget about dirty political games and play a plain commercial game. This is now recognised by the majority of professionals, but it's late – there have been a few years of feuding and bad publicity."

At that point Kasparov was whisked away to the BBC studios for a brief appearance on the children's programme *Blue Peter*. John Henderson, IM Mike Basman and I headed for a luxury hotel in Chelsea Harbour, where Kasparov was due to give an interview to a reporter from *Young Telegraph*. I had been told that he wouldn't speak to any other journalists after that, so gate-crashing the interview was our last chance for a quote. "Perhaps he won't mind talking to you, as you're a professional chess player," I said to Basman. "I don't think so," he replied. "I said hello to him in Armenian and he ignored me." "Are you sure he knows Armenian?" I asked. (Kasparov's mother is Armenian, but he was brought up in Azerbaijan.) "Possibly not," said Basman. "That was the third time!" "In that case, you've probably set a new record for saying hello to Kasparov in Armenian and not getting a reply," I said.

We asked the hotel receptionist if Kasparov had booked a room for his interview, and she said no. At that very moment, the man himself emerged from the revolving doors. I approached him and said hello in English, which I was certain he knew. He looked in the other direction. He greeted the *Young Telegraph* reporter silently and they got into a lift. The lift ascended. "We could have followed them just now, but I got the feeling Kasparov didn't want me to get into the lift with him," I said. "I think *you* didn't want to get into the lift with him," Basman remarked astutely.

Kasparov was obviously giving the interview in his own room. "We can go up there," I said. "What's the worst he can do to us?" Silence. "There are three of us, we can overpower him." "No, there's one of you," said Henderson. Undaunted, I asked the receptionist if she could tell us Kasparov's room number. She wasn't allowed to. "OK, then," I said, "could you ring Mr. Kasparov, please?" "Certainly. How do you spell that? K-a-s-... it's ringing." She handed me the receiver and I shoved it towards Basman and Henderson. They shrank back in the direction of Armenia.

Before I could get rid of the dreaded thing, a familiar sombre voice had said a Russian "Allo?" on the end of it. If I'd had time to think I would have feigned a near-fatal heart attack that rendered me incapable of movement or speech. Instead, I pretended to be the champ's best friend. "Hi, Garry, it's Sarah Hurst from *CHESS* magazine," I said in dulcet tones. Not giving him a second to grunt or come downstairs and pound me into the floor, I said, "I'm here with John Henderson and Mike Basman and we'd like to come up and sit in on your interview with *Young Telegraph*." "Sarah, I'm busy, I've got no time." "I know, but you are giving an interview now, and we'd just like to listen to the interview." "No questions!" "No, fine, no questions. Can we come up?" And Kasparov resigned! "Yes, come up," he said despairingly. "What's your room number?" "114."

The *Young Telegraph* reporter was waiting nervously in one room of Kasparov's suite and Kasparov was behind a closed door in the other room, talking on the telephone. I took the opportunity to gently suggest a question to *Young Telegraph* man, explaining our delicate situation, and he kindly agreed to ask it for me. He had 20 of his own, so Kasparov was bound to answer one or two of them. As expected, he brushed aside some of the more banal ones. Of course he's heard it all before, but when you're world champion and you speak in public, you ought to put on an act. Kasparov wants to encourage more people to play chess – in the interview he said more about that than about anything else – and yet he comes across as intimidating and indifferent.

Kasparov is in a dilemma. He wants to keep on winning, but winning can bring him no more glory. He is defensive. He knows the only direction he can go from here is down, and looking down from a great height is never a pleasant thing to do.

"You've been world champion for 10 years now," the *Young Telegraph* reporter began. "Eleven years, let's be honest about it," Kasparov replied. "What inspires you to play chess?" the reporter asked. "Chess is a part of my life and I have to keep playing to feel confident. You have to keep on with your profession; otherwise your integrity will be in trouble. Almost all my adult years I have been world champion and it's very difficult to separate myself from the duties and responsibilities of the title. My mother still inspires me to play, and my own determination, a driving force inside me. You can go for the longest duration of holding the title, or winning the most matches – but none of it's the same as winning the title for the first time." I wished I could ask Kasparov whether he sometimes yearned to be free of all those responsibilities.

Kasparov said he trains every summer for four to five consecutive weeks, five to six hours a day, with two coaches and three computers. He checks analysis with the Fritz program. "It's a very efficient way of working. You can't concentrate in the analysis as you do in the game, you make blunders. If you have a strong chess-playing program on a PC, it dramatically improves the quality of the analysis. In many positions I'm reaching what I call the final conclusion. I still feel that in many opening lines I'm ahead of my colleagues, even though they only play chess and I do thousands of other things. I'm still capable of mobilising my forces, despite the fact that in most tournaments today I'm the oldest participant, apart from Karpov, who's 45. Most players are under 30. How would I describe my style? Dynamic and aggressive." Kasparov searched for an analogy for a moment. Then he found the right one. "Like a tank division," he said, smiling proudly.

My question was, "Have you ever considered making a film about yourself or another famous chess player to popularise the game?" Kasparov said, "I was approached to make a documentary about myself. But I don't believe that random events can make a big difference, I mean, there was an American film of the book *Searching for Bobby Fischer* and that didn't change anything. Films and big matches should happen regularly. We've had many, many great momentums, high peaks of public attention, but the next day nobody was around. Like when I played Deep Blue [IBM's chess computer] in America.

"Chess players are quite happy with this little life, this little community. Federations have their own control and are scared of expansion. There was no serious force for a long time to bring chess from obscurity to the world stage. Nigel Short was a product of the great chess enthusiasm in England in the late '70s, the momentum after the Fischer-Spassky match. The British Chess Federation kept this going. But another great momentum was missed in 1993 after my match with Nigel. The TV programme had great ratings and very good demographics from a sponsor's point of view, and nothing happened."

The *Young Telegraph* reporter asked if Kasparov had a hobby. The world champion sneered derisively at this affront. "I do not have a hobby. I don't have time for pastimes or hobbies. I have interests. I don't collect anything, don't waste my time on computer games. We live in such a fast-changing time, our universe is being shaken. Most of our views on the world changed since we got these information highways changing our lives. I am going to work hard to bring chess to the Internet – it's a special box which chess has been awaiting for a long time. I'm working on a special site with IBM. We have a huge, hidden, silent majority of chess funds and forces which have never really spent time on chess because the chess world didn't work for their convenience. It's a white-collar audience. With the Internet you can solve some social problems: Many people don't want to go to a chess club, but they have the Internet in their workplace. We must create a loyal, stable audience.

"Chess must be in the school curriculum, one year of chess. It's very easy to do. It teaches kids so many qualities: logic, it helps them to focus on targets, discipline, and the No. 1 quality is responsibility, responsibility about the paradoxes of modern civilisation. We're wasting our most sophisticated technologies on mindless games, and that's a great paradox."

We got up to leave and Kasparov shook hands with all of us. I had nothing to lose now, so I asked another question. "A Russian in the chess centre said you would have been a good candidate for president. Have you thought about that?" This time Kasparov looked at me when he answered. "I'm still young. That should be my last aim in life, I think." With that we released the world champion from his responsibilities until the evening's reception in the hotel. At the reception Basman finally found out that Kasparov doesn't speak Armenian. Henderson persuaded him to sign some books as competition prizes.

I still nurtured faint hopes of talking to Kasparov informally, so I didn't carry my notebook, to show that I came in peace. A woman was asking him if it was true that he could remember every single game he had ever played, and he said, "No, I haven't got room for all that crap in my head." Surely if her conversation was worthy, my conversation was worthy? I said, "Garry, I'm thinking of writing a film script about Alexander Alekhine." "NO!" he said, raising the palm of his hand like a shield. I said, "It's not a question, I just wanted to…" "NO!!!" "In that case, would you please sign this book for me?" He did it.

I thanked him, and I went home happy. After all, he's my hero, too.

Kasparov is still the highest-rated player in the world, although he was defeated 8½-6½ in a match with Vladimir Kramnik in 2000, so Kasparov conceded his world title to Kramnik. Kasparov never played a reunification match with Karpov and has not yet participated in the FIDE knockout World Championships. Kasparov was absolutely right in saying that the Internet would be perfect for chess. His own KasparovChess.com is one of the most impressive chess websites.

I became gripped by the story of Alexander Alekhine after reading a Russian biography of him. Jimmy told me that chess historian Ken Whyld was working on a collection of Alekhine's games and a biography, so I went to see him at his farmhouse in Lincolnshire. He had a table covered with books and articles by and about Alekhine, photographs of Alekhine, actual Alekhine game scores, documents relating to Alekhine's birth, marriages and death…

While writing my mammoth article, I also drafted some scenes for a film about Alekhine's life. A documentary producer in London did show an interest and we met to discuss it, but he was a bit of a maverick and knew very little about chess, and the project never got off the ground. The article was published in three installments in *CHESS*.

Alexander Alekhine: Only Human
(*CHESS*, January, February and March 1997)

An undefeated world champion, obsessed with chess to the exclusion of all other activities, whose games were and still are an inspiration to millions, an enemy of the Soviet state, sympathiser with the ideals of Nazism… Bobby Fischer? No, we are talking about Alexander Alekhine, dead for more than 50 years but a giant of the chess world whose status has not been diminished by time – or by his controversial and mysterious personal life.

Born into an aristocratic Russian family, blessed with a phenomenal chess talent, Alekhine's 53-year slide into despondency, disgrace and alcoholism must rank as one of the most precipitate failures of the 20th century. But his ignominious end in a Portuguese hotel room, friendless and penniless, did not come about only because of weaknesses in his character. It was Alekhine's misfortune to be swept from world crisis to world crisis, always finding himself in the wrong place at the wrong time, having to survive wars and adapt to life under tyrannical regimes, when all he wanted to do was play chess.

All this trouble might have been avoided if Alekhine had succumbed to the severe illness that afflicted him when he was about seven years old. He was born in Moscow in 1892 and was taught chess as a small child by his mother. His older brother and sister also played chess; the brother, Alexei, showed considerable aptitude for the game and went on to become a leading Soviet chess publisher and writer.

Both Alexander and Alexei played correspondence chess as children, signing their names on the entry form "A. A. Alekhine." It is possible that little Alexander did this so that people would assume he was Alexei – he was probably playing before he was old enough to do so officially. Their sister, Barbara, speculated that Alexander's "inflammation of the brain" (which could have been meningitis) was caused by his fanatical chess playing. Alekhine's latest biographer, Yuri Shaburov, writes that Alexander used to get out of bed in the middle of the night to look at a game, and that his parents had to hide the chessboard to keep him away from it.

The illness forced Alekhine to give up chess and all other activities for a while, and postponed his entry into a prestigious boys' school. In 1901 he did go, and became one of the best pupils there without exerting much effort in his studies. Instead of listening to his teachers, he analysed chess positions in the classroom. He had a photographic memory, which meant that a quick look at a textbook was enough for him to answer any question the teacher posed. But occasionally he was so engrossed in his chess that he caused hilarious incidents.

"I remember once when we were all working on an algebra problem," recalled an old classmate of Alekhine's decades later. "All the boys were quiet... Suddenly Alekhine jumped up, his face beaming, surveyed the class with his eyes and, simultaneously, the way he always did, twisted a strand of hair with his left hand which was hanging over his forehead. 'So, Alekhine, you've worked it out?' the teacher asked him. 'Oh yes... I sacrifice a knight... and White wins!' We all shook with laughter. Our usually restrained teacher chortled through his long moustache."

Fyodor Duz-Khotimirsky came to Alekhine's home to give him chess lessons, and the teenager's progress was remarkable. At the age of 17 he won the All-Russian Amateurs' Tournament. He also continued with his studies, graduating from the Imperial St. Petersburg School of Jurisprudence in 1914. In the same week that he was given a job with the Ministry of Justice, he came third in the famous St. Petersburg tournament, after Lasker and Capablanca.

There was more good news for the Alekhine family when Alexander's father (also Alexander) was elected to the Fourth Duma. But Europe was on the brink of war. In the last days before the assassination of Archduke Franz Ferdinand in Sarajevo, Alekhine and many other Russian chess players were in Mannheim, at the 19th Congress of the German Chess Union.

Alekhine was leading the Mannheim International Tournament, on 9½ points to Milan Vidmar's 8½ and Rudolf Spielmann's 8 points, when war broke out. Alekhine was declared the winner and he was interned along with the other Russians who had participated in the congress. In one of the prisons Alekhine shared a cell with Efim Bogolyubov, Abraham Rabinovich and Samuel Weinstein.

Alekhine later wrote, "Life in prison was rather monotonous – there were no books, no newspapers, and, of course, no chessboard. Bogolyubov and I played chess from memory for hours. Our duels were interrupted when I was placed in solitary confinement for four days because during our compulsory walk I had the audacity to smile once."

Fyodor Bogatyrchuk says the punishment was for something quite different: Alekhine had been rather distracted by the beauty of the jailer's daughter, she had not been entirely immune to his masculine charms, and she had permitted herself certain liberties "which were not included in the list of prison rules."

A number of Russian players were interned for the duration of the war, which meant they were in Germany when the February and October revolutions took place in Russia. Bogolyubov was one of these: he married a German and never took up residence in Russia again. When the Bolsheviks came to power, he was denounced as a "renegade". Alekhine would suffer the same fate, but he had no inkling of this in 1914.

The stories Alekhine told of his daring escape from Germany, travelling without papers, fearing that he could be arrested and shot at any moment, were completely untrue. Like the other Russians, he was examined by a German medical commission in September 1914. Unlike the others, he was declared unfit for military service in Russia and given permission to return home. He even had the means to travel in style via England, rather than getting on a crowded ship with other refugees.

Bogatyrchuk, who was also released on medical grounds, found it rather surprising that Alekhine was allowed to join him. "Apart from me, two others were released – Alekhine and Saburov. Saburov was an elderly and not completely well man, but I can't imagine why they let Alekhine go. It could only have been because the doctor was an admirer of Alekhine's chess genius. I ought to point out that Bogolyubov and Seleznyov were amongst those who had to stay behind, both of whom were exempt from military service in Russia."

Back in Moscow, Alekhine began working for a committee that provided clothes and other essential items to wounded soldiers returning to Russia. In his spare time he visited the Moscow chess circle, giving a simultaneous display on 32 boards in 1915, at which he won 23 games and lost five. In the same year two deaths occurred in the Alekhine family: first Alekhine's grandfather, then his 46-year-old mother. She died in Switzerland, where she was being treated for her chronic illness.

Throughout Alekhine's early life, his parents had travelled extensively around Europe. The absence of parental love may well have been an important factor in his character as an adult; biographers have pointed out that he constantly sought a mother figure, which was why his last two wives were two decades and three decades older than him. But that was later on.

In 1916, Alekhine volunteered to go to the Galician Front with the Red Cross. He was given medals for helping the wounded under artillery and machine-gun fire, including the Order of St. Stanislav, for dragging a wounded officer from the battlefield. Alekhine himself was shell-shocked and taken to hospital, where he recovered enough to ask for local chess players to be invited to his ward. His request was granted and he played regular blindfold games with them.

Alekhine was in Moscow at the time of the February Revolution, when Tsar Nicholas II abdicated and was replaced by a provisional government. In March 1917, Alekhine's father made a speech calling for a united, free Russia. In May, he died. Alekhine lived with his brother for a while and even played chess in Moscow during the cold, difficult months that followed the October Revolution.

Throughout the country the White armies of former tsarist officers were massing to fight the Bolshevik Red Army. Ukraine was a particularly dangerous region – Kiev was captured and recaptured several times in the Civil War – but in autumn 1918 Alekhine set out for Kiev and Odessa on a chess tour. Ukraine was in a state of violent anarchy. In early 1919, the Red Army shot 1,300 people in mass executions.

As a member of the nobility, it was hardly surprising that Alekhine was one of those arrested in April of that year. Shaburov says that the arrest might also have been provoked by an anonymous letter written by someone who envied Alekhine's talent, reporting his alleged anti-Soviet activity. He was interrogated by the Cheka (predecessors to the KGB) and locked in a cell. This was one of the murkiest episodes of his life and very little is certain about it.

Bogatyrchuk writes that only one thing is known about Alekhine's arrest in Odessa: he was sentenced to death. A rumour has been repeated in many sources that Alekhine was saved by Trotsky, the Bolshevik commissar for war, who supposedly came to his cell and demanded that Alekhine play chess with him. Alekhine couldn't decide whether to win or lose, played hesitantly at first, knowing his life depended on the outcome, and eventually won the game. Trotsky was so impressed that he ordered Alekhine's release.

It's a great story, which may well have been put about by Alekhine himself, but it is a fiction. Trotsky was nowhere near Odessa at the time. According to Bogatyrchuk, Alekhine was saved by a request from Jacob Vilner, a chess master from Odessa who also happened to work for a military tribunal. Vilner told Bogatyrchuk that he heard about Alekhine's sentence hours before it was due to be carried out and immediately sent a telegram to Rakovsky, the head of the Ukrainian administration.

"Fortunately, Rakovsky had heard of Alekhine's chess genius and got straight in touch with the Cheka in Odessa on a direct line. After that, all we can be sure of is that Alekhine was freed the very same night… It is possible that Alekhine didn't even know about the death sentence."

Alekhine made his way back to Moscow in July, weeks before White forces entered Odessa. Alekhine began dreaming of a career as a film star, and applied to the newly opened State School of Cinematography, along with hundreds of other young people. The head of the school was a famous director, Vladimir Gardin.

"I had loved chess all my life and, of course, had admired Alekhine's genius for a long time," Gardin recalled in 1960. "But he was accepted into the school not only because of that. A talented man brings his individuality into everything he does. This was also true of the great chess player's acting."

While studying at the school, Alekhine married for the first time. The identity of his first wife has been disputed. Shaburov says he has seen the documents and that the woman was Alexandra Batayeva, a widow to whom Alekhine was only married for about a year. But Shaburov is the only person to mention Batayeva. All of Alekhine's previous biographers give a completely different name. Some even say that he had a daughter by his first wife; again, there is no proof of this.

Alekhine never finished the course at the film school. Lectures were interrupted by organisational problems – new premises had to be found for the school. This gave Alekhine free time, in which he played chess. There was no club in Moscow, so chess players gathered in private flats. One of the players who was inspired by Alekhine was Vladimir Lezerson, who described the future world champion as "a very friendly, sociable person, untainted by the usual self-importance and pomposity of a grandmaster. He willingly played casual games with chess players who were obviously much weaker than him, examined and analysed games and individual positions, and demonstrated his own.

"Once he showed us his game with Duras from the Mannheim Tournament. Someone asked him how he rated Duras as a player. 'Well,' Alekhine replied, 'Duras is a very strong chess player, of course, but when he plays me, I always know what he is thinking about.' To the question: 'Really, Alexander Alexandrovich, don't you know what all the masters are thinking about when you play them?' came this answer: 'Not at all. When I play Lasker or Capablanca, I can't even imagine what they're thinking about. Many of their moves are a revelation to me.'"

The first Moscow Championship held under the Soviet regime took place in late 1919 and early 1920. The conditions of play were extremely difficult: there were frequent power cuts and the building was unheated due to a shortage of firewood. Even heavy winter clothing couldn't protect the players from frostbite. "Our noses, hands and especially our feet froze," wrote Ilyin-Zhenevsky. "When we were thinking about a move, our feet had to dance a polka-mazurka under the table at the same time, so that they didn't become completely numb. But our love for chess was so great that no one complained, everyone sat through whole evenings of tournament games calmly and with great pleasure."

Alekhine was the only grandmaster amongst the 12 competitors and played outside the tournament, winning all his 11 games. Soon afterwards, he was struck by a bout of typhoid measles. Then he found a new job that somehow involved his law degree, although the Soviet criminal justice system was radically different from the pre-revolutionary system.

Alekhine worked for the Moscow police force's Centre of Investigations. Some biographers have said he investigated crimes. Shaburov points out that the purpose of the Centre of Investigations was something entirely different – to search for people who had gone missing during the Revolution and Civil War. As with the other events of this confused period, facts about Alekhine's activities as an investigator are notable by their absence. The same is true of his simultaneous work as an interpreter with the Comintern (Communist International).

In the form that he filled in when he joined the Comintern, Alekhine wrote that he was able to speak, read and write French, German and English, that he was married, and that he had been exempted from military service due to illness.

Alekhine won the All-Russian Olympiad in 1920, ahead of Peter Romanovsky, Grigory Levenfish and Ilya Rabinovich. He was the first chess champion of Soviet Russia, but his career in the country of his birth was about to come to an abrupt end. Through the Comintern he met the Swiss journalist Annelise Ruegg, and they were married in March 1921. Five days later, Alekhine received permission from the People's Commissariat of Foreign Affairs to travel to Latvia. He gave a simultaneous display in Riga, losing just two games out of 54.

From Riga Alekhine and his wife went on to Paris, via Berlin. Alekhine undoubtedly wanted to live outside Russia for a while, and true love may not have been his only motive in marrying Ruegg, but he did not know that he would never set foot in his homeland again.

What would have happened to Alekhine if he had stayed in Russia? The Civil War was over. Millions would die in Stalin's purges, and although Alekhine could not foresee the extent of the killing, he knew from his arrest in Odessa that the Soviet authorities did not look upon him too kindly. He could not know how important chess would become in the Soviet Union from 1925 onwards, thanks to chess organiser and public prosecutor Nikolai Krylenko.

The likelihood is that Stalin's government would have turned a blind eye to Alekhine's aristocratic origins, as long as he agreed to represent the Soviet Union in its struggle with world capitalism, as Botvinnik did later on. Krylenko saw to it that the world chess title became synonymous with Soviet prestige on the international stage. Alekhine would have led a privileged lifestyle and been a Soviet hero before his death, not just after it.

Of course, if Alekhine hadn't behaved himself, if he had forgotten to praise Stalin at the appropriate moments, his life would have been in danger. But Alekhine had the ideal personality to play the role expected of him. He was never a rebel. When the Bolsheviks seized power, he worked for them. When he found himself in France at the outbreak of World War II, he joined the French army. When the Nazis occupied France, he wrote Nazi articles and played in Nazi chess tournaments.

Alekhine was basically an apolitical person who did whatever he had to do to continue playing chess. That was his prime motivation in life.

Chess was the reason why Alekhine left Russia in 1921. The man who studied chess "eight hours a day on principle" and never looked up from his pocket chess set when he was taken to the theatre for an evening with Capablanca (who never took his eyes off the actresses' legs), must have found chess life in Russia barren in 1921. He had beaten all the best players in the country, and there was little hope of meeting any foreign masters on Russian soil in the circumstances of the time.

Also, as I have already mentioned, Alekhine was justified in fearing for his safety in Russia. It made sense to go to France for a few years and perhaps return when the situation had stabilized.

Another significant event took place in 1921: Lasker, the world champion, lost his title to Capablanca in Havana. Lasker didn't win a single game of the match. Capablanca was known as the "chess machine" – he had a natural ability to evaluate any position and find magnificent combinations without working too hard on his game. Alekhine, who already harboured World Championship ambitions, knew that this was the daunting opponent he would have to face.

At this stage, the two were on relatively friendly terms. Later on, Capablanca would grow to become a demonic figure in Alekhine's mind, and their rivalry would last until the Cuban's death in 1942. The story of their feud makes Korchnoi and Karpov look like bosom buddies.

Immediately after the match with Lasker, Alekhine sent his first world title challenge to Capablanca. In those days, the world champion not only had the right to set his own terms for the match (which included making the challenger raise the funds for it), but could also decide to accept or refuse any challenge without jeopardising his status.

Capablanca had waited 10 years for Lasker to accept his challenge, so understandably he was in no hurry to risk it against Alekhine. It was up to Alekhine to prove himself by winning a series of international tournaments. If he could do that, he would demonstrate that he was the rightful challenger and put pressure on Capablanca to play him.

In 1921 Alekhine won tournaments in Triberg, Budapest and The Hague. The following year he shared 2nd-3rd place with Spielmann in the Czech town of Piestany, where the winner of the tournament was his former cellmate, Bogolyubov. But Alekhine suffered a far bigger setback in London three months later. Before the tournament began, Savielly Tartakower wrote an article that praised Alekhine highly: "'I win, therefore I am' – that is the best way of describing Alekhine's chess philosophy… The person with the best chances in London, in my opinion, is the bold Muscovite."

Alekhine played superbly in London, but Capablanca played even better. Their game ended in a draw, which was a disappointment to Alekhine, and he finished 1½ points behind the world champion. To make matters worse, Capablanca announced his conditions for a world title match and the other players at the tournament had no choice but to agree to them. Two of them were excessively harsh for the challenger: the match would be played to six wins, draws not counting, and the world champion was not obliged to defend his title unless a minimum of $10,000 was raised.

Alekhine, barely scraping a living in Paris, had never won a game against Capablanca. What chance had he of winning six in one match? There was nothing he could do except to continue playing in tournaments and hope that his fortunes would change.

For most players, Alekhine was an intimidating opponent to face across the chessboard, even more so because of the constant nervous gestures and movements he made. During the London tournament a journalist wrote, "He is a hatchet-faced blond giant, with a sweep of hair over his forehead, and several inches of cuff protruding from his sleeve. First he rests his head in his hands, works his ears into indescribable shapes, clasps his hands under his chin in pitiful supplication, shifts uneasily in his seat like a dog on an anthill, frowns, elevates his eyebrows, rises suddenly and stands behind his chair for a panoramic view of the table, resumes his seat, then, as the twin clock at his side ticks remorselessly on, sweeps his hair back for the thousandth time, shifts a pawn, taps the clock button, and records his move."

Alekhine's obsession with winning sometimes led to violence. In his book *The Human Side of Chess*, Fred Reinfeld wrote, "Sometimes, when he lost a game, he picked up his king and hurled it across the room. On at least one occasion, according to Kmoch, he fell into such a rage that after the loss of a very important game he smashed the furniture in his hotel room. If he lost at ping-pong, he would crush the ball in his anger."

William Winter, in *Kings of Chess*, recalled that he "had an irritating habit of transferring to his pocket any box of matches which might be left unguarded in the vicinity of the chessboard." Winter also heard Alekhine make a telling comment when he was in a more reflective mood: "You call me Grand Master. I am not Grand Master, I am not even master. Chess will always be master of me, of Capablanca, and of all of us."

Alekhine had been fascinated by blindfold chess ever since 1902, when the American master Harry Pillsbury visited Russia and gave a blindfold simultaneous display. In 1925 Alekhine set a new blindfold record, winning 22 games and losing three on 28 boards. He played for 12 hours without a break, eating nothing and drinking only black coffee. Asked how it was possible to keep so many games in his head at once, Alekhine replied that in his memory each game was in a separate drawer, and that all the drawers were shut until it was time to make a move in a particular game, when he opened the relevant drawer and saw exactly what was in it.

This was probably one of the entertaining stories Alekhine made up for the benefit of the press. He put his amazing creativity to use in more ways than one. In his chess books he "improved" some of the games he had played, changing some of the moves when he found something he hadn't seen at the board.

The story of Alekhine's doctorate is a similar "improvement" on the truth. Alekhine is often referred to as "Dr. Alekhine", as he claimed to have been awarded a doctorate in law from the Sorbonne in 1925. He was certainly working on a thesis (the subject was the Chinese prison system), but the Sorbonne records show that Alekhine did not complete his degree.

As is true of most top-level chess players, Alekhine had little time to devote to his personal life. His wife, Annelise, was also busy with her own profession. She gave birth to a son, Alexander, but the marriage ended soon afterwards and Alexander was brought up in Switzerland. He is still alive and has been a guest at Alekhine memorial tournaments. Alekhine himself was quick to find a new love. He married a general's widow, Nadyezhda Vasilyeva, who already had a daughter from her first marriage.

Alekhine continued travelling around Europe to tournaments and Vasilyeva frequently accompanied him. In Austria he was asked by a journalist to write something on the theme "How I became a maestro." In his reply he linked the principles of chess with the principles of life.

"I developed my character through chess. Chess, in the first place, teaches objectivity. In chess it is possible to become a great master simply by identifying one's own mistakes and weaknesses. Life is exactly the same. The aim of human life and the meaning of happiness is to do the maximum that a human being can do. And as I, so to say, subconsciously felt that my greatest achievements would be in chess, I became a chess maestro. However, I must point out and emphasise that I only became a professional after I left Russia, and that I intend to continue with my legal career."

That was rather an optimistic prognosis. By 1926 Alekhine had won nine out of 14 international tournaments since London, come second in three of the remaining five, third in another, and fourth in the last. He was indisputably the only person capable of challenging Capablanca for the world title. In August he was invited to Buenos Aires by the Argentinian Chess Union, and he accepted, hoping for financial support for the match. Three weeks after his arrival, the question of the match was decided. Alekhine was admired by influential Argentinians, including President Marcelo Alvear, and he received a guarantee that the $10,000 would be provided. There was a delay of a few months after that because Aron Nimzowitsch had also challenged Capablanca and only withdrew the challenge at the end of 1926.

Alekhine returned to Europe and won a match with the Dutch player Max Euwe by 5½ points to 4½. Then he came second to Capablanca in a tournament in New York. In September 1927, he and his wife arrived in Buenos Aires for the World Championship match. The result of the first game was a shock: Alekhine won with the black pieces. Capablanca had risked a king's pawn opening, and when that failed he returned to his usual Queen's Gambit for the rest of the match.

Near the beginning of the match Alekhine had to have six teeth removed because of inflamed gums and he endured terrible pain and a high temperature while he was playing. When he recovered, he was in excellent form. He won the 11th game as Black with four queens on the board. Capablanca's morale sank and he lost the next game as well. Now Alekhine had three wins to Capablanca's two.

By the 34th game Alekhine was leading by five points to three. As Black, Capablanca put up a stubborn resistance for two days, but when the game adjourned for the second time he was playing with a rook against a rook and two pawns. The next day the arbiter started the clock with Capablanca absent. Everyone in the hall was startled when a messenger rushed in and delivered a note to Alekhine. It read, "29th November 1927. To Dr. A. Alekhine. Dear Alekhine, I resign the game. Consequently, you are the world champion, and I congratulate you on your success. My regards to Mrs. Alekhine. Sincerely yours, J.R. Capablanca."

Capablanca's decision not to resign in person signaled the beginning of hostilities between the two grandmasters. If Capablanca had attempted to avoid Alekhine's challenge, Alekhine would make it infinitely more difficult for Capablanca to obtain a World Championship match, despite prolonged negotiations. It was so difficult, in fact, that the two never contested the World Championship again. Nevertheless, they were both generous in their assessments of each other immediately after the match.

Capablanca wrote, "He demonstrated enormous strength of will in every game; he persistently sought a victory and was steadfast in defence. Without doubt, he played better than I did in this match, and his achievement deserves nothing but admiration." Alekhine, after praising his opponent's game, wrote, "Finally my life's ambition has been fulfilled and I have been able to harvest the fruits of my long efforts and labours."

Alekhine's victory was greeted ecstatically in the Soviet Union. Letters of congratulation poured into the offices of newspapers and magazines. "The perfection of form and the richness of ideas which permeate Alekhine's games make them real pearls of chess art," gushed Grigory Levenfish in the Soviet magazine *Shakhmaty* (*Chess*). "He is the greatest chess artist of our times." Surely it would not be long before Alekhine would return to the Soviet Union and take his rightful place as the inspiration of its flourishing chess movement? He had missed the Moscow International Tournament of 1925, but there would be plenty more opportunities. Fame and fortune beckoned. Then things began to go horribly wrong.

On the path to the summit Alekhine had been through life-threatening illness, a revolution, two wars, two arrests, one death sentence, and three wives. No wonder the 35-year-old Russian émigré was proud of himself. The carefree life of a wealthy celebrity in Paris couldn't be further removed from the freezing cold flat he had left behind in his native Moscow.

While Alekhine was enjoying freedom and Western decadence, his compatriots were learning to keep their mouths shut if they wanted to stay alive. But Alekhine hadn't lived under Stalin's regime. "The myth of the invincibility of the Bolsheviks has been dispelled, like the myth of Capablanca's invincibility," he remarked casually at a banquet in the Russian Club in Paris. The next morning, the comment was reported in émigré newspapers. Shortly afterwards, it became known in Moscow. Not for the first time in his life, and not for the last, a judgment was passed on Alekhine without any possibility for him to defend himself.

"We must draw only one conclusion from Alekhine's behaviour: anyone in the chess circles of the USSR who still cherishes the hope that Alekhine will return some day, must give it up now... Alekhine is our political enemy and no one should forget that. Whoever supports him, even to a small degree, is against us... Talent is talent but politics is politics and we shall never associate with renegades, whether they be Alekhine or Bogolyubov."

That was the damning statement of Nikolai Krylenko published in *Shakhmatny Listok* of March 1928. Krylenko was a force to be reckoned with. He founded the mass chess organisation that would produce a string of world champions from Botvinnik to Kasparov. He convinced the Soviet leadership that chess was an integral part of proletarian culture deserving of virtually unlimited financial support from the state. He wielded this influence because he was a leading revolutionary who became a public prosecutor in Stalin's show trials.

Krylenko's loyalty was aptly rewarded in 1938, when he was executed. All mention of him was removed from Soviet books and newspapers – his introduction to the book of the 1936 Moscow International Tournament was ripped out of most copies – but his chess policies were lasting. Alekhine remained an enemy, even though he was called an enemy by an enemy. Such was the logic of Soviet life.

Krylenko's declaration meant that all of Alekhine's contacts with Russia were severed. He could not communicate with his family or friends and he could no longer work for the Moscow magazine *Shakhmaty*. He certainly had no hope of being invited to tournaments in Russia. Alekhine's biographer, Yuri Shaburov, points out that this decision had in fact been taken by Krylenko in 1926, two years before the notorious remark at the Russian Club.

A decree on Bogolyubov contained the words, "…we did not enter into any negotiations with Alekhine about his participation in the International Tournament in Moscow, as we consider this master to be a hostile element and enemy of Soviet power." The decree was published in Soviet chess magazines and Alekhine probably saw it. But at that time most of Krylenko's rage was directed against Bogolyubov, because he had decided to live in Germany even after visiting Russia and winning the Soviet Championship in 1924 and 1925. These titles were stripped from him in the decree. But Bogolyubov was completely overshadowed by Alekhine when he became world champion. That was why Krylenko's reaction to Alekhine was so explosive in 1928.

An extremely unusual source gives us an insight into Alekhine's actual political views in the late 1920s. It is the *Minutes of the Astrea Lodge. Paris. 1927-1928.* Alekhine and another Russian chess player, Osip Bernstein, applied for membership to this Masonic lodge and their political views were assessed by the other Masons. One wrote of Alekhine, "By the time the revolution broke out, his political views were rather vague and unclear, even to himself. When the Bolsheviks seized power, he thought that it was the beginning of something new, though he had no clear idea of what it might be. Till 1921 he served the Bolsheviks as an interpreter. Finally he realised that there was a deep gap… between Communist ideas and their application. He then decided to leave Russia."

Another Mason agreed that Alekhine was confused about politics: "In spite of his rather extensive scientific knowledge, he is unable to understand a complex political situation. He has no concrete political wishes with regard to Russia. He approaches all political phenomena 'intuitively', as he himself put it. For him political truth is when people can freely express their will and where there is sovereignty for nations and no violence and lawlessness." Alekhine admitted that his "spiritual loneliness" was the motivation for his desire to join the lodge.

Alekhine and Bernstein were initiated into the lodge in May 1928. Shaburov provides a chilling description of the ceremony. The chess players wore blindfolds. "Bleak candlelight was drowning in black walls. The writing on the walls warned: 'If you have been driven here by mere curiosity, better leave,' 'Beware if pretence is your middle name: you'll be exposed,' 'If you have fear in your heart, don't go any further.'"

Alekhine rolled up his left trouser leg and swore an oath to keep all the secrets of the lodge. "At that moment the band was torn off from his eyes, and in the light of funeral candles he saw the picture of a bloodstained body pierced with a sword on the floor - the fate of anyone who would dare break his oath." Alekhine did keep the oath and never told anyone that he was a Freemason. But he rarely participated in the activities of the lodge and was expelled in 1937 because of his poor attendance.

Although Alekhine took French citizenship and made Paris his base, he travelled constantly. In the summer of 1929 he won a small tournament in the United States before making a successful defence of his world title against Bogolyubov in Holland and Germany. America made a big impression on Alekhine. Films had always excited him (he had studied in Moscow at the School of Cinematography) and in New York he promised a thriller writer that he would take the role of a chess player in a "talkie" based on his novel, *The Crime of the Black Officer*. "As the chess player is a foreigner, I won't have a problem with language," Alekhine told a journalist.

After America, Alekhine shaped up for the World Championship match. "For three months I haven't eaten anything except vegetables, salad and fruit, I haven't touched a drop of wine, and I don't drink anything with my meals: I've lost 12 kilograms."

Alekhine won his match with Bogolyubov by a comfortable margin of 11 games to five with nine draws. He was vehemently opposed to a rematch with Capablanca and used his power as world champion to avoid playing in a tournament with the Cuban. In *The Psychology of the Chess Player*, Reuben Fine, the American grandmaster-turned-psychologist wrote, "Once he had beaten Capablanca, Alekhine's attitude towards him took a sharp about-face. He avoided a return match by any trick that he could think of. Once when Capablanca had raised the $10,000 purse required, Alekhine demanded that it be paid in gold because the dollar was no longer of the same value!... In 1937, at a chess tournament in Margate, England, Sir John Simon, then Home Secretary, made some opening remarks... he happened to mention Capablanca's name in passing. Alekhine immediately got up and left the room."

Alekhine deferred playing Capablanca by accepting a second World Championship challenge from Bogolyubov in 1934. They played in Germany and Alekhine again won without too much difficulty, by 15½ points to 10½.

The Soviet government's hatred of Alekhine and Bogolyubov intensified after the World Championship match. They had shown that the world's top two chess players were Russian, and yet one of them represented France and the other represented Germany. It was a humiliation for the new regime. A torrent of insults was unleashed in the press and the magazine *Shakhmaty* was closed down because it had once employed Alekhine and because it devoted too much space to international chess life while publishing hardly any ideological articles.

The vilification of Alekhine in Russia had a devastating effect on him. He questioned GMs Salo Flohr and Andor Lilienthal about their visits to the Soviet Union. "Even I – no psychologist – read in Alekhine's eyes that he missed Moscow very much," Flohr recalled. Lilienthal confirms this impression: "Once I was sitting in a café with Flohr when Alekhine came in. In conversation with us he said that he dreamt of returning to his native land. It wasn't the only time he spoke about this, it was his ardent desire."

A close acquaintance of Alekhine, the writer Lev Lyubimov, noticed that "something about his fate constantly exasperated him. He was genuinely inspired on the subject of chess, and if he was talking to a foreigner he always emphasized that the most advanced chess culture was in the Soviet Union."

Alekhine sought consolation with a new woman, a chess-playing American widow called Grace Wishar. She was considerably older than Alekhine, like his wife Nadyezhda, whom he divorced to marry Grace. Then, at the end of 1934, Alekhine received a challenge from the 35-year-old Dutch GM Max Euwe. Dr. Euwe, who took his job as a mathematics lecturer as seriously as his chess, was not expected to be a dangerous opponent for Alekhine. But the world champion had become increasingly frustrated and depressed.

According to Fine, "he began to drink fairly heavily, his play deteriorated, and he began to show some signs of megalomania." In preparation for the match with Euwe, Alekhine played top board for France at a team tournament in Warsaw. Supposedly he arrived at the Polish border without a passport and told officials, "I am Alekhine, chess champion of the world. I have a cat called Chess. I do not need papers."

Fine claims that Alekhine was found lying in a field drunk before one of his games with Euwe. I ought to point out that Fine was one of the angriest critics of Alekhine in the 1940s when his Nazi articles were published, so he may have had a tendency to exaggerate (he also called Alekhine "the sadist of the chess world"), but on the other hand there are plenty of reports of Alekhine's drinking.

Euwe caused a sensation, winning the World Championship from Alekhine by 15½ points to 14½. He denied that Alekhine drank excessively – if that were true, it would obviously have tainted his achievement. In one important respect Alekhine's manners were impeccable. He came to the last game in a frock coat and when it ended in a draw he stood up and announced, "I congratulate the new world champion!"

Flohr, Euwe's trainer, was more concerned about Alekhine's nerves than his drinking. "Alekhine's health at that time could have been better," he said. "A Dutch doctor who examined Alekhine during the match announced, 'I am afraid that Alekhine will not live for long – his weak heart – his nerves!'"

When he was still leading the match, Alekhine made an attempt to win favour with the Soviet authorities. He sent a letter to the Soviet chess publication *64*: "Not only in my capacity as a long-serving chess worker, but also as a person who understands the enormous significance of what has been achieved in the USSR in all fields of cultural life, I send my sincere greetings to the chess players of the USSR on the occasion of the 18th anniversary of the October Revolution." The letter was published in *64* and the national newspaper *Izvestiya*. It made no difference to Alekhine's status as a political enemy.

Alekhine had the right to a return match with Euwe and he prepared very seriously for it. He gave up smoking and drinking and went on a diet. He had some tournament successes, but also a major disaster at Nottingham in 1936. As he was no longer world champion, he could do nothing to prevent his archrival, Capablanca, from playing in the tournament. The rest of the lineup was equally formidable, including Euwe, Lasker, Botvinnik, Reshevsky, Fine, Flohr, Bogolyubov, Vidmar and Tartakower. Four world champions and one future world champion.

The joint winners were Capablanca and the new Soviet prodigy, 25-year-old Mikhail Botvinnik. Alekhine trailed in sixth place. "I was far from satisfied with my game at Nottingham," Alekhine wrote in the *Manchester Guardian*. "But what happened here with me has happened to other world champions. After a defeat (and especially because my defeat by Euwe last year was completely unexpected) a certain amount of time has to pass for me to regain my playing strength, to recover from the blow I have suffered."

Witnessing the brilliancies of Botvinnik at first hand must have driven Alekhine to desperation: Botvinnik was a visible symbol of the fantastic Russian chess boom that Alekhine was excluded from. He wrote two more letters to *64*. The first was brief, an offer to work for them and participate in the chess life of the USSR.

The second letter went into more detail. Alekhine confessed to his "mistakes" in true Stalinist style and expressed hope that these mistakes would not prohibit him from future involvement in the Soviet chess movement. He said the press had labelled him anti-Soviet and he had failed to oppose this. His other mistake was misrepresenting Soviet chess in articles and speeches, which he had done because he hadn't seen the Soviet Union for himself.

It is clear from these letters that Alekhine knew exactly how to use Soviet jargon and how to approach a Soviet editor – he adopted a tone of relentless self-criticism with a liberal sprinkling of superlatives in his descriptions of Soviet chess achievements. This underlines both his overwhelming desire to return and his unprincipled nature. When Botvinnik won at Nottingham he wrote to Stalin thanking his "beloved teacher and leader" for his victory. Undoubtedly Alekhine would have had few qualms about doing the same.

Alekhine's efforts were in vain. In 1936 the Soviet Union was in the grip of Stalin's worst terror, and it would literally have been suicidal to publish letters by an enemy of the state. They were kept by one of the editors of *64* and were published in the Soviet Union for the first time in 1967.

The World Championship match with Euwe took place in 1937, and this time Alekhine was the underdog. "To be honest, this time I had no doubt about my victory over Alekhine," Euwe said later. But Alekhine surprised the world again, winning by 15½ points to 9½. He was the first world champion to win the title back after losing it. "I loaned my title to Euwe for two years," Alekhine joked. After the match FIDE announced an official challenger for the first time.

Up until then, anyone could challenge the world champion if they met the conditions set by him. The world champion also had the right to reject a challenge. When FIDE took control, its members voted eight to five for Flohr as challenger rather than Capablanca. Alekhine was happy with this result and went to Prague in 1938 to sign an agreement to play Flohr on the same conditions as his matches with Bogolyubov and Euwe. The match was planned for the end of 1939, but tragic political events intervened – Hitler invaded Czechoslovakia and Flohr went to live in the USSR.

Yet again, Alekhine's fate was determined by circumstances beyond his control. The final years of the man who had travelled thousands of miles to avoid politics and play chess were to be dominated almost entirely by politics.

Alekhine, 47 years old and in poor health, volunteered as an interpreter with the French army in 1940. Six months later France surrendered and at the beginning of 1941 Alekhine managed to travel from occupied Bordeaux to Marseille, in Vichy France. Chess historian Ken Whyld has mentioned something that may have had an important influence on Alekhine's actions in 1941. Up until June 1941, *Germany and the Soviet Union were on the same side*. Naturally this was completely forgotten by Soviet writers after the war, who first condemned Alekhine's Nazi articles and then overlooked them altogether.

It is usually argued that Alekhine wrote the articles in order to get an exit visa and then to protect his wife. But was his wife really in danger? She was an American citizen in France, but America was not yet at war with Germany and France was already under German control, so there were no immediate threats. In any case, why had Alekhine escaped without Grace? Apparently she had stayed behind to look after her property.

By some accounts, Grace, who was 64, was no longer interested in Alekhine. He himself had never shown too much attachment to a woman in the past. Alekhine's wish to ingratiate himself with the Soviet government could have been a much stronger motive for writing the articles. He would kill two birds with one stone, buying himself the freedom to travel and possibly the friendship of the Soviet chess organisation. We have already seen that Alekhine could take on the style of a Soviet writer. When it suited him, he could also take on the style of the Nazis.

The articles were written in German for *Pariser Zeitung* and *Deutsche Zeitung in den Niederlanden* in March 1941. English translations were published in *CHESS* between 1941 and 1942. The editor, B.H. Wood, had been referred to in one of the articles as a Jew. He responded with humour, "We believe few readers would vote against the opportunity to see these articles; that anybody should take them seriously, however, astonishes us… Incidentally, in case people wonder, we are not Jewish as stated in the foregoing article. We should find it more difficult to refute the charge that we play dull, defensive chess, but we have always blamed that not on any tainted blood, but on our opponents, who never seem to permit us to work up a proper attack."

The central argument of Alekhine's articles, entitled *Aryan and Jewish Chess*, was that Aryans played attacking chess full of brilliant sacrifices and that Jews played defensive chess. Apart from that, Alekhine was venomous about the personalities of his Jewish colleagues and came up with feeble explanations as to why some Aryans played defensively and some Jews did not. Capablanca, in New York, "assimilated there, in the Jewish capital, the professional methods of the chess-Yankees." As for Botvinnik, his chess, "as far as the attack goes, is just such an excellent copy of the old masters. Even so… Botvinnik can be called an exception."

It is hard to believe that Alekhine would slander Jewish players whom he knew and respected. Lasker "was a natural heir to Steinitz, the biggest grotesque that chess history has experienced." Reshevsky "represented the worst type of chess professional and utilized the nastiest tricks." He was "systematically exploited… by his equally Jewish managers." Alekhine was shocked that "the peaceful, businesslike and sporting Aryan Euwe would let himself be abused as the plaything of a Jewish clique." Alekhine's victory in 1937 was "a triumph against the Jewish conspiracy."

Alekhine concluded his articles magnanimously, "I would like to emphasize forcefully that my chess fights do not bear a personal character – against no individual Jew himself – but are directed against the collective Jewish chess ideas. And also the last-mentioned match was not directed against Euwe as a person, but against a man who, only temporarily it is to be hoped, was under Jewish influence and was used by the Jews for their purposes."

These statements could have come straight out of Goebbels' propaganda machine. But there is documentary evidence that Alekhine did write the articles. Grace Wishar was looking through Alekhine's notebooks in 1956 and found one containing a draft of one of the articles in Alekhine's handwriting, with the word "Jew" nearly always underlined.

Pablo Moran in his biography of Alekhine has considered this question in detail. He writes, "Alekhine neither sympathised with nor was troubled by Nazi ideology, which he may not even have understood. Nothing interested him apart from chess, his only authentic reason for being. Manuel de Agustin, an excellent chess player and journalist, and the champion's great friend, best defined him... 'I am sure that among Moslems he would have wound up with a tan and sandals.'"

But Moran also notes that Alekhine repeated the views expressed in his articles to a Spanish journalist in September 1941. He was asked which player he most admired and gave the reply, "All. But among them I must stress the greatest glory of Capablanca on depriving the Jew Lasker of the world chess sceptre."

From my own experiences in Russia I can add to this debate that I found that many educated Russians I met are mildly anti-Semitic. Jews have always been categorised as a separate nationality in Russia and successive regimes (Tsarist and Communist) encouraged people to blame the Jews for their country's problems so that the government would have a scapegoat. When Alekhine was born, Russian Jews were confined to certain areas of the country and lived in constant fear of pogroms.

If people have an innate antipathy towards Jews but don't know where this comes from or what the rationale is behind it, then they can quite easily associate with Jews as friends without even connecting them with their feelings about Jews in general. I am sure that these were the contradictions that existed in Alekhine's mind. It would be surprising if someone of his background were not anti-Semitic. This in no way excuses him, but it partly explains why he was able to make the leap from subconscious anti-Semitic feelings to outright hatred of Jews when such opinions were expedient.

To make matters worse, Alekhine also played in chess tournaments in occupied Europe organised by the "Chess Union of Greater Germany." Moran draws attention to the fact that "many famous players took part in these tournaments without being labelled Nazis. The most important were Keres, Bogolyubov, Samisch, Stoltz, Lundin, Opocensky, and Pachman." But as world champion Alekhine brought a powerful element of legitimacy to the tournaments. In total he played in eight such tournaments between 1941 and 1943, mainly in Czechoslovakia. He also gave simultaneous displays, blindfold and sighted.

Alekhine was struck by scarlet fever in 1942 and was taken to the hospital where Richard Réti had died of the same illness. Being terribly superstitious, Alekhine was convinced that he was going to die, too. He survived and in October 1943 he travelled to Madrid for a tournament. It was already coming to an end. Shaburov writes that Alekhine came late deliberately because he didn't want to play in it as a representative of "Greater Germany". He was finally out of the Nazis' jurisdiction, but he was still in a Fascist country, led by General Franco.

Spanish chess players greeted Alekhine enthusiastically and organised several events for him to participate in. He defeated the Spanish champion in a four-game match, won five tournaments and shared second place in another. The last tournament of his life was at Caceres in Western Spain. It was contested by eight local players, the world champion, and the Portuguese champion Francisco Lupi. Lupi won his game against Alekhine, so Alekhine finished in second place. The reason for his poor form was the hopeless state of his health.

"In August 1945 Alekhine reached [the Spanish city of Almeria] in a lamentable alcoholic state," writes Moran. "Thanks to the doctor's care, he managed to play in a tournament after a few days' rest and detoxifications, but soon reverted to his old ways." Alekhine had been told in July that his condition was terminal. He asked Dr. Casimiro Rugarcia to examine him. "The examination revealed a grave cirrhosis of the liver. 'He had an enormous liver,' related Rugarcia, 'so big that it almost reached his right nipple. There was no cure and his days were numbered.'"

Rugarcia told Alekhine to quit drinking. "'And if I quit drinking, how long may I live?' 'If you quit drinking, look after yourself and lead a well-ordered life, you may still live a few years.' Alekhine looked at the physician with obvious compassion, put on his jacket, turned away and as he left, said, 'Then it is not worthwhile to quit drinking.' And he continued to drink during his sojourn in Gijón and Spain, though clandestinely, like a mischievous boy. At the Commerce Hotel in Gijón, the whole staff was frightened by that tall foreigner who would order a bottle of cognac upon retiring, leaving it empty in his room each day."

Alekhine moved to a hotel in the Portuguese resort town of Estoril in late 1945. While he was in Spain he had tried to obtain an exit visa for Grace so that she could leave France, but the Gestapo refused to grant it. When the war ended Alekhine wanted to return to Paris, but this was also impossible because the border between France and Spain was closed. More bad news came to Alekhine from the USSR – his older brother and sister were dead.

Alexei Alekhine had been chess champion of Kharkov in Ukraine, secretary of the Ukrainian Chess Section, and the editor of several chess publications, including a book on his brother's World Championship match with Capablanca. Barbara Alekhine lived her whole life in Moscow, fulfilling one of Alexander's ambitions – to become a film star. She appeared in six films between 1926 and 1934.

Overcome by misery, physically and emotionally destroyed, Alekhine was about to give up the ghost. Then, in November 1945, the British Chess Federation offered him a lifeline: an invitation to the first postwar tournaments, in London and Hastings. Alekhine immediately agreed to play. A short time afterwards his invitation to

London was cancelled. Max Euwe and the American chess players Reuben Fine and Arnold Denker had announced that they would boycott the tournament if Alekhine played in it, on the grounds that he had collaborated with the Nazis and written anti-Semitic articles.

Alekhine replied to this accusation in a letter to the organiser of the London tournament, published in *CHESS* in January 1946. Alekhine denied that he had ever willingly collaborated: "…any disinterested person must realise what must have been my real feelings towards the people who robbed me of everything which gives life meaning; the people who destroyed my home, robbed my wife's chateau (and evidently everything I possess) and finally stole my very name!

"The charge 'collaboration' is generally directed against those who fell in with the Vichy Government. But I never had anything to do with either that government or its officials. I played in Germany and the occupied countries because that was not only our only means of subsistence but also the price of my wife's liberty… Of the articles which appeared in 1941 during my stay in Portugal and which I learnt about in Germany through their being reproduced in the *Deutsche Schachzeitung* nothing was actually written by me…

"Only when I knew what incomparably stupid lucubrations had been created in a spirit imbued with Nazi ideas did I realise what [the reaction in America] was all about. But I was then a prisoner of the Nazis and our only hope of preservation was to keep silent. Those years ruined my health and my nerves and I am even surprised that I can still play chess… I am particularly sorry not to be able to come to London and speak for myself."

A debate in *CHESS* about Alekhine's wartime activities had already begun in November 1945. The Austrian chess player Hans Kmoch, who spent the war in Amsterdam, condemned Alekhine in an article called "Chess Under the Nazi Jackboot". Referring to the so-called "Jewish committee" which Alekhine claimed had supported Euwe, Kmoch wrote, "These cowardly invectives, published under circumstances which precluded any reply, were more than disagreeable for us. They meant danger for us all, for those once exposed in connection with the word Jew at least, had priority when the Germans needed hostages, etc. Although nothing like that happened in direct consequence of the articles, Alekhine may yet have the satisfaction of knowing that Mr. Levenbach, chairman of the defamed committee, disappeared in a concentration camp like Landau." (Salo Landau was Alekhine's second in the match he lost to Euwe.)

The editor of *CHESS* reported on reaction abroad. Dutch writers were unanimously hostile to Alekhine: "Alekhine's articles shall not be forgotten, nor pardoned, and this small-minded drunkard with his lust for money (withal, it is true, a chess player of genius) must be reproached with the insulting and slanderous products of his poisonous pen as long as he lives," and, "This makes it impossible for any self-respecting chess organisation among the Allied Nations to entertain relations with a man who played such a shameful part against the English and Jews, who were fighting for their lives in a fearful and almost hopeless period of the war."

Alekhine somehow gathered the strength to give a blindfold simultaneous display against 29 opponents in the Canary Islands in December 1945. These were some of his very last games. He followed them with a short match against Lupi in January, which he won. By now the tournament in London had begun and a special meeting was convened there to discuss the Alekhine "affair", without the involvement of FIDE or Alekhine himself.

Euwe chaired the meeting. Arnold Denker wrote about it in his memoirs recently. "I found myself in anguish. Back in the Depression years of the early 1930s, Alekhine lavished me with kindnesses – free dinners, superb analysis sessions, instructive practice games and so on. He even chose me as his partner in consultation games. This king of chess treated a young, unknown player like a prince. He became my hero and chessic guiding light. And now, I found myself going along with the condemnatory herd, repaying the currency of kindness with the coin of unproved accusation.

"To this day, nearly half a century past, I regret that more of us did not act like a certain officer in De Gaulle's Free French army, whose parents had been murdered in 1911 at Rostov-on-Don in a Ukrainian pogrom. I'm speaking about Dr. Savielly Tartakower, who publicly pleaded Alekhine's case and then, facing down the entire group, proceeded to take up a collection for the stricken champion, who was penniless in Portugal."

Tartakower was an exception. The other chess players voted to take the title of world champion from Alekhine and not to invite him to tournaments or publish his articles. "In those last weeks, grief, sickness, and poverty entirely crushed him," wrote Lupi. "In desperation some of us decided to appeal again to his wife. 'Since his arrival here a month ago,' we wrote, 'your husband has been in an impossible situation – sick, with no material resources, and living virtually on charity in an Estoril boarding house.' Days went by, and nothing new happened. Alekhine spent his time in bed, or pacing his room like a lion in a cage… Fifteen days before his death, I was called on the telephone and heard Dr. Alekhine ask me sadly whether I wanted to work with him on "Comments on the Best Games of the Hastings Tournament," adding, 'I am completely out of money and I have to make some to buy cigarettes.'"

There was to be one last, tantalising hope for Alekhine to cling to. He was invited to the British Embassy in Lisbon on March 9, 1946. There he was handed a telegram from Mikhail Botvinnik that read, "I regret that the war prevented the organisation of our match in 1939. But I herewith again challenge you to a match for the world's chess championship. If you agree, a person authorised by myself and the Moscow Chess Club will conduct negotiations with you or your representative on the question of conditions, date and the place where the match should be held, preferably through the British Chess Federation."

This match never took place, of course, but the thought of it cheered Alekhine up a little. He played his last game of chess in the embassy, against a Foreign Office employee called Anderson. When he returned to his hotel he talked to Lupi excitedly about the openings he would play against Botvinnik. "This was the old Alekhine," Lupi recalled. "But 24 hours later, at about one in the morning of Friday, March 22, as I climbed the stairs of my apartment in Lisbon, I saw, leaning against the door, somebody whom a few steps closer I recognised as my friend. When I was near him, his hands grasped nervously the sleeves of my coat, and he said, in a voice I shall never forget, 'Lupi, the loneliness is killing me! I must live. I must feel life about me. I have already worn down the floorboards of my room. Take me to some nightclub.'"

That was the last time Lupi saw Alekhine alive. "All I know is that on Sunday morning about 10:30 I was awakened and asked to hurry to Estoril, because something had happened to 'old Dr. Alex'. I entered his room together with the Portuguese authorities. There he was, sitting in his chair, in so calm an attitude that one would have thought he was asleep. There was only a little foam at the corner of his mouth. The medical verdict as to the cause of death – that a piece of meat had caught in his throat – had no meaning for me. To me he looked like the King of the chessmen, toppled over after the most dramatic game, the one played on the board of Life."

A famous photograph was taken of Alekhine, wearing an overcoat, dead in his armchair, with a chessboard and an untouched meal on the table in front of him. Ken Whyld has discovered that Alekhine was posed like that for the photograph and that he actually died outside in the corridor. He was 53, and the only world champion to die undefeated. Alekhine never saw the telegram informing him that FIDE had decided on March 23 to allow the match with Botvinnik to go ahead, nor did he know that a French visa had been sent to him.

No one knew where to bury Alekhine, and after much discussion his coffin was placed temporarily in the tomb of a Portuguese chess player. The Portuguese Chess Federation paid for the funeral. Ten years later, Grace Wishar arranged the transferal of Alekhine's remains to a cemetery in Paris, and when she died in 1956 she was buried with him.

Immediately after Alekhine's death, some readers of *CHESS* wrote in with pleasant memories of him. J. du Mont, a chess editor, met the world champion in 1938 and showed him the proofs of a book. Alekhine spontaneously offered to read them and check the analysis, which he did for no fee within a few days. Fred R. Leicester wrote, "For myself, as poorly as I play, I have derived many hours of enlightened entertainment at the foot of this great master… The whats and whys of politics can be forgotten – as he has paid the debt with his life's work over and over again."

Alekhine's life was full of irony. Perhaps the most poignant was the way the Soviet government's attitude towards him changed after his death. The first Alekhine Memorial Tournament was held in Moscow in 1956, and Alekhine's son, also Alexander Alekhine, was the honoured guest. Further tournaments were held in 1971 and 1975. In the post-Soviet era, Alekhine's son was a guest in Moscow in 1996, when tournaments were held to commemorate the 50th anniversary of the world champion's death.

GM Alexander Kotov wrote a biography of Alekhine and a novel about him, *White and Black*, which was made into a film of the same name. History was rewritten to portray Alekhine as the inspiration of the Soviet chess movement – which, in a way, he was.

* * *

At the beginning of the year I had again interviewed players at the Hastings Congress. As the Alekhine article was so long, these interviews were published in the spring.

The Chinese Connection
(*CHESS*, March 1997)

Chinese ex-women's world champions are thin on the ground in Hastings, so when I spotted one I had no intention of letting her get away. Unfortunately, a layer of ice was also thin on the ground, and Xie Jun was daintily disappearing into the distance down a very steep hill. I'd seen her in the Cinque Ports Hotel where she was playing in the Premier Tournament. She had her coat on and was halfway out of the door when I asked her if she'd stop for an interview. "I'm going to the pier," she said with a smile. "You can catch up with me there. I walk slowly."

By the time I had picked up my bag and wrapped myself up to combat the biting cold, Xie was already several hundred metres ahead of me. I wasn't worried – I'd see her on the pier. I'll take my time, I thought. Better watch my footing. But after only a few steps I began to pick up speed and regretted that I hadn't brought a bobsled with me. I was sliding down the hill uncontrollably and Xie was right in my line of descent, blithely unaware that her life was about to end in a messy heap under an over-enthusiastic, inappropriately shod journalist.

Clinging desperately to each litterbin on my route, I negotiated the bends like champion skier Alberto Tomba and braced myself for the moment when I would soar off the end of the pier and plunge into the sea with the non-existent finesse of ski jumper Eddie "The Eagle" Edwards. I was almost on top of Xie when I managed to make an emergency turn and veered off the pavement into the middle of the road. "Hi!" I shouted, waving to Xie as I slid past her.

I skidded to a halt just before the pier and had enough time to assume a completely unruffled expression before Xie joined me for the far simpler walk to the bar. I immediately went for a stiff drink, while she headed for the fruit machine. When I came back she was grinning, holding out a fistful of 10-pence pieces. "I like this, I'm going to have another go," she said. I wondered if gambling was popular in China. "No," she replied. "It's forbidden."

Xie Jun is 26 years old. Last year she lost the title of world champion, which she had held since 1991, to Zsuzsa Polgar. She won the World Championship from Maya Chiburdanidze of the Soviet Union, ending the 41-year Soviet dominance in women's chess. "I never thought I would become world champion, and I never think of winning the title back," Xie told me. "Perhaps I will, I don't know. I've never concentrated so much on chess. I don't think I will play for a very long time. Every tournament is a long journey, as most of them are in Europe, in different time zones. It makes you tired and you can't avoid that."

Xie got married a year ago, but not to her trainer, as has been reported. "Where did you get that idea? Please tell everyone I didn't marry my trainer. My husband used to be a chess player, but he's not now." Xie was reluctant to give any more information about her husband. "After I got married, life didn't change so much," she said.

When she was a child, Xie played Chinese chess. "I won some competitions in Chinese chess and they chose me to play this chess. I was very young. Someone chose me when I was at school." I asked her what sort of a game Chinese chess is. "It is more attacking, the position is more open, the king can only come into a certain position, but the idea is similar to this chess. In the street in China you can make money playing Chinese chess." Xie doesn't think that the game will become popular in Europe, though. "There are some problems with the rules," she said. "But Go could get popular here."

Xie said life has become more relaxed since she lost the world title, and she certainly appeared relaxed in Hastings, laughing with her opponents even while analysing complicated games. She seemed to prefer talking about subjects other than chess – "I like Holland most out of all the countries I've been to," she said. When I added that it was a strong chess country, she quickly replied, "No, not because of chess. It's just that the people are so friendly. I visited it in 1994 and I liked the countryside. I like quiet places." As for England, which Xie visits rarely, Xie said, "I quite enjoy it here. I meet some friends, practise my English, and I've had some interesting games."

Xie has a degree in English from Beijing University and is now studying Comparative Education as a postgraduate. "I chose it because it's easier than the other subjects to learn. I don't think I have enough time to study."

When I tried to delve into political questions, Xie became extremely reticent. I was interested in how much choice she had about the tournaments she played in – had she suggested that she would like to play at Hastings, or was she told to? "We have a contract with our Sports Committee. It's a secret. I can't talk about it. I can't tell you how trips to tournaments are funded. But life is very hard in China as a professional chess player. Yes, I had duties and privileges as world champion, but I'm not world champion any more."

Would the Chinese authorities put pressure on Xie not to give up chess? "I get nothing special from the government, so they can't force me to play." I asked Xie what life was like for a successful woman in China. "Everyone has to work in China," she said, "so life is heavier for women than in other countries because they have to have a job and do the housework." As for women chess players in general – "Women can enjoy life more, because they don't think they have to be the best."

Xie got on well with GM Paul Motwani in Hastings, another player in the Premier Tournament. They had more than chess in common, as Motwani also got married recently – to a Chinese woman. The top chess player in Scotland, he and his wife Jenny now live in Belgium, where she works for Procter & Gamble. "I first saw Jenny in a Thai restaurant where I went with the secretary of the Scottish Chess Association," said Motwani. "They both did chemistry at Napier University. Jenny was serving in the restaurant part time. He arranged a blind date for us – Jenny didn't remember me at all because I had my head down playing chess during the meal."

They were married in July 1995. "The day of our wedding she didn't know that she would be graduating 12 days later with a Ph.D. in chemistry, but then she found out, so her parents saw both ceremonies, in Perth and in Edinburgh. We're just about to go on a trip to China, which will be the first time I meet her family at their home."

Motwani is learning Mandarin and has developed another Chinese speciality: he is an expert Chinese cook. "I asked Jenny to teach me and she was reluctant at first, but now she says I'm a better Chinese cook than her. She doesn't play chess, but she gives me good advice on how to approach the game. She tells me not to think about ratings or let the result worry me. She's very sensible, she gives me practical advice. We have one mutual hobby – we both love films. Where we live, in the top left-hand corner of Brussels, the Strombeek-Bever district, we're a stone's throw away from one of the biggest cinemas in the world, with 28 screens. Brussels is quite an expensive place to live, but we go once a week to the cinema."

Are Paul and Jenny planning to have children? "My wife showed how flexible she was – she said she wants two children, first a girl, then a boy!" It is obvious from Motwani's easygoing manner and keenness to explain his ideas that he must be an excellent teacher. "I still feel like I'm a teacher," he said. "I miss the contact with pupils a little bit. When I was here I really enjoyed chatting with the pupils at a school in Perth and I've recorded a couple of audio chess cassettes to send them." When Motwani moved to Belgium he had to give up his job teaching mathematics and religious education, but he has compensated for this to some extent by coaching young chess players and writing books. "It's worked out well for me because I always wanted to write books," he said. "My first book was recently published by

Batsford, *H.O.T. Chess*, standing for Highly Original Thinking. My second book, *C.O.O.L. Chess*, is coming out in April – Creative Original Opening Lines. I've proposed two more.

"Although I'm a good player I like writing most of all because it combines my love of teaching with my love of chess. I've aimed the books at a very wide audience. I try to give material of a high level but with clear explanations, so that even grandmasters would get something out of it but lesser players would, too. It's how I always tried to teach in the classroom, so that the brighter pupils would be stretched by interesting puzzles and the weaker ones wouldn't get lost. Using mnemonics is something completely new in chess."

C.O.O.L. Chess includes a tribute to some of the most creative chess players, but Motwani is keeping their names a surprise. When I suggested David Bronstein, who played in the Hastings Challengers Tournament again this year, at age 72, Motwani said, "Bronstein features in a special way in the second book. I limited my tributes to players over a certain age and I admire him very, very much."

Motwani said the books are full of anecdotes and puzzles, "a nice blend of things, so they're not dry books at all, their purpose is to make people enjoy the game. The emphasis in the second book is more on actual games, less writing in between the games."

As the capital of the European Union, Brussels is a good location for chess, Motwani says. "I do miss my friends in Scotland, but this is the happiest time of my life. I like coming back for Christmas, which we've done for the past few years." French is no problem for Motwani – "It was my second best subject at school. I coach an English boy in Belgium and his friend heard the coaching was good, so now his friend comes and I coach them in French."

When he was 16, Motwani won the World Under-17 Championship in a little town in Holland and by coincidence he now plays for that town in the Dutch league and for another town in the Belgian league. "I'm doing a modest amount of playing," he said. "I'm finding this tournament quite tough."

Motwani coaches a group of Belgium's best 16- to 19-year-old chess players. "I used to give prizes in the classroom; I do that now with the Belgian juniors and they are very motivated. I wouldn't be very good at enforcing discipline – I try to get the pupils on my side so that they won't misbehave."

I asked Motwani to tell me his philosophy of chess. "Chess develops logical thinking," he said. "The game is also far better from a social point of view than some people realise. I've travelled to 30 countries and have hundreds of friends. It's very, very absorbing. I love chess for the beauty of the game. I like to do the best at everything I do, but I would like to be remembered as a good person most of all. I would never like to lose the human touch. Some players have a more ruthless side than I do. I'm quite peaceful about chess these days. If I have an interesting drawn game, I regard it as a point shared."

Due to a dispute between Zsuzsa Polgar and FIDE, Polgar did not defend her world title. Instead, a match was held between Xie Jun and Alisa Galliamova in 1999 and Xie once again emerged the victor. She retained the world title the following year by winning the new knockout format World Championship, but she did not play in the 2001 knockout, which was won by her compatriot Zhu Chen. With up and coming male prodigies like Bu Xiangzhi too, China is rapidly becoming the successor to the Soviet Union as an unstoppable chess force.

Paul Motwani continues to write unusual chess books, including S.T.A.R. Chess *and* Chess Under the Microscope, *a conversation between the author and a one-micron-tall extraterrestrial called Mr. Fab.*

Out of the USSR
(*CHESS*, March 1997)

The first was Tigran Petrosian. The second is Garry Kasparov. And the third Armenian world chess champion, if the man himself has anything to do with it, will be Sergei Movsesian. If he achieves his ambition, Sergei will follow another tradition: he won't be representing Armenia. Petrosian played for the Soviet Union and Kasparov plays for Russia. Movsesian emigrated to the Czech Republic in 1994 and has been welcomed onto that country's team.

This year Movsesian was invited to the Hastings Premier Tournament and on the day I interviewed him he had just qualified for his grandmaster title, at age 18. Receiving congratulations from tournament director Stewart Reuben, Movsesian said that his parents had been getting more and more nervous during the year because he couldn't get his last grandmaster norm. Now that he has done it, the sky's the limit.

"I've always had World Championship ambitions. Not everyone can be world champion, but I have enough time," he told me in his fluent English. He also speaks Armenian, Georgian, Russian and Czech. "I speak Czech without problems, almost like the Czechs do, although I didn't know it until I moved there."

Movsesian has some relatives in Armenia, but he has never actually lived there – he was brought up in Georgia. "Sometimes it was difficult being an Armenian in Georgia," he said. "Not everyone looked at me as playing for Georgia, even though I won the Under-12 Soviet Championship in 1989. I wasn't allowed to play in the World Junior Championships in Puerto Rico that year when some other Soviet juniors did play. I never found out why."

Movsesian had problems in the former Soviet Union again last year, when he arrived in Armenia to play for the home country in the Olympiad, but ended up having a month's holiday instead. "The Armenian Chess Federation gave me ridiculous conditions. I found out two days before the Olympiad that they wanted to put me on board 6 when I had the highest rating in Armenia, and that I would receive two times less pay than the other members of the team because I was too young. So I didn't play. I suppose they thought that the others fought for their places for a long time and I was coming from Europe and wanted to take everything."

Living in the Czech town of Pardubice (the local club invited Movsesian to play for them when he came over for a tournament) with his parents and 14-year-old brother Levon, who is hoping to have a career in tennis, Sergei has many advantages. "You can get all over Europe in two or three hours from the Czech Republic. They have chess leagues there and the level of chess culture is higher than in Georgia or Armenia. The principles of life and chess playing in the Czech Republic are completely different. You have choices, like in Europe.

"In Armenia and Georgia there are no tournaments, and it's more important to earn money just to survive, not to play chess. Also you have to have an Elo of 2600 to live well in Armenia and when I emigrated I had only 2400. But I wouldn't want to change countries again. To leave everything after 15 years was maybe not so difficult for me as for my father, but even for me, I had friends, I was going to an absolutely strange country."

The Olympiad must have given chess in Armenia a boost, I suggested. "That was a special year for Armenia, and it won't happen again for 30 or 40 years," said Movsesian. "The Olympiad was really good, but it's a Far Eastern country by mentality. I have a 90 percent European mentality now. Here you might ring a friend occasionally and invite him over. There, he's in your house all the time."

In the Czech Republic there is no danger of the kind of civil conflict occurring that Movsesian witnessed in Georgia. "I saw the fighting in Tbilisi – it was my worst New Year's Eve ever. You shouldn't see such things – but maybe you should know what is possible."

Movsesian had few good words for Petrosian and Kasparov. "I always looked up to Petrosian, but then such terrible things began to be published about him, things you don't want to know about your hero, like the letters he signed against Korchnoi. As for Kasparov – such a person can't be an inspiration to me. Maybe the world champion must be this kind of man. He makes everything for his own profit, in the name of chess. You are presenting chess, so it's not so pleasant. I know what results and good chess playing do, you begin to think you're the best, but you're not. No player wins all the tournaments he plays."

Movsesian learnt chess from his father, a chemical engineer, at the age of four. His trainer in Georgia was also Armenian, but since he has been in the Czech Republic he has been studying by himself, using a PC. "It's impossible without a computer, it's one of the most important things in chess. It's like using a book or looking at any other game, it's like a really good and fast book."

At the start of the Premier Tournament Movsesian's Elo rating was 2635, the second highest after Michael Adams. "Now 2500 players who didn't want to make a draw against me a year ago do want draws," he said, "but I like this tournament because there's no respect to me and my Elo." Movsesian considered that his performance "could have been better, could have been worse." He lost to Xie Jun. "That was the first time I'd played her and I hope the last. No, I'm joking. I made some kind of hand mistake; I took a knight with a pawn instead of a knight. But I won against Sofia Polgar in July. If you want to win you have to know what it is to lose."

To build up his stamina for chess Movsesian runs two mornings a week and plays football. His hobby is reading. "I would like to read as many books as I can, mainly novels. At the moment I'm reading some quite exotic ones, Portuguese, Greek, Irish, Finnish, Italian novels. I read them in Russian, English and Czech. I don't like Czech writers too much, even though it's not very patriotic. I need to be out of everything to go deep into a book, it's not so easy, I normally read when I'm travelling."

I asked Movsesian what he was going to do when he got home to Pardubice. "I'll take a week's rest from chess and play computer games with my brother," he said, grinning.

After our conversation Movsesian showed me his Round 7 win against a friend of his in the Premier Tournament, Eduardas Rozentalis, the top player in Lithuania. Rozentalis shared first place in the tournament with John Nunn and Mark Hebden, coming through very strongly in the last rounds. In the final round he defeated Hebden, denying the British player an outright win.

Rozentalis started playing chess at the age of seven, and in the same year a chess school opened in Vilnius. He studied there with Vladas Mikenas, who was also the trainer of Paul Keres. Both of Rozentalis' parents played chess; his mother was twice champion of Lithuania. But chess was never as popular in Lithuania as it was in Russia, Rozentalis told me – basketball is the No. 1 sport.

"Funding is a big problem for the Lithuanian Chess Federation. There's no support for young players going to the World or European Championships, they must provide their own tickets." Rozentalis wasn't allowed to travel abroad to tournaments in 1990. "Someone in Moscow decided who could go abroad. Now there is freedom for everybody. I very seldom play in Russia, though. For Russia I need a visa but for England I don't."

Rozentalis likes using the Internet, for instance to watch the Las Palmas and Groningen tournaments. "The most important thing is that I like chess," he said. "It's a very pleasant job. I can decide what to do."

In the 1999 Las Vegas FIDE knockout World Championship, Movsesian was a quarterfinalist, losing to fellow Armenian Vladimir Akopian. In 2002 Movsesian won a very strong tournament in Sarajevo, probably his best tournament first to date. Rozentalis achieved his highest-ever rating in 1997 and his Elo declined in subsequent years, although he continues to play in tournaments all over Europe.

Dedication Is What You Need
(*CHESS*, May 1997)

If you've ever doubted that chess is addictive, look no further than Paul Bloom. I first encountered him at a weekend congress in London, where he was pondering the problem of how to find the time for a haircut. "I play in a tournament every single weekend and I'm on six teams," he announced to the diners around him in the canteen. "Do you ever have to play yourself?" I asked him. "What? I thought you said, do I ever have to play myself?" "I did," I confirmed. "Oh!" Comprehension dawned. "No, they're all in different leagues, otherwise it would be difficult."

It came as no surprise to find Paul playing in the 9-day World Amateur Championship at Hastings, which is open to anyone who does not have an Elo rating. This time I decided to question him more deeply, to try and probe the mind of the most fanatical amateur chess player in the country. I also interviewed the youngest of all the participants in the World Amateur Championship, 10-year-old Thomas Rendle. He turned out to be quite experienced at handling the media, having been interviewed three times since he played a game with Kasparov in Dixons recently.

"No one will choose you for the newspaper if you're casually dressed," Thomas explained as he posed unselfconsciously for a photograph. He is never seen in public without one of his multicoloured bow ties and often a chess sweatshirt. "I was chosen to play Kasparov because of my bow tie." The temperamental world champion was supposed to let lots of children take turns making a move, but Thomas picked up the game on move 11 and continued with it until the end.

"I was already a pawn down," said Thomas, "so that didn't help. Also it was a Trompowsky, I think, and I'm not a d-pawn player. Kasparov won with king, rook, f-pawn and h-pawn against king and rook. I didn't know the theory, but Kasparov said it was drawn."

Thomas has a grade of 110, which is fourth best in the country for his age. He has been playing since the age of 4½. Paul is graded 119 now, but because of his phenomenal number of games he expects to be graded about 140 next season. He didn't play chess at all until about four years ago, when he was watching two players in a pub and one of them invited him to have a game. "I found that I knew the moves just from watching and I took it up. It's only this year that I've played every weekend, and three to four evenings a week. I've played over three hundred games. I don't know of anyone else who plays that much chess."

Thomas learned chess from his father (his parents helped organise a junior tournament at Hastings this year) and honed his technique with some visiting students from Russia. He has three brothers and a sister, including a twin brother called James, who gave up on chess at an early stage. "He didn't really have any aims in chess after beating me in the first game we played. He thought he'd done enough."

Thomas gets taken to three tournaments a month – "My dad's relieved when he gets weekends off." He plays for Kent as there is no Sussex junior team, and has lessons from GM Chris Ward, a four-hour session every two months. "Last time in my lesson we did mainly endings, but next time it'll be middlegames, because I'm not doing too well at that in this tournament," he said.

For Paul the biggest difficulty in the World Amateur Championship was the endgame. "I've lost a lot of drawn positions through worse endgame technique than my opponents," he said. Paul believes that the best tuition is to go over your own games at least two or three times. "I had about half a dozen lessons from a guy graded about 200, but it was quite expensive, £10 an hour. It's quite similar to driving lessons – you only benefit if you take two hours at a time. We looked at some of my games and decided which openings suited my style of play: the Ruy Lopez as White and as Black the Sicilian Dragon and the King's Indian. If they play the Sicilian I usually play f4 – it avoids all the theory."

Thomas prefers the Sicilian as White and the French or the Queen's Gambit Declined as Black. "I'm solid, but I do go for attacks," he said. "I'll go out of my style to play the correct move." His favourite game is one he played last June at the King's Head club in London. "I had a lovely sac on h3 to the Queen's Gambit Declined and won lots of pieces on the back rank."

Both Thomas and Paul have witnessed their share of bizarre and controversial chess incidents. As he has been in so many tournaments around London, I asked Paul if he was at the King's Head when a player hit his opponent over the head with a chess clock. He wasn't, but he did have a story to rival that one. "I was playing at Torquay and my opponent was beating me by two pieces. I'd more or less given up on the game and I went off to see some of the Premier Tournament. When I came back there were about 50 or 60 people around my board and pieces all over the place. My opponent had had a fit, hit his head on the board and knocked himself unconscious. I was awarded the game. I thought they should have called it a draw, but the rules said it was a win for me. That's the only time I've won when I was so much material down."

The two controversies that Thomas was involved in have both gone against him, but he isn't too discouraged. "Once I was cheated against. My opponent touched his knight and it was pinned to his queen. He claimed he hadn't touched it. I called the stewards and every single steward agreed with me. The controller came over and he agreed with my opponent. He got away with it and it put me off. Another time I knocked a piece and it was claimed that I touched it, and I was forced to move it. I did manage to win that game, but I was very tired and it lasted a long time, longer than it should have. But the arbiter has to make a decision and if he's got no proof then he has to upset someone."

The conditions on the pier at Hastings were a real concern for Paul. "It's appalling," he said. "There's been no rest day, there are no toilets, it's very cold, the players are wearing coats, walking around to keep warm, and it's worse because we're playing in the morning. Weather-wise it's been really bad." Congress organiser Pam Thomas told me that she'd had very few complaints about the pier this year. In any case, there is nowhere else to hold the tournament. "People used to complain, but we've measured every possible venue in Hastings and we've proved to them that there's nowhere else big enough. We can't split the tournaments amongst more venues – it's complicated enough already with the hotel and the pier."

Paul said he'd been to tournaments where the conditions were worse because of the organisers. "At Kensington three months ago they told us to start White's clock and there were no boards or clocks set up, and no score sheets provided. We had to rip up scraps of paper for score sheets. Maybe I'm a bit spoilt. I play in quite a few Spectrum tournaments in four-star hotels. You have to treat it as a weekend away. The hotels are heavily subsidised, £25 per night rather than £70 or £80."

Incredibly, Paul manages to fit in a 9-5 job in the stocks and shares department of a bank between playing chess. He isn't married: "I couldn't do this if I was." He doesn't play in tournaments abroad: "If I go abroad then I go for a holiday, not chess. Yes, I do that sometimes." In daily life he says he doesn't have any free time, "but chess is a form of relaxation. I like the social side of it. Is it stressful? It depends how seriously you take it. It's just a game, I'm never going to achieve any great heights. Chess gives you something to look forward to rather than work, eat, sleep, bed.

"I want interesting games and friendly opponents. When your opponents are not friendly they spoil the game. There's been only one game I haven't enjoyed. My opponent was graded 180 and he hacked me off the board from the first couple of moves, treated me with contempt, pushed all his pawns at me and there was nothing I could do about it."

Paul's next ambition is to play in Major rather than Minor tournaments, because he says it will give him more chance to use the opening theory he has learned. "If I worked really hard, hopefully I could get to 180 or 190. I'm beginning to wonder how high you can get by learning as you go along and at what stage natural ability takes over. If you play too much, some people say you can get stale, but I'm playing at a low level so I can improve."

Thomas is keen on a career as a chess professional. "It can't be bad being paid to play in a tournament even if you don't win," he told me. At home he uses the chess computer program Fritz 4 ("I can't beat it on the highest level") and reads chess books in bed with his pocket set. "All my rivals I laugh with. I'm still friends with Luke McShane even though he's better than me" – he paused for emphasis – "at the moment." Luke, just turned 13, hit the national newspapers recently when he achieved his final international master norm.

"I had a really good laugh with Luke at the Metropolitan tournament in London," said Thomas. "He was reading a poem with a funny expression on his face and afterwards I looked for the poem in a book, but I couldn't find what page it was on." Thomas is sure he will catch up with Luke because, "you tend to slow down as you get older." His other ambition is to become the youngest-ever grandmaster.

Paul's chess hero is David Bronstein. "He plays chess for the fun of chess, creates wonderful mating attacks, it's more like an art than a science. As he says, you can play whatever opening move you like. *The Sorcerer's Apprentice* is the best book I've ever bought – it's not tied up with reams and reams of theory, but it has lots of very exciting, interesting games. It's written in a way that everyone can understand."

Thomas says his hero "used to be Nigel [Short], but now I think it's Stuart Conquest." Stuart comes from Hastings and was playing in the Premier Tournament this year. He went to the same school as Thomas. "He was smartly dressed for a change," Thomas added approvingly.

The most striking thing about Thomas, apart from his bow tie, is his self-confidence. In the analysis room for the Premier Tournament he rushed to the front to demonstrate his ideas in front of a crowd of people, and at one point had to be told to be quiet for a few moments. He doesn't get nervous during games, either. "I've been on stage – I used to be in pantomimes, I was usually just a villager, but that gives you confidence and you're not that scared. I've hardly got any time for acting now."

Paul is notable for his modesty and total dedication. "One thing I really do dislike is people withdrawing from tournaments," he told me. "The same people do it all the time. Sometimes they don't even tell the organisers. They do it when they realise they're not going to win the tournament. It's not just weaker players; some professionals do it as well. I've seen Bogdan Lalic do it. I don't think these people come to play chess; they come for the money. Today I'd been up all night being sick, I could have withdrawn, but I didn't."

I asked Paul why he liked chess so much. "It's the fascination of trying to outwit your opponent, to achieve something on the board better than someone else. The more you know, the more you realise you don't know."

The Hastings organisers did manage to move the tournaments off the pier, to the YMCA, in subsequent years. Then they changed the venue to the Horntye Sports Complex, providing modern excellent conditions and bringing the Premier back into the same hall as the other events, as was the tradition in the past. Hastings entries have gone up as a result.

The three-digit ratings referred to in this article are the British Chess Federation's ratings. Mine was just under 100, beginner level. Minor tournaments are usually for players rated under 120 or 130 and Major tournaments are for players with a rating above that but under about 180. The strongest players compete in Open tournaments. An international master would probably be rated in the 220s according to the BCF system, or in the 2400s according to the international Elo system. A grandmaster would be in the 230s, or 2500s and upwards in the Elo system.

3. Hungary for Chess

Somehow I discovered that an editor named Andrew Harvey who had once published a couple of my non-chess articles in *The Times* had moved to *The European*, a newspaper that went out of business a few years ago. In early 1997 he was editing *The European*'s magazine-style review section. I offered him my Hastings interviews, but they didn't excite him. He asked me what else was going on in chess. I mentioned the Polgar sisters, three Hungarian former child prodigies who were among the strongest players in the world. Andrew said he would like an article on them. There was one small problem: I had no idea where they were.

With Jimmy's help I learned that the Polgar sisters were in Israel, the United States and Hungary. It was relatively easy to interview them by telephone, but I really wanted to meet their father, who was notoriously reticent of the media. So I decided to go looking for him in Budapest, and while I was there, Jimmy suggested a few more famous chess players I could add to my metaphorical trophy room. He especially hoped that I would track down the reclusive Bobby Fischer, but that proved to be beyond my powers.

As usual, I paid all my own expenses for the weeklong trip. The ebullient First Saturday tournament organiser Laszlo Nagy found me a cheap room in the home of an elderly couple in a block of flats; I also interviewed participants in one of his tournaments. It was a long time before all the resulting articles were written and published. The Polgars made the front page of *The European* magazine and a year later I won the John Anstey Prize for the article, presented by *The Sunday Telegraph* as part of the Catherine Pakenham Awards for women writers under 25. The prize, a laptop computer, accompanied me in all my travels from then on.

The article from *The European* was also purchased by *YOU* magazine in South Africa. This expanded version of the article appeared in *CHESS*.

The Polgar Sisters
(*CHESS*, December 1997)

The Spice Girls of chess were brought up to be global megastars by an ambitious manager: their father. Like today's record producers, Laszlo Polgar believes it is possible to achieve international fame and fortune without any talent at all. Education was everything. But he could never prove the theory because, unlike the Spice Girls, the Polgar sisters *were* talented – enormously talented.

When the Polgars were very young they were an absolute sensation. Good-looking, exceptionally bright, fluent in several languages – and they played fantastic chess. The media doted on them. They brought glamour to a scene that badly needed it, as top-level chess had previously been dominated by unsmiling Soviet men and a few wildly eccentric Westerners.

Laszlo Polgar was more genial than genius.

Now that the Polgars are grown up, their lives have changed considerably. Judit, at 21, is still in the spotlight, but her older sisters Zsuzsa and Sofia are no longer the celebrities they used to be. As they plan their future, away from the dominating influence of their parents, it is worth looking back at the Polgar story and asking whether it was all worth the effort. I spoke to the three sisters by telephone and met their father in Budapest.

Remarkably talented kids have amazed the world throughout history: Sammy Reshevsky toured Europe giving simultaneous displays at the age of eight, in 1919. Laszlo Polgar believes there is no such thing as natural talent and that any child can match the Polgars' achievements if they have the same upbringing. His book, *Bring up Genius!*, explains this theory, but unfortunately it has not been published in English. I asked him if he would like to sell the rights and he said he would do so for an advance of $200,000.

Laszlo's controversial methods, his combative nature and his propensity to demand huge sums of money have given plenty of ammunition to his critics. He and his family see their whole lives as a struggle against adversity, and their success as a reward they deserve.

Laszlo and his wife Klara, both teachers, started out in a one-room flat. When Zsuzsa was five, the police came to their home to make her go to school. The Polgars persuaded the communist government that she should be allowed to be educated at home, but their next opponent was the Hungarian Chess Federation, which objected to Laszlo's insistence that Zsuzsa must play in mixed tournaments. As punishment, the federation banned her from going abroad for three years. Laszlo was determined to prove that women were equal to men in chess.

When the girls began to earn money from chess, their parents bought them each a flat in the same building as their own. In the past few months Laszlo and Klara have moved out of that building and into a luxury flat with a beautiful view of Hungary's royal palace across the Danube, next to a Marriott hotel. It will house Laszlo's vast chess library and the family's collection of hundreds of chess sets. At the time of my visit Klara was away, accompanying Judit at the Dos Hermanos tournament in Spain.

My meeting with Laszlo was arranged by chess historian Gyorgy Negyesi, who knew Laszlo's new number and sweet-talked him into seeing me. "This is the first time I have known Lazie to give an interview without charging," Negyesi confided to me. I expected a tough, rather embittered businessman, but found nothing of the sort. Laszlo was more genial than genius. Smiling as he opened the door, he greeted us with an enthusiastic "Hello!" – which was about as far as his English stretched.

Negyesi translated for me from Hungarian to Russian. "Judka has to play Nigel Short today," he said, an excited sparkle in his eyes. "She should win; she has a nine-one score against him in their previous games." She did. On the other hand, Judit has so far found it impossible to crack the defences of Vladimir Kramnik: her dismal record against him is 17 losses, six draws and no wins.

Laszlo looks like a cuddly teddy bear, but he can turn into a far fiercer creature when provoked. "Laszlo thinks the whole world is against him," I was told by one Hungarian chess player. "You must think of him separately from his daughters. The girls are fine, but the father, well, he is a different matter…" Andras Adorjan, a leading Hungarian grandmaster, was sued twice by Laszlo after Adorjan criticised him on the radio. Adorjan won the first suit but lost the second one. Sitting in the empty room in his leather cap and overcoat, Laszlo gives the impression of a weary man fighting a lonely battle.

Laszlo spends his time managing Judit, lecturing, and writing about chess and education. "I write one or two books every year," he said. Recently he has been trying to promote chess variants that would be played on boards of different sizes: six by eight squares or nine by six. Some of the variants allow the players to start with two queens each. "There is a very big chance of draws in normal chess and a lot of time is needed to study openings," Laszlo explained. "Handball was played on a football field 50 years ago, now it is played on a pitch half the size. All sports change. I don't want to replace normal chess, but I want this chess to exist alongside it."

The idea of making chess less dependent on knowledge of openings is also shared by Bobby Fischer, who enthusiastically promotes random chess, where the pieces start on random squares on the back rank. Fischer has been living in Budapest for a few years and he stayed with Laszlo when he first arrived. Laszlo got fed up with him after hearing his anti-Semitic opinions. The Polgars are Jewish, like many Hungarian chess players.

I asked Laszlo why he thought that Fischer had become anti-Semitic. "I think he had problems with the Jewish organisers of tournaments, and he had friends who exerted a very strong influence over him, and he also has that inclination himself."

Laszlo's teaching speciality is psychology and his educational theory applies to all subjects and activities, not just chess. "Sometimes I wonder if it would have been better if my daughters had been cancer specialists instead of chess players. Whether they would have been as happy, I don't know." His great hope is that he will find a sponsor for an institute to test his ideas, but so far no offers have been forthcoming. The intensive teaching put in by Laszlo and Klara is hardly a realistic option for the average family. The girls used to wake at six each morning, play table tennis for two to three hours, then study chess for six to eight hours.

The results of the Polgar experiment were stunning, nonetheless. Judit was the youngest ever international master at the age of 12 and the youngest ever grandmaster at 14. Two years later she won a match against former world champion Boris Spassky. Today she competes in tournaments with the chess elite, commanding an appearance fee of $10,000 before she has even made a move. Judit is the only one of the sisters who has remained in Budapest. Zsuzsa, 28, lives in New York with her husband Cobi, a computer expert. Sofia, 23, has moved to the Israeli city of Holon to be with her boyfriend, GM Yona Kosashvili.

This year Zsuzsa and Sofia have made some crucial decisions about their future. Both may be drifting out of competitive chess, having reached the limits of their abilities and developed other interests. Their great advantage is that they have plenty of time to embark on new careers. Zsuzsa and Cobi have just published the book of her life story, *Queen of the Kings* [sic] *Game*, and Zsusza has opened her own chess school in New York.

Sofia is learning Hebrew and starting university in Israel. "Of course it would be a shame if Zsuzsa and Sofia gave up chess," said Laszlo, looking sadly at the floor, "but that's not the main thing. I want them to enjoy themselves."

Queen of the Kings Game provides a new perspective on Zsuzsa's extraordinary career, as well as some revealing details of her personal life. It is beautifully produced, with a stunning picture of Zsuzsa on the cover and a number of other photographs inside. (Zsuzsa with Mikhail Tal, Zsuzsa with Bobby Fischer, Zsuzsa with Mikhail Botvinnik, Zsuzsa with Rajiv Gandhi...) Chess players won't be disappointed by the selection of Zsuzsa's 25 favourite games and all the games from her World Championship matches.

Unfortunately, there are some serious flaws in the book's English language. Zsuzsa and her Israeli husband are not native English speakers, but there is a page of acknowledgements to grandmasters, friends and relatives who helped with the book, including two editors and proofreaders. None of these people noticed that *Queen of the Kings Game* is missing an apostrophe on the cover and on every page of the book.

Some of the phrases used by the authors aren't exactly wrong, but sound strange, such as the caption, "Sophia Polgar receiving her gorgeous trophy in Rome." It is a shame that Zsuzsa's admirers don't get the accuracy they deserve from her – although they do get some amusing moments. Former world champion Tal agrees to a quick draw during a tournament so that he can play blitz with 12-year-old Zsuzsa.

"The playing hall became almost empty from 'kibitzers' and spectators. Obviously they were all amazed from the attention Mikhail Tal is paying to the girl. As for the games themselves, they were all very exciting. Zsuzsa gave the champion a monumental struggle. Tal was 'sweating' and the people around were having a bliss."

A chapter by Laszlo Polgar in *Queen of the Kings Game* directly contradicts what he said to me. He makes some very true statements about schools, but he emphasises that certain children have more potential – or talent – than others. "School has a levelling out, uniforming effect. It is very dangerous for talented children, because the levelling out happens at a low standard...

"Repetition over and over again of material that is already understood is torture for the specially talented child. The uncomprehending pedagogue often destroys specially talented children. Often they are considered by teachers to be extremely untalented, retarded, as prisoners of dreams, very unsocial, slow-witted, destructive, insane and furthermore as below average. Mostly, they fail to perceive the giftedness of the children."

The other side of the coin is that the majority of children, who are without special talents, need a varied education and probably benefit from the social life at school more than they would in a hothouse with their parents. Laszlo refuses to draw this conclusion. He would like the world to see his daughters as living proof of his educational theory, not just as three incredible individuals. That ambition may well be impossible even for Laszlo Polgar to realise.

Another chapter in *Queen of the Kings Game* is devoted to Bobby Fischer's stay with the Polgars. The family persuaded him to cross the border from war-torn Yugoslavia to Hungary in 1992. "The next time the Polgars crossed to Yugoslavia, Zsuzsa joined them and at the border control they asked the guard nonchalantly if there would be any problem if they had with them an individual called Robert Fischer when they returned. The guard, who had no idea who Fischer was and was most likely half drunk, answered something to the effect of 'I don't care if you bring back Napoleon Bonaparte.'"

Last year Zsuzsa won the women's world title from China's Xie Jun. By then, no one doubted that the Polgars could compete on equal terms with men, and Zsuzsa was tempted by the prize money. "All my life I was fighting for women playing together with men," she says. "I would prefer it if the international chess federation would cancel the women's World Championship altogether – even though financially I would be worse off," Zsuzsa told me. But it was there, so she entered it.

"If they don't cancel it, the prize fund should be the same as for the men's World Championship. The women's championship can be even more entertaining because there are more mistakes and the games are easier for the audience to understand, so there is no reason why there shouldn't be a sponsor. It would be a temporary motivation for five or ten years, until another couple of dozen women are in the top one hundred."

Zsuzsa won the world title on her second attempt. In her first challenge she tied her Candidates match with Nana Ioseliani and was declared the loser by drawing of lots. Zsuzsa was expected to beat Ioseliani, but *Queen of the Kings Game* explains what was distracting her during the match. She had been living with Peruvian GM Julio Granda Zuniga, who came with her to the Candidates tournament but hardly spoke to her. He had decided to end their relationship. She only discovered afterwards that Zuniga was seeing another woman in Peru – by whom he had three children.

The Zsuzsa-Cobi marketing team is now exploiting Zsuzsa's status as world champion to the maximum. Their efforts set an example that other high-profile players (notably Kasparov) might do well to follow. Zsuzsa is improving the image of chess and promoting it throughout the world by means of a website which was set up in the last few months (www.polgarchess.com).

Kasparov avoids the public as much as possible, and when he does meet people he is often sullen and rude to them. Zsuzsa must surely be the most accessible world champion in chess history. She invites Internet visitors to send a game to her by e-mail, and she will annotate it for a fee of no less than $50, depending on the game.

Admittedly, Zsuzsa's services don't come cheap, but who can blame her if there is sufficient demand? She will give a one-hour private lesson in person or on the telephone for $150; a two-hour lecture for $1,500; a 30-board simultaneous display and talk for a minimum of $3,000. When I wrote to Cobi to find out what the chances were of having some free lessons at Zsuzsa's school for the purposes of an article, this was his reply:

"Until not too long ago, journalists had to pay Zsuzsa in order to conduct an interview with her. Recently we decided that for the time being the fee will be waived and of course many took advantage of that. Also in light of our chess school we welcome more publicity. I'm sorry if I sound cynical but if the chess world champion pays the expenses of a journalist to get publicity, this would probably get Zsuzsa in the front pages of the papers. We run our ventures as a business and not as a philanthropic organisation. Therefore we expect to earn money, not spend. The bottom line is that in order to come here and learn about our activities you would have to pay your own expenses. The one-week course if you or anyone else is interested is $400."

Obviously the women's world title is extremely important to Zsuzsa, and she is very serious about defending it. She turned down her invitation from Kirsan Ilyumzhinov to play in the FIDE knockout World Championship with the explanation that "…as the Women's World Champion every chess competition is very important for me and I need to prepare at least six months in advance. This event has caught me by surprise, as the target of my preparation so far has been to defend my title as a world champion against the next challenger.

"In addition, it seems to me that to play in the first round of this competition would be belittling my title and stature in the chess world. I would consider playing at a higher round if I may, closer to where Mr. Karpov enters the event."

[In the first knockout World Championship the reigning FIDE world champion, Anatoly Karpov, who had defeated Gata Kamsky in a FIDE World Championship match in 1996, played only in the final round against India's Vishy Anand. Karpov won in a blitz play-off. In subsequent knockout World Championships, whoever was reigning champion had to play in earlier rounds.]

At the chessboard, Zsuzsa appears to suffer more stress than her sisters, hunched up and intense, while Sofia is the most relaxed of the three; Judit is serious and focused during the game, but full of fun afterwards. She often gets up and walks around the tournament hall for a think, then goes back to her seat and tucks her legs underneath her in a half-kneeling position. When her games are over she loves to analyse them cheerfully with her opponents. All three Polgar sisters have an abundance of confidence, charisma and class, which are apparent as soon as they walk into a room.

Sofia is a weaker player than her sisters and has often indicated that she would like to escape from the rigorous lifestyle of a chess professional. "If my parents had chosen tennis for us I would have been really rich now," Sofia said, adding that she didn't regret becoming a chess player. Sofia's victory with 8½ points out of 9 at the Rome Open in 1989 was hailed by chess journalist Cathy Forbes as "arguably the best performance in an open tournament by anybody ever".

These days Sofia is entering fewer tournaments. Most recently she shared 4th-8th place in the Hoogovens Open. She also plays for a team in Israel and a team in the

Netherlands. But perhaps chess will eventually take second place in Sofia's life to some other career, as her interests are so diverse.

Sofia plays chess with her boyfriend "for fun", but doesn't see him often as he is serving in the Israeli army. "I go to the movies, listen to music, see friends, and I like drawing," she told me. "The usual things that young people do." A watercolour by Sofia is reproduced in *Queen of the Kings Game* – an imaginary picture of Zsuzsa's world chess crown. When I asked Sofia which chess player she admired most, she answered without hesitation: "Judit!"

The three sisters have always had a very close relationship, untroubled by professional rivalry. "At the beginning we had too many enemies to fight between ourselves," said Judit. The Polgars had to contend with the sexism of famous players such as Lajos Portisch (No. 1 in Hungary until Judit overtook him), who once said that a woman as world champion among men would be "against nature".

British GM David Norwood has never forgotten his ordeal at the chessboard with the ruthless Hungarians. "Some years ago I played against the three Polgar sisters. Before the match I bought each of them a bunch of flowers. They returned the compliment by each of them crushing me in turn. Then the smiling girls gave me a present – a computer printout of all my games which they had used to prepare for me. It was signed, 'Love from the Polgars.'"

No chess player likes to lose, but male players find losing to a woman especially humiliating. The magazine *New in Chess* described Judit's defeated opponents at a tournament in Madrid as "lamentable figures reminiscent of the gloomiest Goya pictures". Judit sat motionless as she accepted their resignations, "only occasionally throwing back her long auburn hair with a twist of the head". It was as if they had lost to a 12-year-old girl, Judit says, even though she was 18 at the time.

Judit was particularly frustrated when world champion Garry Kasparov refused to treat her with the respect she deserved. "He ignored me completely. It was as if I was not there," she says. "Now we have a normal relationship, we say hello, but we don't talk much."

Spain hosts more top tournaments than any other country (it is also Judit's favourite place to play), and Hungary is also a very strong chess country, but there is no rich Hungarian sponsor who is willing to finance tournaments at a level that would attract Judit. "People in Hungary usually prefer to watch football," she said. "The biggest publicity was when I played Spassky in 1993. There was a full playing hall, everybody was very excited, there were 800 to 1,000 people daily, I was really surprised."

Judit feels there is little she can do at the moment to encourage chess in her home country. "It's very hard while I'm playing in the top arena – I don't really have the time or energy to advertise chess in Hungary. We had a lot of scandals between the players and the chess federation – the federation doesn't have money to support things. Of course I'm upset that tournaments are collapsing in Eastern Europe, but

I don't know why. In principle chess is a good sport for advertising things, sponsors can invest less than they do in something like tennis and receive more publicity. They need to spend $200,000 to $300,000. The problem is that there are not too many professional chess organisers."

Judit's playing schedule is hectic. She shared sixth place in the elite Tilburg tournament this October, ahead of Alexei Shirov, Joel Lautier and Loek van Wely. This achievement was followed by her equal second place in the Hoogovens international tournament with Loek van Wely, behind Emil Sutovsky and ahead of veteran former world champion Vasily Smyslov. At the moment she is taking part in the hundred-player FIDE knockout World Championship.

Judit is currently rated No. 12 in the world by FIDE. Judging by her performances, we are rapidly approaching the day when a woman will challenge for the men's world title. When she isn't in a tournament or studying chess, Judit says she tries to do sports, go to the theatre or the cinema, "and I have a dog called Babi, a Hungarian Vizsla, a big dog. She's very nice." She claimed that she has never had a boyfriend – "It just didn't happen" – although a couple of male professional chess players I spoke to about this were sceptical. More likely, she simply prefers to keep her private life private.

I asked Judit if she ever got weary of the media attention she has attracted. "I don't mind journalists," she said. "They're less interested in me than they were before. I usually charge an honorarium, though." In fact she did ask me for £1,500, but when I told her the interview would be published in a chess magazine she waived her fee. She assured me that journalists do pay her that kind of money, "sometimes more".

Would Judit advise other parents to give their children the kind of education that she and her sisters had? "I'm sure parents need a lot of energy and dedication, they have to give up a lot of things; they don't have fun too often. Our parents had to look after us every day, and we had financial problems as well. It brought them a lot of happiness but it was also very tough."

When Zsuzsa has children she intends to do things somewhat differently. "Yes, I would use some of the methods," she said, "not necessarily teaching them at home, though. I don't think I would choose chess for my children, because I've spent too much time on it in my life and there are many other interesting things."

So why, after all, did the Polgar sisters become chess grandmasters and not cancer specialists or tennis stars? Judit gave the answer: "Zsuzsa was good at mathematics and chess at the same time, but at some point our parents had to make a decision. My father said chess is a simple thing: you can measure the results easily. It's just two people sitting opposite each other at a board and whoever wins is better! Later on he realised it wasn't so simple."

At the time of writing, Judit Polgar is No. 24 in the world, with a rating of 2677. In the 1999 FIDE knockout World Championship she reached the quarterfinals, losing to the eventual tournament winner, Alexander Khalifman. Sofia maintains a highly respectable women's grandmaster rating of 2464, while Zsuzsa (now known as Susan) remains at 2565, inactive since her dispute with FIDE when the birth of her first child took precedence over a defence of the world women's title. She now has a daughter and a son. Sofia married GM Yona Kosashvili in 1999 and had a baby recently. Judit reportedly married Gustav Fonts, a veterinarian, in 2000.

Andor Lilienthal
(*CHESS*, August 1997)

You have to travel if you want to catch up with Andor Lilienthal. He walks slowly, which is usual for someone who has just turned 86, but he hops from country to country at a rate that is unusual for anyone of any age. I first met him in St. Petersburg at the 1996 Chigorin Memorial Tournament, where he was serenely observing the clashes taking place around him and selecting the best games. We spoke in Russian, as he doesn't know English. This year I dropped in on him at his flat in a rather monochrome suburb of Budapest.

Lilienthal's wife, Olga, was packing suitcases for their imminent trip to Russia, Sweden and England, where they were going to visit his 90-year-old brother. "Are you hungry?" she asked me. I was, but I could see she was busy, so I said no. But a Russian woman never takes no for an answer. "You don't sound so sure," she said, and minutes later presented me with a sandwich, an apple and a cup of coffee.

Lilienthal asked for a papirosa, a Russian cigarette. "Yes, Andrusha," came the reply. Olga brushed his white hair affectionately. "I must look my best when a beautiful young woman comes to see me," said Lilienthal with a chuckle, demonstrating the charm he is internationally famous for.

"My wife has just one deficit," he said, leaning forward conspiratorially. "She is too old for me! She is only 30 years younger than me!" He sat back again and laughed loudly. "All my wives were Russian. Capablanca was also married to a Russian woman, Olga, who died recently. Réti married a Russian actress; her father was a famous poet. Flohr's wife was a Russian Jew. If foreigners want a good wife, I recommend a Russian wife – although I don't want to offend other nationalities – but you can be sure I'm right."

Lilienthal's sharp grandmaster memory may have failed him momentarily; according to his friend Laszlo Szabo, he was already married to a Dutch woman when he went to Russia and fell in love with a woman who was 20 years *older* than him. "I know he had a Dutch wife, because I saw her when she came to Budapest to arrange the divorce," Szabo told me.

Lilienthal lived with his first Russian wife for 50 years until she died, then he married another Russian woman who also died, then Olga, whom he met at Moscow's Petrosian Chess Club in 1987. "A friend of mine who was the director of the club asked me if I

Andor Lilienthal's charm is internationally famous.

wanted to meet an interesting woman. Her daughter played draughts there. I wasn't too bothered, but Olga was watching while I was giving a simultaneous display on 30 boards. I noticed her and thought, well, she is very nice."

In his long life Lilienthal also found time for some magnificent conquests on the chessboard. He started playing relatively late, at 16, and retired from competitive chess quite early, but he went on to train world champions Vasily Smyslov and Tigran Petrosian, and the Soviet team. In his career he defeated Alekhine, Capablanca and the composer Prokofiev.

Lilienthal was born in Moscow to a family of Hungarian Jews, and when he was two his mother took him to Budapest, where his older brother was at school. When World War I broke out, Lilienthal's father was interned and the children were taken to an orphanage. Lilienthal was already a working tailor at the age of 15, but he had acquired other talents from his parents. His father was an electrician, "but he used to take part in car races and finished second in the Moscow-St. Petersburg run. It is very possible that it was from him that I inherited this competitive streak, this will to win," he commented recently in *New in Chess*.

Lilienthal's mother was an opera singer, and he too has always felt an affinity for music, he told me. "I have a good ear even now. I learnt the piano for a year, but I gave up. I was in Vienna and I missed my mother, so I went back to Budapest. Perhaps I could have become a pianist." Instead, he became addicted to chess, touring the chess haunts of Europe, especially the Café de la Régence in Paris. That was where he played Prokofiev.

"He was candidate master strength. We played chess for money... I had to eat! Of course, I always won." Lilienthal is sure that chess and music are somehow connected, although he doesn't know why. "Oistrakh [the violinist] played chess too, he was a very strong candidate master, he loved chess. Then there was a conductor at the Bolshoi Theatre who was a great admirer of Botvinnik, he looked at all of Botvinnik's games. Taimanov is a very talented musician and Portisch has a wonderful voice. Smyslov sings very well. Philidor was also a famous musician, that's more proof for you."

As a young man Lilienthal spoke to his illustrious opponents in German, not Russian. When he arrived in Hastings for the tournament of 1934 he never imagined that fate was about to lead him to the Soviet Union. At Hastings Lilienthal won an "immortal game" against Capablanca in 26 moves with a queen sacrifice. That success brought him an invitation to the Moscow International Tournament the following year, where he saw his future wife in the front row of the spectators.

I suggested that the victory over Capablanca must be his favourite game, but Lilienthal disagreed. "That game was very effective, good for the public. But if a world champion loses in 26 moves he must have made a mistake, wouldn't you agree? I have much better games, when I beat Lasker, Botvinnik, Smyslov, Bronstein. My favourite game was my win against Botvinnik in the Soviet Championships of 1940. It was stronger than any grandmaster tournament, the 20 strongest chess players were in it, including Botvinnik, Smyslov and Keres. I was undefeated in first place. I've won lots of tournaments, but this was the best."

Mikhail Botvinnik, the official hero of Soviet chess, was so upset at the result that he insisted the top six prizewinners should play in a "Match-Tournament for the Absolute Championship of the USSR" in 1941, which he duly won. Stalin wouldn't have appreciated it if a Hungarian immigrant had too many triumphs. Lilienthal managed to avoid trouble by remaining oblivious to politics. He was rewarded for his naïveté with trips abroad, to play in Hungary, Czechoslovakia and England. He was a model Soviet citizen until 1973, when the authorities began to suspect him of having capitalist connections. They stopped giving him permission to leave the country because they had found out that his brother was living in London.

"I don't want to complain. I lived in the USSR for 43 years, I saw more good than bad, but when I heard that my brother was in London I wanted to come back to Hungary. In 1939 I knew he was in London but a letter he sent didn't get to me and I thought he died in the war. Twenty years later a Russian journalist met him in an Italian restaurant in Soho."

Fortunately Lilienthal also had a very powerful communist connection, the Hungarian party leader Janos Kadar. They had been in the same class at school, so Lilienthal appealed to Kadar for help. "Kadar gave me this flat in 1977 and he requested that the Soviet government also give me a flat. He knew that the USSR was the El Dorado of chess and that I had to live there, too, with my colleagues, grandmasters."

Kadar was generally hated in Hungary for taking over after the failed uprising of 1956, but Lilienthal speaks of him sympathetically. "People always put the blame on one man. Under Kadar living standards were much better than they are now. Kadar loved chess very much. Once when he was in Moscow he said to me, 'I want a break from politics, come with me to the Central Chess Club,' and he met Botvinnik and Smyslov, who showed him their games. He was the only politician I knew who wasn't corrupt. He had a thousand dollars when he died and that was all. Brezhnev gave him a car, but he gave it to the state. He didn't do what he was told by the Soviet leaders, people lived wonderfully, the economy was on a higher level."

Lilienthal took Soviet citizenship in 1939, having previously represented Hungary in the Olympiads of 1935 and 1937. "Half my soul is here and half is in Russia," he told me. "Russia now is chaos, it's awful. It is a mafioso country. They don't pay wages or pensions – certain people have pocketed this money for themselves. We have a niece there, and Olga's daughter, so we go often, but without pleasure. People suffered under Stalin and they are suffering now; what's democracy if people are going hungry? I'm not a politician, so I can't tell you what the government should do, but they should think about the people as they do in the West, you can see that when you go there."

Russian chess is still benefiting from Lilienthal's vast knowledge of the game – he writes articles for Alexander Roshal's magazine, *64*, and gives lectures and simultaneous displays. FIDE President Kirsan Ilyumzhinov gave him a decorative chess set from Kalmykia that is on display in his living room – Lilienthal was the host of a meeting between Ilyumzhinov and Bobby Fischer.

Evidence of Lilienthal's friendship with the elusive Fischer was provided in his photograph album, where, not too far from a picture of Lilienthal with the Russian ultra-nationalist leader Vladimir Zhirinovsky there was one of Fischer at the dining table in Lilienthal's flat, taken last New Year's Eve.

I asked Lilienthal which chess players he had got on best with over the years. He began with Salo Flohr, who immigrated to the USSR from Czechoslovakia at around the same time as Lilienthal. "Flohr was a great friend, my first from my youth, and I was friends with Lasker and Capablanca. I learnt a lot from Alekhine, I was at his house. Tal was a virtuoso like Paganini on the violin, a very nice, enchanting person, we were friends. I don't think he had any enemies."

As for Fischer, Lilienthal turns a deaf ear to his anti-Semitic remarks and his claims that the games between Karpov and Kasparov were fixed. "Fischer is a particular special person. You can't take away the fact that he is a genius. He was the first foreigner who managed to destroy the Soviet hegemony."

Fischer lived in Budapest for some time and had some problems with his American passport, which was about to expire, but Lilienthal said he has now renewed it. He added that Fischer is popular among women aged between 19 and 24, "even though he's 54." Fischer's main interest is popularising random chess, and he discussed this with Ilyumzhinov. I wondered whether this was because he found ordinary chess too easy. "No, old chess isn't easy for anyone," Lilienthal said. "It's infinite. It's difficult for me and the new chess is even more difficult, but I think Leko has played it. Fischer thinks his chess is more interesting because it's more complicated than old chess."

Lilienthal was full of praise for Hungary's own chess geniuses, the Polgar sisters. "Five of them lived in a room smaller than this one and they brought up such girls!" he exclaimed. "I played against two women world champions, Rubtsova and Menchik, they played fantastically, but you can't compare them with these three sisters. It's the pride not only of Hungarian chess, but also of world chess, that women can play phenomenally. I'm not sure if Judit can become world champion, but I don't think there will be another female chess player like her, she plays like a fantasy, like the three tenors, Pavarotti, Domingo and what's-his-name? – oh yes, Carreras."

I mentioned the amazing achievement of Etienne Bacrot, who had just become the world's youngest ever grandmaster at 14, and Lilienthal said he had heard about it but didn't know how Bacrot's name was spelled, so he asked me to write it down. Then I told him about Luke McShane gaining his international master title at 13 – this was news to him and he asked me to write McShane's name as well.

Lilienthal didn't even know the moves of chess when he was Bacrot's age. Did he think chess had changed beyond recognition since he learnt to play? "You needed intuition in my time to play chess. Now computers help with the analysis up to the 20th, the 22nd move of the opening. I never used a computer, it was too expensive, I couldn't afford such a toy. But it's fantastic technology, it's a miracle, it's beautiful. There are fireworks in today's games, I see them in magazines, but in the past there was much less opening theory, and now people can play the opening without thinking."

Lilienthal has no doubt what the best time of his life was, or is: now. "I have a good life, thank God. I live a very peaceful, good life, and what can be better if a person is old and can say that?" He laughed when I asked him whether there was anything he still wanted to do. "I don't think you can have too many ambitions at my age, but I would like to be healthy enough to live a bit longer."

After our conversation Lilienthal showed me his book, *My Life in Chess*, published in Hungarian, pointing out all his friends in the photographs, faces from history. In his stately manner he posed for photographs, concerned that he wasn't wearing a tie, but I reassured him that he looked fine without it. As I left he asked me how much I was paying for my accommodation. "That's too much," he said, shaking his head disapprovingly. "Next time give me a ring and I'll arrange for you to stay with my neighbour for less."

Lilienthal's Hundred Best Games *was published shortly after he celebrated his 90th birthday.*

Chess In Hungary
(*CHESS*, September 1997)

Training Libyan terrorists and developing secret supplies of chemical weapons seemed like a good idea at the time to Laszlo Nagy, a captain in the Hungarian army. He served the communist regime loyally for 10 years until his personal beliefs began to crumble along with the foundations of the system and his thoughts turned to chess. Nagy left the army in 1991 and since then he has become Hungary's leading chess organiser, attracting talented players from all over the world to his monthly First Saturday tournaments.

A bearded hulk of a man with a personality to match, 40-year-old Nagy is truly Mr. Big ("nagy" means "big" in Hungarian). He has enlisted a battalion of his neighbours in the blocks of flats around his own who are willing to host chess players at very reasonable rates – about £6 per night. Nagy is now a born-again capitalist. "Money is freedom," he told me. "In the communist system it was social security to be an officer, I had a salary, a flat, I felt like a good man in the society. Every day we were bombarded by the idea of the communist system, so of course I believed in it."

Exposure to Western influences in the late 1980s convinced Nagy that his energies had been wasted. His main job was teaching chemistry to troops trained in chemical warfare, but he also taught English to Libyan terrorists because they wouldn't have accepted a woman teacher. "The Warsaw Pact was not supposed to have any chemical weapons, but it was a lie," he said.

Nagy, a candidate master, persuaded his wife to give up her job as a Russian teacher so that she could take on the day-to-day running of the tournaments. "She would have been earning £100 a month – it's nothing." Nagy's income from chess is also more than the salary of a high-ranking officer. This is because of the discrepancy between the Hungarian and Western economies, which he expects will continue for another decade.

The prize funds for First Saturday tournaments are very low, but players enter for norms and titles, not for the money. British players Neil McDonald and Matthew Sadler achieved their grandmaster titles at Nagy's tournaments. The strongest grandmaster to play in the First Saturday tournaments was Valery Loginov from St. Petersburg, but after his rating soared Nagy couldn't afford him any more.

The biggest difficulty for Nagy when he started was that he lacked contacts and a reputation. "Chess players didn't want to believe that I was organising the tournaments," he said. "The most important thing for a chess organiser is to be reliable." He has made a success of his business by constantly communicating with players and journalists in every country by telephone and e-mail. "Let's communicate!" he proposed, a few minutes after my arrival at his flat from England.

"Who would you like to meet? Portisch? Shall we phone Portisch?" He asked a friend for the number of the former Hungarian No.1 and dialed it.

I suggested that Nagy should wish Portisch a happy birthday, as he turned 60 that day. There was a sharp exchange in Hungarian between Nagy and Portisch's wife. Nagy looked glum. "She says there is no birthday. She knows nothing about any birthday. He is not giving any interviews. Forget him."

Fortunately some other Hungarian grandmasters were more responsive. Nagy phoned Andor Lilienthal, Ildiko Madl and Andras Adorjan for me. All three were happy to be interviewed. "OK, that gives me an excuse to straighten up this flat," Adorjan said in his excellent English. Once we had made contact with the famous names of today and yesterday, Nagy was anxious that I should talk to the famous names of tomorrow – the young players in his April tournament.

The tournament started the following day at the headquarters of the Hungarian Chess Federation, a formidable old building with wrought-iron gates and a spiral staircase, a short distance from the Hungarian parliament. Janos Kadar, the post-1956 Communist Party leader, gave the building to the chess federation because of his personal enthusiasm for the game.

On our way in we met a young man with curly blond hair and a determined look on his face, 15-year-old Peter Acs, whom Nagy introduced to me as the best player in Hungary for his age. He was a FIDE master and was hoping to make his third and final international master norm at the tournament. Acs, an admirer of Vishy Anand for his chess style and human warmth, learnt chess at four and started to play seriously when he was nine. His ambition is "to be a member of the Hungarian Olympiad team and to become one of the best chess players in the world."

Acs took a leap towards the attainment of those ambitions by winning Nagy's grandmaster tournament with an extremely impressive score of 9/11, a clear two points ahead of Yevgeny Agrest and Peter Lukacs. He easily made the international master title and also his first grandmaster norm.

Jiri Stocek, 19, comes regularly to First Saturday tournaments from the Czech Republic. His hero is Alekhine – "I like his style of play," he said, but Jiri doesn't play Alekhine's Defence – "Alekhine also played it rather rarely." Alekhine won a tournament at Karlovy Vary (also known as Karlsbad) in 1923, which is near where Jiri lives.

Two of the other young players in the April tournament came from a rather more distant part of the world. Ooi Chern Ee, 18, and Mas Hafijulhilmi Agus, 16, looked like a pair of Olympic athletes in their official Malaysia team jackets. The secretary of their chess federation recommended the First Saturday tournament as a way of getting an international master norm and they received some sponsorship from a bank. The Malaysian Chess Federation has also helped by buying them computers.

"Chess isn't that popular in Malaysia like badminton or football, but it's getting better," Ooi Chern Ee told me. "We have just one IM, Jimmy Lieuw." They have both travelled widely; they had already been to Hungary once before, for the World Youth Championships. Ooi Chern Ee's favourite tournament was the Goodricke Open in Calcutta, "a very pleasant tournament, but I generally enjoy most tournaments."

They are not yet certain about whether they will take up chess as a career, and are hoping to go to university in the United States. Ooi Chern Ee is studying electronic engineering. "I think chess helps me with my studies more than my studies help with chess, although it goes in two directions," he said. Mas Hafijulhilmi Agus had a superb result at the April international master tournament, coming first with nine straight wins. Ooi Chern Ee found the grandmaster tournament too strong and languished in 11th place.

Nagy often has Vietnamese players in his tournaments – a Vietnamese diplomat in Budapest who is keen on chess has brought up a chess family. He has an adopted son who is a grandmaster and a daughter, Thanh Trang Hoang, who beat GM John Nunn in a rapidplay game when she was 12. Now she is 16 and has some more scalps behind her, including that of Alisa Galliamova-Ivanchuk, whom she beat at last year's Olympiad in Yerevan.

Zoltan Ambrus, general secretary of the Hungarian Chess Federation, was in an office next to the tournament hall, so arranging an interview with him wasn't too difficult. He is the only paid employee of the chess federation and he has been in the job for seven years. "We receive nothing from the government," he said. "According to the sports law which was passed last year, the Hungarian government said that an activity is only recognised as a sport if it is included in the Olympic Games, unless its international federation is a member of the international sports federation. FIDE is not a member, because chess is a mind sport like go, bridge and other card games." The federation keeps going through gifts from sponsors, membership fees and other income, such as the rent that Nagy pays.

Hungarians have always been fanatical about chess – they even play in the swimming pool – and this lack of state support hasn't dampened their spirits. "The Hungarian population is 10 million and the number of people who have played a minimum of one game in their life and know the rules of chess is half a million. The number of official players in clubs is 10,000. There are more than 1,000 players on the FIDE list." New strong players such as Peter Acs emerge every year, following in the footsteps of the Polgar sisters, Zoltan Almasi, Ildiko Madl and Peter Leko. Like Western players, they are funded by their parents or by private sponsors. Peter Acs is sponsored by the nuclear power station in his home town of Pecs.

Sadly, the Hungarian Chess Federation can't afford to host super-tournaments that the country's best players could enter. "Judit Polgar, Peter Leko, Zoltan Almasi and Lajos Portisch have very high appearance fees – Judit's is $10,000," said Ambrus. "They don't play much in Hungary. Almasi played in the Hungarian individual championships two years ago and won by two points. Portisch last played here in 1991, in the super-final of the individual tournament. We can't find this big sponsor in Hungary and a big tournament is big money. There aren't many rich men in Hungary. We can organise only little tournaments or big opens. Closed tournaments are very dear."

The federation may be short of cash, but it does still own a priceless treasure trove of chess books. A library of 16,000 books and magazines is open to the public every Monday afternoon and books can be borrowed for a deposit fee. Most of the collection was given to the federation by the widow of a man who edited a Hungarian chess magazine in the early part of this century. He exchanged copies of his own magazine for publications from around the world. Now the federation is adding to its library by collecting new tournaments on CD and disk.

Almasi and Portisch both declined to be interviewed by me. Almasi said he was too busy. I phoned Portisch to see if he confirmed his wife's "no interviews" policy. "Where did you get my number?" he asked accusingly. "It's a secret!" But meeting a cheerful young woman, Ildiko Madl, was ample compensation for missing out on a grumpy grandmaster. Madl, 27, is married to IM Jozsef Dobos and they have a four-year-old daughter with an unusual Hungarian-Turkish name, Fruzsina.

Madl's career has inevitably been overshadowed by the extraordinary feats of the Polgar sisters. She bears no grudge, although for two years Laszlo Polgar didn't speak to her. "I don't know why – probably because at the 1992 Olympiad in Novi Sad I told journalists that he had been behaving as if he was the captain of the team. Now he says hello, but we don't speak much."

Madl was being left out at the Olympiad and Judit Polgar seemed to be overworked. "Laszlo knows his daughters, so maybe he knows Judit can play 14 games without a rest. The other teams have four players and they always change, even the first board. The girls are very nice. Judit and Sofia were nice to me in the last Olympiad and helped me to prepare my games."

Unlike Judit Polgar, Madl doesn't mind playing in the women's World Championship; she hopes to get into a women's Candidates tournament. "I think the women's World Championship should continue because men players are stronger than women players. Judit trained for eight hours a day – what woman can do this? Most women don't have the time."

Madl has been in the Interzonal three times and narrowly missed qualifying for a Candidates tournament when she came fourth and the first three went in. "Interzonals are very long tournaments, 15 rounds, and it's very difficult to play well all the way through," she said. Madl has been to three tournaments in England, and particularly liked being at Hastings. "Maybe the biggest tournament of my life was the Hastings Premier in 1995," she said. "I started very well, I played John Nunn and drew. My husband was with me, he was playing in the Challengers, and it was a very nice 10 days. My result was OK, but to see Hastings was very interesting."

The richest country Madl has played in was the United Arab Emirates, where the Olympiad was held in 1986. "We stayed in the Hilton in Dubai, we had a beach and everything we wanted – and our team finished second."

Madl's most unpleasant chess experience was at a youth tournament in Vilnius, when Lithuania was still part of the USSR. She suspects she was a victim of dirty tricks. "I had stomach problems and I think they did something with the food," she said. "I was leading the tournament and finally I won. I played five Russian players and it was very unsuccessful for them." Beating the Russians brings her great satisfaction, and her favourite game was her win against Litinskaya. "Because of the situation, not the game. With this point we beat Russia in the Olympiad in 1988."

Since Fruzsina was born Madl has been playing in fewer tournaments, but she has been teaching chess to her daughter. "She can set up the pieces and make a few moves, then she wants to do something else. She likes memory games very much, sometimes she beats us!" Madl likes to play in the same tournaments as her husband so that they can travel together and help each other. She says it is impossible to make a living from chess in Hungary – she plays for a team in Croatia, and one of her teammates is Zita Raiczanyi, the woman who made friends with Bobby Fischer and helped to make his match with Spassky happen in 1992.

"We always ask her what happened out there in Montenegro, but she won't tell us," Madl said, laughing. Fischer is Madl's chess hero. "I am a tactical player and I like his tactics. I think he was good in everything, though, a positional and a tactical player. His behaviour is strange, of course." Fischer hasn't given Hungarian chess players any opportunity to benefit from his low-profile stay in Budapest, but they aren't worried: they are doing quite well by themselves.

Laszlo Nagy is still organising First Saturday tournaments and his website is http://home.hu.inter.net/~firstsat/. Peter Acs is now a grandmaster. In August 2001 he became the first Hungarian to win the World Junior Championship. Jiri Stocek is also a grandmaster who plays regularly in tournaments around Europe. Ooi Chern Ee appears to have given up playing seriously, not having obtained a title. He became an actuarial science undergraduate at Wharton School of Business, University of Pennsylvania. Mas Hafijulhilmi Agus is a FIDE master. IM Thanh Trang Hoang won the Asian Women's Championship in India in 2000. IM Ildiko Madl is still playing: she won the 2001 Tel Aviv International women's event.

Laszlo Szabo
(*CHESS*, October 1997)

The scene: a magnificent villa high in the hills above a city somewhere in Central Europe. It is spring, and the newly painted building, resting among brightly coloured plants and flowers, shimmers in the morning sunlight. A workman (or so he would like to appear) casts a furtive glance at the foreign visitor. She announces her identity through the intercom, as instructed. The front door swings open, but there is no one behind it. The visitor treads cautiously through the hallway, past a housekeeper who gazes only at her laundry. Could this be a trap?

A light flashes over the lift, indicating that someone is descending. The visitor's instincts warn her to go no further. She has arrived at the meeting point – there is no escape. Only seconds remain before she must come face to face with the Grandest Master, armed with three ballpoint pens to which she had thoughtlessly forgotten to attach a rapid-firing, strychnine-squirting self-defence mechanism. Oh, füstkö, [smog] she cursed in her limited Hungarian...

Unless Laszlo Szabo had been stroking a Siamese cat, with an evil glint in his eye, accompanied by a huge man with iron teeth, his home in Budapest couldn't have been more like the den of a James Bond villain. In reality he is a lovable, funny and immensely dignified man, restricted to a wheelchair since the recent amputation of his right leg. The idyllic lifestyle may be considered a just reward for his chess victories and the hardships he has endured over the past 80 years, but in fact it is the result of his wife's success in business. Szabo would be a poor man indeed if he had to survive on the money and praise he has received in Hungary for his enormous contribution to chess.

The *Soviet Chess Encyclopaedia* has calculated that Szabo scored 1,762½ points out of 2,707 serious games (65 percent) played between 1934 and 1979. It fails to mention that Szabo did not play at all during World War II: he did forced labour in Hungary for three years, followed by another three years in a Russian prisoner-of-war camp. Politics also interfered in his later career, when he fell out of favour with the Hungarian chess authorities.

"After I left tournament chess nobody was talking about me, despite the fact that between Maroczy and Portisch there were 30 years which were my era," Szabo said. "Now, a little late, when I was 80, they invited me to parliament and the president of Hungary gave me a very high decoration, the Officer Cross of the Hungarian Republic. I should have had it 20 years ago, when I was playing."

Szabo was Hungarian champion seven times and joint champion a further three times. He came first in 21 postwar international tournaments, played in World Championship Candidates tournaments, and constantly represented his country in Olympiads and European Team Championships. As we discussed the fateful twists and turns of his life, he rolled across the polished floors of his upstairs rooms, showing me selections from the wall-to-wall shelves of chess books and the database on his computer. Szabo's chess library of six or seven thousand books and magazines, some dating back a century or more, is second only to that of the Hungarian Chess Federation.

The story of how Szabo became a chess player is told in his book, published in English as *My Best Games of Chess*. He was recuperating from a fever he caught after a swimming competition and had to take lots of walks. These led him to a square where people played chess on park benches, a sight which sparked his interest. When he was 14 years old his father took him to a chess club. He threw himself into the game, playing for the club team and studying a book on opening theory by the Soviet master Romanovsky. Within a year he made it to the final of the Budapest Amateur Championship. At 17 he achieved the master title with a win against Füster. Because of its significance, it is still one of Szabo's favourites.

When Szabo wrote his autobiography many of his games from the 1930s were missing – he lost them in the war. He did not know that they had been saved in the notebooks of an admirer. "Somebody who liked me very much collected my games from the thirties," he said, carefully turning the yellowing pages of meticulous handwriting. Szabo has already put more than half of the games into ChessBase on his computer. He would like to add some of them to his book because they are better than the ones that were included.

Szabo is enthusiastic about his computer and tried to demonstrate his familiarity with it. "It is wonderful, you can find any game in seconds. What opening would you like to see?" I made a suggestion and he hammered at the keyboard, but the screen obstinately refused to change. "Well, you can usually," he conceded. "In my time when we prepared for a tournament we had to write every game out of a book. It was a tremendous work. Now youngsters push a button on a computer and they have all the games collected. So the talent of the players comes earlier. On the other hand, it makes youngsters mechanical."

Before the war, Szabo was a clerk in a British-Hungarian bank in Budapest. He imagined this would give him a reasonably secure future and provide an income for his parents in their old age. He also played in international chess tournaments. "Hastings was my favourite town. I won four times there – only Gligoric won more Hastings tournaments. In 1938 they invited me for the first time. I went to the stone where William the Conqueror sat and I wanted to be a conqueror in Hastings, too. I knew Golombek, B.H. Wood, Ritson-Morry; they were all nice fellows. Martin Blaine, who died three or four years ago, was a very good friend. He left Hungary in 1938 and I always visited him when I went to Hastings. He wasn't a very strong chess player, but he wrote a chess book for beginners with Euwe."

Szabo is angry about what the war did to him – not so much because of the terrible way he was treated, but because of the damage it did to his chess. "I think I should have done a lot more. When I appeared on the chess stage they said I had the potential to become world champion. Then came the working company and the prisoner-of-war camp. After my first appearance at Hastings an English lawyer, Mr. Brown, wanted to make papers for me to stay in England, but then my father was very, very ill and the president of the Hungarian Chess Federation told my parents that because the Hungarian team was first in the Olympiad of 1936 I will have special treatment by the authorities, I won't be called to a working company."

Szabo was Jewish, so he knew he was in danger, but he believed this promise. He returned to Hungary. "They called me to a working company. During those six years I didn't play chess. The Soviet players had very strong tournaments in the Urals, and they improved. So it was terrible in connection with my chess career, but you cannot know your fate in advance. Maybe I wouldn't be alive now if I'd stayed in England. Vera Menchik was in a chess club when a German bomb killed her." [In fact, although Menchik was the manager of the National Chess Centre in central London – which was destroyed by a Luftwaffe bomb – she was at her home in south London when a V2 rocket struck, killing her and her sister Olga.]

CHESS reported the first postwar news of Szabo in March 1946. "He was sent to the Russian front in 1942 in one of the so-called 'working companies' which were really 'mobile concentration camps' specially run for Jews... his weight came down to about 100 pounds... Szabo is now in good health once again and longing to play in another English Congress." Straight from his ordeal, Szabo was runner-up to Gedeon Barcza in the Hungarian Championship. His prize was 10 kilograms of lard.

On another occasion, Barcza was Szabo's second at a tournament. Andras Adorjan tells a hilarious story about this in one of his books. "Grandmaster Barcza showed [Szabo] the prepared variation, and, arriving at an unclear position, said: '...and then the better player wins.' Szabo replied: 'My goodness, but that's exactly what I want to avoid!'"

The bank where Szabo used to work was destroyed by a bomb, so in 1945 he decided to become a professional chess player. The first strong international tournament after the war was at Groningen in 1946, where Szabo finished in joint fourth place with Najdorf, after Botvinnik, Euwe and Smyslov. Last year the surviving players reunited for the 50th anniversary of that tournament – and Szabo came fourth again, in rather more relaxed circumstances.

In his career Szabo has won, lost and drawn against many great players of the 20th century. The most difficult opponents for him were Korchnoi and Petrosian. "Their style was terrible. I couldn't play against them," he said. But the player who upset him most is not well known at all. "Lundin, a Swedish player, took my first prize in a tournament in 1948. I was in first place and he was last. In the last round I lost to him. It was a terrible shock to me."

There was an even bigger shock for Szabo in 1955, when he was reported dead, despite coming third at Hastings. He recalls this incident in his book. "'An excellent performance by a dead man,' remarked a London friend of mine. Well, it turned out that many people believed me dead and buried in England. When Istvan Szabo (Romania) died, the press agencies announced me dead by mistake. The outstanding English chess player, Alexander, had already written my obituary for his column, when I turned up at Hastings."

The British press got it wrong again when Szabo was mysteriously absent from the 1971-72 Hastings tournament, but this time the journalists were not to blame. Lacking any information from the authorities in Hungary, they wrote that Szabo had disappeared. At the time, he was editor of the chess magazine *Magyar Sakkelet*. "There was always a problem with the chess federation in the communist era," Szabo told me. "They used me as they used all the sportsmen, for propaganda purposes, but Sandor Szerenyi, the president of the chess federation, didn't like me – he was a party man. It was impossible to go against him. I was invited to Hastings. I had a passport, a visa, flight tickets. It was usual in Hungary that all these documents were with the Sports Committee and only at the last minute they gave them to the sportsmen. The president wanted to throw me out of *Magyar Sakkelet*, but I didn't want to leave because he had no right to throw me out.

"In the first days of December 1971 suddenly a friend of mine called me from the Sports Committee and told me the chess federation had told them not to give me the passport. I had a letter from the secretary of the chess federation saying they thought it was better if I didn't go to Hastings. The international federation wrote to say I should stay in Hungary to clear this up. Everyone went on Christmas holiday. I think they forgot to send a cable to Hastings Chess Club to say I wouldn't come."

Szabo reluctantly left his job at *Magyar Sakkelet*. "Szerenyi had such power. He was a friend of [Hungarian leader] Kadar. He had no reason to sack me, according to the law they couldn't do anything, but he made the presidium [standing committee] of the chess federation tell me stupid things, why I should leave the magazine. I had an answer to everything, it wasn't true, but they had so much power. One day the trade union president invited me to see him with two other gentlemen. They said, 'Lazie, we were studying this case, we know you are right, but the man can put everything against you and if you write white, he will say black. You have a family, you have children. We offer you a position as chief trainer and suggest you accept this.' So I became chief trainer of the trade union club."

Szerenyi's behaviour may have been motivated by an unpleasant moment at the 1968 Olympiad in Lugano, Szabo believes. "Sandor Szerenyi was a person who waited a long time when he was hurt by something and then got revenge. In Lugano we lived together with the German team. One evening Petrosian, his wife and other Soviet chess players came to visit the Germans. It was a little strange because the next day the Russians had to play the Germans. It was important for the Germans because if they didn't lose they had a better place than the Hungarian team.

"On the adjournment day before the last round I was in the tournament hall and Petrosian asked me, 'Why did you say that we went to visit the Germans to agree the result of our next meeting?' I said, 'I didn't say that, who told you?' Szerenyi overheard this. I went to him and started to ask why he said such things. He became very nervous and went out to the toilet."

Competition was acceptable between Hungarians and their Soviet "comrades" at the chessboard, but in the wider world nothing could be allowed to upset harmonious Warsaw Pact relations. When Szabo was invited by the Dutch Chess Federation to tour the Netherlands giving simultaneous displays, his planned visit coincided with an international scandal.

"A Soviet couple, a scientist and his wife, wanted to stay in Holland. The Soviet ambassador wanted to see them at the airport and they said it wasn't possible. The newspapers said a policeman slapped the ambassador. The presidium of the Hungarian Chess Federation said, we don't give you permission to go to a country where the Soviet ambassador is beaten. I couldn't do anything with these people. I had a nervous breakdown and left this gathering. Stupid things happened which shouldn't have. Also I was a bit lazy in studying opening theory and these things hindered me, but I'm satisfied with my life, my family, this is all in the past."

Szabo opened a large photograph album that his 30-year-old son sent him from Israel. "We always were very happy when our children made us presents instead of buying them," he said. Szabo's son is a computer specialist in Israel. His daughter, who studied in New York, is one of Hungary's leading Yiddish experts. Their mother is the director of a tie factory called Cathy Ltd, and she was away in Italy buying materials when I met Szabo.

A relative always stays in the house with Szabo at night in case his disability causes him problems. Without any warning he developed a thrombosis in his right knee. He was in intensive care for seven days and the doctors couldn't save his leg. "I tell myself the words of Grünfeld, who had a wooden leg, 'Chess is a sport in which a man with bad legs can have better results than healthy people.' But I don't play tournaments now, so it doesn't help."

We went out to the balcony so that I could take some pictures of Szabo. He stood up and looked towards the Danube. "My wife insisted that we had to move here because our last flat had about 50 steps to the street. My car was adjusted so I could drive, but it was stolen from outside the house." He became more cheerful when he talked about his 80th birthday party. He was presented with a cake in the shape of a chessboard with pieces in the final position of a game he won against Botvinnik.

The late Laszlo Szabo enjoying the sunshine at his home in Budapest.

On my way out we passed through a large living room where Szabo sometimes plays bridge. I stopped to admire a glass cabinet full of his medals and trophies accumulated in 40 years of chess at the highest level. "I wouldn't do this, but my wife wanted them there," he said. Somehow I got the impression that he wasn't too sorry about her decision.

Laszlo Szabo died in August 1998.

Red, Yellow, Green, Blue – and Black – are OK!
(*Kingpin*, autumn 1998)

It was kind of funny to see the world's most avid proponent of the black pieces analysing on a rainbow chess set with Peter Leko. Hungarian GM Andras Adorjan always prefers the unconventional, even if that means battling alone with those who criticise him or ridicule his ideas. Quite like British IM Michael Basman, in a way, except that Adorjan doesn't agree with the weird openings expert, naturally. "You can still find new moves, and not just me, anybody, chess is democratic," Adorjan told me. "All we know is that there are some moves that are definitely wrong, like 1.g4."

No, Adorjan prefers far more sensible lines such as 7...b5! in the Grünfeld, a move which he is proud of inventing. Adorjan's protégé Leko used it to beat Loek van Wely at Groningen in 1995, when Leko was 16. "I like to attempt the almost impossible," said Adorjan, demonstrating his novelty for me. "This is very unlikely. But after 8. Nxb5 Nxe4 9.Nxc7 e5 Black is winning in all the variations."

I was talking to Adorjan in his flat in Budapest in April 1997. When I arranged our meeting on the phone, Adorjan said it would give him an excuse to tidy the place up. What I saw was rather like an artist's studio: Adorjan had his books on display above the piano, his chessboard out on the desk – but otherwise the room was quite bare, as if furniture and other practical items were of far less importance than his aids to creativity.

Leko let himself into the flat halfway through the interview, arriving for a training session. Adorjan himself looked like an ageing rock star, spiky hair and beard covering an impish but tired face. "In the past two years I went through a kind of crisis in my life, I divorced, and anyone who has done that knows what it's like, with two kids," he said.

A former World Championship candidate, second of Kasparov, two-time Hungarian champion and translator of pop songs, Adorjan is also famous internationally for his series of books entitled *Black is OK!* Their purpose is to provide a repertoire for the black side of a chess game, but the philosophy behind the series goes further. He was inspired to write it by the death of his mother in 1985.

In an article called "The Way It All Started", Adorjan explains the impact of this event on him. "Experiencing this way the finiteness of existence, I thought about the meaning of us being here... I figured we should merit the oxygen we breathe in and transform into carbon dioxide during our presence on earth; and that we must leave something lasting, something living on after our death."

Adorjan decided to start his "life's work" but he was unsure about the subject. "I am extremely extroverted, as a psychologist would put it – my desire for self-expression is enormous. So I didn't have to force myself to take pen in hand. What I wanted to write was something original, sort of a series which has something in common, some kind of 'meaningful harmony', but still, each piece can be taken for a whole, with an essence of its own."

Compiling a list of opening ideas, Adorjan realised that most of them were for the black side. He compared prejudice against the black pieces to apartheid, and in his *Black is OK!* magazine he included an article by Botswana resident Rupert Jones on the resurgence of South African chess.

The magazine folded after just one issue, so Adorjan wrote books instead. "Somehow it didn't work, like so many things in my life. I had to give it up." The first book, *Your Black is OK Repertory*, appeared in a Hungarian edition and a four-language edition (English, German, French and Spanish). According to Adorjan, the Hungarian version is "the only chess book in history with poems, written by me in Hungarian, on black pages." The Black is OK! theme reached a wider audience when a book was published by Batsford.

In our conversation Adorjan was not modest about his achievements, although the ever-present blackness of pessimism in his nature also crept in. "I think the only thing I have to do is die to be recognised at least as much as Nimzowitsch's *My*

System, because this is revolutionary. But unfortunately I'm still alive, you don't get credit so easily. My personal success as a writer and analyst is satisfaction, but the idea is more important. Very few ideas are great, only a few out of millions, and you ask why should mine be right – but then why shouldn't it?

"I deny that to play with Black in chess means any kind of handicap – except one – if White plays for a draw. Both sides are involved in choosing the opening, then you reach a complex position in which the colour of the pieces doesn't matter at all. If you are more talented than I am, if you are in better shape and if you're especially well oriented in that position – that is what matters. If there is a possibility for active counterplay then it doesn't matter who is White and who is Black.

"One of my good friends, a grandmaster, told me you chose such a narrow subject – Black and White. But even the very best players in the world play worse or much worse with Black. Number one, it's psychological, they don't believe they can win. Number two, everybody concentrates on the White repertoire, they try to survive as Black and tomorrow they'll be White again." Many strong players have fallen victim to Adorjan's ruthless play on the Black side.

Leko was the ideal pupil for Adorjan, as he preferred playing Black even before they met in 1993, or so Leko claims. "I am mostly preparing openings with Andras," Leko said. "Our whole work together is good. People say my Black repertoire is much, much sharper than with White. Almost all my Black games are decisive." [The truth is that Leko draws more games than any other top grandmaster – including those with Black.] Leko didn't fully share Adorjan's enthusiasm for rainbow chess, however. "This rainbow chess is funny and not worse than the other one. It's not as boring as the other one, there's more life," said Leko.

Rainbow chess is played in the same way as ordinary chess, with black pawns and white pawns, but the pieces all have their own colours. For example, the white bishops are light blue and the black bishops are dark blue; the white rooks are light green and the black rooks are dark green. After a few minutes it's easy to get used to. But is there any point to it? Adorjan's arguments are not theoretical, as with Black is OK!, but practical. He claims it helps people to remember positions and to plan their moves without losing track of where pieces will be in the future.

"This multicoloured chess was invented by a Hungarian," said Adorjan. "Five years ago I got a letter and a photo of multicoloured chess fell out. For two years I couldn't take it seriously. Then I thought, people are too dogmatic, I wasn't very different from them, I rejected something without actually testing it, just like many people do with my ideas. I got together with the inventor, he gave me a couple of chess sets and I started to test it. Although I didn't really think it was anything remarkable, I wanted to be fair. The result was amazing. In a week or so I not only forgot all my prejudices but only trained with this chess and played with it when I could.

Andras Adorjan with his rainbow chess set and the
copy of *CHESS* I gave him, at his flat in Budapest.

"The point is that by having pieces of different colours, the colour will help you to perceive and store the position." Adorjan held up a pocket rainbow set so that I could see what he meant. "People really go by colours – movement and colours. This sticks. Most blunders happen because you think a piece is there but it's not, or vice versa. You imagine it in the position incorrectly. Most of these blunders can be avoided with the help of these pieces. I use this set for training. It's not as tiring as black and white." For Leko the rainbow set doesn't make much difference, though. "It could be without the pieces and I would remember the position anyway," he said.

The inventor of rainbow chess, Pal Suvada, died in 1995, but Adorjan is continuing his crusade by organising rainbow chess tournaments. Colour-blind people aren't excluded – you just have to put black and white strips on the pieces. There is another advantage, Adorjan pointed out. "It's very good for TV, very good for demonstration. If you are a long way away, you can see the position. With black and white you see a grey mass." This sounded convincing. If one-day cricketers can do it, chess players should be able to adapt, too.

Like another resident of Budapest, Bobby Fischer, who advocates random chess, Adorjan is turning his back on conventional chess tournaments. "I never really played too many tournaments apart from three or four years. I miss chess and will play now and again. Tournament chess for a long time has been going in a direction that I always hated. You either make it to the top 20 and play in civilised tournaments or you belong to the crowd and take the shit. Conditions in tournaments are much below any expectations. If you were offered a job in an office in such conditions you would go on strike with all your colleagues. An open tournament should be in a big room. Usually there should be an oxygen can for those people who would like to breathe. There's no space for the elbows. It's not a chess tournament, it's making money by playing chess. It has nothing to do with art, it's disgusting."

Fortunately for Adorjan, he has another way of expressing himself – through music. He translated the musical *Godspell* into Hungarian and it was performed. "I've also translated songs I like, for instance songs by Bonnie Tyler and "It Must Have Been Love" by Roxette. I'm not so good at selling things and I could never really find the person inside me who could do these things." In the magazine *Black is OK!* there is a review of *Chess* the musical and a copy of the score for Adorjan's song, which he composed for his ill-fated charity Moving Aid.

In the mid-1980s Adorjan wanted to raise money for people suffering from famine in Africa, by holding charitable simuls and donating one percent of the prize money from tournaments over a six-month period. He attempted to recruit Garry Kasparov, but the world champion was unresponsive. Adorjan blames Kasparov's friends and advisers for talking him out of it. In vitriolic tone, he writes in *Black is OK!*, "Moving Aid could have been a good chance for both Africans and chess players with very little energy on Kasparov's side, but the petty-minded, cynical and greedy people around him couldn't see the possibilities of it."

Another factor caused relations between Adorjan and Kasparov to sour. "I had been a good friend of Kasparov's for a long time and then we parted," Adorjan said. "I wrote a book he didn't like, *Quo Vadis, Garry?*, and we didn't speak for a long time, just a couple of words recently breaking the ice. He is doing a lot for chess but he doesn't forget his own interests." As for Fischer, Adorjan is sympathetic towards him. "I've only talked to Fischer on the phone. I pity him, such a great man, homeless, lonely, sad, depressed. He makes it difficult for other people to help him."

Adorjan is not without problems, either. For all his talk of hating prejudice and helping Africans, he has been successfully sued by Laszlo Polgar on a charge of anti-Semitism. "The first time Laszlo Polgar sued he lost and the second time he won, in 1987," said Adorjan. "It was something I said about him and his morals which I still hold, and I think I'm in very, very big company, only other people don't take chances. Yes, some Jewish people suffered from communism, but not because they were Jewish, because they were members of society, and society suffered."

This was the last of my interviews with several people from the world of chess in Budapest, and one thing I can say is that they all enjoy some controversy. Fischer fell out with the Polgars, Adorjan fell out with the Polgars, Fischer offended the late Laszlo Szabo, Andor Lilienthal introduced Fischer to Kirsan Ilyumzhinov.

Therefore I would highly recommend Budapest as a venue for the next-but-one knockout World Championship. With randomly arranged rainbow pieces, of course.

This interview was published in the British satirical chess magazine Kingpin. *I had become friendly with its editor, Jon Manley, and happily supplied him with articles.*

At the time of writing, Peter Leko was No.12 on the FIDE list, rated 2713. In 2001 he beat England's Michael Adams in a Fischer-Random match.

I looked for references to Andras Adorjan on the Internet but all I found was a report in the newsletter of the National Empowerment Center, a U.S. organisation that helps people with mental illness, that said in 1999 Adorjan was leading a patients' group called Way Out based in the ward of a psychiatric hospital in Budapest. I contacted Adorjan by e-mail via Laszlo Nagy and asked him how he was doing. He sent me some articles and poems and a long message. This was part of it:

"Well, it is true, that I do not play tournament chess for two years. It doesn't mean I retired, but I hate the direction the World of chess goes, among many things the awful playing conditions, which are practically guaranteed in any Open tournaments. And since about 90 or maybe even 95 percent of the whole are this type of events, it is very hard to find a round-robin grandmaster tournament with modest finances, but human conditions. My rating is only 2505. So it seems, I can only play in some rapids, and something I organise myself. And it is going to happen sometime next January [2003], when the World's First Rainbow-Chess GM Tournament will take place...

"Funny, I do not read newspapers or waste my time for gossip magazines, but I still not find enough spare time. That's I write a lot myself. At the moment I'm in two books, one is about Queen Pawn Opening, the other is more personal and exciting: My Best Games. Considering that I have got no less than 8 brilliancy prizes, and had many pieces of beauty in tournaments, where there was no brilliancy prize, I was expected a number around 100 of the (more than) good enough kind. It is – to my pleasant surprise – much more!

"I recall the article in which you painted a realistic picture of me... There was however something you misunderstood. I DID say that all I have to do about my BLACK is OK thesis to be recognised [is] to die. You took it, and interpreted in a way as it sounded immodest to your ears. Just the opposite! I'm just one of the poor devils, who discover something, which somehow doesn't fit to the trends of that time... my idea, thesis and me will not be recognised till say 50 years from now. I'm 52. Do you think I can make it?

"And yes, let's talk about depression. This is an illness every 7th citizen of Hungary suffers. Me too, thanks. More accurately I have bipolar rapid cycled depression.

Peter Leko playing on Andras Adorjan's rainbow chess set in Budapest.

In the periods when you are down it is something like Hell could be. And with this burden on my shoulders (diagnosed by the age of 29, but recalling certain memories it goes back to my teenager time) I achieved what I achieved. I'm not proud, neither modest. I did try to give my best to the people in many ways not only in chess. And still do. Regrettably all psychological illnesses are still stigmatising those who suffer from them, as if it would be something like a punishment belonging only to the sinners, evil people. At the moment I am the only so-called famous person in Hungary, who doesn't hide, and is not ashamed about it. I'm a founding President of an organisation called 'Way Out'.

"Finally, what I am doing is writing and writing and writing. I write essays, short stories, fairy tales, poems (sometimes in English, although my English doesn't entitle me to do it...), songs and lyrics, funny but it was at my age of 50 when my first CD has been released! With two co-authors we write a rock-opera titled *1956*, and the second CD is still to come, while the 'libretto'... is ready for a year. Frankly speaking I have no idea when it goes to stage... since we do not have any sponsor, just a very fine guy whose business may provide the complete material. To make it to the stage would need a hell lot of money, and it's very clear we need a support of the Ministry of Culture. After all this is the first and so far the only rock-opera of our Revolution in 1956!"

After receiving that message, I asked Adorjan what he thought of FIDE. This was his reply:

"I don't like what I see in FIDE and in the chess world. I'm sure, soon or later there will be a global collapse. Now it's very much like 'bolshevism' in the late Soviet Union – 2-3 percent lives like a king, others try to earn their daily bread. I thank God I'm out of this filthy business. I love the wonders on the chessboard, but apart from that I don't try reasoning, fight, 30 years has been just enough."

4. Opening Files

A Shrimp Learnt to Whistle was published in spring 1997 and shortly afterwards I took out another bank loan to finance a move to London. I'd applied for a number of full-time media jobs, but no offers, or even interviews, had been forthcoming. Instead of remaining with my parents in Goring-on-Thames, I decided to attempt survival as a freelance journalist.

Each weekend I searched the classifieds for affordable accommodation in London and several times I took the train and tube to some remote, litter-strewn suburb to view a shabby room, smiling at sceptical strangers in the hope that they'd condescend to live with me. One bunch of girls were fellow history graduates from the University of Birmingham, so I was confident I'd be chosen to share their smelly old house. No such luck. When I got home there was a message on the answering machine saying that having met me, actually, they'd prefer a guy.

One visit to London was marginally more successful, in the long term, at least. I called the magazine *Literary Review* and asked to speak with the editor, Auberon Waugh. He immediately came on the line and I offered to review a book for him. "Have you appeared?" he demanded. I told him my articles had been published all over the place and he invited me to come to the office, where I could find something to cut my teeth on.

Ascending the creaky wooden staircase a few days later, I felt like I'd been transported into a scene from a Dickens novel. Evelyn Waugh's most notorious son, known for his flamingly right-wing satirical columns in the *Telegraph*, was leaning back in his chair in the musty Soho office, surrounded by bookcases. He indicated that I should pick out a novel and when he saw what I'd taken, said, "Don't piss on it too much!" because it was by someone who had written reviews for the magazine.

The fee for a review was £25, very little when you consider how long it takes to read a book and condense your opinions of it into 600 words, but the prestige of seeing my byline alongside famous British writers like Martin Amis appealed to me. I took great care over my first review and the proofs were sent back to me to check, indicating that the article was scheduled for publication. But the next issue of the magazine did not contain my review. I called, spoke to someone in the office, and found out that at the last minute there had been no room for it. I asked for a "kill fee", to compensate for my effort and the cost of the trip to London, but was told the magazine didn't pay kill fees.

I wrote a letter to Auberon Waugh complaining about this, describing how expensive it was getting to London and adding that I was so poor, I had to borrow money on my credit card to make the minimum payment on my loans. Bron, as he was known to friends – not to me, obviously – replied with a typewritten letter saying the magazine never paid kill fees, but he was so touched by the account of my poverty that he was enclosing a £10 note from his own funds.

Months later *Literary Review* published a kind review of *Shrimp*. I'd sent out about 50 review copies and, as far as I know, this was the only review that resulted, apart from a nasty one in the *St. Petersburg Times*, which called it "mountains of banal ramblings". Again I offered to write for *Literary Review* and this time saw the deputy editor, Nancy Sladek, who noted the book I'd taken and my name in an enormous leather-bound ledger. That second review was published, as were a few more, and eventually my fee was increased to £35. Nancy also commissioned and published my "Letter from Kalmykia", which talked about chess and literature in the Russian republic. I never saw Auberon Waugh again. I was very sad when he died in 2001, as his £10 gesture and the review of *Shrimp* had meant a lot to me.

A bizarre coincidence brought me my first room in London. In response to an ad I went to a house in the pleasant suburb of Muswell Hill. It was only one bus ride and one tube journey from the city. The landlord, an ageing opera buff, showed me one of the upstairs rooms, which was furnished with a bed, a desk, a chair, a fridge and a rusty cooker; the tenants shared a semi-cold shower and provided their own toilet roll upon each use of the facility (if you left your toilet roll there it would be used by someone else, which was presumably deemed too socialist).

As I was leaving, the landlord introduced me to a Russian woman who was renting the basement room. It turned out we had met before. She was the mother of one of my friends from university, and we'd been out to dinner with my other friend Amy Spurling. Once we'd recognised each other, the room was mine. I think the rent was £200 per month, about the cheapest you could get in London. The other tenant was an elderly man who spent his days combing the banks of the Thames for Roman artefacts. Later a young Kosovo Albanian woman moved in too, but all she got was a mattress on the floor, with nowhere to cook or store food.

Fortunately, I quickly found some decently paid freelance work for a market research consultant named Vincent Nekhaev who became a good friend. I called Russian companies and interviewed them about their soft drinks or packaged cakes manufacturing processes, and helped Vince compile weighty reports full of boring statistics that would be purchased by Western corporations such as Coca-Cola Co.

Meanwhile, I continued writing chess articles and played for Edmonton Chess Club. As well as competing in club matches in the evenings, I often entered one-day rapidplays or weekend congresses around London, and these were excellent opportunities to sell copies of *Shrimp* to my hapless opponents. Faced with the author sitting across the board from them, it was difficult to say no. There was a constant supply of new victims. Sometimes I travelled to tournaments as far away as the British Rapidplay in Leeds.

The 25th anniversary of the Fischer-Spassky match was approaching. Bobby Fischer was *CHESS* editor Jimmy Adams' hero. We wanted to do something big. Jimmy supplied me with some books and articles to read, as I had been born four months after the match took place, and he told me his own memories of it. He accompanied me to interviews with other people who had met Fischer, like *Guardian* chess columnist Leonard Barden. Jimmy also contributed the rhyming couplets, which were extracted from his epic poem about Fischer.

That Little Thing between Fischer and Spassky
(*CHESS*, November 1997)

Americans had little to cheer about in summer 1972. Demoralised by the Vietnam War and on the brink of the biggest political scandal in their history, Watergate, they badly needed a boost to national morale. And on the first of September, 25 years ago, they got it. FIDE arbiter Lothar Schmid walked onto the front of a stage in Reykjavik to make an announcement. "Ladies and gentlemen, Mr. Spassky has resigned by telephone at 12:50. This is a traditional and legal way of resignation. Mr. Fischer has won this game number 21, and he is the winner of the match."

Bobby Fischer had become world chess champion. His victory shook the Soviet system to its foundations, inspired millions of people across the world to take up the game, and turned Fischer into a living legend. Then the new American hero disappeared from the scene, finding his own act a hard one to follow. He left the crowd screaming for more, but instead of Fischer chess, they had to satisfy themselves with Fischer myth and Fischer rumour.

Fischer's image may have been tarnished by his bizarre statements and behaviour in recent years – but that is another story, with an ending that has not yet been written. Whatever Fischer's reputation today, nothing will detract from the brilliance of his performances all those years ago, and nothing will dim the memories of those who knew him or faced him across the board when he was at his peak. And there was also a significant English connection to Fischer's remarkable chess career...

Fischer was never plagued by time trouble in his serious games and loved blitz chess, although in his younger years he wasn't unbeatable. Leonard Barden, British co-champion of 1954, first met him at the Leipzig Olympiad in 1960. "During the Olympiad the top grandmasters played five-minute games for several hours every night in the foyer of the Hotel Astoria, watched by an awed crowd of ordinary masters," Barden recalled. "Bobby was better than Byrne, Najdorf or Lombardy, but found it hard to cope with Korchnoi's in-depth defence or Petrosian's ability to sneak pieces round the board in complex manoeuvres.

"Bobby was a quirky but likeable young man. I got on well with him. He was 17 years old, rather gawky and simplistic, but if you were a knowledgeable chess player he was relaxed, open and frank." Barden was at the Olympiad as a member of the England team and wanted to interview some of the players for the weekly BBC Network Three radio chess programme. This was no time for Barden's tape recorder to break down – even with a brand new set of East German batteries it wouldn't work – but a local radio station in Leipzig fixed it for him, thereby enabling the BBC to offer its listeners their first opportunity to hear Tal, Fischer and other grandmasters on the air.

"I gave people memory tests," Barden said. "I knew Tal had a fantastic memory, so I asked him about an obscure game from his first Latvian Championship, and he not only knew the opening, the strategy and the number of moves, but he also remembered what he and his opponent said to each other afterwards. Bobby was poor on other people's games, but he had good recall of his own games from early U.S. Junior Championships."

Fischer was into collecting suits, and he heard that Savile Row made the best. After the Olympiad he decided to stop on his way home in London, where the U.S. champion accepted an invitation to play a radio consultation game, with Barden as his partner, against British champion Jonathan Penrose and Peter Clarke.

The two teams were in separate rooms and the game was stopped after six or seven hours, when studio time ran out. Edited highlights were broadcast over a period of several weeks in 1961. "Unless you were very experienced on radio, which we weren't, you couldn't make yourself interesting," said Clarke. "You tried to be just as natural as you could and hoped for the best."

Barden adds that Fischer did most of the talking on their side. "I would prompt him with questions like how you should play with the bishop pair against bishop and knight, and he would explain. Once he agreed with a move I suggested. Bobby was articulate, opinionated, and spoke in this loud, nasal voice. He was constantly expecting a win, but Jonathan and Peter were resourceful in defence. The BBC paid Bobby £50 for the broadcast, and he was very pleased as this was more than the cost of his new suit. The producer had many complimentary letters from listeners."

Max Euwe later adjudicated the radio game as a draw. After the recording session, Fischer visited the house in south London where Barden lived with his parents. "We had six blitz games – he gave me odds of three minutes to five minutes – he won all six and then, apparently bored with beating me with Bc4 against the Sicilian, he allowed my favourite Boleslavsky Variation and I won one," said Barden.

"We played another five games, I got a draw, and he didn't want to play any more. I recall his long arms and fingers and how he could pluck a piece off the board without moving his body forward. He had a colossal appetite. My mother always had a well-stocked fridge and he virtually ate the entire contents of it."

Barden has a gift for identifying young players with a potential to make it to the top. He predicted in the *Guardian* that 12-year-old Harry Weinstein would be world champion in 1990; in fact he won the title in 1985, under the more familiar name of Garry Kasparov. But Fischer's talent was obvious. "Everybody realised Bobby could be a world champion," Barden told me. "In 1956 an American friend sent me cuttings of [13-year-old] Bobby in the U.S. Open and then of his match the following year against the Filipino Rodolfo Cardoso. Fischer was very easy to spot. I'm more proud of discovering someone like Nigel Short or Michael Adams."

An English chess player witnessed Fischer's blitz abilities in America. Stewart Reuben, now chairman of the British Chess Federation and a professional poker player, worked in New York as an industrial chemist from 1963 to 1965. Sitting in the bar of a plush London casino, with the clatter of the roulette wheel in the background, Reuben recalled how he met Fischer in the Manhattan Chess Club and played chess with him for money.

"The first time I met Fischer I felt I was meeting a great person. He was obviously a world-class player. He had been a major personality since the 'game of the century' with Donald Byrne." That win by Fischer at 13 had even drawn comparisons with Capablanca's quality of play at a similar age.

"The only grandmasters I'd ever known had been O'Kelly and Donner, meeting them at B.H. Wood's *CHESS* festivals," Reuben continued. "One day, rather falsely, I interpolated into a conversation Fischer was having and he showed me a game where he'd beaten 'this English fellow Bob Wade'. He was very much into dressing well in those days, having got over an adolescent jeans and sweater stage when he was sneered at by the Manhattan Chess Club. He particularly liked the suit I wore that I had made in England. He seemed to need something to look up to in people – either their talent, or the way they dressed, or something else."

Fischer was on good terms with most of the chess players in New York, including Reuben, who was five years older than him. "In my presence Fischer always behaved normally – and impeccably at the board. Fischer wasn't snobbish; he'd talk freely to people. He'd get a 19th-century book down from the shelves of the club library and ask me what I thought of a position. It would not be a modern game, there were pieces en prise all over the place – positionally grotesque from our point of view. He was a bit paranoid about giving his secrets away, he would seldom express his own opinion, but he suffered fools quite gladly. Possibly he might find a kernel of truth in what they had to say."

When Fischer played blitz with Reuben Fine, Stewart Reuben and a friend would write down the games together, taking a colour each. The two American grandmasters sometimes deliberately slowed down so that the games could be preserved. Stewart Reuben also played two sessions of blitz with Fischer for a dollar a game, at 10-1 odds. "There was no point my playing with the black pieces," he said. "Playing White I was at least equalising from the opening. I drew with Fischer in one game, I had a winning king and pawn endgame, I should have won it. In the second session there was no point in me playing with White either. He had learnt more from the games than I had. I believe we played nine games altogether – I lost eight."

A hundred miles an hour was Bobby's creed,
Fastest clock alive – a king of speed.

Later in his career Fischer was virtually invincible at blitz, as he demonstrated at the unofficial "World Lightning Chess Championship" held in Belgrade in 1970. He scored an amazing 19 points out of 22, far ahead of Tal, Korchnoi, Petrosian, Bronstein, Hort, Matulovic, Smyslov, Reshevsky and Uhlmann. Tal's praise for this victory is quoted in the new book *Russians versus Fischer*: "Throughout the tournament I think he did not leave a single pawn en prise, whereas all the others managed to lose a whole set of pieces in this way. Fischer's result is very, very impressive."

Playboy journalist Brad Darrach was in Reykjavik to cover the Fischer-Spassky match and subsequently wrote a book on it, *Bobby Fischer versus the Rest of the World*. This book, which Fischer wanted banned, provides an extraordinarily vivid description of Fischer's appearance. "Bobby is tall and broad-shouldered; his face is clean-cut, masculine, attractive... Yet there is a sense of danger about Bobby. When he is angry or confident his face is alert but unthinking, the face of a big wild animal that hunts for a living... I have rarely seen him register sympathy, invitation, acknowledgment, humour, tenderness, playfulness. And never love.

"Bobby wears a business suit about as naturally as a python wears a necktie... Bobby functions like Frankenstein's creature, a man made of fragments connected by wires and animated by a monstrous will. When the will collapses or the wires cross, Bobby cannot execute the simplest acts... Once, when I asked him a question while he was eating, his circuits got so befuddled that he jabbed his fork into his cheek.

"Energy again and again escapes in a binge of anger. Every night, all night, it escapes into chess. When he sits at the board, a big dangerous cat slips into his skin. His chest swells, his green eyes glow. All the life in his body flows and he looks wild and beautiful. Sprawled with lazy power, eyes half closed, he listens to the imaginary rustle of moving pieces as a tiger lies and listens to the murmur of moving reeds."

Fischer's presence and status could attract women, but his attitude towards them has always been ambivalent. His friends and colleagues closely guard details of his personal life. Stewart Reuben used to go out to dinner with Fischer and other New York chess players at a Jewish delicatessen: Fischer talked more about baseball than girls. Fischer was at school with Barbra Streisand (he was famous; she wasn't), and they share the same biographer, Frank Brady, but there is no suggestion that they knew each other well.

Chess fans loved him, the girls did too,
Proposals of marriage from chicks he never knew.

Brad Darrach claims that Fischer suffered from fear of maraschino cherries, fear of homosexuals – and fear of women. The latter phobia was something he was keen to overcome, a desire which Larry Evans exploited at Buenos Aires in 1960. Evans, twice U.S. champion, was friendly with Fischer but wanted to finish ahead of him, and took the initiative by introducing his rival to an attractive prostitute.

The affair had a disastrous effect on Fischer's play at Buenos Aires, where he finished 13th in a field of 20. Evans shared 4th-7th place. Fischer had found it hard to concentrate on his games, making the only finger slip of his career. In a game against Wolfgang Unzicker of West Germany he absent-mindedly touched the h7 pawn in front of his castled king and had to move it, wrecking his defensive position.

"That settled it," said a grandmaster who knew him well. "If it was sex or chess, sex had to go." Fischer's exploits were the talk of the tournament, but the gossip never reached the Russians, and *Russians versus Fischer* gives some ponderous chessboard explanations for the American's poor form in Argentina.

Mikhail Tal broached the delicate subject of women when he attempted to interview Fischer for his Latvian chess magazine, *Sahs*. "I asked, 'You'll soon turn 20 – are you thinking of marrying?' He glanced at me innocently and said that this was the very problem occupying him at the moment. In fact, he didn't know quite what to do: buy a second-hand car or marry... He repeated that he was planning to marry, but not an American girl (they, according to him, spend all their time in beauty parlours). He felt attracted to girls from Taiwan or Hong Kong, something exotic... A second-hand car in those days cost about $700. The same sum would cover the travel fare of a bride, who could – if things didn't work out – be sent back."

Such frivolity would never have made it to the pages of a Moscow chess magazine, but fortunately for us the scandalous revelations have now been published in *Russians versus Fischer*. The conversation says more about Fischer's friendly attitude towards Tal than about the young American's love life. A few months previously, at the Candidates tournament in Curaçao in 1962, Tal had been greatly offended when none of the Soviet grandmasters came to see him in hospital. Fischer was his only visitor.

One wrong move and the win was no more,
With Geller's analysis Botvinnik got the draw.

At the same tournament, Fischer had a heated argument with Pal Benko over their shared American second, Arthur Bisguier, who was spending most of his time with Fischer. They even squared up to each other, and the quarrel had an unfortunate sequel for Fischer. When he adjourned his first and only game against then-world champion Mikhail Botvinnik at the 1962 Varna Olympiad, Fischer had a favourable rook ending. The Russians analysed all night and the English team, seated between the Americans and the Russians in the hotel restaurant, saw Efim Geller showing variations to Botvinnik at breakfast.

"Both looked subdued and hollow-eyed," according to Leonard Barden, "but in fact Geller had discovered a wicked trap a few moves into the play. Benko, a renowned endgame specialist, had also speedily found this trap, but Bobby was still bearing his Curaçao grudge and refused to look at Benko's analysis. At the board, Fischer fell into the trap and, with tears in his eyes, had to agree to a draw."

"Fischer has only spoken three words to me in his life," Botvinnik told Barden. "When we were introduced at Leipzig, he pointed to himself in the continental style and said 'Fischer.' When we sat down to play today, we accidentally bumped heads and he said 'Sorry.' At the end of the game, he said 'Draw.'"

Chess players who admired Fischer for his talent and for his conduct at the board were often frustrated by the contradictions in his character. Boris Spassky summed this up in 1970: "I hold him in high esteem... Fischer is rather modest, very serious, and very hard-working... Fischer is also ingenuous and proud. He speaks his mind. Such people are not easy mixers, and it seems to me that Fischer is very lonely. That is one of his tragedies."

Benko and Fischer resolved their differences and a lasting friendship developed between them. Benko was also the man responsible for putting Fischer on the path to the world title. Fischer had refused to play in the qualifying Zonal tournament, the 1969 U.S. Championship, because he thought the number of rounds should be increased. Benko knew he didn't have a realistic chance of becoming the challenger to Spassky, so for a payment of $2,000 from the U.S. Chess Federation he allowed Fischer to replace him in the Palma de Mallorca Interzonal of 1970. When Fischer won this, 3½ points ahead of the field, the Soviet chess organisation moved into top gear.

A propaganda campaign against Fischer in the Soviet press was sparked off by an otherwise unknown party hack, Anatoly Golubev, in the chess magazine *64*. "Unintellectual, lopsidedly developed, and uncommunicative, Fischer wittingly or unwittingly stimulates that 'intellectual hippiness' that is, like a malignant growth, spreading in the chess world," he wrote, looking forward confidently to Fischer's bout with Mark Taimanov. The result, as we know, was devastating – Fischer won 6-0. He crushed his next opponent, Bent Larsen, in exactly the same manner.

Anatoly Karpov claims in *Russians versus Fischer* that the Candidates match between Tigran Petrosian and Viktor Korchnoi was rigged. Sports Committee officials asked Petrosian and Korchnoi which of them had better chances against Fischer. Petrosian was more optimistic, so Korchnoi was told to lose. "Such is the story of what happened," writes Karpov. "Needless to say, there are no documents confirming this deal. But the quality of Korchnoi's playing – and, most important of all, the fact that, having lost to Petrosian, he continued to maintain good relations with him... confirms that there was no struggle: Korchnoi simply stepped aside."

There are plenty of documents that show how desperate the Soviet chess establishment had become by this time. While Taimanov was publicly disgraced, grandmasters were privately very sympathetic towards him, well aware that the same fate would probably have befallen any one of them. In a meeting to discuss the Taimanov débâcle they grasped at every possible excuse, but eventually had to conclude that Fischer's win was due not only to the presence of too many Russian trainers, Taimanov's over-optimism, and a poor choice of variations – but also to the genius of Bobby Fischer.

Alexander Kotov opened the discussion by admitting that they had suffered "the biggest setback in the history of Soviet chess". Taimanov responded, "I was aware that the match with Fischer was the chief contest of my life. I had prepared myself thoroughly, and I enlisted the services of the best specialists (Botvinnik and others). I normally play in a relaxed manner, but here I was aware of a sense of mission. This was probably the main mistake." Spassky asked with typical honesty, "When we have all lost to Fischer will all of us be dragged on the carpet?" and Petrosian replied, "Yes, but not here."

It emerged that Taimanov had been deliberately encouraged to underestimate Fischer because the coaches believed he would be deterred if he knew Fischer's true strength. They acknowledged afterwards that this strategy had failed. "Fischer is not only a powerful chess player, he can be very challenging as a personality – because he fights to the last and never gives up," said Paul Keres. "We didn't pay enough attention to this trait of his character... I could name no more than two other chess players who are as tough as he is."

A detailed file on Fischer's repertoire was drawn up by the Soviet team in preparation for Petrosian's match with him. Petrosian held his own for the first half of the match, but then collapsed and lost the last four games, so Fischer won by 6½ points to 2½. Now all energies were devoted to Spassky, who, however, was a reluctant saviour of his nation's chess honour. Provided with a dacha outside Moscow, funding, meals, medical supervision, and the support of every leading Soviet player, the world champion was lulled into a stupor.

Karpov, who visited the training camp, was shocked by Spassky's laziness. "Usually the morning would begin with him enthusiastically recounting, over breakfast, another episode from the Greek myths, which he dearly loved and read before going to bed. Then there would be tennis. Then something else. Anything except chess. At the time he was expounding the 'theory' of a clear head. With a clear head and refreshed, he would, with his talent, outplay anyone."

He was given a raw deal by the world chess press,
The truth from the false was anybody's guess.

As the scheduled date of the first game drew closer, Fischer agreed to a rare interview, with questions posed by well-known BBC presenter James Burke. It was remarkable that the interview took place at all, since Fischer had an intense dislike of journalists, many of whom had in the past misrepresented and misquoted him. Burke was the man who had done the TV commentary for the Apollo moon landing, although his status probably held little sway with Fischer, who kept him waiting for hours.

When Fischer finally sat down in front of the cameras, though, he made a big impression, showing the public his best human qualities and setting the scene for a dramatic East-West confrontation. Jimmy Adams recalled: "Some of my friends didn't have a television, so I invited them round to my place to watch the programme and we made an occasion out of it. One of our enthusiastic group of viewers was sufficiently impressed to write to the producer afterwards to praise him for presenting Fischer in a fair light.

"The James Burke interview was a worthy prelude to the big match. 'This little thing between me and Spassky is like a microcosm of the whole world political situation,' said Fischer, and it was in fact this Cold War angle that captured the imagination of the whole country. After all the bad press Bobby's eccentric behaviour had attracted over the years, many people were surprised how well he came across on screen. He answered all the questions in an easy, sincere and confident way and displayed a great sense of humour.

"For example, in reply to James Burke's enquiry as to why he was so particular about playing conditions, Fischer recounted an incident in Germany where a spectator had put his head right over the board to get a closer look at the position. Bobby was chuckling to himself as he mimicked this fellow, who was pushing him further and further away from his own game. Then he told of the time when an onlooker whispered a move in his ear during an American tournament. Bobby's conclusion: 'These things are not really conducive to high-class play!'

"But the interview also showed that there was an underlying element of isolation and seriousness in Bobby. He acknowledged that he had few friends outside chess and led a disciplined lifestyle, since 'if you start partying around, it just doesn't go'. He talked at length about his Soviet rivals. 'I'd like to show the Russians... That's what I'd enjoy most about winning the title – reading the Russian magazines, what they'd say about it. Either they're going to say nothing or they're going to have some involved nonsensical explanation.'

"Fischer's feelings about the Russians were mixed. On the one hand he admitted, 'When I first started playing chess, to me the Russians were heroes, and they still are as chess players. I used to study all their literature; most of the first books I read were Russian chess books.' On the other hand: '...they started attacking my character. They'd never even met me, or knew anything about me. So this kind of attitude really turned me off – they have the title, and the title belongs to them in perpetuity because it's theirs – that's their attitude. They don't have a sporting attitude about it. Their attitude should be: he's the best, he should have the title. They don't believe in giving foreigners a chance to play for the title.'

"Burke had begun the interview asking Fischer whether he thought calling himself the best chess player in the world was arrogant. Fischer didn't seem at all offended by the question, which he parried with the same simple logic that he applied to his chess games: 'If it's true, then it isn't arrogant.' Then he quickly followed this up with a realistic assessment of the likely outcome of his match with Spassky. 'It's not 100 percent, but it wasn't 100 percent that I was going to beat Taimanov or Larsen or Petrosian. I think I am definitely the heavy favourite according to all the past results.'"

> *The world title fight was scheduled for Belgrade*
> *But Bobby wasn't satisfied with the wages they paid.*
> *Iceland took over but still that financial account*
> *Kept Fischer in New York just hanging about.*

Fischer, now 29, was notorious for arriving late for his games, and even missing the first rounds of a tournament on occasion, but would he really miss the opening ceremony of the World Championship, the moment he had been striving for all his life? The answer was yes. He wasn't satisfied with the prize fund ($78,125 for the winner, $46,875 for the loser), and cancelled his June 25 flight to Iceland at the last minute. He booked another flight, cancelled, booked another flight, drove to the airport – and changed his mind.

Possibly the match would not have generated so much excitement had it not been for Fischer's antics. "The shenanigans added fuel to the press fire, helped to intensify it, like pre-fight talk," said Jimmy Adams. "The hype was feverish. No one knew if Fischer was going to play or not."

Over in Reykjavik, Fred Cramer, former president of the U.S. Chess Federation, took on the unenviable task of facing the media. Brad Darrach describes his attempt to lighten the atmosphere: "'I have been authorised to inform you,' he announced to a circle of newsmen, 'that Mr. Fischer is on his way to Iceland. He is being brought by submarine from Greenland and will come ashore in a kayak after a rendezvous at sea with the Icelandic Navy. Har! Har!'" The joke was not appreciated.

Lothar Schmid, the German arbiter, made meticulous preparations for the match. He was determined that the players would have no complaints, according to Darrach. "When Schmid had inspected the playing hall, for instance, he'd sat on six or seven hundred chairs and wiggled back and forth in each to see if it made any noise. After more than an hour he had hauled his aching pelvis to Thorarinsson [head of the Icelandic Chess Federation] and announced with grave concern, 'Chair number 222 squeaks.'"

The opening ceremony took place in Reykjavik on July 1, as scheduled, but colours could not be drawn because Fischer was still in the United States. Determined to save the match, FIDE President Max Euwe breached the rules and allowed Fischer a two-day postponement. By this time few people believed that the 1972 World Championship would take place at all. They hadn't counted on a startling announcement by the British investment banker Jim Slater, who offered to double the prize fund.

Jim Slater's generosity knew no bounds,
He stepped up the kitty by fifty thousand pounds.

Slater asked Leonard Barden, as *Evening Standard* chess correspondent, to contact Euwe with the news. Slater had played chess as a boy, and was a friend of John Fuller, who tied with Leonard Barden for the London Under-18 Championship. "Slater had backed Fischer against Spassky with Ladbrokes at odds of 5-4 on," said Barden. "When he told me about the $125,000 I said, 'Jim, that's a rather expensive way of winning your bet!' The telephone facilities were antiquated in those days and I had to phone Reykjavik through a British Telecom operator. Assuming the call was going through, I rang the *Evening Standard* and told them.

"To my astonishment they made the story the lunchtime edition front page lead. That afternoon, both television stations, many radio programmes and every Fleet Street paper rang me. Then I remembered about this call to Reykjavik and it turned out that BT had lost the original phone call. The offer reached Iceland via news agencies. Eventually I got through to Dr. Euwe. At first he was very suspicious, he wanted the money in an Icelandic bank account as soon as possible, but when I told him how Slater had already helped Hastings and British juniors, he was persuaded it was genuine."

Robert Toner, Barden's BBC producer, was the person who rang Fischer's lawyer and passed the offer on to the nervous challenger. "Bobby's afraid, basically, he has this fear of action," Barden said. "This was clear throughout his career. He froze before the match, but he was galvanised by the money."

"The money is mine," Slater told the press. "I like chess and have played it for years. Many want to see this match and everything was arranged. If Fischer does not go to Iceland, many will be disappointed. I want to remove the problem of money from Fischer and see if he has any other problems." Fischer replied, "It's stupendous. I have to accept it."

Hours later Fischer flew to Iceland with his newly appointed second, GM William Lombardy. *Sovietsky Sport* didn't identify Lombardy as the 1957 junior world champion, only calling him "a Catholic priest". While Fischer slept in his villa, Lombardy attended the drawing of lots. This was the final straw for Spassky, who refused to draw.

Come weigh-in time Fischer didn't materialise,
Spassky got mad and made him apologise.

Spassky issued a statement calling for Fischer to be penalised. "Fischer... has insulted myself personally and the country I'm representing," he wrote. "Soviet public opinion and I, personally, are full with indignation at Fischer's behaviour... he has, in my opinion, called in doubt his moral rights to play the match."

Lombardy apologised on Fischer's behalf, but Spassky was unimpressed. Fischer then composed a contrite letter that was pushed under Spassky's door in the middle of the night by his lawyer, Paul Marshall. "Please accept my sincerest apology for my disrespectful behaviour in not attending the opening ceremony. I simply became carried away by my petty dispute over money with the Icelandic chess organisers," the challenger told the world champion. He appealed to Spassky's sense of sportsmanship, requesting that no forfeit be imposed on him.

In the original draft, Fischer even proposed "that we both will give up all prize money and play the match for the sake of chess alone!" Brad Darrach was called in to advise on the wording, and Fischer read out the draft to him. "When he came to the part about giving up the prize money and playing for the love of chess, his voice skidded up the scale and hit a note of earnest lunacy."

Lothar Schmid had agonised over his extreme decision to start Fischer's clock for Game Two. While Fischer was composing his letter, Schmid was tossing and turning in his bed, racked with guilt, according to Darrach. "At 4:30 a.m. he awoke, sobbing, from a nightmare in which he 'destroyed' a great genius."

To Schmid's enormous relief, he was let off the hook. A compromise was reached. Marshall eventually persuaded Fischer that giving up the prize money would destroy everything he had worked for throughout his chess career. Fischer was unconvinced until Marshall added that all the money would go to the organisers. Then Fischer backed down and removed the explosive line. The toned-down letter achieved the desired result. Spassky and Fischer shook hands and drew colours that evening, with the black pieces going to Fischer. Spassky dropped his forfeit demand in return for Fischer's consent to postpone the first game until July 11.

Stewart Reuben was working as a teacher at this time and couldn't get to Iceland until term finished. "I came into the staff room one day and someone asked me if I had ever beaten Fischer. I said no, I've only drawn, and the whole room went quiet. In a way it was even better than saying I'd won." The whole world was gripped by chess fever, and Britain was no exception.

"You can't get a realisation of what a big event it was in Western society without looking at the press cuttings," said Reuben. "You could compare it to a small war – everybody knew about it. While my younger nephew was waiting in a car he was throwing a dice and saying 'Fischer, Spassky, Fischer, Spassky.'"

Meanwhile, Leonard Barden invited Jimmy Adams to work on the move-by-move, game-by-game teleprinter service from Reykjavik to London. This was a new idea at the time, organised by a sports agency, Ray Davis Promotions, which operated from a luxury flat in Mayfair, and had the BBC as one of its principal customers.

Fischer had been Adams' hero ever since the American qualified for the Candidates at the age of 15. His admiration for Fischer had increased still further after seeing him play in a tournament in Monte Carlo in the 1960s and he had set himself the task of writing *The Bobby Fischer Story*, a 200-line biographical poem first published in the club magazine *Bayswater Chess* in 1971.

"One early appreciative reader was the Reverend Peter Kings from Norfolk, who came up to me at a weekend tournament with the endorsement: 'Adams, I do believe you have a talent for rhyming slang.' Nowadays, of course, I would prefer to call it rap, but this was nevertheless sufficient encouragement for me to offer it for publication in *CHESS*.

"The editor, B.H. Wood, told me 'some of the lines don't scan properly' and he would fix that. But what he actually did was a complete rewrite in very old-fashioned style. Terrible. He totally ruined it. However, later on the poem was to have some significance, since, after reading it, Leonard Barden got me involved with the media coverage of the Fischer-Spassky match. And a little later still I got a chance to put the poem right when Stewart Reuben and David Levy included an authentic, expanded version in their book *The Chess Scene*.

"I worked at Ray Davis Promotions with a smashing girl named Kathy Blaker. She worked all day in the sports agency and had to put in a lot of overtime in the evenings and weekends to cover the Fischer-Spassky match since the games were played Tuesday and Thursday from 5 to 10 p.m. and Sundays from 2 to 7 p.m. Not to mention the extra sessions for adjournments. Kathy wasn't a chess player so we stuck labels on a big chessboard to indicate the notation of each square so she could still play the moves on the board without having to ask anyone.

"Unlike today's ease of communications via the Internet, getting the moves by teleprinter was a very cumbersome process. There was a great deal of long-number dialing and the line would often be busy," said Adams. "Even so, seeing the match unfold before your eyes was fantastic. It was the next best thing to actually being in Reykjavik.

"Ray Davis Promotions was the only move-by-move service on the match in the world. As the moves came in, we relayed them not only to the BBC but also to newspapers, the American 'educational' television Channel 13 and even the pop music 'station of the stars', Radio Luxembourg, where, sponsored by the *Daily Mirror*, the latest moves with summaries were announced in between records. I remember that Birna, the Icelandic girl operating the teleprinter from Reykjavik, even had a request played on Luxembourg – it was Neil Young's 'Heart of Gold.'

"The BBC had started its first regular chess television programme, providing weekly commentary on the match. With his experience of radio broadcasting, Leonard Barden was a natural choice to provide expert commentaries – but also making his television debut was Bill Hartston, then a total novice but now established as the BBC's regular chess commentator. The programme went out on Sunday evenings and, in addition to coverage of the week's play, was timed to coincide with the end of the playing session of the weekend game.

"The sports agency provided the moves, Harry Golombek was called up via a telephone link to Reykjavik for his summary of the goings-on, and the games were discussed on manual demonstration boards. C.H.O'D. Alexander, then already a sick man, was also a guest on the show. He wrote a very attractive book on the match but died 18 months later."

The sports agency also supplied the moves, as they came in, to nearby Notre Dame Hall, off Leicester Square, where Michael MacDonald-Ross, a regular British Championship contender, was involved with a public analysis of the match. "I commented on one of the games, I think Andrew Whiteley did most of them. Somebody ran to and from the telex, so it was immediate. We had one board for the actual position and another for the analysis. There were about 30 to 40 people in the audience, chess fans rather than super strong players – people who played in the London League and county matches.

"There was no real question as to what the real psychological heart of the match was – it was when Fischer played 11...Nh5 in the Benoni in Game Three. It was a position where White could play Bxh5, shattering Black's pawn structure. That hadn't been seen in grandmaster play before. Later Petrosian worked out how to deal with it, but it was a tremendously difficult decision for Spassky over the board; he couldn't manage it. If you can destroy someone with the black pieces and you're very good with White, as Fischer was, then your opponent never feels secure in the match again."

The British tabloids, including *The Sun*, which had previously devoted little or no space to chess, became caught up in the wave of Fischer-Spassky mania. One or two even started to carry chess columns, explaining how the pieces moved and basic tactics. However, these columns were short-lived. It was the personalities and antics that attracted the newspapers. For the first time chess fans were treated to front-page headlines such as "Spassky Walks Out on Fischer!", "Spassky Smashky" and "Bobby Wins!"

The cartoonists also had plenty of material to work on both from the Russia vs. America angle and Fischer's never-ending demands for perfect conditions. "I remember a cartoon in one paper showing a man looking intently at a shop window overflowing with chess pieces which were labelled as 'Chess sets rejected by Bobby Fischer'," said Adams. "I don't think we'd had chess cartoons hitting the national press since the time the beautiful American player Lisa Lane withdrew from the Hastings Congress because she was love-sick."

Iceland, which hadn't been besieged by foreign visitors since the Vikings lost their way in a gale, was set alight by the match. Stewart Rcubcn still has some of the souvenirs he bought in Reykjavik: first-day covers, postcard-sized cartoons, and a heavy Icelandic sweater with chess pieces on it. "They also had chess sets and plastic tumblers with positions from the match on them," he told me. "The Game Two end position was quite popular because it was also the starting position!" The events surrounding Game Two are a saga by themselves.

> *Shapes and sizes, colours, heat and light,*
> *For Fischer every detail had to be right.*
> *Even the candy squad came to keep out the noise,*
> *No unwrapping of sweets by the girls and boys.*

Fischer had reached a drawn endgame in Game One, but then miscalculated a pawn capture and lost his bishop – the first of two celebrated "poisoned pawns" at Reykjavik. During the game he complained that his orange juice wasn't cold enough and that a television camera was disturbing him. At one point he left the stage, with his own clock running, until the camera was dismantled.

Fischer's struggle for perfect playing conditions had a long history. Sometimes he claimed he was fighting for the rights of all chess players; at other times he was obviously out for himself. "I like to do what I want to do and not what other people want or expect me to do," he once said. "This is what life is all about." He became a follower of the Worldwide Church of God in 1962, which forbade any form of activity between sundown on Friday and sundown on Saturday. Fischer would not play or travel during these hours, but tournament organisers invariably rescheduled games to meet his religious needs.

Other demands by Fischer were more difficult to deal with. Soviet GM Evgeny Vasyukov relates the controversies leading to Fischer's withdrawal from the 1967 Sousse Interzonal in *Russians versus Fischer*. "From the very start he had begun putting forward claims to some kind of exclusive treatment... There were rounds during which Fischer would move from table to table several times... either his seat was too close to the audience, or he was disturbed by the noise (in such cases he threateningly pointed a finger at the culprits), or he was displeased with the lighting... The American was particularly furious about people with cameras. One might have thought that Fischer was simply afraid of having his picture taken, like some major criminal sought by the police."

Vladimir Tukmakov witnessed similar behaviour at Buenos Aires in 1970, where Fischer was one of his opponents. "Our game was played during a day of adjourned games. It began half an hour late: the American grandmaster had demanded that the lighting be changed. His demand was satisfied. This atmosphere of a 'Fischer cult' (one had to get used to it) had an effect on me, and my playing was appalling. Of course, losing to Fischer is no disgrace. But it's a great pity we didn't have a normal game."

It would be possible to sympathise more with Fischer on the question of lighting if it were not for a game in the Candidates match with Petrosian, when a fuse blew and the playing hall was plunged into darkness. Petrosian left the board, but Fischer stayed in his seat and agreed to leave his clock running as he was still considering his move. Fischer could play in adverse conditions when he wanted to. He was determined to participate in the Capablanca Memorial Tournament of 1965, but the U.S. State Department would not allow him to visit Castro's Cuba. So Fischer played all his 21 games by long-distance telephone, finishing just half a point behind the winner, Vasily Smyslov.

Fischer wasn't the only grandmaster to insist on ideal playing conditions. Botvinnik demanded a special lamp for his board at the Munich Olympiad in 1958. FIDE and many leading players agreed with Fischer that cameras could be distracting, so a rule was introduced limiting photography to the first few minutes of a playing session.

Whenever Fischer did agree to play, his attitude towards his opponents was universally admired. "Fischer is a very correct and pleasant partner," Tukmakov added after his comments on the lighting incident. At the 1970 Olympiad, Spassky said, "Fischer himself may have unwittingly contributed to my high spirits. It has always been a pleasure to play against him. His conduct during games is usually irreproachable, and he shows respect for his opponents, especially if he considers them strong enough for him."

> *What Bobby wants, Bobby gets,*
> *Conditions take precedence over TV sets.*
> *Too bad about that lawsuit from Chester Fox,*
> *Bobby can't concentrate while they film for the box.*

The film and television rights for the match had been bought by Chester Fox, but after his defeat in Game One Fischer insisted that all cameras should be removed from the hall. This didn't happen, and Fischer's clock was started for Game Two with the challenger absent.

The mystery of what happened after Game Two of the Reykjavik match has remained unsolved to this day. After Fischer defaulted, making Spassky's lifetime score against him five wins, two draws and no defeats, there was widespread belief that he would quit the match. But while he remained incommunicado in his villa, there was frantic activity elsewhere. The U.S. Chess Federation urged fans to bombard Fischer with cables and telephone appeals to continue.

"Jim Slater was appalled at the thought that Bobby might receive his share of the doubled prize fund after playing just one game," said Leonard Barden. "Slater's money hadn't been sent to Reykjavik yet, so on his instructions I sent Euwe a revised sliding scale of payments: if either player pulled out before four games, 90 percent of Slater's prize would be forfeited. Between five and eight games – 75 percent – and so on. Euwe would surely have informed Paul Marshall of this news."

U.S. Secretary of State Henry Kissinger telephoned Fischer, probably at the request of President Nixon. But perhaps the decisive appeal was by the woman known as Fischer's Californian mother, Lina Grumette, at whose home he often stayed. The international moves did the trick. Fischer booked a flight out of Iceland, then cancelled it. At the eleventh hour Lothar Schmid granted a big concession – he arranged for the third game to be played in a backstage room, away from the cameras and the audience. Fischer turned up, won the game, and his mood suddenly became much more cheerful. The television cameras were removed from the main hall and Fischer agreed to play the remaining games there.

> *Bobby's opening repertoire had always been tight,*
> *A few lines as Black and P-K4 as White.*
> *But now he decided it was time for a change*
> *And knocked Spassky's preparation right out of range.*
> *Those queenside starts got Boris really confused*
> *So did those brand new defences he used.*

Psychologically, Spassky was already badly damaged. If this was the desired effect of Fischer's protests, then the American had achieved his aim. As Karpov put it, Fischer's Game Two forfeit was "a stroke of genius. A stroke tailor-made for Spassky. A stroke proving that Fischer knew Spassky inside out. Had it been Petrosian instead of Spassky, he would simply have licked his chops and swallowed the extra point. But the philosopher Spassky, the unruffled Spassky, the highly experienced Spassky was no longer able to maintain a stiff upper lip... It would now take at least 10 games, some agonising, some helpless, some tragic – for him to recover his poise and self-control, but the match could no longer be saved, the bus had left..."

After his bad start Fischer responded immediately by winning two crushing games with Black. But the game for anthologies was the sixth, where Bobby took the lead after playing a queen's pawn opening for the first time ever in a serious game. It wasn't long before Spassky went from being two up to three down, although it must be said that he never gave up and in fact played very strongly in the second half and thus made the match exciting to the very end.

When Stewart Reuben arrived in Reykjavik to watch the match he found that his services were in demand. "Nowadays staging these big events is commonplace, but at Reykjavik they hadn't arranged for anyone to do commentary in English. B.H. Wood suggested me, so I commentated on this dreadful English game. I explained what Spassky couldn't play, it was very obvious – but he did it. He'd blundered horribly, it was an awful game."

> *The twenty-first game was Spassky's darkest hour*
> *When the Russians saw a shift in world chess power.*
> *Bobby had proved that he was the best*
> *And had opened the door to chess in the West...*

Chess would never be the same again. World champion Bobby Fischer inspired nine-year-old Garry Kasparov in Baku, who recently acknowledged him as "the greatest chess genius of all time". The Soviet Championship of 1973 was reorganised on a stricter basis, and Spassky won it. He was a sympathetic character who had won over many chess fans when he applauded Fischer's win in Game Six. But a new Soviet hero was already being cultivated, Anatoly Karpov, a man who would willingly abide by party discipline.

Documents in *Russians versus Fischer* show that the Central Committee of the Communist Party and the USSR Sports Committee conspired to prevent a match between Karpov and Fischer – a plan that succeeded. So the USSR managed to regain the world title with the help of devious methods, but Fischer's impact on the international chess scene was permanent, with an increasingly professional attitude among the masters and an unprecedented explosion of chess interest among the rank and file.

"And that James Burke interview turned out to be prophetic," said Adams. "Fischer seemed rather taken aback when Burke asked him whether winning the match would be an anticlimax. Bobby appeared not to have thought about that before and for a moment was lost for a reply. The irony was that the aftermath *was* an anticlimax. Fischer had told Burke, 'I think that if you keep yourself in good shape physically, and you keep in love with the game and keep studying, you should be a top player till you're in your 60s.' As we know, Fischer in fact withdrew from chess. He'd reached the height, put in such a colossal effort, and saw that there was nowhere else to go but down. He'd burnt himself out. He didn't want to go through it all again."

In many ways, Fischer's early retirement did no harm to chess, as the impact had already been made. "Fischer brought real professionalism into chess. Previously it had been treated as an amateur game," said Adams. "But money wasn't the main thing with Fischer. His primary objective was to overthrow Soviet domination of chess. In this way he also gave other players confidence that they too could beat the Russians. For example, in the 1970s England's Tony Miles began a habit of defeating Soviet players – which even included a couple of wins against Spassky.

"The fact that Bobby had studied Russian chess literature so deeply and so extensively led [IM] Bob Wade to quip, 'Bobby Fischer was the finest product of the Soviet school of chess!' Though much was made of Fischer carrying around the 'big red book' – a German collection of hundreds of Spassky's games – it is not so well known that far more comprehensive files on Taimanov, Larsen and Spassky were prepared in England by Wade for use by Fischer on his path to the World Championship title. All in all, English involvement with the Fischer-Spassky match was quite significant."

Fischer may have respected Soviet players, but not their tendency to agree to short "grandmaster" draws. "Bobby played to win every game. You were simply wasting your time offering him a draw," said Adams. "A great fighting player, he would risk playing some very committal, almost dubious lines such as the Benoni and the Poisoned Pawn. But these were calculated risks. He knew for every game he lost he would win 10 or 20 times that number. Even against Spassky one of his Poisoned Pawn Najdorfs went terribly wrong and he got his queen trapped. Yet most of the time he seemed to make chess look so simple, like Capablanca. As Picasso once said, 'The nearer an artist approaches true genius, the more simple becomes his treatment of complex themes.' The same can apply to chess."

Fischer's high profile in the years leading up to the match with Spassky had sparked a chess revolution in Britain. Jim Slater, the millionaire who donated $125,000 to the World Championship prize fund, had begun sponsoring a junior chess programme in 1971. A group of five promising juniors were selected for special attention: Tony Miles, Michael Stean, Jonathan Speelman, John Nunn and Jonathan Mestel.

Slater believed that if England had a grandmaster in the world's top 20, that player would become a role model and spark an impetus that could lead on to a British world title challenger. He foresaw in 1971 that Miles and Stean would be contenders for the biennial World Junior Championship in 1973, but each country was allowed only one player. The host nation could field two, so Slater put up half the money for the contest to be held in Teesside, and Gerry Walsh, now the England FIDE delegate, raised the other half. Miles and Stean won the silver and bronze medals, FIDE then made the championship an annual event, and Miles won gold and the world title at Manila in 1974.

A few months after Fischer beat Spassky, Slater offered £5,000 to the first Briton to become a grandmaster and £2,500 each to the next four to do so. All five juniors became grandmasters, England won the World Student Championship in 1978 ahead of the Russians, and the English chess explosion that made this country the main rival to the Soviet Union was in full swing. The number of people in British chess clubs doubled after the Fischer-Spassky match, according to Bob Wade, who trained the five juniors.

"The Fischer boom showed that chess was not just a Russian game," Wade told me. "For once we had an individual and a small team of people like Colonel Edmonson [head of the U.S. Chess Federation] who could stand up to the Russians. We have 30 grandmasters now – we had none then."

The match was documented in Britain with the help of the world's first instant book, written by Svetozar Gligoric. The idea was David Levy's. Stewart Reuben negotiated with the publisher on behalf of Gligoric, because the Yugoslav grandmaster had agreed to a relatively small fee without realising how important the book would be. It appeared three days after the match. "I brought some of the chapters back to England," said Reuben. "It was better than sending them by post. There were mistakes – half a page was repeated. It was retailed like a magazine, rather than a book, and a quarter of a million copies were sold."

British shops sold out of chess sets during the match, and plastic sets were imported into the country for the first time to meet the demand. This was significant because there had been no absolutely standard chess set before. Jimmy Adams recalled one curious side effect of this: "I watched a simul in the '60s where, after having a rough time against the English juniors, Paul Keres complained that the different-size and different-design pieces had made it difficult for him to concentrate and caused him to make blunders. No doubt the plastic sets used everywhere today would have avoided this problem!"

Peter Morrish, one of the partners in Tournament Chess Supplies, explained how the plastic sets came to dominate the market. "Bob Wade told us that Cecil Purdy in Australia was selling cheap plastic sets, so we bought some from him and then found out the supplier in Hong Kong and got them direct." Over the past 25 years Morrish estimates that Tournament Chess Supplies has sold a quarter of a million plastic sets. But just recently they have started selling their own version, the "London Chess Set", designed and manufactured entirely in England.

A British weekend tournament circuit had been established a few years before Fischer-Spassky. Stewart Reuben and the Islington Chess Club organised the first weekend congress at the En Passant chess café in 1965. "Islington Chess Club had £2 in the bank at the time," said Reuben. "We needed eight people to break even, so we discussed what we would do if we had fewer entrants." Fortunately there were 24 pioneering souls.

"If I'd thought of organising weekend tournaments in the U.S. and had stayed there, maybe things would be different here, but in the U.S. I couldn't get sets and clocks," Reuben explained. "By 1971 the Islington Congress had 484 entrants and we had a network of weekend tournaments. In December 1972 our congress had 1,204 entrants. We set it up in three hours. All the tables and chairs had to be moved from one part of the school to another. In 1973 there were 1,500 entries – we had to hire another school."

Elsewhere in Britain, seven-year-old Nigel Short and nine-year-old Daniel King were also becoming addicted to chess. "I didn't know anything about chess before the Fischer-Spassky match," GM King told me. "I was completely knocked out by it. It was totally gripping, just brilliant." A new generation of British chess players had been born. They were Bobby Fischer's children.

Iceland has attracted little attention since that remarkable summer of '72, though, curiously, that nation's other great media success, Magnus Magnusson, started presenting his *Mastermind* on BBC TV just 10 days after the end of the Fischer-Spassky match. This quiz show has just recently come to an end after 25 years – a period in which Fischer has played only one serious chess match.

That 1992 match was held in Serbia, in contravention of UN sanctions. Fischer had agreed to play Spassky again, and won again. As a consequence of the match, the United States issued a warrant for Fischer's arrest. He moved to Hungary and gave several interviews to a radio station in the Philippines, which he contacted through his friend, GM Eugene Torre. Fischer (whose mother was Jewish) used the broadcasts to rant about Jewish conspiracies. On September 11, 2001, he called the station from Japan and described himself as "happy" about the World Trade Center attacks.

Shortly before September 11, Nigel Short announced that he had played almost 50 games on the Internet Chess Club with Fischer. Short's anonymous opponent won the first eight games they played, and could immediately answer questions about players whom Fischer would have known in the 1960s. Fischer later denied it was him in an Icelandic Internet interview.

My next assignment was to interview players at a tournament hosted by London's exclusive Agency Club. It was the centenary of the first women's international tournament in London, so half the players at the Agency were female, including Bulgaria's Antoaneta Stefanova.

Antoaneta
(*CHESS*, July 1997)

Sexy, self-confident, sociable... can we be talking about a professional chess player? Yes, we can. She's 18-year-old Antoaneta Stefanova from Bulgaria, who caught the world's attention in April by achieving a grandmaster norm at a tournament in Hawaii. She already had five international master norms, but no title, as the Bulgarian Chess Federation was slow about applying for it.

"I get no financial support from my federation – it doesn't have money – not even for the European Team Championship," she told me in her fluent English. "We didn't send a men's team or a women's team there. The situation in Bulgaria is quite bad for everything, not only chess. We have only a few players, not many tournaments, many people gave up chess, but we have a strong team."

I found Stefanova smoking a cigarette in the foyer of the Agency Club after her drawn game with Ketino Kachiani-Gersinska. She was disappointed not to have won, especially as her opponent almost missed the game because she thought it started at a different time. Stefanova also got into time trouble earlier in the tournament, when she got lost on her way to the club from Hendon in north London.

This was her first visit to England and she wished there had been more opportunity for sightseeing, although she did go to Buckingham Palace.

"I don't have a favourite country – I like places where I have a good tournament," Stefanova said. "I haven't lived long in the West, but from what I've seen, the people here think more about business than friendships. It's a different kind of life."

If she could find a chess club to represent, Stefanova wouldn't mind living outside Bulgaria. "In Bulgaria it's almost impossible to live only from chess." Communism was good for chess in Bulgaria, but democracy is better for other things, Stefanova says, and she's glad communism has ended.

"My friends in Bulgaria are not chess players. They are soccer players, basketball players and normal people. I can talk about different things with them, anything, but we talk a lot about politics. We had problems in Bulgaria, we had communism up until a few months ago. Then we had demonstrations after the demonstrations in Belgrade and we changed the government. We have a democratic government, but in Bulgaria you never know who are the democrats and if there are any democrats. It's very difficult in Bulgaria, thinking about how to get money to eat."

Stefanova's chess career has been given a boost by her newfound sponsor, the whisky manufacturer Johnnie Walker. How did she get the sponsorship? "It was quite accidental," was all she would say. "I am happy, they are paying my travel expenses, otherwise it would be difficult to play in any tournaments. Usually I have to wear Johnnie Walker shirts and mention them in interviews, but I don't think it matters, they're a big enough company." What is her ambition in chess? "I don't like to talk about my ambitions." She has just left school and is going to concentrate on chess for a few years, then go to university to study psychology.

Stefanova learnt chess from her father when she was five. "He's not a professional, but he loves chess. I played with my older sister, but she gave up. I didn't have a trainer, I worked only with my father and I used a lot of books, and now a computer. I started to use Informators [a series of professional-level openings books] very early. I can't say my style is tactical or strategic – I try to play both." She has adopted a wait-and-see policy on women in chess: "I think it will be clear after 20 or 50 years whether men and women can be equal in chess, as they are starting to be equal in other things."

I couldn't persuade Stefanova to give me some notes to one of her games – "I'm too tired" – but a few minutes later she enthusiastically challenged organiser Adam Raoof to a game of snooker. She had played billiards before, but not snooker. *CHESS*'s commitment to women's equality prevents us from publishing the result.

Antoaneta Stefanova is now a woman grandmaster. She won the strong European Women's Championship in 2002, held in Varna, Bulgaria. A great win in front of the best Russians, Georgians and other East Europeans – and British WGM Harriet Hunt.

Luke
(*CHESS*, July 1997)

At 13, Luke McShane has probably given more interviews than any other player in the tournament. He is certainly the only one whose picture and exploits have made the front page of national newspapers. Since becoming under 10s world champion in 1992, Luke's chess has gone from strength to strength. He was awarded sponsorship of £12,000 by Psion computers in 1995, money which he used to buy a computer, travel to tournaments, and pay for lessons from GMs Daniel King and Jon Speelman. The investment brought dividends this spring, when Luke became England's youngest ever international master.

Luke has learnt to deal with media speculation about his future, predictions that he will become world champion or break the new record for world's youngest grandmaster set by Etienne Bacrot. "People writing about what I might do used to annoy me more than it does now – now I just ignore it. I suppose it's nice, but I have to be realistic." His score against Bacrot is 1-0 – they played each other in the Under 10s World Championship. "I beat him. I was lucky. I should probably have lost, but I came up with a neat swindle."

Luke's mother is a journalist, Jennifer Selway, who divorced from Australian Rod McShane when Luke was a few months old. She has little interest in chess, but it was her father who taught Luke the moves at five-and-a-half, and Luke has a chess column in the *Sunday Express* thanks to her contacts in journalism. "Mum didn't like me playing in chess tournaments when I was first starting, but she's quite happy about it now. Dad plays, but he hasn't played for ages."

Luke lives with Rod in Folkestone on weekends and Rod takes him to tournaments. During the week he lives with his mother, brother and sister in London. He has just won a scholarship to the City of London School, where he will start in September.

At the chessboard, analysing at length with Richard Tozer, Luke sounded like a hardened professional. Deadly serious, totally absorbed in the game, he demonstrated variations that Richard had missed. "If you take on b6 I get some compensation... How about rook c2 here?" But away from chess Luke is still a little boy, losing his train of thought ("What was the question again?") and worrying about his homework.

"Sometimes school is boring, sometimes it's quite interesting, sometimes I find the lessons deadly dull, it just depends." Luke doesn't want to be treated differently at school because of his fame. "The fact that I play chess is taken into account at school. It's respected and ignored. I don't know how to explain it. I don't usually like to be asked about chess at school, I just want to have fun at school more than talk about chess."

Luke McShane at the London Chess Centre,
where he analysed with Anatoly Karpov.

It's difficult for an adult chess opponent to ignore Luke's age. I asked him if this gave him a psychological advantage. "It depends on the adult player, everyone's different. A few don't like playing children. When I jump up and walk around I suppose I'm a bit distracting, but it works both ways, I can find some players distracting."

Luke had an excellent result at the Agency Tournament, sharing first place. He won his first game with a queen sacrifice. He was generally happy with the venue, but added that it was in a noisy area. "My concentration is not brilliant, and it's not helped by the music outside and the plumbing, or banging, whatever it is. I don't mind it that much. It probably annoys some other people more than me."

Sometimes Luke's mind wanders when he is playing chess. "I think about other things during my games – anything – in one game I was thinking about getting an Italian dictionary because we were told to in a lesson about a week ago and I remembered I had to look up some words. I think it was yesterday, when I didn't have a wonderful position. It's usually when I get a bit fed up. When I'm not better it's annoying. Yesterday I lost to Richard Forster after six hours – it was very annoying, my first loss of the tournament."

Luke supports the football team Tottenham Hotspur and likes "most music", although he denies rumours that he is a big fan of the Spice Girls. At the Agency Club he played several games of shogi (Japanese chess) with tournament arbiter Les Blackstock, which Blackstock won easily, even with a handicap.

"Essentially I like nearly all games," Luke told me. "I don't like sports so much. The only sports I'm reasonable at – I can sort of play table tennis and sort of play snooker. I find chess fun. I get fed up with it after I've lost a bad game, but an hour after I lost yesterday I was fairly happy."

Luke McShane became England's youngest ever grandmaster at the age of 16. In 2001 he received the Terence Chapman Gold Award of £1,000 to further his chess career. He is also successfully continuing his academic studies.

Adam
(*CHESS*, July 1997)

In a short time 30-year-old Adam Raoof has become one of the most important chess organisers in Britain. The Golders Green Rapidplay, which he runs, takes place every month. He has also organised several international master tournaments, a grandmaster tournament, and set up the chess pages on the BBC's information service Ceefax.

Raoof is a big guy – at school he was Raoof by name and rough by nature – and he used to think that chess was for wimps. "I was more interested in football at school, but one day when it was raining I went to the chess club to disrupt a few games, beat up some kids." Instead he played a game with a prefect, which he lost, and it made Raoof determined to beat him.

Raoof's first chess success was in a school match. "I kept nagging until I got in as a reserve. The game ended in stalemate with lots of pieces on the board, which I thought was really good, until someone told me it wasn't, but I was hooked." Then he played his father (an Indian Muslim), who had originally taught him the game using Indian rules. "Dad thought I was cheating. Indian rules chess is a much slower game. For instance, there is no castling and the queens move one square."

Raoof lived near a strong chess club, Lewisham, and he quickly improved after joining it. He became even more involved with chess as deputy editor of *British Chess Magazine*, but he recently left that post to work as a full-time organiser. His game has suffered as a result, which is something he regrets. "My grade has gone down, I'm about 180 now. I've been organising more than playing. I had this fantasy that if I got into organising I would play more chess, organise one weekend and play the next, but it hasn't worked out like that. When I have a free weekend I usually want to do something else."

It isn't easy to make a living out of chess, and organising tournaments is no exception. "I'm surviving," says Raoof. "I have a very understanding partner with a full-time job, she's a committee administrator in a health authority. I used to work in a library, so I didn't mind giving up that job."

Raoof's first international tournament was at Imperial College, London, just over a year ago. It was nearly his last. "I was on a very steep learning curve, I made very drastic mistakes," he admits. "There were problems with accommodation, the venue; every day I would find that the tables had been taken to another part of the building and I had to look for them. When the two Dutch players went home, within a week every single Dutch player made up their mind not to come to England. It has taken four more tournaments for me to get a reputation."

Raoof describes his Caledonian Masters tournament in Edinburgh as "phenomenally successful". Luke McShane got his first international master norm there and Jonathan Rowson beat Keith Arkell in a challenge match. Raoof is already close to fulfilling his ambition of organising a tournament in England, Scotland, Wales and Northern Ireland. Only Northern Ireland has so far eluded him, but his sights are set on Belfast. Tax considerations have deterred other organisers from holding tournaments in mainland Britain (they prefer the Isle of Man, Guernsey and Jersey), so Raoof is pleased that he has brought some back.

There is now more opportunity for players to enter closed international tournaments, thanks to Raoof, but he is still concerned about the future of British chess. "There's a yawning chasm waiting to open up for British chess, there's a generation of players who are at their peak and I don't see where their successors are going to come from. Luke is a fluke, a one-in-a-million. Organisation of chess will be in the hands of entrepreneurs, individuals. If I didn't run tournaments, there aren't that many people who would do it."

The sponsors for Raoof's tournaments have been the British Chess Federation and Friends of Chess, "but their pockets are not bottomless," he says. "In general the tournaments have barely managed to break even, but it has been worth doing. Sponsorship in this country is virtually nonexistent, although since Smith & Williamson put money into the British Championships, perhaps that will attract more sponsors to chess. Chess can have a good image, it can be made to appeal to young people. The problem is the antisocial nature of some chess clubs – dingy, smelly, smoke-filled rooms full of people who don't talk to you. I think that maybe people should pay £100 to join a club, then it could provide better facilities."

Venues don't get much more luxurious than the Agency Club, with its plush carpets, comfortable sofas and snooker room. Sadly, it isn't a chess club. An Agency Club member who is also a keen chess player arranged for the tournament to take place there free of charge.

Raoof believes that women can be as good as men at chess, and that women-only tournaments should be abolished. The existence of a women-only circuit made it more difficult for him to get five players with high ratings for the Agency Tournament, as some women avoid mixed tournaments altogether. "In the world there aren't many women with male international master titles, about 10, so they're always being chased for invitations by tournament organisers. I had to find five women above 2300, and it wasn't easy."

While Raoof welcomes women to his tournaments, he discriminates blatantly against computers. "I was approached by a man who wanted to enter a computer into a one-day rapidplay. I said no. How would it affect the players' ratings? It's difficult to work out how strong a computer is because they usually play each other." I wonder if the Adam Raoof cyber-clone in 2097 will be able to dismiss computers so easily...

Adam Raoof organised many more chess tournaments, then embarked on a bachelor's degree in writing and media at Middlesex University, and he plans to become a journalist, a writer or a teacher.

The Eagle Has Landed... a Job in the Government!
(*CHESS*, July 1997)

A high-flier presented the prizes – Angela Eagle MP, the junior environment minister who was filmed on BBC2's Newsnight as she received her momentous telephone call from Tony Blair. She was British girls' under 18 chess champion in 1976 and her twin sister, Maria (who accompanied her to the Agency tournament), was also an accomplished chess player. Maria was elected to parliament in May, making the Eagle sisters the first identical twin MPs.

The twins were taught chess by their father when they were eight years old. "We beat him straight away," said Angela. Then they joined Formby Chess Club. "The atmosphere at the club wasn't bad, we played in a library, so it was non-smoking. All the other members were men, but that was OK."

The Eagles' first tournament was the Formby Junior Chess Championship. Maria played in an older age group than Angela because they didn't want to be drawn against each other. "When I sat down to play a little boy, he refused to believe a girl could play chess," Angela recalled. "It was the first time I realised how unfair the world is. Boys at eight can't cope with losing to girls. I beat him and won the tournament, and the prize was a Biggles book, which shows that they weren't expecting a girl to win it."

Angela and Maria happen to have been involved in two activities where men vastly outnumber women, but they didn't plan it that way. "When we started we didn't know that chess was male-dominated," said Angela. "Politics is in my blood and the fact that it is male-dominated is something I was determined to change."

Before the advent of the Polgar sisters there were few inspirational women in chess for girls to emulate. "I had lots of women role models in politics, Barbara Castle, for instance, who was in the Cabinet when I was growing up, but not in chess," Angela told me. "The Fischer-Spassky match was on, so I suppose that was something. I liked chess because I was almost instantly good at it. I was intuitively good."

I asked Angela if there were any games she particularly remembered. "There are games that I am proud of because they were really good games, and games I am proud of because I was on a team and it was all down to me. And disastrous games as well. One of the most memorable games was when I beat Jane Seymour in the British County Championships. We were board one for our respective counties and ours was the last game to finish, everything hinged on it. I won and I'd never beaten her before."

When she was 20, Angela gave up playing in tournaments. "There's not really a structure to carry on with chess after the age of 18 or 19, unless you're extremely good," she said. "I miss it sometimes. I play in the annual House of Commons match against the Lords, but I don't play very much any more. I don't want to play if I'm not as good as I was."

Angela is concerned that so many girls drop out of chess when they are around 13 years old. "I have my theories about that. There's no reason why women can't be as good as men at chess. If the same number of women as men played, they could be as good. It's the same question as why there aren't so many women composers. The shape of women's lives usually means they have to take on the practical things that men get out of by having a hobby."

Chess can help young people to think strategically, Angela believes, but she doubts that there will be any room for it on the national curriculum. The government can promote chess outside schools, however, and Angela will be lobbying her colleagues to take action. "I won't be slow in coming forward. I shifted the chess budget from the DFE [Education] to the Department of National Heritage, and I will be trying to get chess recognised as a sport... The Sports Council is very hostile because the legal definition of a sport says it must involve physical exertion... We do a remarkably good job in Britain considering that the government only gives £49,000 a year to chess. We have high standards in men's and women's chess."

Angela doesn't think that chess can contribute much to the TV ratings war. "It's not a natural spectator sport, like tennis. Television coverage of master games has always been very good. There's always a healthy minority who want to watch, but it will never be a mass sport. Yes, other sports have transferred to television, but you don't have to be very sophisticated to understand what's going on in snooker or darts."

Chess in parliament is also a minority interest. "Ray Keene said I was the strongest chess player ever elected to parliament, but that's not saying much. We won when we played the Lords, but we didn't play properly, they don't have clocks. It's amateurish. I tried to get them to invest in clocks, but they didn't."

Staying awake has been the hardest part of adapting to life as a minister, Angela confessed. "We're all so tired. But it's been fantastic, although I am responsible for canals, amongst other things. I have a lot of respect for canals, but they're not at the centre of my political philosophy. We need to get people back to work, that's the key to everything."

Angela Eagle was the first MP to come out publicly as a lesbian, in September 1997. She moved to the Home Office as parliamentary under secretary of state for Europe, Community and Race Equality in 2001. Subsequently she lost her job in one of Prime Minister Tony Blair's reshuffles. Maria Eagle is the minister for disabled people.

The Agency Tournament and Harriet Hunt's victory in the World Girls' Under 21 Championship inspired me to interview one of England's first successful woman chess players, Elaine Saunders. We spoke on the telephone.

Elaine: A 10-year-old World Champion
(*CHESS*, October 1997)

Elaine Saunders was just 10 years old when Lady Margaret Hamilton-Russell presented her with the cup for winning the World Girls' Under 21 Championship of 1936. To prove that her victory hadn't been a fluke, she repeated it the following year. The event was held at London's Imperial Chess Club, which was located opposite Claridge's.

"Nearly all the players were UK, I think there was one Italian," Elaine recalled. "The playing strength of British girls was probably about average in the world – the lack of foreign players was due to the fact that you didn't send your daughter to far-flung places in those days, and anyway I don't think the championship was very well advertised."

Nevertheless, Elaine's achievement at such a young age was fantastic. The other participants in the World Championship were several years older than her. "One or two of my opponents blew smoke in my face," she said. "On the whole, they took it quite well. I just had an ability which the problemist C.D. Locock helped me with. He had written a book on imagination in chess. I had a very attacking style. I still do, although it's not as reliable now."

At London 1927, the Hon. Frederick Hamilton-Russell donated his famous trophy, still played for today, to the World Chess Olympiad. But it is not so well known that a year earlier his wife had also donated a cup for the World Girls' Championship, won by Vera Menchik. After the 1936 prize giving, Lady Hamilton-Russell, the daughter of an earl and a former British women's golf champion, invited all the girls to dinner. "To my horror it was mince," said Elaine. "That's the kind of thing you remember at that age. When you're as young as that you don't think winning is at all remarkable. The standard of play was not too bad, but rubbish in comparison with what they play now, I expect."

Elaine had many more successes as a child. At the Margate Congress in 1938 she beat the Austrian grandmaster and author of the famous *Art of Sacrifice in Chess*, Rudolf Spielmann, in a simultaneous display. "Some people suggested that he might have let me off deliberately, but he was nice enough to write afterwards that it was fair and square, he didn't give it away."

Elaine's impression of Alexander Alekhine was less pleasant. "I didn't like him. I sat in the same compartment with him on the train to Margate and he didn't say a word throughout the whole journey." The two had played earlier the same year when, after regaining the World Championship from Euwe, Alekhine had come to England to watch the Hastings tournament and afterwards given a simul against 30 Kent players. Elaine was the last to finish. "I had a drawn endgame, but at one o'clock in the morning I didn't know how to do it. Someone in the audience said in Russian, 'Let her have the draw,' but he said, 'I know what I'm doing,' and he eventually won."

Nevertheless, Elaine's fine performance had been picked up by many of the daily papers, which featured tabloid-style pictures of the little girl, just turned 12, boxing a punch bag, walloping her father blindfold, etc., while Alekhine was even reported in *CHESS* as saying, "She is a genius!" However, "when he played me in another simul, at Bournemouth, he mashed me up – he wasn't going to let the same thing happen again."

Winning the World Girls' twice was enough for Elaine, so after 1937 she set her sights on the British Women's Championship. She went on to win four British titles in 1939, 1946, 1956 and 1965. Her first victory came when she was only 14. "There might have been a press hoo-ha, except that the war started that very week. The ladies' championship ended on August 28, then everything was suspended, we were filling sandbags. I retired into my school shell. I kept the ladies' trophy all through the war and won it again in 1946."

During the war Elaine lost a great friend, the women's world champion Vera Menchik, who was killed in the Blitz. "I was very fond of her, she used to take me to the theatre until she got blown up," said Elaine. "But her play was anathema to me – what I call stodgy – although it was miles better than mine."

The cup for the World Girls' Championship had been given up for lost. "I kept the cup for a couple of years, then my father took it back to R.H.S. Stevenson, who was the leading light in the BCF. Then I didn't hear of it again until it turned up recently. In 1936 it was meant to be worth £50, so it must be worth a good deal more now." The value of the cup does pose a problem. FIDE doesn't want to look after it because of the high insurance.

Winning the cup is bound to be an inspiration for Harriet Hunt, who starts at Cambridge University this year. Elaine approves of that decision. "If I were Harriet I would get a university degree and play in between whiles, see how it goes. It's not a frightfully good idea to become a chess professional at that age. You can be landed with nothing if things go wrong. She is obviously academically brilliant. I did a degree, it didn't do me any harm. I went on at school and did what I had to do, then I was offered a job in GCHQ [Government Communications Headquarters]."

Elaine continued to play chess and considers that some of her best performances were at Olympiads later in her career. She married David Pritchard, a strong chess player and board games expert. She still plays five-minute chess with him and serious games for Godalming Club: "It keeps me from going rusty." Elaine doesn't think that being a woman is a disadvantage in chess. "On the contrary. It's a lot easier to win a women's world title than to be another Polgar." Both genders are affected equally by low prize funds, she believes. "We got sixpence ha'penny and so did Capablanca and all the rest. Ten pounds was the average top prize in tournaments."

The Pritchards' daughter, Wanda Dakin, used to play in international tournaments, but she now has five children, so she takes part in correspondence Olympiads. Elaine is trying to encourage more girls to take up chess. "I teach in a couple of schools. Girls are very keen until the age of 11, then nobody wants to know any more, they get interested in hockey, netball, music. In Harriet's case the Oxford school took it up. It's a hard slog to get girls interested in chess."

* * *

Also in summer 1997, IM Mike Basman invited me to report on his UK Chess Challenge for school kids, the penultimate stages of which were being held at Nottingham University.

Along with the tournament play, several professionals gave simultaneous displays against the kids at the UK Chess Challenge. One of them was IM Gary Lane, a quiet but sharp-tongued Devon lad (in his early thirties), who from his Brussels base made a living from chess writing and playing. We became friends, trawling London for Russian restaurants whenever he visited, and exchanging chess gossip.

A long article about the UK Chess Challenge was published in *CHESS*. This shorter version, focusing on chess in schools, appeared in the *Times Educational Supplement*.

Young Masters
(*Times Educational Supplement*, October 1997)

Losing honourably at sport is something the British have developed into an art form. We've groaned through the penalty shoot-out against Germany in Euro 96, Tim Henman's transient glory at Wimbledon and Mike Atherton's failure to recapture the Ashes. So when the opportunity arises to nurture potential world champions, we shouldn't pass it up.

The activity in question is chess, and the way to make things happen is through schools. British junior chess has never been stronger. Luke McShane, who was under 10s world chess champion in 1992, is now the country's youngest ever international master at 13. Harriet Hunt, 19, has just become world girls' champion. But thousands of children are also taking up chess for fun, thanks to the efforts of Mike Basman, who is responsible for the UK Chess Challenge, a knockout tournament involving 780 schools, which culminated earlier this year in finals held at London's Festival Hall. Next year it will be even bigger.

Basman, an international master, devotes all his time to the cause of promoting junior chess. "At the moment it's still an intellectual minority who play chess," he says. "But if you push kids, it helps to concentrate their minds."

Rotary International in Britain and Ireland (RIBI), a sponsor of the UK Chess Challenge, supports the educational benefits of chess and has launched a national initiative to bring chess into schools, inspired by a study in New York which showed that chess improved academic performance.

The American experiment was carried out in the Bronx and Harlem, New York's most deprived areas. Children who played chess achieved higher results in literacy and numeracy than non-players, and had a better school attendance record. It was also found that the juvenile crime rate dropped and chess players became more self-confident.

This evidence has helped the chess initiative to find enthusiastic partners in some unlikely places, such as Brixton police station in south London. There Sergeant Vernon Allen is helping to introduce its chess initiative in Lambeth.

"You won't find a greater social-ethnic mix anywhere in the whole country," says Allen. "Poverty stands side by side with affluence. We try to build bridges between the police service and the community, and chess is a natural extension of what we already do – we help kids become good citizens. Chess extends brain power: it makes people think."

Allen has made contact with 20 schools, 17 of which expressed an interest in starting extracurricular chess classes. The RIBI chess initiative will try to raise funds to provide them with equipment and will help them to find a coach.

The chess initiative estimates that the annual cost of running a chess club for 20 children is £2,500. Chess sets, clocks, demonstration boards, trophies and fares to tournaments come to £1,000, and the remaining £1,500 goes to the coach. Different schools approach the matter of paying for a coach in different ways. Some charge parents a fee of about £2.50 for every session their child attends, others devote school funds to chess, and still others find parents or teachers who are willing to give their time voluntarily.

Tony Ighodaro, the father of three girls in Richmond, west London, is one such volunteer. Ighodaro learned chess from a friend at school in Nigeria. He set up a chess club at Hampton Hill Junior School in Richmond in 1993. "I found my lack of expertise to be a bit of a help in communicating with kids – top players move their hands so fast on the demonstration board that it's difficult to follow. I used to mark where a knight move started with a pebble."

Variety is the key to successful chess teaching, Ighodaro believes. "I teach what checkmate is, I illustrate the distinction between trapping something and eliminating it. I show them the moves of the pieces, I use puzzles from *The Times* and *The Daily Telegraph*, we do chess-related activities, friendlies, and an all-play-all."

Natasha, Ighodaro's youngest daughter, won the school's chess championship every year until she left. As there is no chess in her secondary school, the chances of her continuing with the game are slim. Many children drop chess in adolescence anyway, but especially girls.

"A lot of girl players start changing their interests around the last year at primary school," says Ighodaro. "They do gym and other games, they are making friends and being sociable. Chess becomes an uncool activity. Only the keenest boys continue, but they have more opportunities – there's more chess in boys' schools."

Mike Basman hopes to change this situation by a policy of positive discrimination in the UK Chess Challenge. Eleven-year-old Claire David travelled from Swansea to Nottingham for the final of Basman's event. She automatically qualified for the final because she was the only girl from the region in her age group.

Those girls who do play chess will find similar advantages at every level. If they achieve the international master title, they are likely to be chosen to represent their country and travel to tournaments abroad. They can consider turning professional, while boys of the same strength are overshadowed by the growing numbers of grandmasters. All the more reason for girls to keep playing.

Secondary school teachers need to help children of both sexes overcome their embarrassment about chess, so that early promise doesn't go to waste. "Teenage chess is so dismal," says Basman. "Teenagers are ashamed to mention that they play chess. It's like when baby turtles are immediately eaten by birds before they can run to the sea. That's what happens to chess at secondary school – it's the killing zone!"

The UK Chess Challenge has continued to grow year by year, with 58,826 entrants from 1,646 schools in 2002.

5. Some Unusual Positions

Spending a winter in the draughty bedsit [studio apartment] didn't appeal, so I moved to a more comfortable house in the unsalubrious suburb of Edmonton. The house was owned by a young Turkish Cypriot entrepreneur whose mother kindly did our washing-up for us whenever she visited, and his ironing, too. For a slightly higher rent I was even further from central London, but at least this time there were carpets and a bathtub, and a separate kitchen.

My involvement in the British chess scene grew deeper when I got the job of editing the British Chess Federation's monthly newsletter, *ChessMoves*. The previous editor had been GM Julian Hodgson, who concentrated on annotating games rather than writing articles. The BCF chose me because they wanted a journalist, not a professional player. I could always ask titled players to annotate their games, so that wasn't a problem. Readers contributed plenty of news items and letters, and each issue only took me a few days to do. It was fairly easy. At first I didn't realise how controversial an eight-page newsletter could become.

Meanwhile, the publisher B.T. Batsford had a new chess editor, David Cummings. When I heard he was arranging an appearance by Anatoly Karpov at the London Chess Centre, I requested a separate interview with Karpov, because the previous attempt to catch Kasparov had gone so disastrously. Cummings invited me to dinner with Karpov and a few other people, so I was able to engage him in one-to-one conversation. The following article was reprinted in the American magazine *Inside Chess*, and the U.S. Chess Federation later gave me a Cramer Award for it.

The Disneyfication of Karpov
(*CHESS*, January 1998)

Santa Claus and Mickey Mouse are best pals of FIDE world champion Anatoly Karpov. So is Ron Henley, an American grandmaster. This is rather strange, considering that Karpov was a hero of the Soviet regime for nearly two decades, supported by all the resources of the state in return for his unfailing loyalty. The first incarnation of Anatoly Karpov – a leading member of the Komsomol, the communist youth organisation – publicly reprimanded his colleague Viktor Korchnoi for defecting to the West in 1976. The new Karpov earns thousands of dollars from book and publicity deals with Western companies. More than a touch of the Walt Disney magic has got to him, it seems.

Karpov was in London last month on a flying visit to promote his new book, *Disney's Chess Guide*. He strolled into the London Chess Centre with a grin on his face and tirelessly signed copies while posing for photographs. Then he watched, still smiling, as some of England's most promising juniors were puzzling out the moves in a Dragon Sicilian that he himself once used against Korchnoi. He followed this by analysing with Luke McShane and answering questions from the public.

Looking relaxed and dapper in a pinstriped suit with a chequered blue-and-yellow tie decorated with little furry animals in funny costumes, it was hard to associate this man with the worried, serious youth he used to be. He has added quite a few pounds to his formerly slim frame. Even though he had just arrived from Indonesia, via Singapore and Italy, giving a press conference in Milan that morning, he never once got irritated. "Do you find that you are treated like a god, and that women will do anything for you?" someone asked. Karpov laughed. "Do you study your opponents' games before you play them?" another fan enquired. "Yes," said Karpov.

I asked Karpov whether he was on good terms with Korchnoi. "More or less," he said. "Is it more, or is it less?" a heckler demanded. "More than less," he said, and laughed again. "Does Kasparov say hello to you?" Karpov was asked. "Kasparov *never* says hello!" he retorted.

When the official question-and-answer session was over, Karpov answered more questions informally and discussed his training match with Indonesian GM Utut Adianto, consisting of normal, rapid and blindfold chess, which he drew 3-3 after a last-game equaliser. "There was huge interest in this match, there were 50 journalists at the press conference, it was on every television channel," he said, as he set up a position from one of the blindfold games on a chessboard.

The following day, Karpov was due to play another training match with GM Eric Lobron in Germany, which he went on to win 2-0. He was preparing for the unusual format of the FIDE World Championship final, in which he was supposed to play six full-length games with his challenger, the winner of the 100-player knockout in Groningen. If the match were to end on a score of 3-3, they would have to play tiebreak games at rapid time limits: two games at 25 minutes each, then if the scores were still level, two games at 15 minutes each, and finally sudden-death games with four minutes for White and five for Black. This idea was dreamed up by FIDE President Kirsan Ilyumzhinov to make the event more exciting for sponsors, the media and the public.

"I would have preferred a longer World Championship match," Karpov said. "I'm sure the system will be improved next time around. The draughts World Championship system is good. One year there is a match and the next year there is a tournament. I don't like the combination of classical chess, rapid chess and blitz. It's like you run a marathon, you are equal, then you run a sprint. Separately I like all types of chess. But rapid games have a lot of mistakes and you lose quality."

Karpov isn't the only person who is dissatisfied with the FIDE World Championship. Zsuzsa Polgar, women's world champion, was unhappy not to be seeded further than the first round and refused to play. In any case, she preferred to spend her time preparing to defend her women's title. Vladimir Kramnik, the hot favourite to win the knockout tournament and play Karpov in the final, pulled out at the last minute. He told the Russian newspaper *Sport Express*, "Any privileges, especially seeding directly to the finals, are not acceptable. In this case one person (I do not care what his name may be) is declared champion before the start of the tournament. I do not intend to participate in this." In other words, Karpov's advantage is too great. Kramnik added that he would certainly take part in a future FIDE World Championship if the conditions were fairer.

The final is scheduled for the first week of January at the Olympic Museum in Lausanne, Switzerland. This represents a publicity coup for Ilyumzhinov, who has been cultivating his links with IOC President Juan Antonio Samaranch, hoping to associate chess with Olympic sports. The loser of the final is guaranteed a prize of $768,000 and the winner takes a cool $1,373,000. At this year's FIDE Congress, Ilyumzhinov promised the incredible sum of $55 million to finance World Championships for the next 20 years, but no one knows where his money comes from – neither his vast personal wealth, nor the money he has allocated to the World Championship.

Ilyumzhinov is president of the tiny Russian republic of Kalmykia. A few months ago the tax inspectors dropped in to investigate him, but he and his entire government were taking a holiday in the Crimea.

The most notable absentee from the World Championship is, of course, PCA world champion Garry Kasparov. Since Kasparov and Nigel Short broke away from FIDE and formed the PCA in 1993, there have been several unsuccessful attempts to plan a reunification match between Karpov and Kasparov. José Fraguela, president of the Canary Islands Chess Federation, offered $3 million to hold the match in Las Palmas. Kasparov "destroyed the negotiations," according to Karpov. The French city of Compiègne outside Paris also considered making a bid, but couldn't raise the money. Karpov went there and saw "a fantastic theatre, which would be the best site for a match." Spain and Switzerland are the other countries where Karpov would like to play, if he had the chance.

In a recent interview Kasparov announced that he was no longer willing to play Karpov because of the decline in Karpov's chess strength. This decline is relative. In 1994 Karpov won the elite Linares tournament 2½ points clear of Kasparov. Last year Karpov came last in the Las Palmas tournament, which Kasparov won – but on both occasions when they faced each other over the board, they drew. Karpov is still in the world's top five and is the strongest player in history for his age, at 46. His rating on the latest FIDE list is 2745, the same as Topalov's. Kasparov is rated 2820.

"Even Professor Elo said his system has a lot of problems," Karpov said. "It can't be used as a main measure of chess players. For me it was always more important that someone was a candidate than 100 points more." However, he was quick to point out that Linares 1994 was the only tournament ever where someone gave a performance rated over 3000 – himself.

The truth is that Kasparov is simply fed up with playing Karpov, and he doesn't think the public will be interested in yet another World Championship match between them. They played five protracted matches between 1984 and 1990. Karpov was the champion in 1984 and was one game from victory, but couldn't clinch it after three months of trying. Against all the rules, FIDE halted the match on the grounds that the players were tired. Karpov was on the verge of physical collapse, but the more robust Kasparov protested against the decision. Kasparov won the title a year later and defended it from Karpov's three consecutive challenges. All the matches were decided on the last game. "It was always a problem to make good preparation against Kasparov," Karpov said.

Karpov commented on Kasparov's match with Deep Blue this year on Roman Dzindzichashvili's website. He wasn't impressed with Kasparov's performance and doesn't argue when it is suggested that he might have been a more suitable player to challenge IBM's supercomputer. "There was not one good game in the Deep Blue match," he said.

If Karpov is relieved not to be playing Kasparov again, he doesn't admit it. "I don't fear any opponent, only myself," he said. "When I'm in good form I'm not afraid of anybody. When I'm in bad form, I can lose to anybody." A few months ago he gave a simultaneous display in Beijing against a Chinese boys' team and lost more games than he won. "We had 2½ hours for the whole game for both players, which is less than the amount of time Kasparov uses when he gives a simul. I ran out of time in two games. But the level of chess in China is growing very fast. They have over one million registered players and they believe that in five years they will have ten million. The Chinese do what we did in Russia a long time ago, they prepare together, exchanging ideas."

Karpov had already seen the Chinese boys in action at Disneyland Paris, where he makes a regular guest appearance at the European Junior Speed Chess Championship. It takes place in December and one year Karpov even took pride of place, sitting alongside Santa on a giant sleigh, as guest of honour in the Christmas parade. That same year he thoughtfully brought several beautiful limited-edition Russian chess tournament books to give as special prizes for the winners. Last December he even broke off in the middle of the Las Palmas tournament to visit Disneyland.

Karpov's efforts have paid off. *Disney's Chess Guide*, a new book for beginners illustrated with Disney cartoons, is being published in more than a dozen languages and sold thousands of copies in its first month. The Russian edition has already sold 15,000 copies. "All Russian children know the Disney characters," Karpov said. "Russian cartoons were fantastic in the '70s and '80s – we had rabbit and wolf – but the cartoon industry there is dead now."

Citizens of the great Cold War rivals have always been fascinated by each other. Very few Russians had the opportunity to visit the United States before 1991, but

Karpov did. On a trip to Washington, D.C., his hosts asked him if he had ever been to the White House. He hadn't, so they arranged a VIP ticket for him. Alexander Roshal, editor of the Soviet chess magazine *64*, wanted to go along as well, but as a journalist he was concerned that he wouldn't be allowed in. Roshal went as Karpov's interpreter, not knowing a word of English.

"Our guide became confused when Roshal asked me what was going on and I interpreted for *him*!" Karpov recalled. "We came to the door of the Oval Office and walked in. There were documents on the table – it was obvious that President Carter had just been there. Can you imagine if someone walked into Brezhnev's office like that?!"

In London Karpov had dinner with representatives of his British publisher, Batsford, at the exclusive Rib Room in Knightsbridge. Also there were IM Malcolm Pein from the London Chess Centre, GM Jon Levitt and myself. Fortunately the service was very slow, so we continued to grill Karpov for hours while we waited for the chefs to grill our T-bone steaks. The waiter offered us an aperitif. Karpov ordered a Campari and orange, which coincidentally was exactly what the others were in the mood for. I had a gin and tonic.

"I don't have any relations with the Russian Chess Federation for four years now, but I'm working for chess," Karpov said. "They cannot disturb my work. Before, this would have been impossible. They would press me terribly. But I always was a more or less free person. I always did what I want and made what I want. I had only one obligation – to play for the national team."

Karpov likes the Beatles and bought their albums when they first came out. He seemed unaware that most ordinary Soviet citizens would have been in serious trouble for listening to such Western decadence. "I also like the James Last Orchestra and Elvis Presley," he added, without a hint of shame. "I don't like hard rock."

Karpov's problems with the Russian Chess Federation began when wealthy businessman Alexander Makarov became its president after the collapse of the Soviet Union. Karpov claims that Makarov was wrongly awarded the international master title. "He's a candidate master. He never played tournaments. He played one game with Atalik, because he thought Turks couldn't play chess. He was beaten terribly in 20 moves with the white pieces. They made a fix. Makarov is a very common name, we have maybe five Makarovs – so many, that people didn't know we have a new Makarov."

Independently of the chess federation, Karpov is setting up chess schools all over Russia, based on the famous Botvinnik chess school, which he attended on three occasions. "I'm trying to restore the system of regional chess schools – I have good support from the Ministry of Education and the local governors. I have one in my home region, the Urals, where Sveshnikov is the coach. The schools will bring together the best players from a group of provinces. For six years I've had my own school for

Anatoly Karpov, Mike Basman and I at the
London Chess Centre. Photo: Mark Huba

kids under 16 who were affected by the Chernobyl disaster, experienced players. I'm
also hoping to open chess schools in Istanbul and Las Palmas."

The first chess book Karpov read was Panov's book of Capablanca's best games.
Capablanca became Karpov's hero. "He was not a very hard worker, but he was
one of the greatest players in history. He refuted the Marshall Attack when it was
introduced and 75 years later the line Capablanca chose is still the best line."

Karpov has a lot to thank the Soviet system for, although nowadays he is happy to
train without a huge entourage of top players catering to his every whim. He works
mainly with Russian GM Mikhail Podgaets. "His understanding of chess is much
higher than his strength in chess," Karpov said of Podgaets. "Ron Henley is an
amateur, but he's my best friend. I don't use a playing computer for preparation,
only databases. I have help from two people on books. I work on my books during
tournaments, making comments after the game. I write books on openings that I
play, and I collaborate on many chess magazines."

The most stressful time of Karpov's life was the period when he was playing a
match with Kasparov every year. But his three matches with Korchnoi were also
notorious. During the first match, the Candidates final, Korchnoi was still living
in the Soviet Union. Relations between Korchnoi and Karpov deteriorated after
Karpov won, qualifying to challenge Bobby Fischer for the world title.

"Korchnoi betrayed me in the negotiations over Fischer's conditions, the number
of wins needed," Karpov said. Fischer wanted the match to continue until one of

the players won 10 games, draws not counting. If the score was 9-9, he insisted that the champion would retain his title.

"When Korchnoi and I were both possible challengers to Fischer, Korchnoi asked me to speak for both of us at the Chess Federation Congress, because I was a more experienced speaker. He asked me to give our mutual position. I said we disagreed with this condition of Fischer's. But when I became the challenger, Korchnoi took Fischer's side on this."

GM Lev Alburt, who defected to the United States in 1979, criticises Karpov's behaviour in the recently published book *Russians versus Fischer*. "Karpov knew he could hardly draw a game with Fischer, never mind winning one or two games. His only chance was to disrupt the match. So a whole arsenal of tricks was worked out, designed to upset the sensitive American, unaccustomed to such methods. As Karpov himself said, 'This match cannot end normally. Either I'll be taken to hospital (Anatoly weighed only 48 kg at the time and even at the end of his Moscow match with Korchnoi required pep pills to keep him going) or else he'll be taken to the insane asylum.'"

The Fischer-Karpov match was indeed disrupted. Karpov today blames Fischer's "psychological problems". They met three times to negotiate the match, in the United States, Japan and Spain, but that condition of Fischer's was the perpetual sticking point. Karpov was declared world champion by default in 1975. The following year, Korchnoi defected after a tournament in Amsterdam. Karpov said that Korchnoi had been at the centre of a controversy over the rebel Olympiad in Tripoli held in protest against the staging of the official Olympiad in Haifa.

The Soviets wouldn't send a team to Haifa because they had no diplomatic relations with Israel. They seriously considered meeting the Arab stipulation to send a non-Jewish team to Tripoli, which would have excluded Korchnoi. In the end, the Soviet Union didn't send a team to either Olympiad, because this would have caused political problems for the 1980 Moscow Olympics. Korchnoi knew that because of his role in the affair, he would not be allowed to travel again when he returned to Amsterdam, so he defected.

"The decision of V. Korchnoi to betray his Motherland was deeply shocking and distressing for me," Karpov wrote in a 1976 issue of *Shakhmaty v SSSR*, under the heading "Soviet Grandmasters Judge the Behaviour of Korchnoi." "Everyone knows that for him, as for all Soviet sportsmen, conditions were created which our colleagues in the West could only dream about... I support the decision of the Soviet Chess Federation to strip him of his titles and rights to represent the Soviet school of chess on the world stage."

Karpov's statement appeared side-by-side with a statement signed by 32 Soviet players, including Petrosian and Smyslov – but not Botvinnik, Bronstein or Spassky.

"I was much softer than the other grandmasters in their letter," Karpov told me. "I didn't sign their letter." The joint statement accused Korchnoi of narcissism and "making a move in a dirty political game."

By the time Korchnoi and Karpov played each other for the World Championship in 1978, they were bitter enemies. Accusations flew. Korchnoi claimed that a hypnotist called Zukhar had been planted in the audience to disturb him and that a yoghurt delivered to Karpov during a game was a coded message. Karpov won the match and fended off Korchnoi's challenge again in 1981, after which their relations gradually improved, especially as Korchnoi's wife and son were allowed to leave Russia, with Karpov's approval.

Karpov attained his position of power and influence in the Soviet era partly by his chess victories and partly by his willingness to conform. Korchnoi and Kasparov were more rebellious and caused the authorities more problems. Famously conservative as a young man, Karpov used to tell interviewers that his favourite author was Lermontov and that his hobby was stamp collecting.

The amount of money Karpov has made from chess can perhaps be gauged from his stamp collection. I asked him what the highest price he had ever paid for a stamp was. "I think, $60,000," he replied. "No, it was $90,000. I paid that for a rare upside-down Belgian Termonde stamp. There are just 14 of these stamps known. I have hundreds of albums, I don't know how many. Through stamps you can learn a lot – history, culture, traditions. For Russian Empire stamps I'm between the first three and four collectors in the world. For the Olympic Games I'm in the first five in the world. For Belgian stamps I'm No. 1. That's on quality, not quantity." He also has a library of 10,000 chess books, which he describes as "smaller than Lothar Schmid's collection, but of equal quality."

Karpov's charm masks a toughness that is just under the surface. Without it he wouldn't have been able to win almost 150 international tournaments. He could survive the destruction of his stamp collection in a fire, he said. "I can stand any attack, ever since I lost a World Championship match in one move in one second." That was in the 24th game of his Seville, 1987 match with Kasparov. Karpov was leading 12-11, but lost as Black and Kasparov retained his title.

Karpov lives in Moscow with his second wife, Natalya, who is an archivist. "She was working in the department of old manuscripts. She made a lot of research for the Cathedral of Christ the Saviour." This enormous cathedral was destroyed by Stalin and turned into an outdoor swimming pool. In the past few years it has been rebuilt. By his first wife, Karpov has an 18-year-old son, another Anatoly, who is studying computing. Karpov feels safe in Moscow. "Why shouldn't I? You need a bodyguard if you've stolen a lot of black money. I haven't, so I don't."

Never far from politics (he was a deputy in the Supreme Soviet in 1989-91), Karpov is president of the Peace Foundation, a Russian charity that distributes humanitarian aid for victims of war. He met President Yeltsin a couple of years ago to discuss the plight of charities in Russia, which are taxed as if they are businesses. "Yeltsin is a strong leader, I know him personally. In the economy he's not prepared. Charities were always in a bad situation. We had a law about charity, but people started to 'improve' it, they created new problems. If more than 20 percent of the budget is administration, you can't be a charity. With all the costs, such as transport, and the changing value of the rouble, this is very difficult to maintain. It's easier not to be a charity, but to be a public organisation. The taxes are the same. The government wants to stop commercial organisations from calling themselves charities, but you can do this by presenting serious audits."

The Peace Foundation sent help to all sides in the Chechen conflict. Karpov's view of the war was indicative of his character. "The invasion of Chechnya was a terrible mistake. It was as if Yeltsin had made a queen sacrifice, then stopped before the finish because someone said it wasn't time to checkmate, it was too early. Of course, you don't do that."

After retaining his FIDE title by defeating Vishy Anand in the final round of the first knockout World Championship, Karpov sued FIDE for making the event annual rather than biannual (meaning he would keep the title for a year instead of two years). He settled the case in January 2001, agreeing to recognise the winners of the FIDE knockout events as world champions in return for a payment of $50,000.

In April 2001, however, Karpov, along with Kasparov and Kramnik, wrote an open letter to FIDE complaining about "unilateral decisions made by FIDE". In particular, "policy changes regarding the official time controls, their treatment of the history of the World Championship, and their open hostility toward the organisers of traditional events". The three Ks called themselves the 12th, 13th and 14th world champions, which went against Karpov's promise to recognise the FIDE titleholders, as Kramnik won the title from Kasparov outside FIDE auspices.

Karpov has been far from consistent in his dealings with Kirsan Ilyumzhinov's FIDE. He was happy to cooperate when they provided favourable conditions for him to obtain the world title in 1996, when he played Gata Kamsky, and again when they seeded him to the final of the knockout event. It appears that he is not troubled by questions of principle, only money. But that is nothing unusual in the world of professional chess.

Karpov's rating was down to 2690 in 2002 and he was the 17th-strongest player in the world, according to FIDE. However, in 2002 he also reached the final of the new FIDE Grand Prix in Dubai, beating Kramnik, Morozevich and Shirov en route, and losing only to Anand in the final. Karpov was still active in politics, signing a petition along with more than 100 other prominent Russians calling for the restoration of the death penalty in Russia.

From time to time I'd go to a "chess editors' night out" at a cosy Italian restaurant, Attilio's, with Jimmy Adams, photographer Mark Huba, *Kingpin* editor Jon Manley, and assorted hangers-on. One such gatecrasher was Tim Wall, who had moved from Newcastle to London to take over as deputy editor of *British Chess Magazine* from Adam Raoof. Tim was a FIDE master who remained perpetually a few rating points away from the international master title. After our first encounter at Attilio's we saw each other at tournaments and started dating.

For a while it was fun to have a chess-playing boyfriend. He was on a team in the 4NCL (Four Nations Chess League) and we would spend occasional weekends in Birmingham, where the 4NCL met. While he sweated over the board, I'd gather gossip from Britain's top players for *ChessMoves*. We also went to Ghent in Belgium to play in a tournament, and on the same trip Australian GM Ian Rogers generously let us stay in his flat in Amsterdam. We visited the Max Euwe Centre and the famous Dutch chess cafés.

Sometimes Tim and I had arguments over petty chess publishing issues. It was hardly surprising, as we were working for rival magazines. Although I was only a freelance contributor to *CHESS*, I was rather prolific. My next subject was London's historic Metropolitan Chess Club, past and present. Jimmy accompanied me to the interview with Jack Moore, asking several questions inspired by his encyclopaedic knowledge of British chess, and, in particular, the London chess scene.

That Was Then...
(*CHESS*, March 1998)

All chess players like to think they are still improving, even when their finest years are long gone. Jack Moore might be expected to have reached his peak some time ago, but apparently he intends to go further. "I'm getting better at blitz chess!" he told me excitedly at the Metropolitan Congress last autumn. "I came second in our club lightning tournament." Not bad for a nonagenarian. "I used to hope God would let me live until I'm 93, when it's the millennium," said Moore, "but now I've decided I want to stay alive until I finish my novel, and that could take a lot longer."

Moore celebrated his 91st birthday on New Year's Day this year. At his council flat in Hackney, east London, he delved into his memory to recount some stories from his long life, in which chess has been his constant companion. He worked hard in his job, got married and brought up two children, but he was lucky enough to have another family, too... the Metropolitan Chess Club, which he joined in 1932. Moore has been president of Metropolitan since 1979. He was club champion in 1978, aged 71.

Moore took up chess during a childhood illness. "But for the trouble my leg caused through my young days – osteomyelitis, inflammation of the bone – I am certain I'd have been playing football or cricket and not chess," he said. "I was in Queen Mary's Hospital for Children in Surrey in 1921. I learnt chess there and made friends with a boy called Victor Claremont, who was in the bed next to me."

Later Claremont would play a significant role in Moore's life. When they met, Moore already spoke with a French accent, a tinge of which he has kept to this day. At the age of seven he had been sent to live with his French grandmother in Bordeaux, in the hope that good food and good air would cure him of his illness. "My mother had five children in five years, which was why my grandmother thought she could look after me better. We used to live in Worthing, and two doctors told me independently that children who lived at the seaside were more liable to osteomyelitis." Moore stayed in France until he was 12, but the illness didn't go away. When he left, he had to relearn English.

"My father was a naval officer," said Moore. "I pride myself that I come from a mixture of middle-class and peasant stock. The peasant stock allowed me to live to this age – my mother lived until she was 96. When my father was invalided from the navy he went bicycling in France with a friend, right down to a seaside resort in the south. He met my mother, who left the village, which was a scandal because you weren't allowed to leave without permission from a priest. And it was a great scandal to go off with a foreigner. My father's pension was enough for him to get a three-bedroom house."

Moore's health problems recurred in 1926 and he went into hospital again: this time St. Joseph's in Surrey. He stayed there for three years. "In the next bed there was a really good player from Manchester Chess Club. He taught me to play chess properly. Not only the moves, but he made me love the game, the beauty of the game. He had something wrong with one side and he could only lie on his other side. Once I beat him because he couldn't see a piece that could take his queen. It made him angry. I beat everyone in the hospital, because they hadn't been taught by him. He taught me so well that I hated losing. Unfortunately, he died."

When Moore finally came out of the hospital he was still limping badly and had to use crutches. He wanted to take up chess seriously, so he went to Lewisham Town Hall and enquired about clubs in the area. "I was in Lewisham because my father got work at Woolwich Arsenal. These were the Depression years. Money was losing its value and they didn't up pensions," Moore explained.

At the town hall someone suggested that Moore should pay a visit to a certain E.G.R. Cordingley, who knew a thing or two about chess. In fact, Cordingley was a pioneer in chess publishing. He ran a small chess shop in Cecil Court, Leicester Square, in the heart of London's West End. At the back of the shop there was a duplicating machine, on which he patiently, if laboriously, produced his own limited-edition tournament books and magazine.

Moore went over to Cordingley's home in southeast London and had a game with him. "I'd swotted up a game as Black from the first edition of *Modern Chess Openings*, and the first 15 moves went exactly as they were supposed to – then he was all over me!" Moore played Cordingley on a few more occasions in a Lyons tearoom. "They used to provide us with a chessboard and we met up at Lyons' until somebody rumbled that we were spending a whole evening on one cup of tea."

Moore became a subscriber to Cordingley's publications, joining a distinguished group whose names were printed in a list at the front of every numbered copy, including C.H.O'D. Alexander, Sir George Thomas and Harry Golombek. Moore sold most of his Cordingley books to the *British Chess Magazine* in the 1950s when he was "strapped for cash", keeping only two. Today they stand on a shelf alongside various classic best games collections and openings books, in various languages, including Boleslavsky's *Selected Games* translated by *CHESS* editor Jimmy Adams, which was a prize for defeating Adams in a simul in 1990.

Through Cordingley, Moore found out about St. Mark's Chess Club in Lewisham. "St. Mark's was in a small crypt. It wasn't cold at all. There were 12 to 14 members. A Captain Dickinson ran it. Then he committed suicide and killed his wife, probably because his pension wasn't enough for them to live on." Moore still owns an original, if battered, Jaques chess set with heavy wooden pieces that he bought from the club for £1. There is a metal plaque on the top of the box engraved with a dedication to a club member who died in the First World War.

The sudden demise of St. Mark's meant that Moore had to look for another club. The Metropolitan Club was advertising itself in *British Chess Magazine*. "Around the same time that I saw the ad, Victor Claremont started up on his own in a business which manufactured leather handbags," said Moore. "He offered me a job. I went to live in Homerton [east London] and I worked there for 37 years. I became partners with Victor. By coincidence the number 22 bus went from Homerton to Holborn, near the Metropolitan Club. For three years I worked from eight a.m. until nine p.m., but on chess nights I left early – at six o'clock."

The worn jeans and moth-eaten jumpers of today's congress players would strike deeply at the pre-war Metropolitan Club member's refined dress sense. "The Metropolitan Club was a leftover from the Victorian days," Moore recalled. "You never saw anything but neckties and wing collars on the players, always a jacket, never any laxity in clothing." No one knew what anybody else in the club did for a living, and they certainly weren't aware of their opponent's first name, even if they had played the same person every week for 10 years.

"Formal address was Mr. Moore and informal was Moore. Most of the club members were elderly men. At 24 when I joined, I was young, there was no such thing as teenagers in chess clubs. You didn't get to your best until you were in your thirties." Mr. Moore was greeted on his first Saturday afternoon session at Metropolitan by Mr. A. Louis, a key member who had joined in 1910, was match captain from 1923 to 1945, and would be club president after the war until his death in 1949.

As Moore writes in his recent book *A History of the Metropolitan Chess Club*, Mr. Louis "was a tall man in his early fifties, with a large presence and curious way of walking which I remember describing to myself as rather crab-like! However, he was most pleasant, asked me if I had played much chess, and getting the reply that I had been playing in Kentish competitions, found me an opponent who, he warned me, 'would make me give a good account of myself'. I don't recall his name, but getting a win in one game and a draw in another, you could say my fortune was made – in a manner of speaking – for the next thing I knew was that I had been picked for the first team and was never to leave it for well over 40 years!"

At this time the Metropolitan's premises were at the Food Reform Restaurant, 2-3 Furnival Street, Holborn. The building no longer exists – it has been replaced by a modern block of shops and offices. Wooden chessboards were clamped over the dining tables and had to be stowed away after each club meeting. "There were 20 boards in those days and I was on Board 13 or 14," said Moore. In 1936 he faced the toughest opponent of his club career up until then, American GM Reuben Fine, who gave a simul at Metropolitan after participating in a tournament in England that year.

The Fine simul was sponsored by club member Mrs. Shannon, the widow of a ship owner. Her enthusiasm for chess was not matched by her ability. In *A History of the Metropolitan Chess Club*, Moore describes her as "a very moderate player" who was in the club championship of 1937 only because of her financial generosity. "In similar circumstances, today, I doubt whether there would be any quibbles either," Moore writes. "But that wasn't my state of mind when ruefully contemplating the scoreboard after my bad start." Mrs. Shannon approached him and said, "Don't be discouraged, Mr. Moore, I'm sure you'll do better in time." She was quite right – Moore cheered himself up by beating her in 12 moves.

Mrs. Shannon was not discouraged either, sponsoring a simul by Samuel Reshevsky the following year, in which Moore also played and lost. The Metropolitan was one of the top clubs in the first division of the London League, but its best players caused few problems for the visiting grandmasters. Fine won 31 games and drew four; Reshevsky won 33, lost two and drew one. "They only stopped for a few seconds at each board," Moore said. "They'd seen it all before."

The Food Reform Restaurant was sold in 1938 and the Metropolitan Club had to relocate to a large cellar below Keen's Restaurant in Portugal Street, Kingsway. This was an unpleasant environment with little ventilation, and club members were very unhappy with it, but high rents prevented them from moving somewhere better. It also broke with tradition because it was outside the city boundary.

The club's poor premises, its financial problems and the opening of the National Chess Centre in Cavendish Square, obviously a competitor, were a cause of serious worry in 1939. But world events soon overshadowed all this. Moore entered one of the last pre-war chess congresses, at Brighton. "I played six training games with Vera Menchik for five shillings a game. I lost five and won one. She was very cautious in the opening, so I managed to survive, and all the games were about 40 moves long. I also played her sister Olga, who was weaker." The women's world champion and her sister were killed by a bomb during the Blitz in 1944.

Blackout conditions prevented the Metropolitan from meeting on Thursday evenings, but Saturday afternoon sessions continued for the first few months of the war. The last committee meeting took place on May 25, 1940; then the club shut down altogether – because opening on a Saturday was considered too expensive. Moore joined Hampstead Chess Club, which did continue to meet on Saturday afternoons.

Attitudes were changing rapidly. "I remember waiting for an opponent in a match at Hampstead. A chap came in – hair down, casual clothing, and, horror of horrors, bare feet and sandals. I thought, he's not going to play me, is he? He was." However, Hampstead did preserve the tradition of preparing score sheets in advance with the players' names already written on them.

Moore won the Hampstead Championship in 1946. He had become a strong player and estimates that his grade in the 1950s was probably around 190. "I was a great analyser. Only twice in my life was I ever outplayed in an adjourned game. In the '30s there was a rule that you shouldn't look at an adjourned game at all, but I couldn't trust that my opponent was observing the rule, so I didn't. But we were more polite in those days. Even in the '50s if you saw your opponent might have gone to sleep, you warned them about time trouble."

Moore studied the games of Alekhine and Capablanca. "Capablanca was a cautious player, which is why he drew so many games, but he never made an error. Simplicity was his style and I try to be simple. It doesn't always work, you also have to be aggressive with unusual moves."

The Metropolitan Club reopened after the war at St. Bride's Institute and Moore returned to it. "St. Bride's was old-fashioned," he said. "There were long tables, everybody smoked – pipes, cigars, cigarettes – I was the only one who didn't. It's a wonder I haven't got lung cancer. It stank of tobacco; it was impregnated with smoke. I think the place was whitewashed once. The heating was abysmal; it made a roar. The British Chess Problem Society met there and had a glass-fronted cabinet in the room, packed with books."

Moore's wife reluctantly tolerated his passion for chess. She died more than 30 years ago. "She didn't play chess. I don't think she was too happy about me playing chess, leaving her with two children in the evenings, but I made a point that I would pack it in if she wanted me to."

After his long career with Victor Claremont at the leather handbag firm, which was put out of business by competition from plastics, Moore moved to a travel agency and then to a firm that made baby seats and ventilation and heating systems for buses. "I retired at the age of 77, perfectly fit, but suddenly fed up of getting up at 6:30 a.m. instead of when I wanted to."

Moore continues to play matches for Metropolitan. He still attends club nights and played in the Metropolitan Championship last summer for what he swore was the last time, although younger members should beware a centenary comeback. In the Metropolitan Congress a couple of years ago he stood in when someone's opponent didn't turn up and won the game – against the reigning British veterans' champion.

Never out of touch with modern developments, Moore was introduced to chess computers by his son-in-law, who had bought a second-hand one. "This was about 15 years ago. Computers were in infancy; some couldn't even castle. It got my king in a corner. I wasn't playing too seriously. It was going round and round trying to mate me, when all it had to do was push a passed pawn, so I showed it what to do."

The Metropolitan Club today is very far removed from the club that Moore joined as a young man. "It has changed absolutely. All those weekend tournaments sprang up after the Fischer-Spassky match, gradings came in – traditions ended. Before the weekend tournaments, strong players used to come to the clubs to get practice. These days there is matey talk at the Metropolitan Club, lots of young people. It's what life is now, more friendly. More noisy, except when matches are playing. It's a different atmosphere. I don't mind it; all I want is for the membership to keep up."

As for the crime novel that Moore is staying alive to finish, well, it's coming along slowly. He has a copy of *One Way to Write Your Novel* on his bookshelf to help with the tricky parts. "I never had any English schooling because I was in France and in hospital – I go over my drafts several times," said Moore. "I have to fit it in around the chess, the cooking and the shopping. I have deliberately kept away from chess players in the novel, but I have made use of my French grandmother, a seamstress. A husband and wife with no children have a very rich cousin who knows painters in Paris, including Van Gogh. The cousin was going to marry this young woman, but he had an unfortunate injury in the 1870 war with the Germans and she married another man. The cousin had a deep grudge. He recommended Van Gogh to paint her portrait, to get his own back. She hated the painting and hid it away. It disappears in the war."

Wait for Moore's book to find out what happens next… publication will be sometime in the next millennium.

...This Is Now
(*CHESS*, March 1998)

Rasul Bagirov follows in the footsteps of Sir George Thomas, William Winter and other celebrated names as Metropolitan club champion. One of the opponents he beat last summer was Jack Moore. But Bagirov had to return his trophy after six months because he was heading home to Baku, the capital of Azerbaijan, having completed an M.Sc. in Health Science and Hospital Management at the South Bank University.

Growing up in Kiev (he is half-Ukrainian), Bagirov was fanatical about chess, playing and studying constantly throughout his schooldays. He became a candidate master, but gave up altogether when he entered university to study medicine. His family had already moved to Baku, where his father was one of the country's leading heart surgeons. After graduation in 1992, Bagirov had to do a year's national service in the army. Unfortunately, Azerbaijan was at war with Armenia over the disputed territory of Nagorno-Karabakh, so Bagirov was flung straight into the front lines.

Smiling as if he were describing a holiday in the Bahamas, Bagirov told me how he narrowly escaped death time after time. "Once we were being bombed from a mountain, the enemy was directing bombs to us. Everyone was trying to get away, and a tank nearly reversed over a sleeping man because the driver was in a panic. It stopped inches away from him. I had to see if anything was broken, and a bomb fell next to us. He wasn't hurt, but he was petrified when he woke up. He couldn't move."

Driving away from the war zone was just as hazardous. "I was in a military car and we couldn't stop, it was raining and we were skidding in the mountains. It was an open car. It couldn't brake or turn. We were falling down the mountain, but luckily there were three trees. The first and second tree broke. The third tree was a big one. The car turned over. We didn't go very far downwards. I was thrown out of the car. I looked around and nobody was there. I was thinking, so I realised I must be alive.

"The others came to me, they helped me. I stood up. I could make some steps. So that was a really happy end. But then we came to the road and stopped a car. A driver pulled up with lots of sacks of potatoes in the back, which we lay on. At a checkpoint some soldiers searched the sacks, and it turned out they were full of grenades and Kalashnikovs. The car had been bumping and we could have exploded at any minute – we were lucky again."

Some people would turn into nervous wrecks after all that, but not Bagirov. He doesn't even drink or smoke. In another traumatic incident, he was blamed by a patient for causing a life-threatening injury. "A soldier came to me saying he was afraid that he would be killed the next day. He wanted me to give him a medical exemption from fighting, but I couldn't, because then all the other soldiers would do the same thing. The next day I was helping people with first aid. I saw that guy. He was wounded in the worst way, in the abdomen. He said, 'I told you something would happen.'

"We brought all the patients to the car. He was sitting near me because he needed the most attention. We were 30 km from the hospital. It was night, the road was very bad, this guy was suffering from pain. I gave him three shots of morphine. He couldn't breathe normally. Again he said, 'I told you this would happen.' The car was very slow. He was dying in my arms. I thought we would never get there, but we did. He had lost a lot of blood, but they treated him in the hospital and he became quiet and happy. I never saw him again, but someone told me later that he saw the guy in the streets of Baku, so he probably survived.

"After the war I lost my fear," said Bagirov. Judging by his subsequent chess results, this applies to chess as well as life. The British Council sponsored him to come to England in 1996, and he didn't find his studies too demanding, so he started playing again. Bagirov had assisted his father as a heart surgeon for a while, but corruption forced them to leave their jobs. "There was a very rapid commercialisation of medicine in Azerbaijan – people had to pay for treatment, sell cars, furniture, sometimes houses. My father, as head of cardiac surgery, had to take this money and pass it to someone else; eventually it went to the president. We refused to participate in this destructive way of life."

The pressures of living in London were not so great. All Bagirov had to worry about was completing his 20,000-word dissertation on time and finding Black's reply to 1. d4 c5 2. d5. For most of the time when he was in England he didn't have a chess set at his house; when he finally borrowed one from the Metropolitan Club towards the end of his stay, he was so pleased that he sat up all night analysing. Like Jack Moore, he discovered the club accidentally. Not understanding the British grading system, he decided to enter the Minor section of the Metropolitan Congress. "My first opponent was graded 89. I got to a winning position and then I relaxed. But I found a beautiful way to draw. Then I realised that my opponents weren't so strong – I won the next four games." For sharing 1st-2nd place, Bagirov was awarded membership in the Metropolitan Club.

Bagirov's next congress was at International Students' House, where he boldly entered the Major section. He shared 2nd-3rd prize. "There is a very big difference between the level of playing here and in Ukraine or Azerbaijan – it's a much higher level there," he said. Scoring 0/5 in the Open section of a rapidplay didn't deter Bagirov, and he went on to score 3/5 in the Open section of the Islington Congress two days before he went home. By then he had a grade of 175, which he expects will be higher next year. He was extremely successful in his matches for Metropolitan, beating several players graded around 200. His best achievement was his win against IM Colin Crouch.

While Bagirov's medical speciality is the heart, his hobby is the head. He is very interested in psychology, and in particular the way that external appearances affect the personality. So he sizes up his opponents from the moment they walk into the room. "I'm using the Lasker approach," he said. "Some people prefer open positions, a lot of tactics; some prefer closed positions. You have to use what people don't like. With patients you look at how he behaves, what he looks like, what his build is – and the opponent is like a patient.

"People have different metabolisms. Tall and thin people don't have a strong nervous system – they're more like artistic people. You have to be very strong in what you're doing when you play them, confident, and they will be hesitant. People who are stronger looking can become overconfident. You have to be more subtle with them. Try to use something interesting, original, not standard. They will be sure everything is all right. They go into your trap and the door is closed."

The different shapes of foreheads also give away a lot, according to Bagirov. "You can understand the way people are thinking. If the forehead is broad and not very high, they have a lot of interests, but they don't go very deeply into things. In a chess game they are considering a lot of variations, but not very deeply. People with a high, narrow forehead analyse a few variations in depth. Don't try to calculate for 10 moves against this type of forehead. Choose something not so obvious." So, what did Bagirov learn from the forehead of Colin Crouch? "He has a well-proportioned face, so this approach didn't work with him."

Several other factors have to be taken into account. "Some people come straight from work, they didn't eat properly, they're tired – so it's better to play a game which will continue for a longer time. A junior has a very big advantage because you will feel very bad if you lose. Like when Kasparov was playing Karpov, even if Kasparov lost, he would have another chance to win. The pressure is on older people. But young people don't use any psychology – it's pure chess. That makes the game easier. You have to play to the end. They sometimes relax and think they have won, but in the end they will make a mistake. They can't concentrate for the whole game. They lose interest when the opponent is thinking."

Bagirov's ambitions in life are limitless. He speaks five languages: Russian, Ukrainian, Spanish, Azerbaijani and English – and he hopes to become "at least an IM", although he doubts that he will have much time for chess in the near future. He would like to build the first private hospital in Baku, subsidised by money from oil companies. The subject of his dissertation was a feasibility study for the hospital. "The idea is to break the monopoly of the Ministry of Health," he said. "Doctors get $10 a month in Azerbaijan."

More realistically, Bagirov might come back to England in March to take an exam which would qualify him to practise as a doctor in this country, but that would mean starting again at the lowest level, while in Azerbaijan he is already a surgeon.

"I'm still very unclear about what I'll do in the future," Bagirov admitted. "Rasul is an Arabic name. Ra means sun, sul – messenger, so I'm a messenger of the sun – but I don't know what the message is yet!"

Rasul, who was 28 when we met (three years older than me), became my friend for the short time he had left in London. We went to the Islington Congress and a Christmas party together. Little did I know that in 1999 I would be working for the BBC in Azerbaijan. Rasul introduced me to his parents, his girlfriend, his sister and his brother-in-law, who took me and another BBC journalist on a trip to the southern region bordering Iran. Rasul had a job in the health section of the World Bank; his father was writing novels based on his depressing experiences as a Soviet and post-Soviet doctor. Rasul's ambition was to become president of Azerbaijan. But he is probably too honest for that.

Some of my chess writing experiences were pure fun. The generous organisers of the Kilkenny Congress in Ireland invited me to report on their event, and put me and Tim up in a luxury hotel. The following article resulted.

If You Ever Go Across the Sea to Ireland...
Remember to Bring a Set and Clock!
(*CHESS*, February 1999)

There's something about Irish chess that makes it slightly different from the staid and formal game we are accustomed to in England. Our more inflexible arbiters would probably keel over in shock at some of the practices I witnessed during my short stay in Kilkenny. And they might as well remain under the table, as that's where the Guinness is going to take them eventually. But if you don't take chess (or life) too seriously, and you've spent years searching for the perfect tournament... then Kilkenny, like the beverage that is indispensable to it, is well worth the wait.

Certainly you need patience to play in Kilkenny, at least if you're languishing in the U1550 section (the James Mason Challenge). Participants in the exalted Masters started the first round reasonably on time, in the plush surroundings of Butler House hotel's conference room. Down the road, in the bar room of the Club House hotel, there was absolute chaos.

"This is completely normal!" shouted Rod McShane, Luke's dad, over the din of people chatting and playing blitz. It was ten past eight on Friday evening, the round should have started at 7:30, and the computer had made a mess of the pairings. When we eventually got going, the organisers gave us 90 minutes for all our moves instead of 105 minutes; otherwise some games would have finished in the early hours.

I was sheepishly hoping that my schoolboy opponent had the sense to bring a set and clock, unlike myself. How was I supposed to know? OK, so "Bring a set and clock" was clearly printed on the entry form, but I thought this was some kind of Irish joke. It was Catch-22: if I lugged my equipment over from England, I assumed I would find all the boards set up when I arrived, and everyone would laugh at me. Instead, everyone laughed at me (in my tortured imagination) because I had to sit at an empty table until each opponent turned up. My second opponent was half an hour late, but I couldn't take advantage, as there was no clock to start.

The stupid ones like me who rely on their opponents usually get a standard clock and roll-up board with plastic pieces; in unfortunate cases you might get stuck with a digital game timer that you can't understand, and you could end up playing on an ornate wooden set from Eastern Europe with a queen and king that look exactly the same, or even someone's chess computer. In other words, when in Ireland, *bring a set and clock*.

When you finally get hold of a clock, you can put it on whichever side of the board you prefer. None of that rubbish about Black's right-hand side. "We like everyone to express themselves, it's part of the craic," explained Jack Lowry, who "is to chess tournament organisation what Rembrandt is to violin-making", according to the website of Kilkenny Chess Club. He "makes Attila the Hun look like Shirley Temple", but "gets more work done for the club in a week than anyone else could manage in a day."

And he's honest, too. "Doesn't Jim Hayes help run the tournament?" I asked Lowry. "No, he doesn't do anything," he said. Hayes is Kilkenny's bard, romanticising the event with his enthralling stories of the misty past – some of which have been published in *CHESS* – while Lowry is the mover and shaker, as successful at inviting ex-world champions as he is at putting up posters.

Lowry spends most of the year hunting, fishing and working in his shop, Jack Lowry's Carpet World, but in November chess is all that matters. His attitude towards the players is brutally egalitarian. While the lucky invitees may get a luxury hotel room and free food, their social skills will be tested to the limits. Grandmasters who prefer to shun the crowds, stay sober and spend every evening analysing on a computer won't be invited back, no matter how famous they are. Popular guys like Michael Adams, Michael Hennigan, William Watson, Daniel King and Stuart Conquest return time and time again.

"Mickey Adams enjoys it here," said Lowry. "He's one of our own now, he's a Kilkenny man – he relaxes. Conquest, Watson and King are the same, tremendous for mixing and talking with people. This is what we half-expect them to do." This year Adams couldn't make it because he was ill, so former British champion Hennigan gave the traditional post-tournament high-speed simul against the organisers.

The superstar who established Kilkenny's reputation was Boris Spassky, who visited in 1991, to celebrate the club's 21st anniversary. "He had to look for Ireland on a map," Lowry said. Spassky reportedly told his hosts that his only blunder in Kilkenny was drinking too many Irish coffees! In return for entertaining Ireland's chess players with his good-humoured repartee and a couple of simuls, Spassky was rewarded with the post of honorary president of Kilkenny Chess Club, something he had dreamt about all his life, he claimed.

"He was a great man to talk to, a real gentleman, but also a real professional," said Lowry, who now corresponds with Spassky. "We get birthday and Christmas cards from him; I send over a smoked salmon occasionally," he added.

Thanks to the publicity generated by Spassky, the Kilkenny Congress has grown bigger and bigger, with 220 people playing this year, the most ever. The playing venues can no longer cope with more expansion. Essential sponsorship is provided by Iona Technologies and Eamon Keogh. "Iona is one of the bright lights of the Irish computer industry," said Lowry. "It's only five or six years old, but it's quoted on the stock exchange here and in America. The company is based in Dublin. My son was working with them and he approached them for sponsorship two years ago. I'm hoping to get them involved more in Irish chess."

The other sponsor, 54-year-old Eamon Keogh, also makes his money from computer software (he has his own company), and he is one of Ireland's great chess players. Not that he looks like someone who has spent much of his life hunched over a chessboard, deep in thought: he's a bulky man with huge shoulders who could probably head-butt an unwanted opponent through the nearest window.

When Keogh sat down at my table in the bar, accidentally knocking a glass onto the floor, drawling, "Are you a bad chess player?" and trying to grab my notebook, I made my excuses. But the next evening I braced myself and asked him for an interview.

"Do you want larger than life, or...?" Keogh enquired jovially. There didn't seem to be an alternative. A few minutes later he was slapping his knee and singing an Irish folk song. Only after that was he ready to start reminiscing about his glory days at the board. "I could have been a chess professional after the World Junior in 1961," he said, "but my mum didn't think I should. And you must always obey mum." Nevertheless, Keogh was Irish champion twice in the 1970s and represented his country in three Olympiads: Tel Aviv 1964, Havana 1966 and Haifa 1976.

In Tel Aviv Keogh became the first Irishman to beat a grandmaster, apart from the late *British Chess Magazine* editor Brian Reilly, who beat Reuben Fine in 1935 when the title hadn't been invented. Keogh defeated the Swedish player Gideon Stahlberg, but not without incident. If he had drawn or lost, Sweden would have gone through to the final round. A win meant that the home team, Israel, would qualify instead. When the game was adjourned, the entire Israeli team descended on Keogh's hotel room to help him analyse. Everybody agreed that Keogh had a winning position, but he got very nervous and phoned Stahlberg at 2 a.m. to offer a draw. Stahlberg didn't answer, so Keogh had to turn up the next morning and he won nine moves later.

At the Havana Olympiad, Keogh chatted with Bobby Fischer and was given $2,000 worth of Cuban money by another American player, Donald Byrne, when he left the island. He played in a giant open-air simul and just managed to finish all his games before the event was rained off. Keogh believes his experience at Olympiads could be put to use by the England team. "Julian Hodgson rang me up and asked me to take over as captain," he claims.

More seriously, Keogh is concentrating these days on supporting Irish chess rather than playing the game. He was instrumental in bringing Spassky to Kilkenny, and also David Bronstein. Keogh was crushing Bronstein in a blitz game, but offered a draw, which Bronstein accepted. In Bronstein's simul that followed, the benevolent Russian offered a draw whenever *he* got a winning position. All his opponents accepted, "but everyone knew the real result of their game," said Keogh.

With backing and encouragement from Keogh, Russian GM Alexander Baburin has made his home in Ireland. Keogh thinks that bringing titled players to Ireland from abroad can only benefit Irish chess. Some Irish players disagree, however. Baburin, 31, is extremely good-natured and doesn't like to complain, but he admits there have been problems. He has played for Ireland just once, at the Yerevan Olympiad in 1996.

"I get on really well with most of the guys in the team," Baburin says, "but a couple of players are very unhappy because they are in a shaky position, they have less chance of being selected because of me. Some others think I shouldn't be allowed to play on principle, because I'm not Irish."

Baburin met Keogh at the Capelle-la-Grande tournament in France, in 1993. "He had the idea of inviting someone to deal with the Irish team, and with juniors," Baburin explains. "Then I started to have private pupils." Irish players have to pay for their own travel to Olympiads, so Baburin went to Yerevan with financial help from Keogh, but he wasn't keen on going to the Kalmyk capital, Elista. "I felt Elista would be unpleasant, unsafe. I thought they wouldn't manage everything up to a decent standard." ·

Being the top player in a small country is very different from Baburin's early chess life, as one of several very talented Soviet juniors. Baburin was born in Nizhny Novgorod and his contemporaries were people like Dreev, Ulybin, Ibragimov and Shcherbakov. "I should have been more ambitious when I was younger, I should have been more hard-working. Maybe I never believed in myself too much. The experience of being with Dreev and the others was a little bit off-putting," he said.

Athletically built, Baburin could have been a sportsman. "I used to play a lot of basketball at school – for a while it was a question whether I would play basketball or chess. Between the ages of six and 10 I was a very good swimmer. I had to quit because I came across a very stupid doctor. I had a problem with my knee and he told me to stop. Later people told me that swimming would have been good for me."

A loss for physical sport was a gain for chess. When Baburin came to Ireland he was an international master with a rating of 2550; he had missed a grandmaster norm by half a point in 1992. "When I arrived here my results came down, I had to learn a few things in life," he said. Although he spoke English, having taken a correspondence course with the Institute of Foreign Languages, Baburin had to adapt to different customs, such as "the necessity to work". Also, he found that the Irish tend to meet in pubs, while Russians like to socialise at each other's homes.

"I felt homesick for a while," said Baburin. "I had to learn how to manage my own time, how to deal with people, potential students, the ability to sell yourself." Baburin has succeeded in those aspects of his life, but he has never managed to grasp the attractions of Ireland's answer to vodka. "I hate Guinness," he said. "I've been told you need to drink 100 pints in order to appreciate it, but I can't survive that many. I like Kilkenny bitter, though," he added diplomatically.

Baburin now lives in Dublin with his wife Elena and children Ivan, nine, and Anastasia, four, and he intends to apply for Irish citizenship. "I am starting to take life a little bit easier now. I used to be a lot more tense," he said. "In 1995 I basically learnt how to deal with my students. Although I had taught some chess in Russia, I never did it on a formal basis. By 1995 I had established a network of students, I knew how to handle it, and I felt I had to come back to playing chess. I changed my approach. Instead of playing one tournament and doing badly, I would play three tournaments in a row, using the first one as a warm-up. I also decided to only go in for strong tournaments."

Baburin achieved grandmaster norms in Groningen and Copenhagen, and finally qualified for the title in Yerevan. "After Yerevan I had even better results," he said. "Exactly the same thing happened when I got my Russian master title – it's psychological."

Along with playing and coaching, Baburin also sells antiquarian chess books, which he buys in Russia, and he has been doing some writing of his own recently. He has a column on middlegames in *ChessBase* magazine, a column on endgames in the American magazine *Inside Chess*, he has written two *Trends* booklets and he has just finished a book for Batsford which took him three years, called *Winning Pawn Structures*. He thinks publishers should be more honest with the titles of their books. "I don't like this 'winning', as if there should be winners everywhere," he says. "If I wrote a book about Alekhine's Defence, I would probably call it *Survival with Alekhine's Defence*."

Unfortunately Baburin didn't survive with Alekhine's Defence in his game against Luke McShane: in fact he lost to Luke for the third time in Kilkenny, having gone down in smoke a week previously at the 4NCL and also been defeated ignominiously in Cambridge when Luke was 12 years old. "It's becoming a psychological problem," Baburin said. "Apart from McShane and Adams I have very good results against English players. I have this feeling that English grandmasters tend to be casual about their moves – you have to check them, there could be something wrong. But of all the grandmasters in the world, the English are probably the best educated, you can actually talk about things other than chess with them. I think they're champions in this respect."

One of the reasons for the sloppiness of English players is their enthusiasm for weekend tournaments, Baburin believes. "I quit playing weekenders one or two years ago – it does certain damage to your chess. And the prize money is lousy." Baburin describes his style of chess as "rather technical, solid". He doesn't go so far as to call his own chess boring, but neither does he portray it as wild and exciting. "A few weeks ago I was in Austria, working with Smirin and Psakhis," he said. "Smirin was telling me about someone annotating his game 'dubious move – typical Smirin'. Typical me wouldn't sound nice, I'd have to sue the guy."

Baburin had the opportunity to speak some Russian in Kilkenny this year, as his compatriot Sergei Tiviakov came over (also to fall victim to Luke McShane), and so did Zhanna Lazehevskaya, a 14-year-old girl who has been awarded the first Kasparov Scholarship to Oakham School in Leicestershire. Jack Lowry invited her, but he forgot about the rather significant matter of an Irish visa. At the last minute, he rang the relevant government department and asked if it would be OK for a Russian teenager to come in without a visa, as she was urgently needed for the Kilkenny Masters. Not entirely unsurprisingly, the government didn't consider her case to be a top priority matter of state. But they hadn't reckoned on Lowry's gift for the blarney. He insisted that Zhanna was going to be interviewed by national TV, radio and all the papers – and a visa was instantly provided.

Zhanna comes from the closed city of Gregorny, which is home to a nuclear processing centre where both her parents work. She has been under-18 Urals champion and she was enrolled at the Kasparov Chess Academy in Podolsk when she was selected to study at Oakham, a private school that is renowned for its chess. A coach at the academy talked to Kasparov about her, and she was chosen. "I was one of the best in my year," she says. "I think Kasparov is the best chess player in the world, I like him," she added.

Zhanna's father and grandfather were both strong players and she started playing "seriously" at the age of seven. "I've wanted to be a professional chess player since about two years ago," Zhanna said. "My most difficult game was the first game in the Minsk Open, when I played against the Ukrainian Under-12 champion, and I drew. He was rated 2400 so I was very happy." Zhanna's favourite player used to be Veselin Topalov, but now it is Peter Svidler, and she also admires Vladimir Kramnik.

Despite the economic crisis in Russia, there are some things that Zhanna misses. "The food at Oakham is not so good as at home," she said. "The crisis wasn't so bad in my town – it was much worse in larger cities, where people panicked." On the other hand, "We had stricter teachers in Russia." Zhanna is already getting plenty of high-level chess experience in England: she plays for Wood Green in the second division of the 4NCL.

The story of chess in Kilkenny wouldn't be complete without talking to the town's most avid chess book collector and supreme socialite, Jim Hayes. The organisers gave me a bottle of wine on condition I didn't repeat anything that Hayes said, but sadly that instruction had to be ignored in the public interest. Sporting a natty white moustache and cravat, Hayes claimed to be 54, but it was quickly pointed out by a "friend" that the Veterans' section for players over 60 had been introduced to the congress this year because Hayes was eligible to play in it. He didn't take up the offer, though, as he prefers to stand back and cast an amused eye over the proceedings.

Hayes stopped playing chess two years ago when he opened a shoe shop called Sole Comfort. "When I get the nuns in I call it Soul Comfort!" he confided. His real passion is collecting – he owns some of the oldest and most valuable chess books in existence. "I have three or four thousand books," he said. "I'm going to catalogue them soon and make my library available to people. A book is valuable not for its content, but for the feel of it, the heft of it, the talent that went into it – the bookbinder's craft, the printer's craft. The best reason for acquiring a book is to preserve it – you're a custodian. The prime criterion is that it should be scarce and worth preserving."

Part of the thrill of collecting is the hunt, tracking down a rare book and acquiring it for a fair price. The close-knit global community of chess book collectors all have their own contacts, and in recent years they have also been exchanging information via the Internet. "Anyone can be a chequebook collector," said Hayes. "But that's not interesting." One of Hayes' most prized possessions is an edition of Greco's book, of which there are probably only 15 in the world, and very few in private hands. Hayes' is the first printed edition, with a portrait of Charles II as a frontispiece, indicating that the printer was a Royalist. Hayes also has the autographs of every world champion – except for Steinitz, his next target.

In the spare few hours between talking to people, I managed to complete all six of my games. The starting times of each round got earlier and earlier, so there would be more precious drinking time. Several of the players in my section stretched Jack's notion of "expressing themselves" to the limits – one of my opponents stopped writing down the moves halfway through the game because he thought he'd lost (he went on to win); another took the pawn in front of my king with his queen, thinking he was mating me, and stuck out his hand to accept my resignation, but he hadn't noticed that I could take his queen with my bishop. "I didn't think you'd give the game away that easily," he said, and I went on to take the rest of his pieces before he finally resigned.

A few boards away from me, a player resigned, then his opponent showed him that he could have played on. "OK, I'll go here, then," he said, and the game continued until the original victor got fed up and claimed the win. But this kind of bizarre practice didn't surprise me any more. As the Irish know very well, not everything in black and white makes sense.

The Kilkenny Congress is as popular as ever, under Jack Lowry's stewardship. Boris Spassky was guest of honour again in 2001. Eamon Keogh still plays enthusiastically. Alexander Baburin writes prolifically and he played for Ireland again at the 2000 Olympiad in Istanbul. He runs the Internet's first daily chess newspaper, Chess Today. *Zhanna Lazhevskaya won the women's prize at Hastings 2000/2001 and is studying four subjects at A-level, as well as playing football for Oakham School girls' team. Jim Hayes has developed a new talent: he is now a published poet. He also helps Baburin conduct regular Internet auctions of rare and secondhand chess books.*

6. Making No Sacrifices

At first FIDE President Kirsan Ilyumzhinov was an enigma to me. Although I had been writing about the former Soviet Union for almost a decade, I had never heard of Kalmykia until Ilyumzhinov's role in chess brought the tiny Russian republic to my attention. I was even more intrigued when I found out the Kalmyks were Europe's only Buddhists, somehow living peacefully within a few hundred miles of war-torn Chechnya. Besides heading FIDE, 36-year-old Ilyumzhinov was also the president of the republic.

I was impressed when I heard that Ilyumzhinov was pledging millions of dollars to chess and readying Kalmykia to host the 1998 Olympiad. I became determined to see Kalmykia for myself, and meet Ilyumzhinov face to face. Fortunately, I could afford to travel there. I was working regularly for Arena, a publishing company that owned some in-flight magazines with titles like *CIS Today* and *North European Businessman*, and I was co-editing a book for Haymarket called *Winning Business Strategies on the Internet*.

My friend Amy Spurling, whose father had accidentally reintroduced me to chess, wanted to go with me to Kalmykia. She was also a freelance journalist writing

FIDE President Kirsan Ilyumzhinov congratulates world champion Ruslan Ponomariov.
Photo: Vladimir Barsky

mainly about the former Soviet Union. Then her rather nervous cousin Nicholas asked if he could come, too. He was a middle-aged photographer who rarely wandered far from his tranquil home town of Berkhamsted. We agreed to take Nicholas as long as he subsidised our flights.

We contacted the Kalmyk government by e-mail. They offered us accommodation with families in the capital, Elista, and promised to show us whatever we wanted to see. We flew from London to Moscow to Elista. Nicholas's suitcase got left behind at the stopover on the way to Moscow and we had no time to wait around for it. So his new-found lust for travel and adventure was somewhat dampened.

In addition to our chess-related interviews, we visited an orphanage and watched some traditional Kalmyk horse-riding events and dances. The orphanage was miserable. Most of the residents weren't orphans at all, but mentally or physically disabled kids who had been abandoned by their parents. They were so excited to meet us and happy to receive fistfuls of sweets. One older boy was quite smart, but hunchbacked, and it was obvious that he had a dismal future. At the bareback riding event we met two young guys who told us about their illegal caviar racket in neighbouring Astrakhan.

A monk showed us around the new Buddhist temple. Nicholas was unmoved: he said it was just like the one in Berkhamsted. The monk had been born in the United States to a Kalmyk family, who couldn't afford to raise him as he had so many brothers and sisters, so they sent him to monks in Nepal or India, and he eventually decided to live in Kalmykia. Amy and I enjoyed meeting this monk and other Kalmyks, but much of our time in Elista was spent sitting on the steps of the presidential palace, waiting for Ilyumzhinov to turn up. One day, while we were sitting there, he drove right to the door in his white Cadillac, followed by an armoured jeep, and walked past us. We followed him in. Our persistence paid off.

Unlike other offices in the building, Ilyumzhinov's was pristine, the polished desk adorned with Buddhist and Kalmyk artefacts. The president smiled and shook hands, but he was strangely tense, as if he were more afraid of us than we were of him. He appeared frail and childlike. Adding to the impression of vulnerability, he had his arm in a sling, having injured it playing tennis. Nicholas took photographs. After the interview, Ilyumzhinov signed a copy of his book for me. He wrote in English, "To Sarah Hurst with best regards. You are welcome always to chess Kalmyk Republic."

It turned out there was no flight from Elista to Moscow on the day we had to leave, so we took an overnight bus to Volgograd. We got the last seats, squashed up with some sweaty soldiers. In the morning Amy and I visited the spectacular memorial to the Battle of Stalingrad (Volgograd is the modern name for Stalingrad), and I played a few outdoor games of blitz chess with an old man in the shadow of the giant female statue that towers over the river. Nicholas wasn't happy with our services as guides and wouldn't come with us.

Promoting peaceful relations at the memorial to the
Battle of Stalingrad in Volgograd, on the way home from Kalmykia.

From Volgograd we flew to Moscow. Amy stayed there for a few weeks and then went to Tbilisi, Georgia, to be one of a handful of Western freelance journalists in the South Caucasus. Nicholas and I returned home safely to England. My feelings about Kalmykia at this point were very mixed. I wrote the following article, my first for the Dutch magazine *New in Chess*, which pays quite well and is generally considered the world's leading chess publication. The magazine used two of Nicholas's photographs with the article. Later the article was reprinted by the Dutch newspaper *Algemeen Dagblad*.

The Steppe-Father of Chess
(*New in Chess*, spring 1998)

This year's Olympiad will be more like Dubai than Yerevan, if the FIDE president is to be believed. Elista might not have much of a reputation as a high-class resort, but in fact it has many attractive features. Although there isn't a beach (was there one in Dubai?), and no sea or even river to admire within a couple of hundred kilometres, there is plenty of sand, which is what "Elista" means in the Kalmyk language. And rising from the steppe, as if a mirage, is Kirsan's glorious creation, City Chess.

Not every chess player is an avid reader of *FIDE Forum* or the little-known glossy magazine *City Chess*, so I visited Kalmykia in early May to bring news of the Olympiad preparations to a wider audience. I had also become extremely curious about Ilyumzhinov himself. FIDE Treasurer David Jarrett seemed to take my gentle

Amy and Nick Spurling dazed on arrival at Elista "international" airport.

enquiries about funding for the 1997 World Championship as a personal insult, and he urged me to read Ilyumzhinov's autobiography, *The President's Crown of Thorns*, to understand more about this unusual man.

Jarrett sent me a copy of the book. It didn't explain how Ilyumzhinov had made enough money to own a Rolls Royce, a sports car and a private jet, but it did contain a small postcard of the president, smiling, in front of some idyllic mountain scenery. Kalmykia immediately metamorphosed into a warm, mountainous land in my imagination, much like the nearby republics of the Caucasus (some readers may have heard of Chechnya, which is to the south of Kalmykia – day trips aren't advisable, as they can turn into lengthy, involuntary stays!). However, I was misinformed. The picture on the postcard must have been taken in Switzerland, as Kalmykia is one of the flattest places in the world. It's also considerably cooler than the surrounding regions, because of the unabating steppe winds.

Nevertheless, foreign visitors are treated like royalty, especially if they are connected with chess or can bring Ilyumzhinov some publicity. My colleagues and I were met at Elista airport by the people with whom we would be staying and Sergey Badminov, chairman of the Olympiad organising committee. They picked us up in two cars, one of which was a Hyundai belonging to Badminov. He was keen to show off all the gadgets in it.

In the evening, Badminov whisked us off to a restaurant with Alisa Galliamova, who had just been knocked out of the Russian Women's Championship in the semifinal. A waiter from Madagascar, of all places, served us with huge plates of crayfish and fish kebabs, and an apparently unlimited supply of wine and beer.

Alisa Galliamova
samples the Elista water.

Unfortunately, the cars that had collected us would both be written off in separate accidents later in the week. One of the cars was smashed up in the centre of Elista. The other, Badminov's, was taken by a government driver to the airport at Volgograd, where he picked up the chess players Maya Chiburdanidze, Zurab Azmaiparashvili and Kiril Georgiev. He crashed a few miles outside Elista, trying to overtake a lorry at high speed.

Ex-women's world champion Chiburdanidze, in the passenger seat, lost consciousness and was rushed to hospital, where Ilyumzhinov visited her (presumably without his usual broad smile). The tournament they were supposed to be playing in, the President's Cup, was postponed for a day. Georgiev played, but Chiburdanidze and Azmaiparashvili withdrew.

The accident, which could easily have been a tragedy, was a bad omen for the Olympiad. Transport to Kalmykia and within the republic is a serious problem. The roads are full of potholes, which cars swerve to avoid. The airport building at Elista is disintegrating into a pile of rubble: the official line is that it is being "reconstructed". Government ministers repeat the mantra that improvements are taking place "step by step", a slogan they all know in English.

Elista airport has "international status", according to the head of the president's administration, with a runway capable of accommodating any plane except a jumbo jet. At the moment the only regular flights are to Moscow and Turkey. We arrived from Moscow in a 32-seater operated by the obscure airline Avia Express Cruise, which serves a plastic cup of fizzy pink water as refreshment.

Players from the former Soviet Union aren't bothered by such details. Neither Alisa Galliamova nor Nona Gaprindashvili had any complaints about Elista. Galliamova had lots of fun with Kalmyk friends and wasn't at all bothered when her estranged husband Vassily Ivanchuk came to town – she just ignored him. Ex-women's world champion Gaprindashvili had been invited by Ilyumzhinov to play in the Russian Women's Championship, even though she is from Georgia. The 57-year-old superstar wasn't particularly successful, losing in the quarterfinal, but she enjoyed herself signing autographs, playing billiards and gambling in the casino.

"I admire Ilyumzhinov," Gaprindashvili told me. "He's doing everything for the development of chess, and to me that means a lot, as chess is my life. I really like him as a person, and I hope he will continue with what he's doing. Something new is being built all the time here." Gaprindashvili welcomes the knockout system, as times have changed and there are no sponsors for long matches, "but there is no ideal system in chess."

The chess federations of Mauritius and Japan will be delighted to hear that the knockout system isn't yet being applied to the Olympiad. There will be some new technology, however. Every board will have electronic sensors that instantly transmit each move to journalists and to the Internet. A few of the boards at the world championship in Groningen were similarly wired, but this will be the largest event yet to have the facility. The cottages and playing hall in City Chess will also be state-of-the-art, providing they are completed on time.

Ilyumzhinov compares City Chess to the legendary land of Bumba, immortalised in the epic Kalmyk poem *Dzhangar*. The front page of the first issue of *City Chess*

City Chess was still being built when I visited Elista.

The main playing hall for the 1998 Olympiad under construction in Elista.

magazine is graced with an Ilyumzhinov photo, interview, and lines from *Dzhangar* that describe the building of a magical palace with foundations of coral, walls of pearl and glass "red as a flame". The centrepiece of the four-story playing hall in City Chess will be a glass elevator. The luxury Western-style cottages have brightly coloured roofs, in striking contrast to the concrete blocks of flats where ordinary residents of Elista live.

Half of the builders of City Chess are from Kalmykia; the rest are Serbian. The chief engineer, a Serb, has no doubt that City Chess will be ready when the teams arrive. Several years ago his company built a hotel in Belgrade very quickly, so he is undaunted by this project. But I also talked to a Russian builder, who was more sceptical. "We are each working seven days a week, 10 hours a day. We can have a day off – if we really need one," he said. "Our salary is $150 a month. To finish City Chess on time, we would need to work exceptionally hard, but to work exceptionally hard we would need to be paid well." They started in April 1997 and have worked in temperatures of –25 C. The buildings have to be finished in August, so they can be tested.

The president's representative in City Chess, Viktor Dzhanzhiev, assured me that there had been no accidents at the site, but I did see a builder with a bandaged nose. Hardly any of the builders were wearing helmets, and we ourselves were taken to the top of the playing hall, where heavy concrete blocks swing from cranes, without being offered helmets. "Legally the builders should wear helmets, but they don't like them, they consider them uncomfortable," said the deputy minister of construction. "Like ice hockey – recently the Canadians took off their helmets in an important match. Amateurs wear helmets, but professionals don't always."

A guard salutes
at the door to
Kirsan Ilyumzhinov's
office in Elista.

With some luck and an enormous amount of effort, the chess players won't see any of this. All they'll see are tastefully decorated cottages with three twin bedrooms, a fitted kitchen and bathroom, dining room, living room, utility room, garage and a neat lawn surrounded by a freshly painted garden fence. After the Olympiad, these will go on sale for $600 per square metre, making a total of $94,680. City Chess is supposed to become Kalmykia's fourth town, with its own mayor and hotel. The playing hall will be the administrative building. For now, it will have a restaurant and offices for the media and FIDE. Journalists who come for the Olympiad will live outside City Chess, in a student hall of residence.

Kalmyk students are being sent on intensive language courses so they can attend to every need of their international guests. Not all Kalmyk women are interested in chess, but most of them seem to be interested in chess players. Their exotic charm, alluring makeup, platform shoes and fashionable clothes from Turkey should make them irresistible to lonely grandmasters. But their passionate desire for foreign men often disguises an even more passionate desire to get out of Kalmykia.

One thing is certain: the Olympiad will not make Kalmykia rich. No matter how much money the visitors pour into the economy (knowing chess players, not a fortune), it won't make up for the money spent on preparing for the Olympiad. The Kalmyk government asserts that all the funding will come from the Russian federal budget, rather than the meagre local budget, but the Russian deputy finance minister stated in April that the necessary documents from the Kalmyk government had not been received. "The estimates for work on the Olympic village in Elista have not been presented for inclusion in this year's federal investment programme," he wrote.

Lenin stands firm outside the presidential palace in Elista.

The Russian government is expecting to spend 94.9 million roubles on City Chess ($15.8 million). If the cost turns out to be more than that, Ilyumzhinov will have to find the money elsewhere, or hope that Yeltsin will bail him out. Kalmyks will have to hope that Ilyumzhinov doesn't decide to take an extended holiday. It was clear from our meeting with Ilyumzhinov that his workload is spiralling out of control. "My wife sees me between three and seven in the morning, and on television," he said.

Ilyumzhinov doesn't spend much of his time in Kalmykia, but he can run the republic from anywhere in the world, he claims. "I could be in Africa or Indonesia, but I have a computer, I can turn it on and find out how much money is in the national bank, how many people have received their salaries." However, there's no time for deep analysis of Kalmykia's problems. "I try to answer questions straight away, I say yes or no immediately. It's as if my life is a game of blitz chess. If I put things off until tomorrow, they'll just pile up. But I'm also raising my professional level, from master to international master to grandmaster. When I was elected president, I didn't know anything about wool, so I read books about it. Every day I spend an hour or two reading about economics, business or politics."

On the rare occasions when the president is in his office, he is besieged with visitors. Orthodox priests and Buddhist monks have to wait alongside pensioners and journalists. A woman who was accompanying an 85-year-old veteran of World War II handed me a note. She wanted me to pass it to Ilyumzhinov, in the hope that he would consider the veteran's request for a flat. There are other government departments, but people justifiably assume that Ilyumzhinov is the only person with the power to get things done. His relatives and former classmates are also in the government, proof of his all-pervading influence.

People are very reluctant to criticise Ilyumzhinov. The only opposition newspaper, *Sovietskaya Kalmykia Segodnya*, is based outside the republic. Igor Shalkhakov, the head of the president's administration, denied that it existed, even though I'd bought a copy in the market. One person did speak out, but she expressed fear that she'd be arrested. Ilyumzhinov claims that he tried to close down the KGB office in Elista, but the Russian government insisted that it stayed open with a staff of 500. "Why do we need 500 KGB officers in a town of this size? You tell me! I don't know what they do – perhaps they catch Japanese and English spies," the president joked. "Were you followed? An American businessman came here and he was followed by three people. He couldn't even go to the toilet."

Perhaps Ilyumzhinov is telling the truth when he says he knows nothing about the KGB, but his credentials as a democrat are not convincing. When he was first elected in 1993, he offered every citizen $100 and promised that Argentinian star Maradona would play on the local football team. This was fantasy, of course. He was re-elected two years later with no opponents, in breach of the Russian constitution. I asked him if he had a political hero. "No one in particular. I like Napoleon, Suvorov, Jesus Christ… probably Jesus Christ most of all, because people have followed him for so long. I also like the teachings of Marx and Lenin."

Sadly Ilyumzhinov hasn't been able to arrange a meeting with Jesus or Lenin. He is very proud of his other meetings – so proud, that there are posters of him all over town with the Dalai Lama and the patriarch of the Russian Orthodox Church. He happily showed us photographs of himself with Mikhail Gorbachev and Saddam Hussein. Saddam Hussein? What was Ilyumzhinov's impression of him? "Very good. I met him in 1994. In the press they said he was a dictator… but he's very cultured, educated, he understands history and politics… I had the same sort of impression with the pope."

Ilyumzhinov knows all about the cult of personality. Schoolchildren make busts of him in their art classes. In the playing hall where the Russian Women's Championship and the President's Cup were held, an inspirational slogan was proclaimed from a banner: "Chess is the most intellectual and most popular game in the world. K.N. Ilyumzhinov." Chess is compulsory in Kalmyk schools.

In FIDE Ilyumzhinov won't have things his own way forever. His powers of persuasion are formidable, but he is staking everything on the success of the Olympiad. For this reason it will probably go ahead on schedule, even if the entire population of Elista has to be mobilised to finish City Chess. The election for FIDE president will take place during the Olympiad. If Ilyumzhinov is chosen again, he promises a glittering World Championship in Las Vegas at the end of the year. Ilyumzhinov is hedging his bets on the participation of Karpov and Kasparov. "If they don't play, maybe it's because they're not on form. I thought Kramnik wasn't on form when he refused to play in Groningen. Often political aspects are wrongly read into things."

Alexei Shirov is also welcome to play in Las Vegas, despite apparently breaching his contract with FIDE by taking part in the rival World Chess Council match with Kramnik. "The only World Championship is the FIDE World Championship, we don't recognise any other," Ilyumzhinov said. "Let Shirov play Kramnik – we'll see it as an international tournament. Anand could have played if he'd wanted to. Kasparov is a usurper, he has become a dictator, he wants to choose his opponent. We need discipline. Individuals can't have their own conditions."

The voice of the individual is rarely heard in Ilyumzhinov's world. A young woman handed me an article criticising him, but didn't want her name to be published. She protests that Ilyumzhinov is neglecting the needs of the Kalmyk people in favour of chess, and worries that he will soon bid to host the Winter Olympics. "Sometimes, it seems to me that someone said to our 'Kira': 'Yes, you are right. The time to organise the Olympiad has arrived. Don't think about the crowd. They can wait or… just forget about them. You should think about your image. Kalmykia should forget about money.'

"OK. I can wait, because I'm young and may be too stupid to understand his politics, the teenagers could be bought by superstars Boney-M, Michael Jackson etc., the other people would not say anything against him, because he may reproach them, that it were they who elected him, anyway they would keep silent, just to be patriotic or because it is dangerous to speak aloud. What is allowed is to cry: 'Greetings to the construction of the century – City Chess!'"

A few weeks after my trip to Kalmykia, I came home one evening to find a message on the answering machine from Australian GM Ian Rogers, who is also an outspoken chess journalist. Ian played on the same 4NCL team as Tim, so we knew him slightly. The message asked me what I thought about the murder of Larisa Yudina. Her name was vaguely familiar, but I couldn't place it.

When I called Ian, he reminded me that Yudina was the editor of Sovietskaya Kalmykia Segodnya. *She had been stabbed to death, Ian said. In Russia journalists are frequently assaulted and murdered. It's a convenient way for the local authorities or mafia, who are usually closely connected, to stifle criticism. So I immediately suspected that Ilyumzhinov was involved in the murder, as he was the chief target of Yudina's investigations.*

The following letter to New in Chess *was published in the same issue as my article:*

Boycott the Olympiad

Since I wrote my article about City Chess in late May, a tragic event has occurred. Larisa Yudina, the editor of Kalmykia's only opposition newspaper, *Sovietskaya Kalmykia Segodnya*, was stabbed to death on June 7. She was a fierce critic of Kirsan Ilyumzhinov and was investigating the alleged misappropriation of funds by a state company at the time of her death. One of the men who has been arrested in connection with the killing, Sergey Vaskin, is a former aide to Ilyumzhinov. The authorities in Moscow have taken over the investigation because they don't trust the police in Kalmykia.

The financial scandal that Yudina was investigating could have serious implications for FIDE. There is a strong chance that Ilyumzhinov's business dealings will collapse and he will disappear in the next few weeks or months. Ilyumzhinov's reputation is in tatters, and he has tried to cover this up by announcing that he is standing for the presidency of Russia (he favours the Communist or Agrarian Party).

Either Ilyumzhinov has been controlling events in Kalmykia, or events are completely out of control. Whichever, he is clearly not a fit person to be running FIDE. Elista is not a safe place to go and it would be morally wrong for the world's top chess players to go there, according Ilyumzhinov the credibility and status he craves. No chess player should take any more money from him until the investigation into the murder is completed and Ilyumzhinov explains where his money is coming from.

I am calling for a mass boycott of the Olympiad in Elista.

For more information, please contact me.

Sarah Hurst

My campaign for a boycott sparked an intense debate in the chess world. Professional players and administrators who were benefiting financially from Ilyumzhinov's deep pockets argued that human rights in Kalmykia had nothing to do with chess. Only a few players (mainly from liberal Scandinavian countries) were willing to sacrifice their chance to play in the Olympiad. My position as editor of *ChessMoves* became precarious, as British Chess Federation Chairman Stewart Reuben was closely involved with FIDE.

The late GM Tony Miles, one of England's top players, sent me an e-mail asking if I would expect the Russians to boycott an event in Britain if my body washed up in the Thames. Despite knowing he had a history of mental instability – he once tried to break into the prime minister's residence, 10 Downing Street, to complain about fellow GM Ray Keene – I decided not to interpret this as a death threat.

Luckily, Malcolm Pein, the proprietor of *CHESS*, was friendlier with Kasparov than with FIDE and he published the following story about the boycott campaign (providing I put a disclaimer at the end saying the editors didn't necessarily share my opinions). The title is a bad pun – by me – on the TV series *LA Law*. Originally I wanted to call it "EListA ConFIDEntial", incorporating a pun on the film *LA Confidential*, but Jimmy preferred the other title. I also gave Sam Sloan permission to publish the article on his tabloid-style website, and it has stayed there ever since.

ELista Law
(*CHESS*, July 1998)

The murder of newspaper editor Larisa Yudina in Kalmykia has convinced me that it would be wrong to participate in the Olympiad there. Yudina, 53, was stabbed to death on June 7 and her body was found the next day in a pond. She had been an outspoken critic of Kirsan Ilyumzhinov, president of Kalmykia and FIDE, and at the time of her death she was investigating allegations of financial impropriety relating to a state-owned company.

Outrage at the murder has been expressed all over the world, in newspapers ranging from the *International Herald Tribune* to *El Pais*, *The Guardian* and *The Times*. In Russia, where in most regions freedom of speech is already taken for granted, the murder has been called a political contract killing and Ilyumzhinov has been quizzed about his involvement on television. His response was to amaze the interviewer by announcing his intention to stand for the presidency of Russia in the year 2000.

A team of investigators has been sent to Kalmykia from Moscow to conduct the murder enquiry, because President Yeltsin doesn't trust Ilyumzhinov's local police. Meanwhile, the chess world has not responded at all. Chess journalists have written about the murder, notably GM Ian Rogers in the *Canberra Times*, but at the time of writing (June 21, two weeks after the murder), as far as I know, no chess federation and no FIDE official has made any statement to disassociate themselves from Ilyumzhinov. When I spoke to FIDE Treasurer David Jarrett in the week following the murder, he hadn't yet heard about it. I explained what had happened, and he replied, "This is nothing to do with FIDE, I don't wish to comment, thank you."

GM Murray Chandler, editor-in-chief of *British Chess Magazine*, refused to publish this article because "it has nothing to do with chess". Twice in the last two months I have been instructed by the British Chess Federation to remove articles critical of Ilyumzhinov from *ChessMoves* (which I edit), because the BCF is affiliated with FIDE and cannot express dissent in its official organ. In this month's *New in Chess* I am calling for a mass boycott of the Olympiad, and on June 20 I attended a BCF Management Board meeting where my proposal that the England teams should boycott the Olympiad was discussed.

In the process of sounding out opinion before the meeting, I made some depressing discoveries. Several members of the Management Board said they knew already that Ilyumzhinov was a repressive dictator and so the murder didn't really change much. I was told the story of Ignatius Leong, the FIDE official who fled Armenia in 1996 after opposing Ilyumzhinov at the FIDE Congress and receiving threats.

When David Jarrett stood for treasurer on Ilyumzhinov's ticket, Stewart Reuben asked him if he felt safe, taking into account the fact that his wife is Russian. Jarrett replied that he did. Nevertheless, on the two occasions when I have questioned Jarrett by telephone about FIDE finances, I have received nothing but hostility, and not a single fact about the source of all the money Ilyumzhinov is pouring into FIDE.

At the Management Board meeting, the BCF's international director David Sedgwick said he had "very grave doubts" about Ilyumzhinov in 1996. But Ilyumzhinov "has been more successful than I expected at that time and less dictatorial within FIDE". If the Olympiad goes ahead as planned, in September, the FIDE Congress and the election for FIDE president will take place during the event. Each federation has one vote, and the BCF's delegate is Gerry Walsh. BCF Chairman Stewart Reuben will also be present, as he is being paid by FIDE to be on the pairings committee for the Olympiad. Although Walsh is supposed to be representing the BCF, in practice it will be up to him and Reuben to decide whom to vote for – if there is a choice at all.

After sitting through an excruciatingly tedious Management Board meeting from 11 a.m. to 5 p.m., the point on the agenda regarding the Olympiad was finally reached. A few days previously, I had spent some time discussing the issues by e-mail with Robin Mackley, the BCF's publicity director, but this time was wasted because Mackley went home at 4 p.m. On Monday, June 15, I sent a letter to all 20 members of the Management Board explaining my reasons for requesting a boycott, and at some point in that week, David Sedgwick sent out a response. However, I was not allowed to see it – it was marked "confidential" – and in fact Sedgwick wanted the entire discussion to be confidential, i.e. without my presence.

Fortunately, Tony Suttill, director of management services (who knows me because he is responsible for *ChessMoves*), asked that I should remain in the room, and the board accepted this. I was never allowed to see Sedgwick's written response to my letter, but the gist of it was that he did not support my call for a boycott. When I spoke to him on the phone on June 19, he made it clear that he was unsympathetic and seemed irritated that his notification of selected players had been held up by my proposal. His public announcement of the teams for the Olympiad, which starts at the end of September, has been set back by about a week.

IM Susan Lalic is certain to be selected for the women's team. Even before notification, she had already cancelled all her coaching commitments so that she could play. "It's my livelihood," she told me on June 19. "I will make statements and give money to poor people in Kalmykia, but I'm still going." She has good reason to be pragmatic. In the early '90s she boycotted the women's World Championship interzonal in Serbia in protest at the war with Croatia (her husband, GM Bogdan Lalic, is Croatian). Susan was hoping that others would follow her example, but, instead, the BCF simply sent Sheila Jackson in her place. So Susan is now disillusioned about the effectiveness of making a political stand, and, having seen how the BCF works, I can hardly blame her.

Susan is not at all happy about playing in Elista, the Kalmyk capital. "Every player would agree the Olympiad should be somewhere else," she said. "It's the last place on Earth I'd want it to be. I am surprised that the Olympiad can be held in a most inaccessible place and recent political disturbances make it even more incredible that the federations allowed the Olympiad to be in such a ridiculous location. I wish to have it on record for the future that a civilised and democratic country is necessary to draw all the top teams and make the event credible and safe."

To make things easier for the BCF and the players, I recommended that the BCF should call for the Olympiad to be moved to another venue, such as St. Petersburg, instead of being cancelled altogether. Then there would be more chance of holding a fair election for FIDE president and no insinuation that the chess world is utterly indifferent to and immune from politics. My true belief is that in the wake of the murder, the Olympiad will not go ahead in Elista. Ilyumzhinov has been publicly discredited and the Russian government is out to get him. He might be arrested in the next few months, or he might fly away in his private jet. Most likely, the Russian government will not provide the necessary funding for the completion of City Chess, the Olympic village.

In that case, why bother to call for a boycott? I think it would be a disgrace if the chess world stands by Ilyumzhinov to the bitter end. When he finally goes, it will be due to his own decision or the action of the Russian government. The chess world is according him the status and credibility that he craves, and shows no sign of withdrawing this at the present moment. "It has been said that FIDE would have been bankrupt if it weren't for Ilyumzhinov," Reuben told me. The fact that the millions of dollars Ilyumzhinov has brought to FIDE are of unknown origin doesn't seem to matter. And this money will disappear as suddenly as it appeared.

If the Olympiad does collapse, there might not be time to find an alternative venue. This is why the best option is to call for a change now. In the worst-case scenario, which has to be taken into account, the Olympiad *will* go ahead in Elista. This would be utterly wrong. From my own impressions of the place and from reading a huge pile of articles in the past two weeks, I shall explain why.

I visited Elista in the first week of May to report for *New in Chess* on preparations for the Olympiad. I had no preconceptions at the time – in fact, I had very little information. I had read Ilyumzhinov's autobiography, *The President's Crown of Thorns*, but his activities in FIDE were left to the last few pages and his business interests from the time when he stopped working for a Russian-Japanese joint venture were hardly touched on.

My assumption that the Kalmyk population would be fanatical about chess turned out to be very far from the truth. Ilyumzhinov has made chess compulsory in schools, but the republic has yet to produce a grandmaster. A teacher of English whom I spoke to gave me her views on chess and Ilyumzhinov very reluctantly.

"Some people must be fond of music, some of ballet, some of art – it's up to the people. We mustn't force… [long pause] maybe the future will show who is right."

A young woman studying English at Elista University told me, "It is very bad when a president has no opposites. He must have, he must know his disadvantages. He doesn't want people to know how he gets his money, his power, and what does he do… If you read our local newspapers, you will not find any article against him, and one of our newspapers is in Volgograd because this newspaper is opposite against him, *Sovietskaya Kalmykia.*" The newspaper that Larisa Yudina edited.

When I was about to leave, the same student gave me a folded piece of paper and asked me not to show anyone in Elista, but to read it on the plane. It was an article protesting that Ilyumzhinov was devoting all the republic's resources to chess and to his own glory, while doing nothing for the people themselves. The roads in Elista are full of potholes, the airport building is a pile of rubble and hot water is only available sporadically. The government's slogan is "step by step" – these things can't be fixed overnight. But Ilyumzhinov has been in power since 1993. And City Chess is being built at breakneck speed, not "step by step".

Chess federations are relying on FIDE for information about the Olympiad, but FIDE information comes from Ilyumzhinov, and Ilyumzhinov's government tells a pack of lies. Igor Shalkhakov, the head of the president's administration, told me there was no such paper as *Sovietskaya Kalmykia.* "How can there be, we have no Soviet Union." According to him, there is no crime in Kalmykia and the airport has "international status". Chess federations will probably have to charter planes for their teams, but there are no guarantees that the runway will be long enough for them to land on. They could fly to a larger airport, such as Volgograd, but that's what former women's world champion Maya Chiburdanidze did – and she was seriously injured in a car crash on the road to Elista.

Ilyumzhinov himself is an admirer of Saddam Hussein. I interviewed Ilyumzhinov, and he proudly showed me photographs of his meeting with Saddam in Iraq. Ilyumzhinov knows the techniques of dictators very well. When someone requests a meeting with him, he makes them wait for days, without indicating when the meeting might take place. Eventually he summons them at 3 or 4 a.m., when they are at their weakest. This happened to David Jarrett, when he agreed to stand for treasurer.

I brought a copy of *Sovietskaya Kalmykia* back home with me, but I didn't read it all at first. I had been asked to write about chess, so I ignored the political content and only drew attention to a few paragraphs about the funding of City Chess, which emphasised that the Russian government had not received the relevant application documents from Ilyumzhinov, who claims that all the money will come from federal funds.

When I heard about Yudina's murder, I immediately read her article in that issue. It was called "Psychiatry is Used in Kalmykia for Non-Medicinal Purposes". She told the story of a group of hunger-striking women who were protesting at not having enough money to feed their children. She interviewed Kalmykia's chief psychiatrist, who forcibly "treated" the leader of the hunger strikers. The psychiatrist said that a hunger strike was an "inadequate reaction" to such a trivial problem. Following the murder, the same woman hunger striker arrived in Moscow, saying she believed she would be next on the hit list.

Ilyumzhinov banned a demonstration in protest at Yudina's murder. She was obviously a prominent thorn in his crown. *Sovietskaya Kalmykia* was forcibly evicted from its Elista offices in 1994 and Yudina complained that her staff members were beaten up by security guards of a bank that has links to the Kalmyk government, according to *The Moscow Times*, the Russian capital's leading English-language paper. Ilyumzhinov once said he didn't understand people like Yudina, who wished to harm Kalmykia. The most damning evidence comes from Thomas de Waal of *The Times*, who actually interviewed Yudina. Following that, Ilyumzhinov said he was "disappointed" and refused to see de Waal, threatening to report him to his editor.

Yudina was not the unlucky victim of a mugging. She received a phone call from a man who offered to give her proof that money had been embezzled by the state company she was investigating. She got into a car to meet him, was driven away, and never seen alive again. These were Ilyumzhinov's comments, on Russia's TV6:

Ilyumzhinov – As head of the republic, I have been informed that investigations are under way and that suspects have been detained, practically on the day of the murder.

Interviewer – Who are they?

Ilyumzhinov – They are being investigated. They are from Kalmykia. Sergey Vaskin. I cannot remember the name of the second...

Interviewer – You did not know these people before?

Ilyumzhinov – I knew them. One was one of my public relations men, an aide, and the other was the same, a representative of the Republic of Kalmykia in the Volgograd Region.

Interviewer – Clearly the decision on whether these people were involved or not is a question for the investigators. Nonetheless, does it not seem strange to you, are you not ashamed that someone working as your public relations aide should be detained on suspicion of involvement in this murder?

Ilyumzhinov – I said at the start of the interview: I answer for everything that happens in our republic.

Later in the interview, Ilyumzhinov made his shock announcement that he wanted to stand for president.

Interviewer – You, the president of Kalmykia, now intend to stand for president of Russia?

Ilyumzhinov – Yes, I intend to, because having looked at the situation, at how several politicians, political demagogues, use one situation or another in the region, I decided to create my own electoral headquarters and start preparing for presidential elections.

Interviewer – Great. And who are you counting on?

Ilyumzhinov – Well, at the moment, I do not have a political party. Either I will create one which will get its support from the regions, from young people, or I will form an alliance with one of the parties, a democratic party, the Liberal Democratic Party, the Communist Party, the Agrarian Party.

Interviewer – The Communist Party?

Ilyumzhinov – Well, I was simply giving the range of parties with whom an alliance can be made.

Interviewer – Well, I do not think that your statement will impress the Kremlin too much, or that, given the situation with freedom of speech in your republic, that people used to reading the papers freely and watching television and who are not used to a country where the editors of opposition papers are killed will be impressed either.

Proof that the Russian government has given up on Ilyumzhinov comes from Belgian businessman Loie de Gruben. I met him outside Ilyumzhinov's office in Elista, where we were both waiting for a meeting. The businessman wanted to discuss the small matter of $750,000 he paid for wool that Ilyumzhinov guaranteed to deliver, but which never arrived. After Yudina's murder I rang de Gruben in Antwerp. He had been urgently summoned to the Russian embassy in Brussels on June 15. There he was advised to sue Ilyumzhinov, and promised the full support of the Russian government.

"Business was very good in 1993-95, but then I saw how things were going wrong," de Gruben told me. "I have worked for Coca-Cola in Nigeria, Congo, the Ivory Coast – but I've never had the sort of problems I've had in Kalmykia. You cannot trust Ilyumzhinov. One day he says yes, another day he says no, and this is very dangerous. The Russians are sick of all those promises and stupid projects for his glory. They find City Chess really stupid – all this big construction, it's selfish. The Olympiad goes on for one or two months, then what will they do with it?"

I have tried to make it clear to the BCF that action should be taken regardless of a definite link between Ilyumzhinov and this murder. Lara Barnes, director of women's chess, was absolutely right when she said in the debate that Ilyumzhinov is bringing the game into disrepute. She pointed out to the Management Board that de Waal's article in *The Times* was called "The President who Pawned his People". There will be hundreds more such articles if the Olympiad goes ahead in Elista.

The editor of *Kinpin*, Jonathan Manley, has written to me saying, "Following Larisa Yudina's murder and other disturbing reports emerging from Kalmykia, I do not believe that the BCF should send a team to the Olympiad in Elista. The ethical and practical reasons for boycotting the event are compelling and I shall be urging others within the chess community to join the protest."

The BCF didn't see it that way. Barnes initiated the discussion. She said, "There has been so much adverse publicity about this man, the president of FIDE and Kalmykia, I wondered why FIDE agreed to hold the Olympiad there in the first place." Reuben replied, "The decision was made in 1994. He was just a very presentable young man, we knew nothing about him." In Reuben's opinion, "it would be a terrible error to unilaterally boycott the Olympiad, for our relations with FIDE. Speaking as an arbiter, because comments are made about somebody in the newspaper, we don't assume those things to be true. Until judicial process has taken place, it's quite incorrect for us to make a judgment. Prime examples are the trials of O.J. Simpson and [British au pair accused of shaking a baby to death] Louise Woodward."

[Reuben may or may not have been aware that Russian regional leaders, as members of the upper house of parliament, are immune from criminal prosecution. It has been a typical ploy for multimillionaire Russian oligarchs such as Boris Berezovsky and Roman Abramovich to get themselves elected to parliament from remote regions (Karachayevo-Cherkesia and Chukotka respectively) to obtain immunity.]

As for safety, Reuben said that the chief arbiter for the Olympiad, Geurt Gijssen, thought that Elista would be safer than London. "[Gijssen] believes the runway is adequate as it is, but it is being built up." Alan Martin, a former BCF president, said there had been similar situations in the past. "The safety of players is paramount. We had the possibility of sending a junior to Medellin in Colombia and we decided this wasn't a good idea. We should consult the players, consult the Foreign Office, and consult our fellow chess federations. We've got sensible people in charge to deal with these things."

Neil Graham, director of congress chess, said, "If we do send a team, players should be happy they're going and not be forced to go. The safety aspect doesn't look particularly satisfactory, but if people are happy, that's up to them. As for the political situation, we're not here to judge the regime a person runs, provided it's not deemed to be dangerous. As president of FIDE, that's another matter. We would have to think about whether we wished to vote for him. But the withdrawal of our team would be a futile gesture."

Graham added that he had spoken to prospective members of the Welsh team and that the Welsh Chess Union was considering very strongly what to do, because of the difficulties of getting to Elista.

Gary Kenworthy, director of coaching, said, "It's a very dangerous dictatorship. We should really be asking, should this guy be head of FIDE? We should be talking to other federations." Sedgwick said he had asked Gerry Walsh to contact other federations, but that Walsh had not succeeded in talking to any other delegates. Sedgwick hadn't yet got around to asking the Foreign Office their advice, but intended to. Furthermore, he believed Ilyumzhinov's popularity in the chess world was such that he would win the FIDE election even if the congress were held in London. "I don't believe that if the BCF takes unilateral action other federations will quickly follow," he added.

Well, I do believe that someone should take responsibility, someone should take a lead, and that others will follow. I was given a fair opportunity to have my say at the Management Board meeting and I voiced some of the arguments contained in this article. However, I failed to persuade the board. In a vote on Sedgwick's proposal not to boycott the Olympiad, six people were in favour and 10 abstained, with no votes against. This is not exactly convincing. It simply means that no one had the courage to do anything.

I am continuing with my campaign – I will write to all the selected England players and urge them not to go to Elista. I will send a press release to chess journalists and other journalists expressing my disappointment with the board's decision, and I will contact other federations to find out what they think. At this moment I am ashamed to be a chess player.

The opinions expressed here are those of Sarah Hurst and do not necessarily reflect those of the editors. Sarah will be donating her fee for this article to Amnesty International.

* * *

When I wrote to the England players, Tim and I were housesitting for some friends and I didn't have access to a printer. We were leaving for Ghent the next day. So I sent the letters on disk to my parents and asked them to print them and send them for me. Later some of the players criticised me for not signing the letters, but this was an irrelevant detail, in my opinion. I regret that I was unable to sign them, but I doubt it would have made any difference.

The campaign gathered some momentum. The BBC World Service's Russian Section interviewed me (in English and Russian). I spoke by telephone from my bedroom/office on a live radio chess programme in Melbourne, Australia. I went to Bristol to speak on a BBC Radio 4 travel programme, but they edited my comments and broadcast mainly descriptions of Kalmykia, without the political angle. It was a shame, because I'd invested in an expensive Sony Minidisk and microphone and taken them to Elista so that I could record a contribution for that travel programme, my first venture into radio journalism; but due to my incompetence the sound quality of my interviews wasn't good enough.

In August 1998 the Russian rouble crashed and Tim and I rented a house together. I had been far too optimistic about the Russian government's commitment to free speech and democracy, and intentions regarding Ilyumzhinov. Yeltsin didn't want Kalmykia to go the way of the North Caucasus, to become another rebel republic, and Ilyumzhinov at least offered stability. When he tentatively threatened to secede over a budget issue, he got a slap on the wrist in Moscow and didn't step out of line again. The Russian government's attentions were focused on the economy. Human rights were increasingly eroded, and this process continued under Putin, who waged a second war on Chechnya.

The decision to move in with Tim was based primarily on practical considerations, for both of us. He was renting a room in a house in north London. Having a house of our own meant more independence. All we could afford was a mews cottage in Woodford Green, so far out of London that it was practically in Essex, one of the home counties. The landlords were two unsavoury entrepreneurs who owned an empty shop in front of the house.

The president of the U.S. Chess Federation, Don Schultz, rang me to hear my opinions on the Olympiad. He referred to this conversation in a letter to USCF members that he wrote in August 1998. The following is an extract from that letter:

"Ilyumzhinov is famous. He is an announced candidate to succeed Yeltsen [sic] as President of Russia. Recently, a journalist, known for her extensive criticism of Ilyumzhinov, was murdered in Kalmykia; and two former employees of Ilyumzhinov have been charged with that murder. Many in the world press have suggested the USCF and other national federations publicly condemn President Ilyumzhinov for possible involvement in the murders [sic] and for human rights violations in his home country. I was told that this issue would be raised at the Delegates Meeting in Hawaii.

"Before going to Hawaii, I called FIDE delegates from friendly countries to see what they were doing. I also called and discussed the concerns with the FIDE Secretariat, members of FIDE's Presidential Board and various journalists including Sarah Hurst, the leading critic of President Ilyumzhinov. My take from these calls was that everyone was concerned but that no countries would stay away because of human rights violations. The feeling by most was that public opinion had not advanced beyond the point of concern and individual decisions, rather than chess federation decisions, should govern participation and cooperation."

Schultz added that he had contacted the U.S. State Department for advice and had been told there was no reason not to send a team to Kalmykia. Of course, this was a purely ethical issue, up to the conscience of chess players, not the U.S. State Department. Unless the State Department (or the British Foreign Office) deemed a region dangerous for foreigners, it would not make judgments in a case like this. Human rights violations in Russia are well known and Kalmykia is a republic within Russia. To me, British and U.S. government advice was simply a smokescreen for chess administrators to hide behind.

I was often confronted with the argument that chess players have to travel all over the world and can't avoid countries where there are human rights abuses. Very true. But Kalmykia is different, because the leader responsible for the human rights abuses is also the head of FIDE. By giving Ilyumzhinov such a prominent role in chess, players endorse him. Moreover, some of the economic problems of Kalmykia are a direct consequence of Ilyumzhinov pouring funds into chess.

Schultz's letter continued:

"I asked many of the players who would represent us in Kalmykia. They all intend to go to the Olympiad. When I arrived in Hawaii, I asked the delegates their opinions on what we should do. Virtually everyone I asked stated that they felt this was an individual decision and that the USCF should send and finance a U.S. team. When the matter came before the delegates, it was debated. My recollection is that only two delegates spoke in favor of the USCF boycotting the Olympiad. I respect both of them for stating so forcibly their minority viewpoint. Nevertheless, after listening to the arguments, a large majority voted that we send our team."

Another perspective on the discussion in Hawaii was provided by U.S. GM Alex Yermolinsky on his website:

"A motion of boycotting the Elista Olympiad was introduced by Bill Goichberg, who happens to be a Policy Board member, and supported by a group of human rights activists, led by Larry Parr, who I think used to be Chief Editor of Chess Life *and also wrote a bunch of teaching books together with Lev Alburt. Bill we all know very well, and it takes me quite by surprise to learn that his interests extend beyond balancing his checkbook. I can't imagine what kind of bearing may the U.S. participation (non-participation) in Chess Olympiads possibly have on Continental chess tournaments' turnout, so it's hard to figure out Bill's motives. Whatever they are he kept them secret until the trip to Hawaii; as we spoke in length during his Continental Open just days before, he gave no hint of his intentions to torpedo the Chess Olympiad. My guess is that he was used by the Parr group for legitimization purposes – after all they needed somebody who's active in USCF politics."*

Yermolinsky made his feelings about Ilyumzhinov clear:

"It is difficult to brush Kirsan off as not a trustworthy person ever since he delivered on the promise in Groningen 1997, single-handedly bankrolling the most lucrative chess tournament in history. Same thing with Garry's talk about 'Kirsan's dirty money' – it's getting old and stale. The new thing in the character assault on the only guy who got the balls to stand up to K-K mafia dealings is his 'dictatorship'. Suddenly the people who normally don't give a rat's ass about anything that is not going to make them richer, speak in unison of the horrible situation with human rights in Kalmykia, shedding crocodile's tears about 'suffering of common folk' who have to work night shifts to complete City Chess project by September 26th.

"The article by a Sarah Hurst, that appeared in New In Chess *and gave a harsh criticism to Kirsan's regime, was apparently an angry feminist's reaction to the murder of a Kalmykian journalist, Ms. Larisa Yudina. Lots of circumstantial evidence were thrown in to accuse Kirsan of assassinating his political opponent – I doubt Ms. Yudina was ever that powerful in the Elista political scene – and a call was sent to all chessplayers to boycott Kirsan's events. One person did answer, GM Ian Rogers is not going to Elista! Oh, boy, Chess Olympiad will never be the same without him!"*

If I recall correctly, it was Don Schultz's suggestion that I contact Garry Kasparov's manager and find out if Kasparov was going to make a statement on the matter. I found out that Kasparov was aware of the situation, but he didn't participate publicly in the debate. He had been an adversary of FIDE since his breakaway match with Short in 1993, but it seems to me that this was for little other than financial reasons, and perhaps personal prestige. If only Kasparov had stood up strongly to Ilyumzhinov on ethical grounds. He might have been a catalyst to end the corruption within FIDE. Professional players would have listened to him.

Although Kasparov was quiet in the chess world on this matter, he did attack Ilyumzhinov in a statement to the House Banking Committee of the U.S. Congress on September 15, 1998. He spoke about the failure of the Yeltsin government's reforms, the "bloodbath in Chechnya", and the return of communists to high office. Kasparov's advice was to stop giving Russia aid. After describing the corruption in government and business, he turned to Ilyumzhinov:

"There is one transgressor who is extravagant even by Russian standards and I have watched his progress because it adversely affects my chess career. Kirsan Ilyumzhinov is president of the tiny republic of Kalmykia, ruling over 360,000 impoverished people in the vast empty steppes in the south of Russia on the Caspian Sea. The president of this under-populated, semi-autonomous state has made an amazing career by attracting over 4,000 Russian corporations, including some household names, to register in his self-proclaimed offshore zone.

"The result is that these companies pay 5,000 euros per quarter to a special presidential fund. This equates to a multimillion-dollar fortune to Kirsan Ilyumzhinov, and a significant loss to the central Russian tax base. This would be like allowing Citibank-Travelers to register on an Indian reservation somewhere in the U.S. and pay no taxes at all.

"At the end of 1995, Kirsan Ilyumzhinov decided to take over the ailing International Chess Federation known as FIDE. His patronage and his subsidy gives him full control over an international federation based in Lausanne. The connection with Switzerland and the conduit this provides for his money is obvious.

"Today, as we speak, he is finishing work on a Chess Village in his capital, Elista, which will play host to the Chess Olympics and 2,000 competitors and officials. This comes at a time when workers are not receiving their salaries and Moscow cannot finance a housing programme for military personnel. Simultaneously Mr. Ilyumzhinov, despite regular revelations of his nefarious business activities in the Russian press, announces that he personally will put up $3 million in prize money for the FIDE Championship in Las Vegas this November 29th 1998.

"Arguably then, my chess colleagues will be playing for prize money provided in part by U.S. taxpayers, in part by the IMF and even more shamefully, for money taken literally from the mouths of many underprivileged Russian citizens."

British GM Jim Plaskett suggested to me that he was thinking of going to Elista to stand against Ilyumzhinov for FIDE president. Plaskett was well-intentioned, but his solo plan wasn't very realistic and it came to nothing. Most entertainingly, Lord Avebury became very enthusiastic about the boycott campaign. He talked to me a couple of times on the phone and wrote an article in a tabloid newspaper calling Ilyumzhinov a "murderer". "He won't sue me," he told me jovially.

As I mentioned before, *The Sunday Telegraph* had given me an award for my article on the Polgar sisters. Afterwards Daniel Johnson, a journalist at *The Times* and a keen chess player, gave me a guided tour of his newspaper's offices. A features editor for the *Mail on Sunday* also invited me in for a chat about famous Russian women and their hairdos. Then I got my biggest commission so far. Dominic Lawson, editor of *The Sunday Telegraph* (and another keen chess player, who had written a book about his friend Nigel Short's World Championship match with Kasparov), called and asked me to write an article about Ilyumzhinov. He offered me £1,000. That was a phenomenal sum to me, for one article.

The story, titled "The Kalmykian Gambit", appeared on the front page and inside of the paper's review section in September 1998 with three photographs, including one taken by Nicholas Spurling. A quote from Nigel Short, *The Sunday Telegraph*'s chess columnist, was lifted from the article and repeated under the main picture of Ilyumzhinov leaning on a Cadillac. "'We all know Ilyumzhinov is corrupt,' says the British chess champion Nigel Short, 'but at least he is putting money into chess. The previous FIDE president was corrupt and taking money out.'"

I had extracted the quote from Short rather deviously. We met at the British Championships in Torquay for the first time, although presumably he'd read my letter, as one of the players selected for the Olympiad team. Short was sitting in the bar after losing a crucial game. I caught him off guard and started asking about the Olympiad. He casually made the comment that turned into the lifted quote, of course not expecting that it would be published in a high-circulation newspaper.

The next (and last) time I saw Dominic Lawson, at an awards ceremony in London, a year after my own award (I was invited again as a previous winner), he told me in a disapproving tone that Short had been upset by the use of the quote. I found this whole episode amusing, as Lawson had once famously written an article based on a secret recording he made of the Cabinet minister Nicholas Ridley comparing the Germans to Nazis at a dinner. But apparently this type of behaviour just isn't cricket when it affects friends of Dominic Lawson.

The article in *The Sunday Telegraph* retold the Ilyumzhinov story for a non-chess audience. I also did some extra research. I quoted the Glasnost Defence Foundation, a group of Russian human rights campaigners who had urged players to boycott the Olympiad: "You will eat and drink on money received by a racket – President Ilyumzhinov's private fund, which is funded by an unlawful tribute by all the companies being registered in Kalmykia's offshore zone," they said. "Your arrival is simply being used as a vivid manifestation of the Kalmyk and chess president's ambitions. The winners will get prizes, but these are paid by unlawful extortion from the Kalmyk people. Every citizen of the Republic is obliged to make a financial contribution to the Chess Olympic Games."

I spoke to a representative of the U.S. oil company Americo, who wanted to be quoted anonymously. He told me that the company had been taken to the verge of bankruptcy by its dealings with Ilyumzhinov. Lengthy negotiations resulted in a contract, signed by Ilyumzhinov, for Americo to exploit Kalmykia's untouched oil resources, but the Kalmyk side pulled out and no work was ever done.

"Ilyumzhinov's supporters were the region's top mafia bosses. I met them," the Americo man said. "When we talked to the Kalmyks in New York, they had to call Kirsan before they did anything, and he wanted to know what his percentage of the profits would be. At one point Kirsan was discussing a possible Kasparov-Karpov match and he proposed that proceeds from the sale of oil would go towards the purse for that. I thought it was crazy."

The article concluded: "The issue of a boycott [of the Olympiad] has been debated by chess federations across the world, and all but one have taken the same decision. Scandal may have shaken Ilyumzhinov, but the grandmasters and their presiding bureaucrats have no intention of unseating him until the funds dry up."

In fact I was mistaken here in implying that one federation had boycotted the Olympiad. I must have been thinking of the Danish Chess Federation. I had been in contact with top Danish players, who were very concerned about the Yudina murder and decided not to go. Due to the lack of players, the federation did not send a team to Elista. But there was no official boycott.

The Olympiad went ahead, starting a day or two late. BCF officials had insisted to me that England must play because the men's team had their best chance yet to win gold. Instead, they were ridiculed in the press for their drunken behaviour under the "leadership" of their laid-back captain, GM David Norwood. The Kalmyk girls proved to be quite a distraction for many of the teams, and some long-term relationships were formed. Also, Ilyumzhinov was re-elected president of FIDE. He was unopposed.

After the Olympiad was over, I was interviewed for a BBC Radio 5 sport programme. The producers were linking the corruption in FIDE with the campaign for chess to be recognised as a sport by the British government. Ilyumzhinov had visited the House of Commons to lobby politicians for this. If chess were considered a sport, it would be eligible for funding from National Lottery revenues. Ilyumzhinov also hoped that his friend, IOC Chairman Juan Antonio Samaranch, would include chess as a demonstration sport at the 2000 Sydney Olympics.

One British MP, who agreed that chess should be a sport, said on the programme that he hadn't received any letters about the plight of the Kalmyks from his constituents in Oxford! The shadowy presence of Russian millionaire Artyom Tarasov was also noted in the programme. Tarasov had gone into partnership with Ilyumzhinov to form an organisation called FIDE Commerce. He blustered over the issue of the various passports he had held.

This was the beginning of the end of my career as editor of *ChessMoves*, and indeed my commitment to chess journalism was in steep decline. There had been other controversies over articles I wrote or published in the BCF's newsletter. Junior chess was a minefield, as was sexism, which the well-known chess player and journalist Cathy Forbes wrote an article about. Her accusation of sexual harassment against another chess journalist, John Henderson, made the national newspapers, and he threatened to sue the BCF for publishing the story first without giving him the chance to reply. Never mind that the national papers made the story far more lurid. The BCF immediately backed down and published an apology.

I also wrote some humorous articles that provoked a mixed response. One satirised a chess organiser and sponsor, Nigel Johnson, who had been embroiled in a series of trivial mishaps. Tony Miles wrote a letter to *ChessMoves* complaining about my brutality towards Johnson, and Stewart Reuben didn't like the article, either. There was always a lively debate on the letters page, involving contributions from big names in British chess like Leonard Barden and Mike Basman, and I was happy to air all sides of a story. I hadn't asked John Henderson to comment on Cathy Forbes' article because she had kept him anonymous, and I wrongly assumed he'd want to stay that way.

All the articles in *ChessMoves* were approved by the BCF before publication. When there was a negative reaction, they blamed me. I looked back on all this when I was in Azerbaijan, working for the BBC.

He Wanted *Pravda*, Not *Private Eye*
(*CHESS*, January 2000)

Now that I'm back in the former USSR, the word "glasnost" or "openness" suddenly looms large. Strange as it may seem, there is considerably more of it in Azerbaijan than in the BCF. I'd like to shed some light on my 19-month tenure as editor of the BCF's official organ, *ChessMoves*, if I may be permitted to do so uncensored.

On the front page of the first issue produced by the new editor, BCF Politburo Chairman Stewart Reuben, Stewart says that I was appointed to add my "individualistic voice to the general clamour for attention". A slightly odd phrase, but in Stewart-speak it means I was expected to make *ChessMoves* more lively. As a professional journalist, not a chess bureaucrat, that is exactly what I tried to do.

Unfortunately, during the course of a few months it became clear to certain members of the BCF Central Committee that I "did not have the best interests of English chess at heart", as Stewart himself regretfully informed me. Apart from the early Nigel Johnson fiasco, when I made the heinous mistake of satirising the activities of a chess sponsor, my first big blooper was to campaign (outside the pages of *ChessMoves*, because nothing on the subject was permitted by Stewart to appear in the newsletter) against the Elista Olympiad held by the FIDE and Kalmyk president, "His Excellency" Kirsan Ilyumzhinov.

Once again, I was hitting a big chess sponsor, who of course should remain untouchable, despite the scurrilous accounts of his activities which have appeared in the Russian and international press. Members of the England team and the BCF management were furious that I had dared to suggest they should forfeit their chance to win gold at the Olympiad for the sake of human rights. But when the England team openly admitted to using the jaunt to Elista as an excuse for drinking and partying, were they vilified as I had been? I think not.

A series of further controversies convinced the BCF that I was truly an enemy of the people who ought to be purged and preferably sent into exile. Junior chess was the main issue being discussed during my time as editor of *ChessMoves*. I published most of the letters I received on this subject, some of which criticised the BCF selection process and also the BCF junior director at the time, Brian Jones. One of the strongest letters was from *Guardian* columnist Leonard Barden, who has devoted most of his life to junior chess.

For some reason, some of the BCF management and also some readers of *ChessMoves* tended to assume that I fully supported the views in the letters, just because I had published them. This assumption could not be further from the truth. To be honest, I have no opinions on junior chess at all. I know nothing about it. I didn't play chess seriously when I was a child, and I have never commented on the subject. I simply gave well-qualified people the opportunity to express their views, so that there could be a proper debate on this extremely important issue.

The same goes for Cathy Forbes' article about sexual harassment and Mike Basman's campaign to have the Croydon girls' chess team reinstated into *The Times* Schools Chess Championship. The latter was a convoluted story, but I tried to provide a balanced summary of it in the newsletter. Far from acting as an agent of Mike Basman, I repeatedly had to tell him that I could not publish his lengthy and frequent letters. When Brian Jones eventually resigned as a result of the dispute, Reuben tried to persuade me not to publish his resignation statement, but I insisted.

Previously the BCF had blamed me for publishing Barden's criticisms of Jones, when he was a BCF director, and now they were trying to keep Jones's statement out of *ChessMoves*! Afterwards it emerged that Jones had managed to go over budget by about £13,000 [later the BCF revised this figure to £6,248], which has plunged the BCF into a financial crisis, which is why Stewart kindly offered at a BCF Management Board meeting to edit *ChessMoves* voluntarily for six months.

The only problem was, Stewart didn't think it was worth mentioning this fact to me. The regular £210 per month that I earned from *ChessMoves* was very valuable to me as a freelance. I also derived great enjoyment from editing it, until it got to the point where I was being suffocated by Stewart breathing over my shoulder. So Stewart had decided to take over *ChessMoves*, i.e. to sack me, and this had been decided at a meeting where probably 20 or so people were present, but I knew nothing about the decision until a rumour reached me several weeks later, by which time I already had a job with the BBC and had resigned as editor of *ChessMoves* for that reason.

To say I resigned "to pursue my career" is an enormous oversimplification. I was forced to stop being a freelance and look for a job because I had concentrated too much on chess writing, for which I was paid a fraction of the amount that I would expect in any other field. This was compounded by the fact that a barrage of criticism was directed at me. Not from the readers of my articles or of *ChessMoves* – if I get a response from something I have written or published I am happy, whether it is positive or negative.

The depressing thing was that the owners of the publications I wrote for, in particular the BCF, were placing all the blame on me when there was a controversy, instead of backing me up for providing exciting copy. I was fed up, and my enthusiasm for writing about chess was waning for this reason, not because I had lost interest in the subject itself.

Reuben obviously doesn't want to make the same mistake again, so he didn't bother to advertise the post of *ChessMoves* editor this time around. He could have advertised it as a voluntary post if the BCF is really strapped for cash, and there would still probably have been applicants, as plenty of people are willing to do chess work voluntarily. But he wanted *Pravda*, not *Private Eye*. *ChessMoves* readers are getting a raw deal.

* * *

In the spirit of Reuben's insistence on absolute impartiality, *CHESS* also published a reply from him. One paragraph is enough to sum it up: "Sarah herself writes with relish about some of the mistakes she made as editor of *ChessMoves*. It became necessary to ensure none further appeared and I undertook this task as chairman of the BCF... It would have been a dereliction of my responsibilities to permit her to continue unchecked with her catalogue of mistakes, misjudgements and potentially libellous comments and also to range outside her brief to concentrate on British chess."

Since my departure from the chess scene, I have followed the continuing saga of Ilyumzhinov via the Internet. As the second anniversary of Larisa Yudina's death approached, at the end of May 2000, Radio Netherlands published a story on their website focusing on Larisa's husband, Gennadi. Margreet Strijbosch wrote: "The actual killers have been put behind bars. But Gennadi Yudin says justice hasn't yet been done. He wants those who ordered the murder to be punished as well.

"The killers and others have given evidence, pointing at political circles. One witness, who is no longer alive, has alleged that President Ilyumzhinov's brother was in Yudina's flat on the evening she disappeared. The official police investigation, however, has been closed and the public prosecutor refuses to re-open the case.

"After the murder of his wife, Gennadi Yudin and two other journalists continued publishing *Sovjetskaya Kalmykia* with foreign financial support from abroad. The newspaper now appears twice a month and is printed outside the republic. Printers in Kalmykia simply find it too risky to get involved in a non-government newspaper. It is illegal to sell the paper, but 3,000 copies find their way to enthusiastic readers."

The 34th Olympiad took place in Istanbul in 2000, along with the 71st FIDE Congress. "President Ilyumzhinov was given unprecedented powers and used them immediately to announce the end of serious chess," Dutch GM Hans Ree said on the *ChessCafe* website. "According to the Dutch federation's report, the congress was badly prepared and chaotic, handled nervously by vice president Makropolous while Ilyumzhinov smiled and sat quiet as if it was no concern of his. Many times

FIDE's own statutes were blatantly violated, but this is hardly a surprise any more. Also no surprise, but still almost incredible when you really think about it, was the transfer of all commercial rights to the FIDE World Championship to the private firm FIDE Commerce, owned by Ilyumzhinov (70 percent) and the Russian businessman Artyom Tarasov (30 percent). These rights were given to FIDE Commerce until the year 2017, with an option for the company to renew it 'til 2027."

Ilyumzhinov also made the startling announcement that all chess games would last two hours instead of six, "from the World Championship and the Olympiads to all local tournaments." This measure was supposed to encourage TV coverage of chess events. Ree then qualified his remark about "the end of serious chess". Chess would survive, as it had done for about 1,500 years, he said, but this was the end of serious chess within FIDE. He concluded his article with the words: "Now that FIDE is really on its way to kill chess, decent national federations should walk out, as quickly as possible."

Obviously the chess world is more concerned about Ilyumzhinov's attitude towards the game than his human rights record. But still no chess federation heeded Ree's call for a walkout. FIDE continued to host lavish annual knockout World Championships and other high-profile events with big prize funds.

The Russian media have also been paying close attention to Kalmykia. The news agency Interfax reported in February 2001 (quoting the liberal Yabloko Party's press service) that opposition candidates running for seats on the Elista city council had received death threats. "These candidates, who criticised not only the policies of the city's leadership, but also the policies of Kalmykia President Kirsan Ilyumzhinov, have been receiving death threats by phone almost every day. The callers reportedly mention the fate of Larisa Yudina… Some opposition candidates have also been dismissed from their jobs, while others… have been unable to register to participate in the election."

Online newspaper *Pravda.Ru* reported in June 2001 that Russia's highest supervising agency, the Audit Chamber, had discovered abuse of the transfer of federal funds in Kalmykia. "In violation of the present legislation, the upkeep of the football club Uralan was financed at 57.7 million roubles (one American dollar equals approximately twenty-nine roubles) from the republican coffers. 53.6 million roubles of the federal resources under a federal goal-oriented programme were spent on building a facility (City Chess) of the 1998 Chess Olympiad and the Uralan stadium… At the same time, one of the main goals, provision of drinking water for the population of Kalmykia, has not been achieved."

However, according to an article in the magazine *Profil* by Inessa Slavutinskaya, the violations found were minor and the Audit Chamber was disappointed. "The 50-member team's three-month effort went for naught, although most politicians questioned by *Profil* said that only a lazy person would not see the lawlessness in Kalmykia." The magazine blamed the failure on the head of the audit team, whose term had already expired, so he was working until a replacement arrived. "Most of the officials in the presidential administration who were questioned by *Profil* believe that sending a man whose term has expired for such a critical audit was a major mistake. It would have been better to wait for the appointment of a new auditor, but [chairman of the Audit Chamber Sergey] Stepashin was apparently in too much of a rush to report a success."

The magazine reported that Ilyumzhinov was still popular in Kalmykia: the people did not seem willing to exchange their president for a solution to the water shortage. Ilyumzhinov plays on the Kalmyks' ethnic feelings, a Kremlin source told the magazine, by constantly reminding them of Stalin's deportation. The Kalmyks have not forgiven Moscow for that. "The Kremlin, however, has an interest in the opposite – it wants to have its own person heading Kalmykia," *Profil* said. "The point is that Kalmykia is of great strategic importance."

The opposition Yabloko Party is also continuing its campaign against Ilyumzhinov. "As for Ilyumzhinov's beloved soccer club Uralan, R70.2m of budget money was spent on it, which is two-and-a-half times as much as the funding for all of the republic's educational institutions, including the payment of child-support allowances," the magazine quoted Yabloko deputy Valery Ostanin as saying. "When a former prosecutor of Kalmykia personally drove one criminal file, involving violations in the work of the Agency of Development and Cooperation, to the prosecutor-general's office, he had an accident en route – and the criminal file burned up along with the car. The former prosecutor himself got away with a mild scare, losing only his prosecutor's job."

City Chess "is empty, bringing no revenues to the treasury, and the international airport still stands unfinished," *Profil* reported. The article came to a depressing conclusion: "Whether the present Kremlin will turn Ilyumzhinov out of office is a very debatable question as of today. At any rate, the presidential administration's big plan – to promote the former TV diva Aleksandra Buratayeva, now a deputy in the Duma from [the party that supports Putin] Unity – attests once again to the overly fanciful imagination of the Kremlin strategists. If there is anybody people in Kalmykia are unlikely to vote for, it is a woman president."

The Audit Chamber's activities in Kalmkyia were also analysed by Jorunn Brandvoll, a writer affiliated with the University of Oslo and the Norwegian Institute of International Affairs. In an article for Radio Free Europe/Radio Liberty, she reported that at around the same time the results of the audit were published, the Russian State Duma passed a law stipulating that Kalmykia was one of 10 regions whose leaders would be allowed to run for a third or even fourth term in office.

"From time to time some people go out on Elista's main square to protest against harsh living conditions," Brandvoll wrote, "but such demonstrations are normally swiftly suppressed by the police. On 4 July, three women were badly beaten up by police for going on a hunger strike in the main square. Too many have lost their livelihoods for criticising the regime, and loss of one's job is a serious threat in a region where unemployment is high. A high school director was recently dismissed after she let her pupils go to school on the president's birthday, which is a republican holiday." On July 25 there was an attempt to set fire to the flat of Yabloko member and *Sovietskaya Kalmkyia* journalist Svetlana Ilinskaya, Brandvoll wrote.

On television, Russia's NTV featured Kalmykia in a special report in December 2001. NTV focused on the risks of being a journalist in the republic, and spoke to Valery Ulyadurov, a correspondent with *Sovietskaya Kalmykia*. "There's no economic base and not even a remotely independent newspaper," the NTV correspondent said. "There's no profit to be made from putting money into the press here. You could lose everything." Ulyadurov agreed: "Here in Kalmykia, since there isn't, or rather hasn't been until recently, any independent political or economic organisation, everything was decided by Kirsan Nikolayevich Ilyumzhinov. Journalists can either sell themselves to Ilyumzhinov or maintain a haughty disdain and die of hunger." The same could be said of chess players.

The list of shady characters who are associated with Ilyumzhinov is quite remarkable. Another name came to light in February 2002, when the newspaper *Vechernyaya Kazan* reported that Kalmykia's new senator – the republic's representative in Russia's upper house, the Federation Council – was Rustem Iskhakov, "a Kazan-based businessman whose dealings are under investigation by local law enforcement authorities." According to a summary of the article by Radio Free Europe/Radio Liberty, "Iskhakov reportedly has friendly relations and joint business projects with Kalmykia's president, Kirsan Ilyumzhinov."

The president's own business activities were scrutinised in an article on the politkom.ru website in March 2002. "One of the main results of Ilyumzhinov's nine years in office is his personal infiltration of all significant commercial and industrial structures in the republic," the article said. "All more or less big business in Kalmykia is controlled by Ilyumzhinov and his people. And small businesses live in fear of pressure from the state and do not dare participate in the republic's political and social life except in Ilyumzhinov's general line.

"Informal control over regional business is exercised through three structures. They are the companies Aris... and Khalzan... as well as the National Clearing Bank. Registration of enterprises in the offshore zone created in Kalmykia is conducted through the first two. The bank handles financial transactions. All three are dependent on Ilyumzhinov and can through joint efforts 'strangle' any local entrepreneur...

"Through these same three structures, the authorities pump shadow money out of the offshore zone. According to varying estimates, it ranges from 20 million to 30 million dollars a year. An investigation by the Audit Chamber which caused an uproar a short while ago merely forced the local structures to act more secretly and cautiously. Significant independent business is simply absent in Kalmykia. That also has an effect on the weakness of the opposition to Ilyumzhinov."

The article went on to describe the criminalisation of business in Kalmykia, alleging that the Kalmyk government collects protection money from fish and caviar poachers. There is no effective opposition to Ilyumzhinov, the article concluded, and he has been triumphant due to his charisma, efficiency, talent, shrewdness and hard work.

Ilyumzhinov even made the pages of *Time* magazine in March 2002, in an article titled "Knights and Knaves" by Lev Grossman. This focused on the rift in the chess world over Ilyumzhinov's attempts to popularise the game, skimming over his rise to power in Kalmykia and FIDE, his hosting of the Olympiad and the World Championships, and the Yudina murder. Grossman apparently saw much humour in the situation, describing chess players as "mad geniuses" and comparing the game to professional wrestling. American GM Yasser Seirawan preferred a slightly different analogy: "You've almost got a situation like boxing," he said. "Speaking as a member of the chess world, it's extremely undignified."

It's worse than undignified. It is inexcusable that chess players can accept their dependence on Ilyumzhinov so readily. In a move that is typical of professional chess players, Seirawan has put moral questions to one side by putting forward a suggestion to reunify the FIDE World Championship with the rival World Championship cycle supported by Kasparov and Kramnik. I requested an interview with Seirawan for this book, but he declined, referring me to his previous comments about FIDE.

In June 2000, Seirawan wrote an open letter to Ilyumzhinov titled "Enough is Enough". "When did [FIDE] last show any respect for the prestige of a game which is many centuries old? Above all, why has it allowed itself to become a laughing-stock through its serial incompetence?" Seirawan asked. "The full catalog of disasters in recent years is too grimly familiar to need repeating here. The bouncing checks of Las Vegas and your unpaid promissory notes are just two well-publicized scandals from the past year that have made FIDE look clownish and tawdry."

Seirawan slammed FIDE for undermining the credibility of the GM/IM title system, antagonising top players, and suggesting Baghdad and Tehran as venues for World Championships. "FIDE is cheapening and destroying almost everything it touches," Seirawan said. "Mr. President, it is time for you and your board to step aside."

In response to the letter, American GM Boris Gulko suggested that Seirawan should be the next FIDE president. Seirawan replied that his preference was Bessel Kok, a leading chess sponsor. "He is wealthy and wouldn't run FIDE with the purpose of increasing his wallet size," Seirawan said.

"All we have to do is circulate a petition by as many Grandmaster colleagues as we can and basically ask Bessel to stand for election," Seirawan explained. "While very helpful and very important, that unfortunately is not enough. The key is Garry Kasparov. It must be Garry who picks up the phone and asks Bessel to stand for office. Garry has to agree to work with a new administration and to support the new President. If Garry is willing to do that and if the majority of the grandmasters agreed to make Bessel their candidate, he would sweep into office... we must recognize that Garry is the greatest chess player who has ever lived."

Needless to say, Kasparov did not heed the call to find a new FIDE president. In his long essay "A Fresh Start", published on Kasparov's website in 2002, Seirawan wrote, "Garry Kasparov is the world's number one ranked player and has been a harsh critic of FIDE's leaders, as well as its Knockout tournament system to determine the official FIDE world champion. Despite fighting against FIDE with great determination, in 2001 Garry participated in a FIDE event and is, as a result, the official FIDE champion for Rapid Chess. (Quite a strange irony...)"

Seirawan then laid out the details of how he would bring Kasparov and the FIDE World Championship together again. However, his previous call for Ilyumzhinov's resignation was strangely absent. Seirawan described himself as a "peacemaker". Yet another opponent of Ilyumzhinov bites the dust.

Now, let's see what we can find out about FIDE from its website (www.fide.com). In a contents list under the header "Official info", there is a section titled "Commissions" which includes the presidential board, the executive board, zone presidents, the qualification commission, the titles and ratings committee, the arbiters' council, the technical commission, the rules and tournaments regulations committee, the Swiss pairings committee, and so on... there is even an ethics commission, a medical commission and a committee on chess philately.

All these 33 "commissions" are liberally staffed by officials. Two familiar names appear more often than most. David Jarrett from England is still treasurer and is also on the committee on chess philately, the "permanent fund" (whatever that is), and the medical commission. Jarrett's colleague Stewart Reuben is secretary of the rules and tournaments regulations committee, chairman of the organisers committee and is also on the World Championship cycle committee.

Bizarrely, there is a Players' Council and a World Players' Council. The Players' Council looks like all the other FIDE "commissions" – a list of names and addresses. These are GM Jan Timman, GM Darcy Gustavo Machado Vieira Lima, GM Efstratios Grivas, WGM Alisa Maric and Branimir Jukic. Out of these, only Timman and Maric are well-known names. The World Players' Council is different, however. Here we have just two names, one phone number and a web address. The names are well-known Russian GM Valery Salov (president) and not so well-known GM Jaime Sunye Neto (vice president).

I was dismayed, but not entirely surprised, to find the World Players' Council listed as an official commission on the FIDE website. I had already discovered the WPC website by accident in a search on materials about Larisa Yudina. There are many fascinating articles on the WPC website (ajedrez_democratico.tripod.com/).

One is titled "Larisa Yudina Murder Case: Just a Smoke Screen?" and unsigned. The following quotes convey the tone:

"Why this sudden hysteria around the murder case of some brave but obscure journalist, head of the Kalmykian branch of the fascist political party 'Yabloko'? Despite non-existence of any kind of incriminating evidence against the FIDE President in this case (at least it has never been officially disclosed) our chess hacks immediately jumped to the occasion to self-appoint themselves investigators, prosecutors and judges and did not linger for long before pronouncing their sentence – guilty...

"Only because of your unreserved racist support to the bloodthirsty, hateful, immoral and goony individuals like Kasparov there is no place to dignity, responsibility and honor in Russian politics (the same as everywhere else)... Why are you so fiercely opposed to the World Players' Council, even more so than to FIDE itself? Why do you only support thieves, liars, drug-addicts, ignoramuses and docile puppets? Because you are horrified by the very idea of existence of an independent organization of Players, directed by a leader of strong will, democratic convictions and impeccable reputation; you are afraid of losing your monopoly on brainwashing us."

The diatribe concludes with an article on the shooting of Palestinian journalists with rubber bullets by Israeli troops in March 1998. Naturally, I wondered how many famous chess players were on the World Players' Council. On close scrutiny of the site I found that Valery Salov was the only famous player with his name on any of the articles (most of them, in fact), which was encouraging. Most players are not daft enough to join Salov, but FIDE nevertheless considers the WPC a legitimate entity.

The sycophancy towards Ilyumzhinov continues unabated. "His Excellency" celebrated his 40th birthday on April 5, 2002. The participants in the Dubai Chess Grand Prix wrote him a letter:

Dear Mr. President,
On behalf of the chess fraternity, many happy returns on your today's 40th birthday, we offer our sincerest congratulations and warmest thanks for all your hard work as FIDE President for the last 7 years.
We wish you continued success and happiness for many years to come.
Best wishes,

G. Makropolous
FIDE Deputy President

I. Al Bannai

President, Arab Chess Union

P. Nikolopoulos
Chief Arbiter, FIDE Grand Prix

Zhu, Chen (CHN)
Anand, Viswanathan (IND)
Shirov, Alexei (ESP)
Short, Nigel D. (ENG)
Karpov, Anatoly (RUS)
Dreev, Alexey (RUS)
Georgiev, Kiril (BUL)
Leko, Peter (HUN)
Lautier, Joel (FRA)
Khalifman, Alexander (RUS)
Topalov, Veselin (BUL)
Azmaiparashvili, Zurab (GEO)
Grischuk, Alexander (RUS)
Ivanchuk, Vassily (UKR)
Bacrot, Etienne (FRA)
Radjabov, Teimour (AZE)

A historic meeting took place in May 2002, finally bringing Kasparov and Ilyumzhinov together. How long this marriage made in hell will last is anybody's guess. It's an incredible feat of hypocrisy by Kasparov (who turns 40 himself in 2003), considering that he has achieved everything that one player can possibly achieve in chess, and isn't exactly strapped for cash. If he didn't want to oust Ilyumzhinov, he could have stood aside from the fray and become a distinguished spokesman for international chess. He preferred to make a pact with the devil, in return for a little more fame and fortune.

Resolutions of May 6, 2002 on the Unification of the Chess World

- All parties and persons present at the meeting of May 6, 2002, in Prague have expressed their willingness to support the process of unification of the Chess World.

- This process accepts the main principle that FIDE is the custodian and owner of the World Chess Championship title and that there should be only one federation – FIDE – recognized by the IOC and the world of sports representing the Chess World.

- The unification process has to lead to only one undisputed World Champion recognized by FIDE.

- The professional chess world requires a professional management body to be constituted on the basis of a business plan, which will be submitted by Bessel Kok and to be discussed and agreed with the World Chess Foundation and the FIDE

Presidential Board within 90 business days after May 6, 2002. On approval of the business plan, FIDE shall issue a license (excluding Einstein Group Pre-unification events) to this body to manage professional chess as a profitable business.

- FIDE supports the principles of unity plan (Annex A) presented by Bessel Kok and will cooperate to help with the acceptance of the principles on which the unity plan is based and the implementation thereof, by all players concerned, including the FIDE World Champion, and all organizers involved.

- All parties and persons present agree to the principles put forward during the meeting with respect to the post-unification World Championship system.

- All parties and persons present at the meeting of May 6, 2002 in Prague have agreed that they will do their utmost to achieve the unification of the Chess World.

Made this day in Prague, May 6, 2002

Signed by:

H.E. Kirsan Ilyumzhinov, FIDE President
Bessel Kok
Garry Kasparov
Vladimir Kramnik
Yasser Seirawan
Alexey Orlov, President World Chess Foundation

Ilyumzhinov was scheduled to face an election in Kalmykia in October 2002. On July 30, 2002, the Yabloko regional leader in Kalmykia, Ivan Ryzhkov, sent an appeal to international human rights organisations. He wrote:

"Unbelievable as it may seem, there has been a totalitarian regime for nine years now in one of the regions of democratic Russia… Since 1994 an offshore zone has existed in the republic, but this hasn't benefited the people - its revenues, $20 million, have never passed through the budget of the republic. All this money has gone into the pocket of one person, the president of Kalmykia. Moreover, the offshore zone has brought large-scale economic crime to the republic, such as money laundering, a network of drugs dealers, the caviar and fish mafia, illegal oil exploitation and other criminal activities the like of which we had never seen before."

Detailing the restrictions on the media, absence of human rights and manipulation of elections by Ilyumzhinov, Ryzhkov concluded that there could be a chance for free and fair elections to take place if international observers came to Kalmykia on October 20.

"This could threaten Ilyumzhinov's main asset, his image, his fear of appearing before the eyes of a wide international audience as he actually is - a provincial dictator, a dull-witted, ambitious man, willing to use all possible means to retain power - and thus temper his administrative fervour."

Putin's attitude towards Ilyumzhinov is highly ambivalent. Ilyumzhinov's erratic behaviour is sometimes damaging, sometimes helpful to the federal government. In August 2002 Russia refused a visa to the Dalai Lama, who had been invited to Kalmykia by Ilyumzhinov. Clearly the Putin government did not want to upset China. However, in the same month, Russia and Iraq were preparing to sign a $40 billion economic cooperation plan. Ilyumzhinov's friendly relations with Saddam Hussein would presumably be valued in that context.

Also in August 2002, Ignatius Leong from Singapore, the 46-year-old president of a FIDE zone that comprises 14 Asian countries, announced that he would oppose Ilyumzhinov in the FIDE presidential election in November 2002. This was encouraging news. The following statement appeared on his website (www.ignatiusleong.org):

"Chess is his life. Nobody gets rich in chess administration (unless you are crooked), and his source of income is open for everybody to see: Mr. Leong runs a chess school/training center with several hundred students...Mr. Leong says: 'My keyword is REFORM, my slogan is REFORM for a BETTER FIDE... If the electorate feels that the... money of Mr. Ilyumzhinov is the greatest benefit for FIDE, then FIDE will have to wait till another billionaire comes by.'

"You see, FIDE cannot continue relying on President Kirsan to put in more and more money. This source has already shown signs of drying up, and when it does, sooner or later, it will mean complete collapse for world chess."

I interviewed Leong by e-mail:

Q. What made you decide to run against Kirsan in November?

A. First there were the press releases of the French Chess Federation which called for reform. These were followed by numerous calls persuading me to join the reform group. Then I was informed that Kirsan would assemble exactly the same team for the elections. This goes to show that Kirsan remains indifferent to worldwide opinions despite advice that he drop at least Makropolous and even Jarrett. I actually applaud his generosity to chess but he is oblivious of some persons whose actions bring disrepute to FIDE - and I mean specifically Makropolous. I have seen before my own eyes on several occasions how Makropolous would walk past delegates who belong to the smaller federations. Noticeably, how I saw him deal with the Chinese organisers at the Shenyang World Cup. And how he belittles even some of his closer friends during the sessions of the General

Assemblies. And since Kirsan cannot do without Makropolous, there's no better way than to run against Kirsan, whom by the way, I still consider a friend.

Q. How would you finance FIDE, and would you keep the knockout World Championship going?

A. I don't have the wealth of Kirsan. But I believe I have better credibility as I have been able to find organisers and sponsors for events in my zone. I would like to set up an international trust fund managed by a committee who have no vested interests and who do not hold any FIDE positions. Better still would be that they are either individuals or representatives of organisations who themselves contribute towards the fund which shall be kept in the banks for the sole purpose of earning interest. The funds shall only be used to help FIDE in emergencies and only the interest derived may be used for development purposes.

I would like to consider the possibility of organising the World Championship with different formats in alternate years. But I prefer the top players in the world and a specified number of players in each country to be consulted on the qualification process, the time controls, tiebreaks, etc... They are the ones working for their meals so they should have a say. Geurt Gijssen should have no say at all in these matters. If at all, he would simply be appointed, and to carry out his function, period.

Q. Is it true that you were subject to intimidation by Kirsan in Armenia? Do you feel safe opposing him now?

A. We signed a Memorandum of Understanding in Lausanne during the Karpov-Anand match. Hence this subject is closed.

Q. Do you have any opinions on Kirsan's alleged corruption and possible involvement in the Larisa Yudina murder?

A. I was not living in Elista any more at the time of the murder. I have not done any research on his wealth. So on both matters I cannot derive any opinions. My contest against Kirsan is purely based on chess and how he manages FIDE.

It was rather disappointing to me that Leong did not intend to bring up Ilyumzhinov's corruption, and that he preferred to focus on trivial issues relating to lesser FIDE officials. I even began to wonder whether Leong's campaign might actually benefit Ilyumzhinov, by making FIDE look more democratic. I find it difficult to believe that chess officials will strangle their golden goose by voting him out. Ilyumzhinov is an arch-manipulator, a grandmaster of dictatorial tactics. He can thank chess players for being as compliant as his own Buddhist people. FIDE may well have many more years of its beloved Kirsan's reign to look forward to.

A brief history of FIDE's new knockout format World Championships:

1997-98 Groningen (Netherlands)/Lausanne (Switzerland)
Total prize fund: $5,000,000
Number of players: 97
Winner: Anatoly Karpov (RUSSIA)
Runner-up: Viswanathan Anand (INDIA)
Karpov said: "For chess fans following this match throughout the world, and especially those on the Internet, this new World Championship format became the Super Bowl of chess."

1999 Las Vegas (USA)
Total prize fund: $3,000,000
Number of players: 100
Winner: Alexander Khalifman (RUSSIA)
Runner-up: Vladimir Akopian (ARMENIA)
Khalifman said: "I think Las Vegas was a good tournament, very tense and exciting. The level of chess was high enough although at the latter stages the players were rather exhausted. However, I never said this format is perfect for the World Championship. I think that the system needs some improvements and it's a bit disappointing that FIDE is not working in this direction."

2000 New Delhi (India)/Tehran (Iran)
Total prize fund: $3,000,000
Number of players: 100
Winner: Viswanathan Anand (INDIA)
Runner-up: Alexei Shirov (SPAIN)
Anand said: "This is so very special. It's something that I have been chasing for and I feel just wonderful."

2001-02 Moscow (Russia)
Total prize fund: $3,000,000
Number of players: 128
Winner: Ruslan Ponomariov (UKRAINE)
Runner-up: Vassily Ivanchuk (UKRAINE)
Ponomariov said: "Perhaps the shorter time limit does lead to more mistakes, but in my subjective opinion, it makes chess events more lively."

7. Breaking Down the English Defence

My obsession with Russia had led me into chess journalism, but Jimmy Adams was equally enthusiastic about the British chess scene. After I moved to London we hatched a plan to write a book about British chess, past and present. We interviewed several key people, and I spent a week at the BCF office in Hastings, photocopying articles from old chess magazines, but we never got further than the research stage because we were both too busy.

A couple of the interviews were published in *CHESS*. The bare transcripts of the other interviews languished on my shelves for years. This book gives me the chance to bring them into the light of day for the first time. I'll start, though, with an interview with chess historian Ken Whyld that appeared in *CHESS*.

A Walk on the Whyld Side
(*CHESS*, November 1998)

Ken Whyld's farmhouse lies on a Roman road near the village of Caistor, Lincolnshire. But don't go and visit him unless you have a very good reason. It's quiet out there, and that's the way he likes it. No traffic, no hawkers, only the occasional phone call – this way of life gives Whyld more time to read books, write articles, and add to the encyclopaedic fund of knowledge that has earned him the nickname "The Omniscient One".

His real name, Whyld, was an adaptation by his great-grandfather of the original Wild. Apparently, in the middle of the 19th century, confusion was caused when two cousins with exactly the same names came to live next door to one another in a street in Derbyshire. Today the name Whyld is respected the world over as that of an authoritative chess historian – although he can talk with equal confidence about a whole variety of subjects, ranging from the origins of language to politics in the Middle East and the plot of *Trainspotting*.

And he has a keen sense of humour, too. Whyld thought he saw something rude in the picture of a whistling shrimp on the cover of my book about Russia. "A dirty mind is a perpetual feast," he told me. That's a saying I won't forget, especially after hearing it from a wise and outwardly respectable septuagenarian, but one whose looks and attitude to life are those of a man some 20 years younger. Maybe that's all down to the dirty mind, or the fresh country air he breathes, or perhaps the fact that his estranged wife, who visits him from time to time, *is* 20 years younger than him.

"I've had three lives, really," Whyld says. He is a prolific writer and indefatigable researcher, a former computer programmer, and the father of three children. In his spare time he became a strong chess player, amassed a huge collection of chess books and magazines, and did some downhill skiing. The cost of all this activity was the breakup of his two marriages.

Sitting in Whyld's kitchen, which is heated by an Aga cooker and packed with chess books from floor to ceiling, we discussed these eventful lives. "When I was a teenager I always used to think I was a completely average person, but now I realise I wasn't average at all," he said. "I was an only child. When I was 12 I read *Das Kapital*; at 13 or 14 I read Einstein's Theory of Relativity. I read Lenin and Freud when I was 14 or 15."

Whyld's father set him an example in life. "He didn't believe you couldn't learn something. He was an electrician. He taught himself a lot of things, like how to become a radio engineer. If something went wrong with an appliance he didn't telephone for help, he tried to find out how it worked. When I was learning the violin at school, he learnt as well."

Whyld also learnt chess from his father, who used to play with a neighbour. "My father had a *Daily Express* book on beginner's chess and he loaned it to someone who gave him back instead a book on the openings by the old master Gunsberg. My father was furious because he wanted a beginner's book, but I was fascinated." As a teenager during the war, Whyld would play blindfold chess with a friend while walking through the streets of Nottingham. "Any decent player can play one game blindfold," he believes.

When he was 19, Whyld married the woman he would later sacrifice for chess. This was during his national service. "I was due to be posted to Palestine and we knew we'd get a better allowance if we were already married when I got there. Since Germany surrendered the day I finished my basic training, and Japan in the week that I completed my officer training on the Isle of Man, I always say the Arab-Israeli conflict would have been resolved if I'd gone! But I didn't – because of an injury.

"This happened on a training exercise while I was showing groups of men how to throw a grenade. I had given the order: 'Pull the pin out, throw it, then get down.' They had about 10 seconds and, in turn, all of them did it – except one. I went up to this fellow and repeated 'PULL THE PIN OUT,' upon which he extended his hand with the grenade in it and said, 'I already have'! It turned out that he'd done it while he was waiting, to save time. I snatched the grenade out of his hand and threw it, but I wasn't quick enough and it exploded just as I let go, and I had burns all the way up my arm."

In the army Whyld began playing correspondence chess, and as a young man he was even profiled in *CHESS*, with his photograph, as "Postal Chess Club Personality of the Month". Whyld had been a student at Nottingham University during the war, but didn't graduate, and only got his degree in English literature from the Open University in the 1970s. In 1949 his first son was born. "On my way to the maternity hospital I stopped in at a secondhand book shop where there were shelves full of chess books – it was George Hume's library."

Hume was a Scottish problemist who settled in England and died in 1936 – according to the *Oxford Companion to Chess*, by Ken Whyld and David Hooper. "I took a suitcase and filled it, they were so cheap," Whyld continued. "In today's terms I bought £5,000-worth of books for £50. Half the books were on problems, which I sold, but the other half were main line, including a long run of *British Chess Magazines*. I've never had another marvellous opportunity like that!"

The chance find sparked off a lifelong passion for collecting. Whyld started to buy books at auction. But there is one book that means more to him than the others. "I won some tournament and they offered me a prize – up to a certain amount. I chose Murray's *A History of Chess*. After you've read that, you find that people will fill a book with what is three pages in Murray. I became interested in the older forms of the game, like the Arabic form. I did a list of corrections to Murray and gave it away to chess collectors."

This in itself must have been a time-consuming endeavour, considering that Murray's book is 900 pages long and contains information about everything from medieval problems to 18th-century chess player and musician Philidor. But then, even today, Whyld is still researching, writing and lecturing on the mysteries surrounding the origins of chess in China and India.

In the immediate postwar years Whyld found someone else who was equally fastidious about preserving chess history, albeit of a more modern kind. This was E.G.R. Cordingley, a pioneer of chess publishing in Britain. As Whyld wrote in his obituary of Cordingley for *British Chess Magazine*, he was the first person to produce a duplicated tournament book, *Hastings 1932-3*. Limited to 30 copies, it turned out to be the first of a whole series.

After the war Cordingley also brought out his own magazine, *The Chess Student's Quarterly*, which consisted mainly of well-annotated contemporary master games. Whyld was among the small number of subscribers to Cordingley's publications, and the two of them struck up a friendship, first by correspondence and then in person. Later, when Cordingley began suffering from arthritis, Whyld even took over the editing of the magazine while Cordingley reduced his own workload to printing and distribution. *The Chess Student's Quarterly* ended in 1952 with Cordingley retiring due to ill health. He died about 10 years later.

"In the '40s, Cordingley had a typewriter with figurines – he was one of the first people to use figurines," said Whyld. "Hungarians had used them a long time before in a magazine. Everyone else used descriptive notation. I was very hostile to using 'N' for knight instead of 'Kt'. I thought it was very vulgar, like writing 'Niteclub' on a sign. Later on I took the figurine keys and put them on another typewriter. Now Lothar Schmid has them."

Lothar Maximilian Lorenz Schmid ("A collector of chess books and paraphernalia, he has the largest private chess library in the world" – *Oxford Companion*) became another great friend of Whyld's. They first met in the 1950s and shared a mutual interest in chess books and history. Schmid had originally come from the Dresden area of East Germany, but in the austere postwar years he had gained permission to travel abroad to play in chess tournaments. On one of these trips he smuggled his mother out in the boot of his car and defected to the West, where he made his fortune from publishing children's books. In 1958 Whyld was invited to attend Schmid's wedding to a woman whom the Finnish GM Heikki Westerinen described as "the most beautiful wife of any chess master I know".

Whyld remains eternally grateful to his German friend for offering to take care of his youngest son while he himself was going through a divorce in the early 1960s. Schmid had a son of about the same age. Whyld recently paid a visit to the Schmids, who have not yet fully recovered from serious injuries sustained in a car crash about a year ago.

In the 1950s, continuing Cordingley's pioneering work, Whyld produced several duplicated books of his own: *Meran 1926*, the Bronstein-Boleslavsky match of 1950, and a joint venture with William Winter and David Hooper on the Zürich Candidates of 1953 – a major work which, remarkably, came out within a month of the end of the tournament.

Whyld also met James Gilchrist, a strong county player with an interest in World Champion Emanuel Lasker, and they compiled two volumes containing all of Lasker's "serious" games. Gilchrist died in 1963 with only Whyld and David Hooper attending his funeral. But Whyld had a third volume in mind, containing other games played under match and tournament conditions, as well as those of the simultaneous display and casual variety, something that had not interested Gilchrist.

When this was published a few years later, Whyld asked the publisher, The Chess Player, Nottingham, if he could have a special copy, interleafed with blank pages, so he could insert extra games as he found them in readiness for the next edition. Whyld subsequently carried his Lasker manuscript around the world in search of more and more games, and it was only recently that the new edition appeared – over 30 years later and under the same publisher.

Throughout the 1950s Whyld had also produced his own magazine, *The Chess Reader*. This was quite different from *The Chess Student's Quarterly*, being exclusively devoted to reviews and discussions of chess books, but it had the same effect of keeping the editor in touch with chess buffs around the world. Whyld was simply doing something he wanted – keeping a record of new chess publications and obtaining a few free review copies along the way. Long before the invention of the PC and desktop publishing software, he laboriously typeset the pages. "I typed everything out with dots to the end of the line to see how many spaces I had to leave, then I typed each page out again with right-hand justification."

Subscribers to *The Chess Reader* paid similar attention to detail, in a section called "Points from the Post". M.V. Anderson wrote from Australia, "In your last *Chess Reader* at page 59 you commence the third paragraph 'it states that Alekhine played a simultaneous at Riga in 1937', and later query it. According to my records, Alekhine played a simultaneous at Riga in September 1936. My authority is *Schach-Echo* 1936 page 216." F.J. Skoff from the U.S.A. was more succinct: "*Chess Reader* continues on a high quality level, but I disagree with one review. Marshall's best games do contain instructive points."

Side by side with his interest in chess history and publishing, Whyld was also an active and strong competitive player. "In my club matches I always used to look for unusual lines in openings that were not the natural move. I played one against Znosko-Borovsky in the Spanish and he eventually won. It turned out that the stem game was Znosko-Borovsky-Alekhine, 1926!"

In the days when tennis players wore long trousers and Olympic athletes were amateurs, Whyld used to politely warn his opponents if they forgot to press the clock, and wouldn't argue in the postmortem when the loser tried to show him how he would have won if it were not for that one mistake… "But I wouldn't say I lacked the will to win," he added. "I believed that if you can really thrash someone then you're winning that game and the next one as well."

Whyld followed Lasker's approach, playing the sort of game in which your opponent is uncomfortable. "I'd play something sharp if I knew he liked positional play and vice versa. I was a great believer in playing an opening which looked like you were insulting your opponent, like 1. a3. Lots of people think that as Black they must have a winning game after that. It just means perhaps you've lost the advantage of the first move, you've got an equal game. Your opponent is so desperate to prove he is winning that he starts going for silly, desperate measures."

The atmosphere in chess clubs was quite different then. "In the '50s there was a member of Nottingham Mechanics called Beadles who I played a lot. He always sat leaning backwards because he had some kind of physical problem. He died and I went to his funeral. I regarded him as a friend, but I realised two things: I didn't know his first name, only his initials; and I'd spent more time face to face with him than I had with my wife." There were times when etiquette simply couldn't be observed, however. "Once I was in a match and the man sitting next to me was so shocked by his opponent's move that he was sick on the board."

Whyld was once the only participant in a simultaneous display to beat the great Soviet player Paul Keres. After the game, Whyld left the playing hall with Keres to go for a meal, but found his car hemmed in tight, front and back. Though Keres willingly helped him "bounce" the car out, Whyld later had cause to reflect on whether or not Keres knew then of the heart condition that was eventually to kill him.

By the end of 1963 Whyld's life changed abruptly. He divorced, gave up collecting chess books and went to work in Switzerland. He also ceased editing *The Chess Reader* and it was not until the 1980s that an equally high-standard chess self-publication appeared. This was Edward Winter's magazine *Chess Notes*, presently carried in serial form in *New in Chess* magazine [and subsequently on the ChessCafe website].

Indeed, Edward Winter is one of the few people in the world whose vast knowledge of chess history rivals Whyld's. But the two great chess historians have had a number of differences, for example their view of the role of British grandmaster, chess writer and organiser Raymond Keene. "I see him as an impresario, entitled to bullshit to get the punters hooked, whereas Edward Winter sees him as a chess scholar who lacks accuracy," Whyld said.

Switzerland is Edward Winter's home now, and Whyld also lived there during the period 1967-71, while he was working as a project manager, responsible for harmonising international systems for Nielsens. "That was the time I was a normal person for a while," he said. Instead of chess, his hobby was downhill skiing.

Whyld had worked in computers since the early '50s, when he set up Boots the Chemists as the first company in Europe with a fully transistorised computer. "I drafted this scheme, which was for stock control," he said. "It was accepted and I was put in charge." At Boots he was also very active in the sports club, which included chess. One day a programmer working under him, named Max, asked Whyld if he would give his son some private chess tuition. At the time Whyld's view was that a five-year-old should not get hooked on chess, and anyway he would probably never get any good at the game – so he declined. That little boy, Yasser Seirawan, went on to become one of America's top grandmasters. Max had come from Syria to work in England and had married a girl from Nottingham. He later emigrated to the U.S.A. to work for Boeing in Seattle, where Seirawan still lives.

From 1971 to 1973, Whyld worked in London as a management consultant and then the following year went to South Africa, where he was responsible for computerising a bank. "I was in charge of the conversion of the bank from manual records to computers. It had branches all over the country. We did it so quickly, at one point I worked for two-and-a-half days without sleep."

By this time Whyld had married his second wife, Janie, and they had a baby daughter named Abigail. Before his family moved to South Africa, Whyld started playing chess again. It had been a long layoff, but now he joined a chess club for something to do in the evenings. "I captained a prize-winning team named 'Goodbye FIDE' by one of its members as a reaction to South Africa's expulsion from anti-apartheid FIDE. That member, Kurt Dreyer, also happened to be captain of the South African Olympiad side. I had a few games published, one in the *Rand Daily Mail*, and was the highest-placed foreigner in an Open tournament in Johannesburg… which was one of my best ever results.

"In Johannesburg people weren't as racist as in other cities, except in public places like the post office, where there were separate entrances. In supermarkets there were two different piles of booze for white and black people, but it didn't really matter which pile you took from – that was just to conform with the law. It was essentially an English city. We played teams with black members. It was illegal for blacks and whites to drink at the same bar, but we always mixed at prize ceremonies. Not a lot of black people were interested in chess – draughts was much more popular."

Also on the subject of apartheid, Whyld recalls the ironic comment of his longtime friend and fellow chess writer, Wolfgang Heidenfeld, who had escaped pre-war anti-Semitism in Germany and gone to live in South Africa: "It was as bad being the oppressor in South Africa as the oppressed in Nazi Germany."

Whyld really did manage to give up playing chess when he came back to England, apart from a couple of tournaments in Cleethorpes. But he was still infected with the collecting bug and found that it was incurable. He was also embarking on his most ambitious project, a modern Murray – the *Oxford Companion*. David Hooper had suggested the idea of co-authoring the book, and they started researching it in 1973. Hooper and Whyld had known each other since 1950, and, as mentioned above, had already collaborated on the Zürich Candidates project.

"It took us 10 years to do the first edition of the *Companion*," said Whyld. "We both had jobs when we started, then David retired as an architect and began working full time on it. Abigail was born on the first of January 1972 and when we moved here the following year I was looking after her at home. I'd missed out when the boys were growing up because I was busy working, so I wanted to spend time with her."

Considerable detective work was required to make sure the *Companion* didn't repeat past errors. "At first we thought it wouldn't be a huge job – it would all be taken from existing sources. But we found different accounts in different sources, different dates of birth and death. We had to start doing basic research. For British players I spent days in Somerset House looking up wills. You gradually learn that some sources are nearly always reliable and some are nearly always not reliable – for example, Edward Lasker's *Chess Secrets* wasn't reliable.

"We had a lot of trouble with where Alekhine's last wife Grace was born and we established this – New Jersey. Even tombstones can be wrong on occasion – Alekhine's date of birth and death are both wrong by one day on his tombstone, and the Latvian player Mattison's date of death is two years out on his.

"Trying to find out details of some of the French people was quite hard, going through early 18th-century military records. We had to be selective when deciding which people should be in – you look at results. I've compiled a lot of statistics about performance. You had to perform at a certain level to be in as a player – being a GM wasn't necessarily enough. But [British player and journalist Harry] Golombek was in as a writer and administrator. [American author Fred] Reinfeld wasn't in the first edition and there were a lot of complaints.

"[British player Matthew] Sadler wasn't in. He wasn't an international master yet and I thought, wrongly as it turned out, he had too many interests to concentrate on chess. Some, like Bird, are more famous than other players even though they're not as strong. Bird had to go in even though he often played rubbish. It's like in motor racing. Stirling Moss is well known, although he was never world champion, but he captured the public imagination.

"For the *Companion* we did a lot of work tracing the reasons for names of openings. Often the Soviets wanted to claim openings, and sometimes it was the other way around, they weren't credited for openings. The Ufimtsev Defence, for instance." This is the Soviet name for the Pirc Defence. It was named after a man who was born with the surname Ufintsev, but when the secret police took his father away for execution in 1937 they recorded the name as Ufimtsev. This mistake may have kept the son safe, as it disassociated him from an "enemy of the people".

"In those days I didn't have a computer, of course," said Whyld. "Everything was handwritten, then typed and typed and retyped. David did most of the problem and study composition entries, but all the other entries were done jointly – one of us would write it and then send it to the other to change, so it was impossible to tell who had written what in the end."

The first edition was published in 1984 and reprinted twice. There was a new, revised, second edition, which has so far been reprinted once. The words of Edward Winter are proudly displayed on the back cover: "It is a masterpiece representing a landmark in the literature of our game." David Hooper died earlier this year and in his memory Whyld is arranging for an annotated collection of his best games to be published. [Since the interview, the book has been published.]

Shortly after finishing the *Companion*, Whyld wrote another popular chess reference book, *Guinness Chess: The Records*. Cross-tables and lists are interspersed with entertaining stories about the world's greatest players, plus a chapter of unusual records. Apparently the shortest game was between Miles and

Reuben at Luton, 1975, when the players agreed to draw without playing a move – assuring themselves of first and second places respectively. The slowest move was made by Francisco Trois, after two hours and 20 minutes. His opponent was Luis Santos. "As there were only two moves worth considering, Santos said he could not see how it could take so long. Trois replied, 'Yo tampoco' (me neither)."

Whyld's most borrowed book is *Learn Chess in a Weekend*, a pocket-sized hardback with lots of photographs. "*Learn Chess in a Weekend* brings me the most public lending right fees of all my books," he said. "There was a stipulation that there should be an illustration after a certain number of words. There are Dutch, Danish, Norwegian, Polish and German editions, and it's going into Czech."

There are no signs that Whyld is slowing down. He travels abroad to give lectures on chess history, he writes articles and a regular "Quotes and Queries" column in *British Chess Magazine*, while his new edition of Emanuel Lasker's games has just been published. He has a long-term project on the go – a biography of Alekhine, which would complement the enormous collection of Alekhine's games by Skinner and Verhoeven. The substantial amount of biographical material on Alekhine left by the former *BCM* editor, the late Brian Reilly, who knew the world champion personally, has been passed on to Whyld for his use.

When I was researching my article on Alekhine for *CHESS*, I went to see Whyld. "If you were here on a social visit, I wouldn't be interested," he told me. The kitchen table was piled high with books and papers. "These are my Alekhine materials," he said. Whyld has Alekhine's original game scores, photographs of Alekhine, letters by Alekhine and even a document proving that a mountain in Australia was named after Alekhine. And, of course, books about Alekhine in a dozen languages.

Whyld buys books for a purpose, not just to line the shelves. "Real collectors aren't interested in what's in the thing, they want a run of something that's perfect or a first edition," he said. "For me a photocopy will do – it's the content I'm interested in. I don't buy something unless I think I'm going to use it. I'm constantly using chess magazines such as *Kagan's*, *American Chess Bulletin*, *Stratégie*, *BCM*. Also I get a lot of queries from people. [Children's TV programme] 'Blue Peter' called – they wanted to know about the history of chess, famous people who'd played. Someone wrote to me wanting me to tell them 'the history of chess', but usually the queries are specific and I can answer them."

Many of Whyld's books contain handwritten dedications from the author: *The Encyclopaedia of Chess* is signed by Golombek – "To Ken Whyld in gratitude for making this book a little less inaccurate." *The World of Chess* is signed by Anthony Saidy – "To Ken Whyld, the world champion of chess historians." *Mezhdunarodny turnir grossmeisterov* is signed by David Bronstein – "To Kenneth Whyld with best wishes." It should be mentioned that Bronstein had been very pleased four years previously to receive an autographed copy of Whyld's own book on the Bronstein-Boleslavsky match.

Once Whyld sent me a newspaper cutting that I couldn't read, because it was in Dutch. But I could understand the headline. The author, Hans Rcc, had decided to call his piece "Ken Whyld – een monument". High praise indeed from the Dutch grandmaster, yet, with characteristic modesty and humour, Whyld has the last word even here: "I told Ree that I thought this was more a comment on my dynamism than importance!"

In April 2002 Ken Whyld married Pat Frankish, a former president of the British Psychological Society, and moved to the village of Kirton Lindsey, 15 miles west of Caistor.

When I was in Nottingham for Mike Basman's schools chess event, I interviewed Cordingley's modern-day successor in the field of specialist chess publishing, Tony Gillam. There are thousands of chess books on the market today, but Gillam was a pioneer. His dedication to finding and preserving lost games is unparalleled. Gillam's story was timeless, and as I had written so many topical articles, it didn't appear in *CHESS* until two years after the interview took place.

The Chess Publisher from Nottingham
(*CHESS*, July 1999)

For those of us who are still on the more energetic side of 30, the era when there were relatively few openings books and games collections is a whole world away. But it's true, there was such a time, and Tony Gillam was one of the innovators who was responsible for bringing chess publishing out of the "dark ages", as he calls it.

Gillam, 55, has dedicated a great part of his life to the preservation of chess games, preferring to live modestly and pursue his passion rather than taking a nine-to-five job. Along with his publishing business, The Chess Player, Gillam earns some money as a Liberal Democrat councillor in his hometown of Nottingham, as well as repping at Foyles, selling books for Chess Direct, and housing a lodger. But it doesn't add up to a fortune. "I don't smoke or drink or drive a car," he told me. "My most extravagant expenditure, apart from my children, is when I go to Holland to look in the library. When I went to Istanbul for three days recently, it was the first thing I'd done for years that wasn't to do with family or chess."

Gillam's unconventional career began when he was a sixth-former at school in Derby. Together with a friend at the same school and four others in Nottingham, they set up The Chess Player around 1961. "I started playing chess as soon as I went to grammar school, but I didn't find the chess club until the second term," Gillam said. "I already thought I knew how to play because I had played with a friend at primary school, but we didn't know the rules properly – we didn't know about castling and *en passant*, for instance. Cerebral activity has always been of more interest to me than physical activity."

The Zürich 1961 tournament was the subject of the first book published by The Chess Player. "That was number 0, because it didn't have a number," said Gillam. "Number 1 was published in May 1961 or 1962 and it was the Budapest 1961 Maroczy Memorial Tournament. It was the old quarto size; the cover was blue. I was getting ready to leave school and the last thing I wanted to do was work. I was too idle to get the exam results to go to university. The only other thing I was interested in was chess."

Unfortunately, publishing tournament books fell far short of paying the rent, so Gillam worked briefly for an insurance company before training as a teacher in 1963. "The business was on the smallest conceivable scale. It was not remotely a full-time business. We knew absolutely nothing about it when we started, none of us had a background in publishing. We were half a dozen enthusiastic young chess players in the provinces. We could only publish things where we could get the information, the bulletins. Slowly we developed contacts to get information from elsewhere. We anglicised things that were in foreign algebraic notation, put them into descriptive notation."

In the 1960s hardly anyone was publishing chess books in Britain, apart from Bell, and occasionally Faber and Pitman. The process of publishing on a small scale was incredibly laborious. "You could either do hot metal typesetting and print them as they used to do in the 19th century, which was expensive, or use a typewriter and duplicator for small quantity, low quality publications," Gillam explained. "Offset litho [a method of printing in which the ink is transferred to a rubber surface and from this to paper] was coming in, it was used initially for facsimile reprints, Dover rehashing the classics.

"Those books were no good for opening theory. The only openings book around was *Modern Chess Openings*. We did typewritten and duplicated books, 200-250 copies initially. In 1965 we had a shot at offset printing. The machine we bought was very poor and it was very unsuccessful. We used it to publish the Candidates matches of 1965, which was appallingly produced but had brilliant content."

The potential for misprints was enormous in those days, due to the difficulty of correcting them. "We went to Hastings and produced the entire tournament. *CHESS* had done that previously, but stopped. We just did the game scores. If there was a typing error in the stencil it was not easy to correct. If you proofread it, you had to take the stencil out and might not put it back properly, so we didn't do much of that. We sold to chess dealers, B.H. Wood and Brian Reilly bought copies and sold them, and so did people on the continent. Fairly soon we went on to English algebraic notation. We did Havana 1963, the Capablanca memorial, in two editions – algebraic and descriptive."

Producing the covers was another challenge. "We did typing, duplicating, stapling, folding and Letraset for the covers," Gillam said. "They were duplicated onto coloured card, called Queen Anne antique board. Most of the books were quarto size – 10 inches by eight. You do know what inches are, don't you?" he joked.

The Soviet Championship of 1963/64 was number 21 in the series, and for this the format was changed completely. "It went onto foolscap paper folded in half, which was a big improvement. By stapling through the fold, the book would open flat. We had to work out where the middle was to type on the other side, by counting the move numbers of every game, so if there had been notes it wouldn't have worked."

Gillam and his friends had some advice from the people who sold them the stencils, paper and duplicator. "The best advice was from Freddy Reilly, the son of Brian Reilly, who owned *British Chess Magazine*. He suggested we went to London to see how they produced the *BCM* quarterlies – they were done on more sophisticated duplicators. We also got some advice on glue-binding books. Freddy was a lovely man, he had a heart operation and never came round."

The loss of Freddy Reilly in 1980 at the age of 50 was a great blow to chess publishing in this country, as he had introduced many ingenious ideas, including a way of adapting the phototypesetting machine to produce figurine algebraic notation. The phototypesetter was a computer-driven machine containing a spinning disk with all the characters on it. When you typed a letter, the disk would stop for an instant and a beam of light would flash, exposing the letter onto photographic paper. "Phototypesetters arrived in the early 1970s," said Gillam. "They were ferociously complicated machines, on which you could only typeset the basic font until Freddy made his changes."

Back in the early 1960s, *BCM* was responsible for another significant development: producing facsimiles of classic tournaments. Later in the decade there were two enormous steps forward in publishing, according to Gillam. "Volume 1 of [Yugoslavia's] *Informator* came out in 1966, a whole new publishing format, a huge leap of imagination. The keen chess player and correspondence player could get something up-to-date for the first time. It had languageless notes, plus and minus signs, the famous triangle, 'N' for novelty, 'TN' for theoretical novelty, the infinity sign on its side for unclear. Short of modern IT [information technology] it is the only way for practical purposes you can produce something of that size and quality for a mass market."

The second major development was the emergence of B.T. Batsford. "The first Batsford book was published in 1968, *The King's Indian Defence* by [British players] Barden, Hartston and Keene, 'a trio of unsurpassed strength', as it said on the blurb!" The chess book collector Michael MacDonald-Ross had told Gillam that there was a big potential market for specialist books on opening theory, but Batsford got there first. "We didn't have the capital or the connections within the book trade to do it," said Gillam. "I was teaching. I stopped teaching at the end of December 1969 and I haven't had a proper job since."

Gillam had bought out the other partners in The Chess Player in 1966, when he left teacher training college. "Since then, apart from my ex-wife and a brief period with David Levy, I have run the business on my own. The address has been my house in Nottingham. I took a positive decision not to get my children obsessed with chess. They know the moves. They're not against the game." One of the original partners became a correspondence international master but died in his 40s. "I can't even remember the names of all the original partners," Gillam admitted.

All of Gillam's chess mania has now been channeled into the search for lost game scores. "I was never really interested in playing," he said. "The highest grading I ever reached was 183, which was off the scale in the circles I moved in, with grandmasters. I would have played better correspondence chess than over-the-board chess. I'm a natural-born ferret, I like looking things up and finding things, like a game by Rubinstein which hasn't seen the light of day for 50 years – I don't necessarily admire it for the wonderful play, I just cross it off on the list of missing games."

Like Mount Everest, which Sir Edmund Hillary climbed "because it was there", Gillam looks for lost games "because they're lost". Although professional chess players are primarily concerned with the latest theoretical novelties, Gillam is adamant that the games of the past matter, too. "You shouldn't lose the basis of your sport. It doesn't follow that what we know is necessarily the right bits. We should have everything that is available to us."

On the other hand, Gillam concedes that old games won't help you to beat Kasparov. "The whole approach of top players is different now. What is definitely superior nowadays is that White plays with the intention of maintaining the initiative. Openings used to be very pedestrian. The opening was about getting it over with and transferring the struggle to the middlegame. Chess now is phenomenally sharper – [Elo] 2700 players of today would wipe out the players of the early part of the century."

Gillam continues his tradition of publishing bare game scores, without notes, but he does sometimes include some colourful background to tournaments. "Chess players buy books obsessively, thank God. Most of them never get opened, I suspect. I wanted to put prose in that they would read so they would feel they got some entertainment out of it. In the Meran 1926 book there are stories about a player who spent all his time in the Alps, and one who took substandard German aspirin sent to Italy as reparations and was ill and lost his last two games."

Some would say that Gillam's determination to track down games that only a handful of people will appreciate borders on fanaticism. "I would love to go to

Warsaw and look in the Polish papers for lost Rubinstein games," he said. "I'm very interested in him because I've spent a lot of time on him. I went to Austria, I spent two weeks looking at Austrian newspapers – I was in Vienna and didn't see the Danube – but I came back with nothing. I can tell you something: all the games of Stockholm 1937 are not lost. It is the only Olympiad on which there wasn't even a book until the one published by *BCM*. A collector in Sweden has the scoresheets. Even more remarkable – the scoresheets for rounds 8-13 inclusive of the Warsaw Olympiad have been discovered, and the games have been published."

Once a game has been found, the circumstances in which it was played have to be verified. "You have to be extremely careful because in those days players had a lot of offhand games, as they called them, during the tournaments, and you can easily mistake them for tournament games. A German player claimed to have won a match against Alekhine – but they were skittles games."

Several previously unknown serious games by Alekhine have turned up in recent years, however. He played a match against Bogolyubov in 1921 that no one apart from the readers of a contemporary Russian chess magazine knew about, and the games were found decades later in Alekhine's notebook. In Budapest he played Alekhine's Defence for the first time and gave the notebook with his games in it to Yugoslav GM Boris Kostic, who sold it to the Yugoslav Federation for their library. They sent a photocopy to Gillam, and afterwards the book was stolen. "Alekhine wrote everything, the times and dates of the games, which was the sealed move," said Gillam.

While most tournament collections appeal to a select bunch, The Chess Player has also published more populist material. When David Levy came into the partnership, he and Gillam launched *The Chess Player* magazine, which was bound into a half-yearly book, like *Informator*, so people could take it as a magazine or a book. It brought Gillam into contact with many of the world's leading players for the first time, and it was part of the basic reference materials of the early 1970s. But The Chess Player's biggest ever coup was the world's first "instant" book, on the Fischer-Spassky match.

David Levy had the idea of asking Yugoslav GM Svetozar Gligoric to write a book that The Chess Player would produce and sell to major publishers. Collins-Fontana bought the British and Commonwealth rights, with Simon & Schuster in New York taking the American side of the deal. There were also German, Spanish and Brazilian editions. During the match, Gligoric telexed the games and annotations across from Iceland to England, so that Gillam and Levy could typeset them day by day. Arrangements were made to print the paperback edition in Manchester at a specialised firm.

The project was formidable anyway, but the intervention of a dock strike stretched everyone to the limit. The strike caused a desperate paper shortage, which Collins coped with by obtaining low-quality paper through business connections. "Someone came up to me at the Frankfurt Book Fair afterwards and described it as Spanish toilet paper!" said Gillam. There were other logistical problems: the German publisher, Droemer Knaur, wanted the book to include some background information, so Bernard Cafferty was employed to translate material from Russian into English. Gillam sent proofs over by airfreight at £10 a time, and the Germans would meet the plane at 10 o'clock in the evening and set to work translating the English into German. Their edition turned out to be a 256-page hardback, twice the length of the English edition.

When it came time to send the first 64 pages of the English edition to the printers, only 63 pages had been written. Gligoric had forgotten to write anything about the playing hall, but luckily Levy had been over to Reykjavik and described the atmosphere to Gillam in conversation, so Gillam wrote a scene-setting page from his memory of what Levy had said – without ever leaving Nottingham. "I remember going to the dentist, but other than that nothing was happening apart from work on the book," Gillam recalled. "There was a lot of running around and telexing."

Collins had to solve the dilemma of how many books to print. This wasn't a problem for Simon & Schuster, as books in America were distributed on a sale or return basis, so tens of thousands could be printed and those that were unsold would be pulped. Collins, however, had to estimate in advance how many books they would sell. "They got it completely wrong," said Gillam. "They thought that because the games had already been in newspapers and magazines, there wouldn't be that much interest in a book. They started off talking about 15,000 copies, the minimum print-run for a mass-market paperback – but I told the printers to do 25,000. When we got to the end of the match, Collins were screaming for every copy they could get."

Simon & Schuster had been more realistic, ordering 50,000 copies and also negatives so that they could quickly reprint the book, which they did. "The Americans immediately printed another 100,000 on better quality paper. It was outselling Reshevsky's book on the match by two to one. My feeling is that the final sale in America was something like 180,000." Collins, meanwhile, got hold of 32,000 copies at first. The printing press had broken down but continued to work – something that might have caused panic, except that Gillam didn't find out until afterwards.

The match finished on a Friday afternoon and the final game was typeset by 10 o'clock that night. Again, Gillam was a page short of the 128 needed, so he put a quote on the last page by *New York Times* chess correspondent Robert Byrne, who had predicted that Fischer would win the match. Someone then drove the artwork to Manchester overnight, delivering it at six in the morning. The books were printed on Saturday and had been bound by midday on Monday. Copies were distributed across Britain that day, well ahead of the rival book by C.H.O'D. Alexander that Penguin was publishing.

"I think they kept one copy for a member of the Collins family who was on holiday, but apart from that, they sold the lot in three days," said Gillam. "A Nottingham bookshop ordered 250 copies; it was only sent 50 and never saw the book again." Following the success of the Fischer-Spassky book, Gillam's business expanded in 1975, when he had a factory and employees in Nottingham's Lace Market, to cast type out of molten lead for figurines. This lasted until 1980, when the typesetting technology changed again and it became possible to work out of an office. Now, of course, the most elaborate publications can be produced on a PC at home.

"Computers are not putting publishers out of business," Gillam says. "Computers require books about computers and books about computer chess. This technology has come at a late stage in my life, but it's a delight to be able to produce books so well in my living room, with no factories, no industrial equipment. Chess diagrams were incredibly expensive to produce until we got computers. I'm now back producing what we were producing in the '60s – tournament books from the 1920s – but they're phenomenally more attractive. Fonts are printed fonts, not typewriter fonts."

Surprisingly, for someone who has trawled the length and breadth of Europe for missing game scores, Gillam hasn't kept copies of all his own books. "The idea is to sell them, so I sell every one," he said. "The Royal Dutch Library asked me for a list – I haven't got a clue. It is several weeks' work to do when I'm very old. I have published 420 to 450 books. If anyone can send me a list I would be deeply grateful, especially numbers 120 to 220 before I started allocating ISBNs."

Gillam did once have a superb collection of other people's chess books, bulletins and magazines, about 4,000 in total, but he became ill in the late '80s, got into debt, and had to sell many of them to pay his National Insurance contributions. "I had the best collection of 1970s bulletins because I exchanged stuff in Eastern Europe," he said. "*The Chess Player* magazine was in demand in Eastern Europe, it was very topical. I bitterly regret getting rid of some of the things, like a book in Estonian called *Chess in Estonia*, copies of *Shakhmatnaya Moskva*, which was sold only at kiosks in Moscow, and I sold a complete run of *Lasker's Chess Magazine* for £13. Nowadays it is worth at least £250 if you can find it. I have still got two walls of my lounge stacked with chess books from floor to ceiling."

One valuable item that Gillam kept was the typewriter that he and his friends used to produce number 1. He now types his invoices on it. "We had it substantially altered so that we wouldn't have to use the shift key to type descriptive notation. We had plus-over-minus signs put on it four years before *Informator*. I can still get ribbons for it."

There has been a publishing revolution since Gillam started in the business, but some things remain constant. He has his circle of loyal readers and he himself remains loyal to the principle of publishing for the sake of it, not for profit. "My stuff is highly specialised. I do what interests me. Older players, chess book collectors, more discerning people buy my books."

Tony Gillam is still devoted to his two main interests: chess publishing and local politics. He has started collecting avidly again, reacquiring all the titles he had to sell off, and now he has more books and magazines than ever before.

If anyone's philosophy is completely opposite to that of Tony Gillam, it's Raymond Keene's. One of Britain's first grandmasters, he is a prolific journalist, author and chess organiser on a lifelong mission to popularise – and profit from – chess. Scandal and ridicule bounce off his balloonish figure without making a dent. He has invoked the ire of fastidious historian Edward Winter and satirical magazine *Kingpin*. Love him or loathe him, Keene's ego is proportionate to his girth.

Jimmy Adams, Mark Huba and I interviewed Keene around the time of his 50th birthday, at the final of *The Times* Schools Chess Championships. This was one of my longest chess interviews, and for a change, I used the Sony Minidisk instead of just my notebook. Keene hardly paused for breath. It took me a week to transcribe the interview, and I never got around to writing it up, until now.

Raymond Keene, OBE: The Most Grandiose of Masters

Raymond Keene decided at the age of 10 that he would one day be *The Times'* chess columnist. He got the job in 1985 and has kept it for almost two decades. Surprisingly, the man with so much drive and ambition was a nervous chess player and gave up the game in mid-career. Keene's personality is complex: there is more to him than the caricature that is often presented in the media, and yet there is much truth in the caricature, too. Oddly for someone so avowedly populist, he never misses an opportunity to show off his erudition.

As a boy, Keene was inspired by *Times* columnist Harry Golombek's book on the 1948 World Championship. "[I] thought, this is wonderfully well written, and it said he was *The Times'* chess columnist, so I thought, right, I'll become *The Times'* chess columnist," Keene said. He had learnt chess from his mother when he was six. "I always remember distinctly... my mother wanted to take a bath and I was whingeing, and she said, 'Here, play with these,' and gave me a chess board and some pieces and I said, 'How?' and she thought I'd just sort of play with them, and I said, 'How do you play?' so she taught me, and she never got the bath. So that's how it happened."

Keene's mother had no inkling that she had spawned a prodigy. "She'd never studied [chess] or anything, but she knew how to play. She wasn't a brilliant player at all... She didn't have a rating or anything, never been to a chess club." Keene was attending Wix Lane Primary School in south London, where academically bright pupils were encouraged to join the chess club. "But I didn't take it terribly seriously until I got to Dulwich College. And then there was a fellow called Sugden, you know John Sugden? I played hundreds and hundreds of games with him, he was quite a bright player, we just played all the time, and, you know, we evolved on the strength of that."

There were few chess books available in Britain in those days. One of the first that Keene came across was *Teach Yourself Chess* by Gerald Abrahams. "By the time I got to see [it], I knew everything in it," Keene said. "The only thing I didn't know were the games collections at the end, when he had some famous games at the end, and those I wasn't aware of. But everything else in it just seemed ridiculously elementary." And this was while Keene was still at primary school. When he went to Dulwich College, he read Nimzowitsch's chess bible *My System*.

"So it was a combination of *My System* and practical play against Sugden. And really *My System* was kind of strange, because I thought it's got to be right and everything, there's this great book, and he's right, so I used to play knight h1 whenever possible on the grounds that it would immediately energise the position. It worked sometimes, you know, the knight suddenly emerged on some great square and won, but once or twice, I had this great attack going and played knight h1, and a few moves later it had to go back from where it had come."

The strange knight move to a corner square had enabled Nimzowitsch to win a great game against Rubinstein in 1926, Keene explained. Another Nimzowitsch move that Keene emulated was queen b8, again putting a strong piece on a remote square at the edge of the board, which contradicts the usual chess rule of centralising your pieces. "I used to play queen b8 whenever possible," Keene said. He retained his fascination with unusual moves throughout his chess career.

Along with *My System*, Keene used to borrow a battered copy of *Alekhine's Best Games* from his local library. "What happened then was that I won a prize at school, I won the prize for literature in the junior school, we had to compare *Animal Farm* with *Treasure Island*, so I won the prize, and usually people were allowed to stipulate what prize they wanted, so I said Réti's *Masters of the Chessboard*, please, and they said bugger off, it's John Betjeman's *Summoned by Bells*, and I developed a longstanding hatred for Betjeman's poetry, and went out and bought *Masters of the Chessboard* instead. So I read that one very avidly, too.

"Golombek's book on Capablanca I thought was excellent, I read that one from cover to cover, as it were. Alekhine's second volume of best games, *Masters of the Chessboard*, *My System*, and I thought Peter Clarke's book on Tal was very good. But paradoxically, I thought his book on Petrosian wasn't. I don't know why. It just seemed to lack sparkle. The book on Tal was absolutely outstanding... And also *500 Master Games* by Tartakower, I thought that was a very good book... There was one more person who had a huge influence, and that was Botvinnik. I read Golombek's books of Botvinnik's World Championship matches... Botvinnik and Petrosian were big influences...

"Nowadays, you want to buy a book of tactical positions, it's pretty easy, but it wasn't so easy then, there weren't so many books around. I mean, when Peter Clarke published his book of Tal's games and Petrosian's games, these were events.

You know, people were sort of waiting for months, has it come out yet? B.H. Wood used to have a little shop in Victoria. I used to roll up there and say, 'Has Peter Clarke's book come out?' and he'd say, 'No, not ready yet,' and I'd go off and come back the following week. And chess publishing then, in this country, was pathetic compared to what it is now. When the books came out they were brilliant books, but they were few and far between."

Keene also read a series of German chess pamphlets on the World Championship matches. "They had a diagram after every five moves, so you could follow the whole game, you know, going on a bus to school, or a train somewhere, you could read it through and see the game as it unfolded. And one of my theories is that you can improve your playing level by studying systematic patterns of advantage and disadvantage. So it's not just, you know, White to play and mate in three – you know, what's the tactic? – it's looking at positions that people agree are better or worse for one side or the other, and getting a mental imprint, a vision of the position."

In around 1961 Keene discovered Clapham Common Open Air Chess Club, near where he lived. "There was a young guy there, about 15 or 16 years old, he said 'Do you want a game?', I said 'Fine,' and I beat him with extraordinary ease. He seemed a bit surprised." Keene was younger than his opponent. "But anyway, we played a whole series of games, I won them all very easily, and he said, 'Do you know who I am?', and I said, 'I've absolutely no idea who you are', and he said, 'My name is Alan Whitbread and I'm the London Under-16 champion.'"

Whitbread advised Keene to enter the event, and the first serious tournament he entered was the London Under-14 Championship. The following year he played in the Under-16 section and was runner-up to another future chess journalist, Bill Hartston. A year later, Keene won both the London Under-18 Championship and the British Under-18 Championship.

"The nearest thing I got to tuition was Peter Clarke, because the British Chess Federation had a scheme in the mid-'60s, where internationals would sort of correspond with promising young players and give them tips," Keene said. "He was quite well-informed and we used to write to each other, he used to send me ideas and I'd send him some of my games, and occasionally I'd go and visit him and we'd go over the games together." Keene and Clarke stayed in touch until 1970, when they prepared for a tournament together by looking at the amazing Spassky-Larsen game from the USSR-World match; later Clarke moved to the southwest of England and Keene heard no more from him.

Keene was at Cambridge University at the same time as Prince Charles, the heir to the throne. There were also several strong chess players, including Bill Hartston and Keene's childhood rival John Sugden. "Apart from the fact that we were all playing each other all the time, there was a lot of competition in club matches and team matches. Nick Paddison was at Cambridge, he was Irish champion at the time." Keene had chosen Cambridge because he thought it was better for chess than Oxford. Chess also influenced his choice of college at Cambridge: he went to Trinity rather than Jesus, where Hartston was.

"I seriously considered becoming a professor of German at Cambridge," Keene said. "I mean, until 1971 I was probably headed for a career at Cambridge, but then I had a sort of strange incident at Cambridge, and I decided to switch to chess full time." Keene expounded at length on this incident, which was a dispute with a professor over his interpretation of the novel *Death in Venice*. After giving a lecture about the composer Gustav Mahler and 19th-century European literature, Keene finally got to the point. His professor had said the hero of the book was a homosexual, and Keene argued that the homosexual love in the story was a metaphor for the quest for an ideal of beauty.

Keene showed the professor a reference to the main character's daughters on page 19 of the book. "My supervisor, the greatest expert in German literature of his day, had not noticed this. So I was told I was stupid, missed the point, and generally thrown out, and told to rewrite the essay I'd just written. And I had a long think and thought, if I pursue an academic career, I'm at the mercy of people who can't read texts properly. You know, it's a lottery.

"If I write something based on my close reading of the text, and the guy has missed it, I'm in danger of not being told, 'Oh, thank you for spotting this' – when if you analyse a chess game and you point out that Botvinnik's 15. h4 is totally unsound, and zap, zap, zap refutes it, it's unanswerable, unless you're wrong. There's an analytical process, there's an objectifying process that says you're either right or wrong. They don't just say, 'You're stupid.' They've gotta say why you're stupid. So I stayed up all night thinking about this and thought, right, time to become a chess professional."

Keene explained how he developed his style of play. "When I started off, I had awful trouble seeing any tactics of any sort whatsoever, and tactical operations were kind of miraculous to me, you know, if I was playing over a grandmaster's game without notes and suddenly they sacrificed something, I thought, Jesus, they've lost a piece. You know, I couldn't understand it. And quite a lot of the early tournaments I played in, I missed fantastic opportunities because I just didn't see the tactics…

"And then I went through this tactical phase where I tried to learn it, and it was done as a corrective – I didn't continue provoking tactics unnecessarily after that, I thought, you know, this is it, I'm going to do it for a while and see what happens, and then I'll emerge at the other end and hopefully the tactics will come. And I found after that I saw the tactics much more easily, and I provoked tactical complications in my games, especially with Black, there were ridiculous complications much of the time, just things that were sort of terrifyingly knife-edge.

"And I think there was a huge amount of tactics in my games. There were always strategic aims, but I wasn't scared of entering tactics if I could work them out. At first, after I'd gone through this phase of provoking them, I'd get into tactical situations where I couldn't foresee what was happening, and I'd just sort of go forward like a sleepwalker, hoping that everything was all right. But gradually I got to the point where I could actually calculate them, and in some of the games I played, I was able to see huge numbers of variations very quickly and very accurately."

Keene had started writing his first book, *Flank Openings*, while he was still at school. It was published in his first year at Cambridge, 1967. Keene researched German chess literature and also Russian tournament bulletins: He had learnt enough Russian to follow chess notes. *Flank Openings* "was very good at the time," Keene said. "It's been superseded a bit... I was very pleased with it... I worked very hard on it... I had a purpose. It wasn't just, this is it, and I had no opinion about it, it was, you know, I have an opinion that these things are very useful openings. And I played them."

During Keene's early career, the top British player was Jonathan Penrose. Keene saw him as a blockade. "I think that he completely buggered his own career by just concentrating on the British Championship... There's only so far you can go in national chess, and I think he did it, and winning the national championship 10 times is pretty bloody remarkable, but he should have stopped. And he should have concentrated on becoming a grandmaster." To do that, Penrose would have had to play in more international tournaments.

"He's become a grandmaster now, I suppose, sort of retrospectively, but he never played internationally seriously. I mean he played in the Olympiads a few times and did well, but whenever he played in a proper international tournament it was usually a disaster. And he was obviously strong enough to be a very good grandmaster, and I think he did himself nothing but damage by not doing it, he certainly squashed the up and coming lot, because the only time I got an invitation to an international tournament was when I won the British Championship in 1971.

"And the Germans thought, ah, new British champion, rang me up and said, 'Do you want to play?' and I said, 'Yes, please,' and I immediately got the IM title, and the fact we went for 10 years without a single English IM was catastrophic, it was absolutely incredible. And getting the IM title then I think was more difficult than getting the GM title is nowadays. But even so, to go for 10 years without getting a single IM is absolutely incredible. And I think that he could have gone a long way in the chess world if he'd decided to just accept a few losses, you know, take it on the chin, and go out and improve. And the fact that people like [John] Littlewood and [Peter] Clarke and [Owen] Hindle could never actually win the British Championship meant that they could never get invitations, because it was the only route to get out of the country, was to win the championship.

"Let's take the World Championship, let's say someone dominated the World Championship. There's nowhere to go from world champion, is there, there isn't sort of grand imperial champion of the known universe, it's world champion and bust, you can't do better than that. And I would say that someone who wins the World Championship and can carry on winning the World Championship forever, more power to his or her arm. And if the others can't take it from him or her, tough shit. But there is something bigger than the British Championship, you know, there's the grandmaster title, there's international tournaments, there's the World Championship, there are other horizons…

"Look at Shirov, he's just achieved his goal of beating Kramnik, what happens, you know, nose-dive in the next tournament. And if you set yourself a tremendous goal, the moment you achieve it, unless you're a really superhuman character, what tends to happen is a rut before you come up again. And what happened with Penrose was, he won the British Championship 10 times, and was hailed in all the magazines as, you know, the supreme, wonderful, marvellous, the greatest ever. Never got another good result in his life. That was the end of it. Bingo. He'd done what he set out to do, and fell off the edge of the plateau…

"In 1975, a mere six years after he won the championship for the 10th time, people, you know, like Ritson-Morry and Golombek, were writing in the reports of the Alexander Memorial Tournament of 1975, you know, that the great players of British chess were Blackburne and Atkins and C.H.O'D. Alexander, didn't mention Penrose at all. Suddenly, the focus had shifted to international chess."

Despite Penrose, Keene progressed. He blames William Ritson-Morry for creating the impression that he played for a draw too often. "Ritson-Morry was a menace… he'd rant on about – that's right, in the '71 British Championship report he was banging on about me agreeing short draws, and he comes to the round where I had this 128-move win against Holt, and says, Keene's amazing incompetence and failure to find the right plan led to an incredibly long game. You just can't win with this man!

"And, you know, my percentage of draws was, you know, no better or worse than anybody else's. With the exception of Basman, who'd go berserk and win half his games and lose the others, but the number of games I won against leading British players was far greater than Basman's, for example. He was the one who was held up as a paragon of virtue, and a wonderful, aggressive player. I won far more games than he did."

Indeed, Mike Basman remained an international master, as did Bill Hartston, while Keene obtained the grandmaster title in 1976. "I'd often thought of giving up, actually, in 1967 almost before I'd started, I had what I considered to be a very bad result at the Churchill Memorial Tournament in Bognor Regis, when I came behind a number of British players. I thought bugger this, I'll never really make a go of this, I'd come behind people like Perkins and Danny Wright. I can't even beat George Botterill, I thought, it's time to give up, and I seriously considered retiring from chess at that point. But I didn't."

The race to become Britain's first grandmaster was a big incentive for Keene to continue playing. Financier Jim Slater, the man who saved the Fischer-Spassky match in 1972 by increasing the prize fund, offered £5,000 to whomever achieved this. "According to current regulations, Bill Hartston should probably have been the first GM," Keene said, "because, you know, now you can freeze your results after X number of rounds, and poor old Bill would have made the GM norm easily in the Hastings '72 tournament. He lost in the last two rounds, and if he'd frozen his result with two rounds to go, he'd have made the first GM norm."

Keene sheds crocodile tears for Hartston, according to *Kingpin*. It quotes Michael Stean, Keene's teammate from the 1974 Nice Olympiad as saying, "It was the first time I was in the England team for the Olympiad. Bill Hartston was number one board, and Ray Keene was on two. Bill was playing very well at the time and he had a good chance of achieving his first grandmaster norm. Bill was more than upset when Keene, who had achieved a norm rating, and didn't want to play on in case he put it in jeopardy, came to an agreement with [captain] David Anderton that he would rest for a few rounds, because Bill was then forced to play a string of difficult games on board one."

Hartston eventually gave up competitive chess. Instead he became the *Independent*'s chess columnist and wrote books. The first British grandmaster was Tony Miles, who obtained the title shortly before Keene by flying to a tournament in Dubna, near Moscow, in February 1976. Miles continued to play in Britain and abroad until his diabetes-related death in 2001, at the age of 46. Stean also achieved the grandmaster title, then stopped playing.

Keene participated in many international tournaments around the world up until 1985, when he ended his playing career at the Lisbon Open. He would look for tournaments in interesting places, like Australia and Indonesia. "The prizes were pretty ropy in general," he said. "There wasn't much difference, usually I didn't make money going to a tournament, I wanted to break even at least. But if you break even going to a tournament, you know, and you go for three months and play in lots of different tournaments, it saves a lot on the expenses at home."

Some of Keene's results were impressive. He won at Dortmund in 1980 and tied for first place at Barcelona the same year. He won the Lloyds Bank Masters tournament in 1981. The British Chess Federation didn't provide much support – except to introduce Keene to his wife, in 1969. "Someone rang up the BCF and said they wanted a chess tutor for their kid, and it turned out it was Annette's brother, and I married his sister, the pupil's sister… The only thing they really did was send me to the Olympiads. There was nothing else they were in a position to do. They didn't have any money. We didn't get paid for going to Olympiads, I mean, we covered our expenses."

Keene drew with former world champion Boris Spassky at an Olympiad. "Against people who were really strong, I felt my thinking was being a bit scrambled," he said. "You know, people like world champions, like Smyslov, Smyslov I had trouble with, Petrosian I had trouble with. Tal, funnily enough, I didn't have trouble with." Keene drew a game against Tal. "I should really have won that game… Gligoric I never had any trouble with at all." Keene won one game against the Yugoslav grandmaster. "I should have beaten him several times. I lost one once, drew lots, and at least one of the draws I was completely winning. You know, if I'd won the game against Gligoric Hastings '68, I would have come second on my own in that tournament.

"I tended to find against really strong players, if I had a completely winning position I'd then make a really stupid move. Or sometimes, you know, I'd play very passively in the opening. I tended to overestimate their chances, I'd think they were doing things they weren't thinking of doing at all… I was devising amazing plans for them that they hadn't actually got at all… I somehow thought they had some sort of magical thing up their sleeve, which actually they didn't have at all.

"I found at the start of my career, when I was playing IMs I'd see amazing things that weren't there, and after a few games against IMs I'd realise that actually they weren't that special, and I started to beat them all the time. And then, you know, against grandmasters I'd tend to sort of see ghosts that weren't there, and after a while I was beating grandmasters all the time. But I never got quite to the stage where I could beat world champions and ex-world champions all the time, that didn't happen."

According to Keene, there is no British champion he has a minus score against. In other words, no British champion has won more games against Keene than they have lost to him. The closest rival was Hartston, who beat Keene twice and lost three games to him, with 26 draws. "And the ones whom I played once, like Julian Hodgson I played once, it was a draw, William Watson I played once, it was a draw. But I think I played 15 British champions and I've got a plus score against almost all of them… Penrose has got a terrible score against me. Four-nil… I think his strategic play was awful.

"I played a huge number of games, I beat Wade once, Penrose twice, Botterill once and Barden once, five games against British champions, where in the final position they actually couldn't move. Almost complete and utter zugzwang. You know, totally run out of moves. Paralysed. It was a strange coincidence."

After losing an interesting game to Soviet defector and World Championship candidate Viktor Korchnoi, Keene considered offering to be his second. "I was thinking about his situation, I thought, he really needs someone with organisational abilities and a lot of imagination to help him. And he had a couple of Dutch guys helping him, Hans Ree was helping him. I know Hans, and he's a nice guy, but he's got the energy of a – well, I mean, he's, you know Hans, don't you? Nice guy, cultured, a writer, but he's not Mr. Dynamic. And he's very sort of laid back, etc., and I thought the combination of talents, I could actually make Korchnoi world champion.

"And I sort of sat up all night after I'd played him and next morning I said to him, I would like to help you become world champion, I think I can do it. And I said, you know, give me carte blanche to invite other people on the team and, you know, get me kind of involved in the process and I think we can do it together. And he said, he thought about it for a while and agreed, and I said, right, I want Michael Stean involved as well, and the first match that he played with our team was the one against Polugayevsky in Evian.

"And I actually think that he would never have destroyed Polugayevsky by that margin if we hadn't been there. He murdered him. And he kept on springing horrible opening surprises on him, too. I actually think that Korchnoi's style was not predicated on surprising people in the opening, it was predicated on surviving until the middlegame and outplaying the other guy.

"And what we did for him, was to give him an armoury of openings ideas that were capable of destroying a classically minded opponent before he got onto the board. And do you remember that English Defence he played against Polugayevsky in game six? Polugayevsky got ripped to shreds in the opening, he didn't know what hit him, you know, you're a Russian grandmaster, you're White, you're supposed to have the initiative by move eight, and, you know, his position had fallen apart."

Keene believes that Korchnoi could have won his World Championship match against Anatoly Karpov in 1978. "Oh yeah. I mean, he needed one major thing, which was not to have [future wife] Petra Leeuwerik there. I mean, Korchnoi was totally paranoid, and she magn-... he shouldn't have had this woman within a hundred miles of an important chess match. He made her his head of delegation.

"So the upshot was that everyone was arguing at jury meetings, you know, what's the colour of the ceiling and can we have a yoghurt, you know [there was a suggestion that different-flavoured yoghurts were being used to signal chess moves]. The last thing Korchnoi wants is to be distracted, and he's easily distracted. He has a fantastic bent towards mysticism. And he needed to be forced rigorously to look at the bloody chessboard. If he'd done that, he would have won, because he was a much better strategist than Karpov in '78. He came incredibly close. And if he'd seen the mate in five, he might have won the match. You know, in this ending when he was chasing Karpov's king round the board, and, you know, played the wrong check, and if he'd played the right check, he would have checkmated the guy.

"It was incredibly stressful, yes, of course it was. Absolutely nerve-racking. You just found out about this problem with the Ananda Marga terrorists, now what was it, there was some bloody problem I cured, oh that's right, we solved the problem with the reflecting glasses and the chairs, and so on, and I invited the rest of the committee round for a drink and said, let's celebrate the end of the problems and getting on with playing real chess, but somebody said there's these terrorists sitting in the front row. I said, 'Oh no,' there were just endless problems. You'd think you'd squashed something, and then something else would turn up.

"It's very strange. It was almost as if he didn't have the confidence in himself to win the match and therefore he wanted to score a propaganda victory against the Russians instead. But the way he went about it wasn't the way to score propaganda victories, anyway – he just made himself look like an idiot."

Some key participants have cast doubt on Keene's version of his role in the Korchnoi-Karpov match. A *Kingpin* investigative article on Keene, "Raymundo Contra Mundum", draws attention to a quote from Petra Korchnoi that appeared in *New in Chess*: "I knew nothing at all about this yoghurt… That was all Keene's doing. He was the one who turned up the heat all the time." In the same article, Korchnoi himself is quoted as saying: "…[Keene's] work for me was not good. After I originally invited him to be my second he said he would complete his work much better if Mr. Stean was invited. But it was clear that while Mr. Keene was writing one book after another, Mr. Stean was doing his work for him… Never in my life would I use him again."

According to *Kingpin*, Stean confirmed Korchnoi's statement in *The Sunday Times*. "I was very disenchanted with Ray because we had been close friends for many years, and had been at Cambridge together. Ray introduced me to Viktor and Viktor and I became very close. Ray and I were on Viktor's team throughout the 1978 cycle of World Championship matches, from the quarterfinals to the finals. At first it was very good, but during the second match [with Spassky] Viktor became concerned at the amount of time Ray was spending writing books and articles. So he said to Ray, if you want to stay in the team you have to choose: are you a journalist or are you a second?"

There was an even bigger scandal over Keene's role as second to Tony Miles at the 1985 Interzonal in Tunis. When I questioned Keene about this, he got defensive for the first time in the interview. "You must have seen the famous [*Kingpin*] cover which said 'First Violin of British Chess or Just a Second Fiddle?'" I asked. "Yeah, I rather like being called first violin of British chess," he quipped. "No, I mean, this was a serious accusation." "I didn't read it." "About the money." "I didn't read it. I don't read *Kingpin*."

"What about this accusation where, you must know about it, where it says that you got about a thousand quid off the BCF for pretending to be Tony Miles' second?" I went on. "I was Tony Miles' second," Keene said. "That's the point. And it wasn't a thousand quid." "Well, how much was it?" I asked. "When I did my accounts after that event, I think I'd made £11 profit."

Why, then, did Miles deny in *Kingpin* that Keene was his second, I asked. "I was completely baffled by this," Keene replied. "I mean, I, the Interzonal he played in was in Tunisia. I had to go anyway, because we were trying to persuade the FIDE executive council there to put the World Championship in London. So I had to be there anyway. And I was discussing it with David Anderton [from the BCF] and said I couldn't arrive before round four or something, or five, or whatever it was, but I'd be happy to be Tony's second, and it would combine the two things and cut down the costs.

"And he said, you know, it may be difficult to – he may suddenly prove difficult, and he said that the way to Tony's heart is always to cut a deal on the money with him. He said, that's how I got him to play in teams before. So when I got there, Miles said, I absolutely don't want a second, and I said, all right, Tony, I'll give you half the fee. And he said, oh yes, that's fine. And then I sat through all his bloody games, he never actually adjourned any games, so I didn't need to do adjournment analysis, but, you know, he got into various scrapes like he tends to, he got thrown out of something and I had to sort of go and defend his interests and things like that.

"Part of the job was sending back reports to the BCF, which I did religiously. I think I made a very good case of recommending us at the FIDE meeting, because we got the World Championship the following year. I thought no more about it. And then two years later I'm accused of stealing money and doing this, that and the other. I was very upset about it."

Miles said in *Kingpin* that he took his cheque for half of the second's fee back to David Anderton, who returned the money to the BCF. "Oh, he should have given it back to me, because it was my cheque," Keene told me. "Well, he says he thought it was unfair to be given this money, and then he sort of links it to you resigning as FIDE delegate," I said. "I got pissed off with them," Keene replied. "I thought I'd done amazing things for the federation [BCF], like get them extraordinary international events... we had a world championship, two world semifinals, a USSR-World match, a gigantic GLC [Greater London Council] tournament, I'd rejuvenated Hastings almost single-handedly by finding sponsors for them, and I thought, the mere thought that they can even remotely suspect me of doing something against their interests was so insulting, I didn't want anything more to do with them."

Kingpin editor Jon Manley analysed this part of the interview in "Raymundo Contra Mundum". Keene must have seen and read *Kingpin*, Manley wrote, because he was sent copies and even contributed an article to the same issue that published Miles' accusations. In fact, Batsford technical editor Ian Kingston showed a copy of that *Kingpin* to Keene, who "read the articles carefully before leaving the building without saying a word".

Keene was telling the truth when he said the fee for being Miles' second wasn't £1,000. It was actually £1,178, Manley wrote. And according to *Kingpin*, this was not the only time that Keene obtained money from the BCF by dubious means.

The first half of the 1986 Karpov-Kasparov World Championship match in London was "a financial disaster for the BCF... the May 1991 *BCM* [*British Chess Magazine*] put the deficit at £17,240 and stated that Keene and Stewart Reuben had agreed to return the fees of £6,000 each received as match organisers".

Kingpin reported that the then-BCF financial director, Mohammed Amin, told *The Sunday Times*: "During the match my belief, whatever they say to the contrary, is that Stewart and Ray set out with the objective of spending the money down to zero and they missed – by about £17,000. They wanted to spend it all and they overspent. They were very lavish."

Keene was at his own chess peak when he stopped playing. "Just before I gave up I achieved my highest ever rating record, I got to 244 on the British rating system. The real thing that convinced me that the time had come to stop making a living out of chess playing was that in 1981, which was actually my most successful year ever... I got a mortgage. And I realised that in order to pay the mortgage I had to win Lloyds Bank Masters twice a month from now on. I thought, this isn't going to work. You know, I'm not going to win the World Championship, it just isn't going to happen.

"It gets more difficult as it goes along, I raced up the rating list when I started, I went phwit, got to number two in the country quite quickly, you know, I think I ended up at 231, which was number two to Penrose in '68, something like that, and the highest rating I ever got was in 1981/82 when I got to 244, so, you know, the last 13 points were by far the most difficult. The rest of it, getting up to 230, was not a problem, it was fighting up from 230 to the middle of the 240s that was the real problem.

"I'd been leading a transient life as a chess player for quite a long time before, I mean, I'd been actually making a living out of it from around 1970, or '68 actually, to 1981, which is quite a long time... I'd been married for seven years. And Annette... she was agitating to get out of Acton [west London], where we were living, and move somewhere more central. And I think she was rather more ambitious than I was in terms of having a normal life, you know, she wanted kids, she wanted a proper house and things like that. And I thought, well, these things aren't really compatible, something has to go. Also, in 1985 *The Times* made me their chess correspondent, so that obviated the need to play in tournaments all the time."

Recovering from two strokes, *Times* columnist Harry Golombek had invited Keene to help him out. They wrote the column together for about five years, then Golombek retired completely. Keene expressed enormous admiration for him. "The thing that I liked about Harry's writing most was that he was a lucid writer who could create a story, and it wasn't just a question of White should go here and Black should do that, and this is better, and what a terrible mistake – it was a kind of narrative. It made the game come alive... I've tried to retain that in everything I write, though I actually think he did it better than I did. His best writing is wonderful."

Golombek was prolific, contributing to *British Chess Magazine* and writing books, but few people can match Keene in terms of sheer output. Nowadays, in addition to his daily *Times* column, he has a weekly column in *The Spectator*. By 1988, according to the blurb on the back of the second edition of Keene's *Leonid Stein: Master of Attack*, he had already authored or co-authored more than 50 chess books. Keene has been criticised, in particular by meticulously accurate chess historian Edward Winter, for paying too little attention to detail. Winter has made long lists of the errors in Keene's books.

"He's trying to get accuracy and he has a very rigid interpretation of what is accurate," Keene said of Winter. "Occasionally, you know, there's a misprint somewhere, and if he points out there's a misprint, that's fine, and it can be corrected, and that's perfectly OK. But some of the things he thinks are inaccuracies, I just don't accept that... Whenever I've made an error in *The Times*, or there's been a misprint introduced by typesetters, which can also happen, er, if someone writes to me and says, this is wrong, I immediately correct it.

"Sometimes the typesetters at *The Times* leave a piece out of the diagram. There's nothing you can do about this. You send in a correct diagram. If they get it wrong, that's it. Sometimes they print the article on the wrong day... I dictate the articles, and I noticed that Giuoco Piano kept on being misspelled... It kept coming out as G-u-i. I realised that the person who was typesetting it thought it was spelled that way, so I said, would you please put an instruction in the computer, from now on, spell it that way. I mean, two days ago I noticed that Peter Svidler's name was spelled with a 'v' and a 'w' on the same day. That's because I write the puzzles separately from the articles, so I said again, please insert into the computer program that we spell – we don't care which way you spell it, but just make sure it's consistent."

Winter savaged the book that Keene co-authored with chess historian Nathan Divinsky, *Warriors of the Mind*. Winter called it "swill", asserting that the authors had "juggled" figures. In *Warriors of the Mind*, Keene and Divinsky applied a mathematical rating system to compare great players past and present. "[Winter] hated it because I think he didn't like the conclusions," Keene said. "I mean, there were some misprints in there. For example, Tartakower got spelled Tartakei, k-e-i... but it was just a misprint.

"I was very upset with the conclusion. But I mean, you know, we set ourselves a certain task, and I didn't like the conclusion that came out the other end, but having done it, we'd asked the question, so we had to wait for the answer... Divinsky and I thought for a long time about what was the right way to establish absolute chess strength, and we decided the right way to do it was to only take games within a certain elite, which we defined as being over 2600, to add a factor into whether people were very young when they played or very old, so that it evened out, you know, gave less weight to those games.

"And I was quite happy that Kasparov came out on top, I thought it was justifiable. When Alekhine came out 18th, I thought, oh shit, you know, there's gotta be something wrong here, but I couldn't work out what it was. I didn't like that, I mean, I think Alekhine is one of the all-time greats, should be in the top five or six. The fact that he'd come out so low really bothered me. And I nagged at Divinsky endlessly to see if there was something we could do about it, but he said, there's nothing we can do, he just lost too many games to Bogolyubov and Euwe.

"And there's no way round that. So I wasn't particularly happy with the outcome, but it's a scientific outcome, reached in a scientific way. And that was the end of it… We asked a question and we got an answer… the figures indicated that Alekhine was not as good as we thought he was… I asked Divinsky to analyse Alekhine's chess strength from, say, 1925 when he won at Baden-Baden until Zürich 1934. That didn't help much. I think the problem was really sort of geopolitical, rather than in himself, in that, I suspect that a lot of people who would have become strong chess masters got killed in the First World War and the Russian Revolution. They were actually wiped out. And the fact that the Soviet Union was isolated from the rest of Europe meant that he wasn't playing their players at all, apart from Botvinnik later on… he was defeating a dying generation."

Keene has even written a book in a weekend, when called upon to do so. "It was a bloody emergency," he said. He was planning to write a book about the Kasparov-Short rapid chess match in 1987, to go with the Channel 4 TV series, when he heard that another London chess organiser, Ali Amin, was going to write one. "And, because we didn't want the games released before they were shown on television, we had to take him to court," Keene said. "And I couldn't start writing our book on the event that was meant to coincide with the TV series until the court case had been cleared up, because I could have written it and then discovered that, you know, there wasn't going to be a book, a total waste of time."

By the time Keene had won the court case, he only had a weekend left to write the book. "You can't normally do it. I mean, there were only six games, lots of it was diagrams, and it was aimed at a television audience, so the comments didn't have to be very deep. I had Annette chained to a typewriter for two days, only allowed to get out for coffee and water and go to the loo. And we managed to get it done. But, I mean, it was a nightmare, I don't want to do that again." This episode is sometimes cited by Keene's critics as an example of his alleged rush jobs on books – but according to Keene, he had no choice, under the circumstances.

Keene's literary talents extend to rewriting Shakespeare. With the Staunton Society he helped raise the money to erect a tombstone for the great 19th-century British player Howard Staunton. "They wanted a quote from Shakespeare to go on the headstone, so I found some quote from Shakespeare, but it didn't quite work, so I rewrote it. And then some gentleman who came along wrote saying, this isn't quite right, it says 'us' and it should have said 'them', or something, but, you know, it works the way it's been done, it fits the context… But, you know, every director does that. Laurence Olivier did that with Richard III, he rewrote Shakespeare wholesale to make it work for the film."

Keene also writes on non-chess subjects. Just before the interview, he had an article in *The Spectator* about intelligence versus appearance. "It's not so much, you know, eat stacks, drink stacks and you'll live for a long time, it was more that developing your intelligence is the way to a better life," Keene said. "And there's this research done in America, as you'll probably know if you read it, that 93 percent of women find intelligent men more attractive than physically attractive men."

On the subject of his chess organising, Keene claims credit for major national and international chess events. "I started organising the Brighton tournaments in 1979," he said. "I got involved in the GLC tournaments in '82 and '84, and from '83 onwards I was organising things left, right and centre. I did the semifinals of the World Championship and in '84 we did the USSR-World match. In '85 we did the Commonwealth Championship in London and in '86 we did the first half of the World Championship. And the other GLC, the final GLC tournament.

"The 1980s was the period when things really took off, with the big GLC tournaments and the World Championships and, you know, the 1980s, all sorts of extraordinary things happened. Many of which, which I say with horrible lack of humility, I actually started and found the money for… I did find the money for the USSR-World and the Korchnoi-Kasparov match, Docklands, the '86 World Championship, you know, things like that."

Humility is not one of Keene's most prominent characteristics. "I think, without necessarily wishing to be, I can be quite dismissive of people," he said. "But if they're, if I find somebody boring or stupid, I find it very hard to conceal the fact. Or even to look remotely tolerant or interested. And quite often when I'm saying we've gotta do this, we've gotta do that, we'll do something else, people can see this as being dictatorial, when in fact I'm trying to be efficient. And often, I try to do things in ways that speed up efficiency, and sometimes this involves cutting corners.

"I don't mean doing things that are illegal, but, you know, not going by what other people consider the rules. So when I was BCF publicity director, for example, I'd often do things that horrified people. Like turning up to a meeting and saying, by the way, we're hosting the USSR-World match next weekend, and things like that… in fact I was thinking, they should be pleased that I've just delivered a world event at five minutes' notice.

"And that sort of thing can terrify people, I mean, if people are, you know, what did somebody say, a foolish consistency is the hobgoblin of tiny minds? You know, if people have that, I have very little patience for that sort of thing, if people can't see the bigger picture, I've got very little patience with them. And I think that sometimes people find this intimidating."

Since leaving the BCF, Keene has shifted his focus towards organising an entirely new annual event, the Mind Sports Olympiad. The first of these was held in London in 1997. Participants compete at a myriad of games, including chess, draughts, shogi, go, Scrabble, memory challenges and cards. "What takes up most of my time is the Mind Sports Olympiad, because I'm determined to establish the Olympic Games for the mind," Keene said. "You've seen what's going on, we just shifted the venue, we had a £400,000 budget last year, it's an enormous event... I think mental sports are potentially capable of generating vastly more interest than physical sports."

Keene disagrees with FIDE President Kirsan Ilyumzhinov's plan to make chess an Olympic sport. "I think that we should have our own Games. I think that to put chess in the Olympic Games is to give it insufficient prominence," he said. I put it to him that mind games don't usually attract many spectators. "The point is that you don't need a stadium," Keene replied. "What you need is a thing called the Internet. That is the modern stadium. In the final hour of the Kasparov game in the Deep Blue match last year, they received 22 million hits. The Internet is the perfect medium for following a mind sport.

"You can play Scrabble on the Internet, that's the point, you don't necessarily have to watch it. You can play it. The thing about a mind sport is that if you're watching a running race, like the 100 metres, and the man you want to win is not doing well, there's only one really valid thought you can have, and that is, run faster. You can't say, oh, you should be doing this, this and this, and when they do that, you should do that. It's run faster. That's all you can do. Or swim faster, or jump higher. If you're following a chess game, it's real time on the Internet, for example, you can be thinking, well, I would go there. And he will go there, and I'd do that and he'd do that and checkmate.

"So by watching, you already become a participant. You elevate your status in the context of the combat to something more than a passive spectator. And I think that mind sports and the Internet in that sense have a tremendous potential synergy." Keene was right about this. Ilyumzhinov has made great efforts to ensure that FIDE has the exclusive rights to show top chess events live on the Internet; Garry Kasparov has organised rival international events on his website, and thousands of people, including most of the world's strongest players, are paid-up members of the Internet Chess Club – playing and watching chess 24 hours a day.

Keene organised the Mind Sports Olympiads with mind games expert Tony Buzan. They also wrote books together: *The Book of Genius*, *The Age Heresy*, and *The*

Book of Mental World Records. Then, once again, Keene landed himself in the middle of a scandal. His sister's husband and longtime business partner David Levy wrote an open letter to him that was published in *New in Chess* and *Kingpin*. Levy said the Mind Sports Olympiad was his idea and accused Keene of misappropriating £50,000 from Mind Sports to set up a new company, Braingames Network plc. The matter was settled amicably. In 2000, Keene and Braingames successfully organised the Kasparov-Kramnik match in London. Later Braingames ran into financial difficulties and was taken over by a company called Einstein, in which Keene is not openly involved.

Ilyumzhinov does not command much respect from Keene. Nor does former FIDE President Florencio Campomanes, who famously stopped the first Karpov-Kasparov World Championship match when Karpov was weakening. "There are degrees, aren't there? I mean, Campo was always short of money, I suspect, and I think his corruption was of one type, but what's happening now is of a different order of magnitude, isn't it?" He correctly predicted that chess players were unlikely to remove Ilyumzhinov. "It's very difficult for chess, which is always strapped for money, to go and kill its golden goose, isn't it?"

Relations between Kasparov and Campomanes strangely mirrored relations between Kasparov and Ilyumzhinov. Keene said it was difficult to oppose Campomanes: "It was an uphill struggle and it cost me a huge amount of money and time. And I was met with universal apathy. No one really cared a toss. And apart from Kasparov, who put his heart and soul into it, but then even he a few years later was forging alliances with the man. That really disillusioned me. And after I saw Kasparov supporting Campo in the FIDE election, I thought, what the hell is the point?

"What Ilyumzhinov has produced, I mean, forget the background and where the finance comes from, and whether or not he's good for female journalists in Kalmykia, what he produced wasn't a World Chess Championship. It was a nice, big, open tournament with lots of prize money. It was not a World Chess Championship. But what Kasparov has produced is not a World Chess Championship, either. He's got Shirov challenging him, which is ridiculous, really, isn't it?" According to Kasparov's World Championship system, Alexei Shirov won the right to challenge him, but the match never went ahead due to the absence of a sponsor.

Keene's son, Alexander, was seven at the time of the interview. Keene was not pushing him to become a chess prodigy, but he did have high expectations. "There are various things I'd like him to do," he said. "I'd quite like him to be a paleontologist. Or an Egyptologist. I think they're superb professions… He wants to be an artist… He's drawing stuff all the time. He's quite well informed, too, sort of does pictures under the influence of Picasso and Cézanne and people like that. But he spells Cézanne S-a-z-a-n.

"He plays Japanese chess, Chinese chess and Western chess. And draughts. And occasionally he plays simultaneous displays, or I play draughts, Chinese chess and shogi, and we each take a board against each other simultaneously. He's very good, he beat me at Chinese chess once. I made a terrible mistake and lost a cannon. And I resigned… It's like losing your queen."

When I met Keene, his book *Samurai Chess* had recently been published. "It's not really a chess book," he said. "It uses chess as a metaphor for strategic thinking. It's not meant to be a book about chess, the chess there is incidental. It's meant to be a book about strategic initiatives… One of the things I like about chess, one of the things that persuades me of the superiority of mind sports, and chess in particular, is that you can do, quite legitimately, what you see choreographed in films by Toshiro Mifune… Thirty people attack the hero…

"You know, he defeats 30 people simultaneously. Whereas in real life that would be a bit hard to achieve. But in chess, you know, a master, a grandmaster, would take on 30 people at once and actually can beat them. Laughingly… It's the laughing, the play, you know, the absorption of the message so thoroughly that you are one with the ethic of the game or the discipline. And when you've reached that mastery, nothing can touch you."

Three Wise Men: A Conversation

It would have been fascinating to bring these three thinkers together in one room, but circumstances did not allow that. Instead, I interviewed them separately and now unite them in a single article. Although they can all remember a wealth of historical events, they are also firmly rooted in the present, highly articulate, and concerned about the future. Despite the difficulties of surviving in chess, journalism and academia in the 20th century, none has lost his lust for life.

Bob Wade was born in New Zealand in 1921. After moving to England he became a chess professional and international master. Three times New Zealand champion and twice British champion, he is also an author, teacher and FIDE official. He was awarded the OBE for services to chess in 1979. Mild-mannered, with a wry sense of humour, Wade generously shares his time and knowledge.

Leonard Barden was born in England in 1929. He was joint British champion in 1954 and achieved the international master title. After giving up competitive chess, he became an author, journalist and junior coach with a reputation for finding and nurturing prodigies. As *The Guardian*'s longest-serving chess columnist, he is meticulously accurate and always on the lookout for unusual stories. Like Wade, he is very approachable, friendly and forthcoming about his successes and failures.

George Steiner was born in Paris in 1929. He has taught at universities in the United States and in England and has held chairs of comparative literature at Geneva

Leonard Barden and Bob Wade at a junior chess event in London.

and Oxford. He is a founding fellow of Churchill College, Cambridge, where I interviewed him. Steiner has had a lifelong fondness for chess and was sent by the *New Yorker* to cover the Fischer-Spassky match in 1972. As a result, he wrote the book *White Knights of Reykjavik.* Steiner frequently alludes to chess in his writings and once said, "Chess may be the deepest, least exhaustible of pastimes, but it is nothing more. As for a chess genius, he is a human being who focuses vast, little-understood mental gifts and labours on an ultimately trivial human enterprise."

HURST: What are your first memories of chess?

WADE: I played a number of years with my father, a farmer, without any literature at all. I had five sisters and one brother, much younger. We did dairy and poultry farming. We sold eggs and milk – if you wanted to buy a chicken to eat at our place you would have been sent packing. I went to a library which had chess rooms, they had magazines, people played. It was in Dunedin. I lived about 20 miles away from there. Some good people came to the chess rooms. The strongest player was J.B. Dunlop, who had been New Zealand champion five or six times. My first game in the New Zealand Championship I beat him.

BARDEN: I learnt chess during bombing raids in Croydon – they sent us down to the school shelters and people in the class started to play chess. I was taught by one of the kids in the class. I went to the chess club at school and Alan Truscott was sitting at the master's desk. The first thing he said to me was, "Can you mate with king and rook?" I couldn't. It really got to me. There was a blitz tournament in the Leipzig Olympiad and I got down to king and rook against an Armenian guy and I had 30 seconds left, I kept thinking about this thing and I couldn't do it in the time.

STEINER: My father was trying to teach my older sister and he let me watch. I was about five, so this was 1934, in Paris. He had as a personal friend the grandmaster Osip Bernstein. Bernstein said whatever move I made he would force me to mate him in a predictable number of moves. This I found awesome. He did it half a dozen times and it gave me a real sense of the light years between a real chess player and an amateur. These were difficult times; he was a refugee.

HURST: Bob and Leonard, what chess books did you read when you were starting out?

WADE: I learnt mainly from chess magazines. *Australian Chess Review* – [Cecil] Purdy, and *BCM* [*British Chess Magazine*]. Purdy used to write a lot in *Australian Chess Review* on the rules of chess.

BARDEN: I used early Fred Reinfeld books like *Chess Mastery by Question and Answer*, books by Znosko-Borovsky. My family was rather poor, I got them from the library. Reinfeld is underestimated, in my view. *Chess Mastery by Question and Answer* I took on holiday to my grandmother's when I was about 14. I felt I was getting better as I read that.

HURST: What else can you tell me about your early playing days?

WADE: In 1945 I went to Australia, almost the first day the war finished. I played in the Australian Championship and came equal second. In 1946 from New Zealand they sent me to the British Championships. I was ill. I went into hospital immediately afterwards, I had arthritis. I was dissatisfied with my performance. I went to Spain, which wasn't so easy in those days. Najdorf won. I played so badly – it took a little while to realise I had a lot to learn in chess. I scored half a point in the first 10 games. Then I got 2½ out of the last three.

[Abe] Yanofsky took me back to Canada, via Iceland and New York. Now I can't understand how I managed to pay for it. I stayed in hotels. In Canada I stayed in Yanofsky's home, travelled the whole length of Canada, went to Texas.

I went to the West Coast of America in '47, then back to New Zealand. I had to see a civil service commission; it wasn't usual to go on three-month leave for 15 months. They found me a new job and after six months I resigned. I came to England in '48. I travelled around Europe for four years. I saw Stalin at the May Day parade in 1950. I was staying at a reasonable hotel as a guest for seven weeks, the Savoy Moscow, I had no knowledge of normal conditions. I always thought the best way to stand up to the Russians, be equal to them, was to learn from them, as Fischer did. I had pneumonia in 1962 in Moscow. Bronstein came to visit me, he brought chess diagrams to show positions from tournaments.

Was I a professional? What do you call someone who enters a monastery – is he a professional? I was available for tournaments. Either Buenos Aires [1960] or the Interzonal in 1952 was the strongest tournament. I drew with Fischer in Havana [in 1965]. I played a lot of chess with Che Guevara. He came and played quick games in Havana. He was [graded] about 170. With the number two, three, four person in a political organisation you can only talk the party line, but with the top person you can actually discuss politics, they can justify themselves, ideas. I didn't agree with him. In the tournament you suddenly realised there were armed guards all round the periphery, that's how you knew he'd arrived. I had a column in the *Daily Worker* and was paid for it, but I wasn't a communist.

In 1954 I started playing for England in the Olympiad. I was a New Zealand citizen. I played for New Zealand in Siegen 1970, and for England in Skopje 1972.

BARDEN: One gets obsessed with chess – I was competitive. I went to Whitgift School in Croydon [south of London], where there was a strong chess player called Alan Truscott who qualified for the final of the knockout championship of London. During the war they had a very strong chess club in the local department store, Kennards, with about 150 members. It met every day, it was run by a retired guy, it had a ladder system. It was down in the basement of the store, next to the hairdresser's.

Julius du Mont, editor of *BCM*, my predecessor on the *Guardian*, was a member, so I inherited the *Guardian* column… I got to know him more after university – I was a strong player and I was writing for *CHESS*. I tended to help him a bit. The *Standard* column started about two years later – they used to have just a problem, no commentary, so I wrote to them about it.

I went down to Hastings for the British Under-18s in 1946, it was a big adventure, I was 16. I had a letter from du Mont saying that G.T. Crown of Liverpool was likely to be my most dangerous opponent. Gordon Crown turned out to be my best friend in chess. [John] Fuller won the tournament, followed by Crown and myself. There were only about 20 players, most of them were local rabbits. Gordon and I played, we had a good game that ended in a draw; you could feel the strength of the guy on the other side.

When I was doing National Service in the RAF in 1947 I had weekend leave in Liverpool and I went to visit Gordon, he was in bed with a stomach problem. We analysed and talked chess. Only weeks later I heard he had appendicitis, he was diabetic, and he died that night. He had beaten Kotov in the Anglo-Soviet match, it was his happiest moment. We met at the British, he knew more theory than I did. I think he would have been better than Penrose. He could channel his energies, he worked at chess, and he was a really nice guy.

Oxford University had the best team in Britain, it won the County Championships and the National Club Championships… I was studying history. My main subject was 16th century history. I trained under good Marxist historians. The first ever Commonwealth tournament was held at Oxford in 1951. Bob Wade represented New Zealand, I was the English representative, and we had the best player from Scotland, South Africa and Canada. I ran the University Team Championship, three boards per team. There were 100 teams, including all the women's colleges.

STEINER: In school I played a lot, at the French lycée in New York. My most interesting experience was about six weeks at the University of Chicago in 1948 or '49. The place was full of people playing at master standard, veterans back from the war who were slightly older than the usual students. They were formidable players. For a few weeks I looked over the edge into the abyss of real chess. They said if you don't want to be a cretinous wood-pusher all your life, be serious. I played chess with them for 16 or 17 hours a day, studying, playing around the clock, blitz, every possible training variety, simuls.

For a few weeks I think I experienced the drug, absolute addiction, where nothing else mattered. Then I returned from the brink, I returned to my studies – I just said "no" one day. I have never in my life touched a narcotic, so I'm at least grateful that I can remember what an LSD trip might be like, absolute closure from the normal world.

HURST: What were some of the highlights of your playing career?

WADE: I got to know Bronstein at Hastings 1953/54, where I beat Tolush and drew with Bronstein and Alexander. At Bucharest in 1954 I beat Kholmov. The chess achievement I am most proud of was when I played Na5 in a game in 1955 against Bhend. I saw what he could do, but he didn't see it himself. I pointed it out after the game to Euwe. At the Olympiad in 1958 I beat Sanguinetti and published in *BCM* the variation that could win for Black if he plays Na5. Two weeks later Fischer beat Reshevsky with it.

BARDEN: I was a late substitute in a tournament, I had to play Keres at Hastings in 1957/58. I was at my best, I spent the best part of a week preparing against d4 and mostly e4. He played c4. He had read that I knew a bit about openings. He put pawns on d3, e3 and f4. He got me with the two bishops. He did exactly the same formation against Tal in the 1959 Candidates tournament. It was my best international result, I finished fourth behind Keres, Gligoric and Filip.

I went through every possible magazine I could and every tournament book, I even went backwards through old books, 19th-century stuff. The opening archives [which Barden famously carried around with him] were about 50 volumes in loose-leaf files. In 1962 on the way to Varna we were going by train, we had to change trains at Munich in a hurry, I had four suitcases.

At my first Hastings in 1950/51 I played Weaver Adams, the guy who believed White could play and win. In the new edition of his book he'd written about the Fried Liver Attack in the Two Knights' Defence. I followed the book against him, I got a tremendous attack, I smashed him up, then I told him I had his book.

I played [C.H.O'D.] Alexander at the British Championships in Buxton, with d4 in the Ruy Lopez. We played a line of my theory and after 12 moves I'd taken one minute and he'd taken an hour. He was psychologically rather damaged by this and I eventually won. I wrote the section of *MCO* [*Modern Chess Openings*] on some lines in the Queen's Gambit Declined. The Barden Archives eventually went to Batsford.

When I won the British Championships the first prize was £35. I had a 10-game playoff with Alan Phillips. [This ended in a tie after one win each and eight draws.]

STEINER: I temporarily got better, but once you don't keep up with opening theory the edge goes very quickly... I could play chess without a board; I could play any variation of the Benoni. It became real wood pushing for me, but always a joy. It led much later to my being sent to Reykjavik. It has brought me pleasure wherever I go. Now I have one or two regular chess partners. I don't play in the Cambridge chess club because the standard is far too high for me, I would make a miserable ass of myself if I played there. I was in the audience at the Kasparov-Karpov match in London. At [Oxford college] Balliol I was an exact contemporary of Leonard Barden.

I played a good deal with Arthur Koestler, who was much stronger than I was. I would love to play Castro once – he's probably far too strong – on a quiet beach in Havana. He adores the game. Once in a simul held in a comprehensive school near here my son and I obtained a draw against a very generous Hartston. I teased Hartston because his wife was with him, she was furious. My son, who was 10 or 11, was so excited and proud of what looked like a drawish position, that Hartston conceded the draw.

HURST: What convinced you to stop playing serious competitive chess?

WADE: I play in the London League [and the 4NCL], sometimes a county match. I'm involved in the organisation of shogi – two of the leading Japanese usually visit me here. I do my best to avoid playing – it's too complicated.

BARDEN: I had very bad results against Golombek, I never beat him... Milner-Barry always had a flask of whisky, I always felt very nervous, I never had good results against him. I had good results against Alexander. Penrose had a plus score against me, but when I was playing White I had a plus score against him. I was a very bad finisher. If all the British Championships I played in had finished in rounds six to nine I'd have had three titles. At one British I was in a terrible time scramble and I also had to write a *Guardian* report, I hadn't looked at any of the games, and I lost. Generally I managed OK to combine journalism and playing.

I had terrible chess vision. In Leipzig we were playing Czechoslovakia, I was adjourned, I took the position down and Clarke said I was the only person in the entire Olympiad who had to take the position down, everyone else remembered them – but some remembered them wrongly. I was very friendly with Clarke and Penrose. We stayed together in the British Championships. We were rivals as well, but it was a good system. More than once we all finished near the top.

I gave up chess because it was very hard work. My last [serious] tournament was in 1964, the qualifier for the Olympiad. I came last. I made the decision to quit on Peter Clarke's doorstep. I decided that was enough. In 1970 I played in the Bayswater tournament, and I was a filler against Gavrikov at the Lloyds Bank Masters when the Russians went to the wrong hotel, where it had been held the year before. In 1994 I stayed with the McShanes, I played about 150 blitz games with Luke, at the time when he played in the Lloyds Bank and got the youngest-ever 2300 result. I had six minutes to his five minutes, then we were about equal. I could still move the bits around. I don't miss it. It's a large chunk out of your day, it's a hassle getting to the venue.

STEINER: In my case it was sheer panic at the notion that I might not be any good anyway. Chess humiliates deeply. I use images, metaphors, similes from chess in my writing. I'm interested in the analogies between war and chess, chess and certain economic enterprises, sex and chess. I once played a very bold woman who offered herself to me as the prize. I drew and I was rather pleased, although I always wonder what really would have happened if I had won. *Luzhin's Defence* is the greatest chess novel we have; I upset [the writer Vladimir] Nabokov when I wrote that the composition of chess problems is to chess what masturbation is to sex. He didn't like that.

HURST: Bob, how did you get involved with FIDE?

WADE: I attended the first FIDE Congress in Paris, 1949. I was put on a subcommittee, and in 1950 I was on everything. I represented Australia and New Zealand. Golombek in '49 and B.H. Wood in '50 were England's representatives. I became an international arbiter in 1958. In 1950 I was one of the five people on the Rules Commission who made up the code. The others were Ragozin, Zubarev, Rogard and B.H. Wood. We rewrote the Laws of Chess. We eliminated old terms. Then they translated it into French – they put the old terms back in. We had a lot of arguments with the translator. Then Golombek came in '52 and he had a good knowledge of French.

We brought in Russian approaches to the rules as well as ones we'd been carrying out. Like claiming a draw by repetition, exactly how to claim it. The rule from 1930 said it had to have occurred three times. But the Russians also allowed you to claim on a move that would make it repeated three times. We changed it to that.

We did this in 1950. We met for about 10 days in Stockholm. We were all practical players, except Rogard.

John Boyd was the first British international arbiter. I learnt a lot from him about rules. I had two main mentors, Boyd and Purdy. Kottnauer was an arbiter. They appointed six from the USSR, one from Yugoslavia, six Dutchmen, the U.S. got three, Germany two, Argentina, Canada, Spain three, England two, France one and so on. A lot were a slight mixture of organiser/arbiter, for instance Sweden had Rogard. They were mainly European-style countries, apart from Argentina. Asia didn't come to an Olympiad until Moscow 1956, unless the Indians played in one before that.

A lot of problems arose – the early ones after the war dealt with the setting-up of the World Championship tournament [to establish a successor to Alekhine, who had died]. The USSR was doing its best to create a monopoly and to some extent was getting away with it. Alexander Rueb, the first FIDE president, was fair-minded. Then there was Rogard, a good lawyer, who had a habit of shaking heads together, making them agree.

We [England] are not producing any people who are good in the corridors of power. This is true of sport in general, the IOC, athletics. We should have more of a say in the direction FIDE's going. Top players in general don't have enough representation in FIDE... Stewart Reuben is part of the World Championship committee and this is an example of where we should be. Our people should talk to players, too. No money is raised for English chess, no appeals are made now. It has to come out of the BCF budget. In the past there have been sponsored simuls. No GM would refuse to give one a year for junior funds.

HURST: Leonard and George, what can you recall about Bobby Fischer?

BARDEN: There were three phases to Bobby's sex life. There was Buenos Aires 1960, where it was assumed he was still a virgin... Then, after winning the World Championship, he decided to search for women and went to a California dating agency. At Varna 1962 he came with a radio, he was twiddling with the knobs. I asked him what he was looking for and he said he was trying to get a Radio Peking broadcast in Spanish, he wanted to learn Spanish. This was how he got onto the Worldwide Church of God. You had to pay tithes – 10 percent of your income. Bobby paid 20 percent and they gave him a flat...

One [girl] was asked how it was with Bobby and she said it was very boring, he could only talk about chess. Then there was the real thing with Zita [Raiczanyi, the much younger girlfriend who helped organise the Fischer-Spassky rematch in 1992].

Barden translated some of Raiczanyi's comments from an interview in German:

"I stayed with him for six weeks in California in 1992. In June 1992 he said OK to the match. He became nervous and grumpy when the chess match was costing him too much energy. We slept separately. I loved him; in the beginning it was just hero-worship, then love grew. He is very difficult and lacks charm, he has a mania, he always says, 'I am the best chess player of all time.' I was repelled by his anti-Semitism and his conviction that there were no concentration camps or gas chambers in World War II.

"He prefers women aged 18 to 20. In 1994 I saw him for the last time, we met on the street, he wanted to propose marriage. I said no, it's too late, I had a boyfriend and I was expecting his child. Bobby went white and walked away without a word. Now I live in the Pest suburb of Budapest. Bobby was a short, unlucky chapter in my life, long since closed."

STEINER: There's one story that I don't think has been published. When he had decided to leave [Reykjavik], after the third game, I think [actually after defaulting game two], and the plane was ready, and everyone was calling him, begging him not to go, but he wasn't answering, [Henry] Kissinger called. [Fischer's second William] Lombardy lost his nerve, said you must speak to him. Fischer was naked, he had thrown his clothes out of the window, but he took the call and then he said to Lombardy, "Who the fuck is this, is he a chess player?" Lombardy whispered, "No, he's the secretary of state," and Fischer yelled down the phone, "Who the fuck are you to talk about chess?" and slammed the phone down. This brought me great joy. He was absolutely right. He was incorruptible at that time.

HURST: Bob and Leonard, tell me about your involvement in junior chess and chess teaching.

WADE: With juniors I had to give them direction and everyone's different, I had to think of things that would unlock doors. I had to teach them to be logical, but also to be different. There are so many different designs of cars now and it's the same thing in chess, so many more openings are playable now. In the Richter-Veresov you create problems for yourself, it's not a flowing development. But you also set your opponent problems. A complete flow is no longer accepted as a necessity, but you have got to still not give up control...

Knowledge is only one part of learning chess – it's not the main part. Knowledge is the enemy of thinking. There's no limit to knowledge, even for a computer. Don't concentrate totally on openings – you get unbalanced. People still think that you can win at chess by knowing – but it will only take you some way. I'm doing a book on thinking...

The most important lesson in chess is the first lesson, where you get taught the moves. If you understand that, you won't spend a lot of time having second thoughts about how they move. You spend a lot of time getting rid of the wrong way of calculating your position. You've got to fit it in so that you don't get blitzed at the end of the game. To write books for a level which you are not at is not hard, you have to put yourself in their shoes, bridge the gap between top chess and their chess.

The Reinfeld books were good, he used to teach chess at night school in New York. You mustn't put people off. They should ask themselves – have I a better move? Look at the whole board, not just at the part of the board you've been deeply engrossed in. Then ask yourself, am I being stupid? Am I ready to present my masterpiece to the world? You should have doubts, not submerge them, but somehow quantify them. You can learn from computer evaluation and apply some of this to the way we approach positions.

BARDEN: [Future GM Nigel] Short won the London Under-10s Championship with a 100 percent score. Most players will take a couple of draws to make sure they don't mess up. When I saw he was getting quite good we had a chance to send a child to Jersey in spring 1974. He got a good score. The thing which really impressed me was that the winner, Gerald Bennett, spent the day after playing blitz with Nigel. Also Short argued with Peter Clarke's suggestions about a game, which is always a good sign. We had a Southern Counties Under-14s Championship and Nigel was one of the top seeds, he was walking up and down with his arms behind his back as GMs do.

I was invited to give the prizes at the London Juniors. We got the *Evening Standard* involved, Stewart [Reuben] was involved, and the thought occurred to have invitation tournaments with masters and juniors. There would always be a trainer to coach people between rounds. [Future GM Julian] Hodgson and other kids were appearing. We took a lot of ideas from what the Russians had done in the '20s and '30s. In a book by David Hooper, *The Unknown Capablanca*, I read that at Moscow 1925 he gave a simul where he lost to Botvinnik. It impressed me that they carted him off to Leningrad in the middle of the tournament, and the next day he lost to Ilyin-Zhenevsky. In 1935 they made him play in Moscow and he got a minus score. Therefore I got the ambition to have simuls with a plus score for the juniors. Petrosian finished only on plus one. He was really angry, he said it was a dirty trick.

In the middle Sunday of the 1977 British Championships, where the juniors were all playing, they had to come up to London from Brighton and Karpov won a clock simul 9½-½. I wanted revenge. We asked Karpov to do a simul the day before Phillips & Drew in Sussex. We had Hodgson and [future GM Daniel] King on the top boards. Anatoly trudged around for about seven hours, lost about five and drew about eight out of 30-something. The next day he drew with Short in the first round. I remember the postmortem, Karpov looked tired!

In the '70s in the junior squad I tried to get these kids all to have a buddy. Nigel always stayed with Daniel King in London. [Future GM Michael] Adams stayed with [future IM] Michael Hennigan, it was an enormous help. I wrote about [future Women's World Champion Maya] Chiburdanidze when she was 12. I wrote about Judith Polgar when she was 11 – a game in Switzerland which I called the female game of the

I reported for *ChessMoves* on a match between prodigy Murugan Thiruchelvam (seated) and IM Andrew Whiteley (standing directly behind him). The other people in the picture are Jimmy Adams (arbiter of the match), Barry Martin (artist and chess enthusiast) and Murugan's father.

century. I first heard about Zsuzsa Polgar when she was five. Szabo came to do the London Juniors' prize giving, he told me about her. When she was 11 I gave a game of hers in a column.

Anand was at a Lloyds Bank Junior Invitational Quickplay. He was a polite little lad with a kind of minder. He was allowed in by Stewart Reuben. At the end of the day he was going to win the tournament, he fought out first prize with Adams. I said he was the first Indian to win in England since Sultan Khan, and he looked bored.

[Current British prodigy] Murugan Thiruchelvam is the second-best eight-year-old I've seen. The BCF is reluctant to put people in for the Under-10s World Championship, we had terrible trouble with Luke McShane [who won the event]... In the '70s I always think I should have pushed the kids harder... People are self-selecting, there is a huge dropout rate among kids between 11 and 18 who realise it's not going to be worth continuing. It's a financial thing, the parents have to be prepared to give most of the support. Adams is a good example, he stayed on to the sixth form at school, after discussions with his father he decided to become a professional. It was the right decision, he wasn't particularly academic.

HURST: George, what's your opinion of British chess past, present and future?

STEINER: The 19th century was a great period of British chess. This question attaches to the absolutely fascinating and very deep anomaly that this is the only country in the northern hemisphere where chess champions are, with certain

242

exceptions, Gentile. The Jewish community in England has been very isolated from the mainstream of intellectual life. That has changed very gradually with the assimilation of British Jews into the full range of British life.

The British chess situation is a very particular one... The sponsorship of young British chess talent, which has flourished, makes this a new, very, very strong and exciting phase, of which Short's bid for the World Championship is a sign. There has been an enormous increase in interest, there is a daily chess column in *The Times*, every serious paper takes an interest in chess.

The future of the game will be computers playing each other at standards of play unattainable to us. Deep Blue will play Deepest Blue. It's the first human aesthetic activity which has been stopped by computers. Kasparov won't beat it, because the drawing power of the machine is so great. Human beings will play each other, but it will be a different kind of activity in terms of the depth of activity available to supercomputers...

We have to accept that chess is finite. Random chess wouldn't help, computers would understand that as well. One is in on a second-rate activity, a very happy pastime at a low level, but I wouldn't study the best games of top players in the same way as I used to hurry to get the latest book by Karpov or Kasparov, I would study printouts... At the moment I'm playing through the two-volume book on Rubinstein, to me he's the most beautiful player of all, but it's like a museum, it's history. I like seeing new things and hearing the music of new composers.

HURST: Leonard, tell me about the various ways you've presented chess in the media.

BARDEN: The first book I wrote was *A Guide to Chess Openings*. I was trying to improve on Fine's ideas in *The Ideas Behind the Chess Openings*. My second book was *How Good is Your Chess?* which I wrote in two weeks – it was very superficial. My best book was *Play Better Chess*, which was published by Octopus. I wrote my third book for Foyles in 1958, it's now published by Dover, *An Introduction to Chess Moves Simply Explained*. I had a girlfriend working for Foyles.

[C.H.O'D.] Alexander approached Pergamon and brought me in on it, we went to see [the late, disgraced publishing magnate Robert] Maxwell, he gave us his visionary thing about how Pergamon would be the greatest chess books of all time. When we left, we said this guy isn't quite right. I did the first Batsford book on the King's Indian with Hartston and Keene. The editor from Pergamon had gone to Batsford and took the idea with him... [Pergamon did, however, publish chess books and also owned *CHESS* magazine for a time.]

In 1965/66 when Spassky came to Hastings just before the first match with Petrosian, I asked him to give me an interview. He talked for two evenings into my tape recorder. He described being adjourned against Tal and looking dishevelled after analysing until five in the morning, and he talked about his first marriage – he told me his first wife had remarried and her new husband was also called Boris Vasilievich. It was one of the best things I ever did as a journalist. I wanted to give him a present to thank him, something special, so I gave him the Barden Archives file on the Caro-Kann so that he could prepare against Petrosian.

In the first game of the match Petrosian played the Caro-Kann and he played something out of the Barden Archives, but unfortunately Petrosian found a way to equalise, so it didn't work out perfectly. Spassky lost that match, so I waited, and when he became world champion the interview got published in [American magazine] *Chess Life*. It showed Boris as a very sympathetic person, which was unusual in the Cold War era. It really helped to get the image of Spassky as a nice guy. The interview is also in the book by Cafferty on Spassky…

I was on [TV chess programme] *The Master Game* up until 1978, for about four years. We had Hodgson and Short on, Short playing Hartston. I was a co-presenter with the BBC guy Jeremy James. It wasn't live. Then Bill [Hartston] took over when the *Guardian* conflicted. It was a very popular programme, better than the things they've done since. As far as the viewers were concerned it was a live game, except when Short won it at 15 the result leaked out.

The games were played normally and the players would do a voice-over giving their thoughts. Karpov beat Miles the first time he was on, but his vocabulary was not very good. Larsen, Gligoric and Lothar Schmid were good. Once we were discussing whether a very long game should continue or whether we should wait until the next day to finish it, and the matter was decided when Hodgson burst into tears, so we carried on the next morning…

The first column I ever wrote for the *Guardian* under my own name was in 1954 – I'd done some when du Mont was ill – I used to give a problem in the *Guardian* which was checked by a problemist in Lancaster, Edward Boswell. I stuck the thing in and the solution was published the next week. I was told that the switchboard was jammed by people pointing out that the key move was stopped by a knight check – it was the first time Boswell had got it wrong in 10 years… and for months later letters came in from all over the world. I was told off by the sub-editor who said the *Guardian* is always accurate, and I narrowly survived with my job. B.H. Wood made two mistakes in a row on the *Sunday Telegraph* and he was sacked from that, although he also did the *Telegraph*.

The *Guardian* deadline is very awkward, I have to write about two weeks before publication. This started during the Fischer-Spassky match – it wouldn't be topical. I used to bash my columns out on a typewriter, but now I have to go into the office and do it on a computer. The *Field* column stopped about two years ago. At one time it was the greatest column in England, it was written by Steinitz, Amos Burn.

Most of the columnists seemed to die in office, while typing – one has this heroic vision of oneself doing the same...

I had an April Fool's mate-in-one problem where there were nine black pawns on the board and whichever one you take off there is a mate in one on the board. I published a problem set by Wade, then published it again 10 years later – no one said anything – then again 10 years later, and it turned out the position was totally drawn!.. People only normally write if they think you've made a mistake.

I haven't been abroad for 30 years. In Varna I would be posting letters home with articles and they just didn't arrive. The logistics were very difficult. By the '70s I had another column to do, for the *FT* (*Financial Times*), and deadlines were stricter... Keene doesn't try too hard. The *Spectator* column is good. Hartston writes well. He's improved over the years, Raymond's got worse. One of the things which encouraged me [as a chess player] was being mentioned in a column – journalists should give more space to British news.

8. Endgame

After *New in Chess* had published my article on Kalmykia, it wasn't difficult to persuade the magazine's amiable editor, Dirk Jan ten Geuzendam, to commission another couple of interviews from me. The first was with Ukrainian prodigy Ruslan Ponomariov, who was playing in the 1998/99 Hastings Premier, where I met him.

Ruslan Ponomariov: No Time to Think about Records
(New in Chess, early 1999)

In its terrible beauty
Towering over the gloomy steppe,
Surrounded by silence,
The anonymous guard of the wilderness
Lies in wait for Ruslan
A menacing and foggy hulk...

...Winter was approaching – Ruslan
Courageously continues on his way
To the far north; with every day
He meets new obstacles:
Either he defeats a warrior,
Or a witch, or a giant.

From: *Ruslan and Ludmilla*, Alexander Pushkin (1799-1837)

Ruslan is a legendary hero, a brave knight who must slay a terrifying warlock if he is to win the ultimate prize. So Ruslan Ponomariov has much in common with the mythical character he is named after, from Pushkin's poem *Ruslan and Ludmilla*. The 15-year-old Ukrainian still has a long path to travel and many battles to fight before he becomes world champion, but he has already attained the grandmaster title – just as Ruslan in the poem must steal a magic sword from a decapitated head, the only weapon that can kill the warlock (Karpov/Kasparov).

In the poem, Ruslan has rivals who are eager to rescue the kidnapped Ludmilla (Ponomariov's eight-year-old sister in real life), but these eager young men fail in their task due to various distractions, including a horde of seductive women. Ruslan the chess player, too, is utterly dedicated to his mission in life. While other children might have shown as much promise a few years ago, Ruslan worked hardest. His first published FIDE rating was an incredible 2550, at the age of 12, and he became the world's youngest grandmaster at 14. "I just played and played, I didn't really think about the record," he says.

When Judit Polgar won the Hastings Challengers at 14, her picture appeared on the front or back pages of nearly every national newspaper in Britain. If Ruslan had won the Premier, we can safely assume that the response would have been more muted. Of course, Judit's victory was extraordinary because she was a girl, not only because of her age. But it is a sign of the times that teenagers are expected to compete at chess on equal terms with adults, and no one assumes that they will automatically become world champion, or even make it into the elite.

Ruslan and his coach are well aware that the real struggle has only just begun. As Paris-based Russian chess journalist Lev Khariton points out, "Ponomariov reminds me of Karpov when he was his age – the same nondescript appearance. But Karpov developed a fantastic tactical talent when he was about 18. Besides, he was brought up by Furman. I don't think today there are such chess players and trainers as Furman around Ponomariov. This is a very important consideration. There are too many competitors today, he has to have a special genius, he has to be charismatic, he has to have a mafia behind his back. No one can reach the top single-handedly."

By coincidence, Ruslan and Karpov have plans to train together for the FIDE World Championship. This is unusual for Ruslan: most of the time he can't afford to work with strong grandmasters. His "senior" coach, Boris Ponomariov (a namesake, not a relative), is rated 2460, well below Ruslan's own rating of 2585. Another coach has also been helping out recently, but at Hastings only Boris accompanied Ruslan. They started working together six years ago, at the suggestion of Boris's father, who runs the Donetsk Oblast Chess Club. He is also a businessman and he paid for the coaching initially. Now Ruslan is sponsored by two Ukrainian companies – AVK, one of the country's largest confectionery manufacturers, and Danke, a metallurgical factory.

Ruslan was born on October 11, 1983, in the town of Gorlovka in the heavily industrialised Don Basin, eastern Ukraine. His mother is a teacher and his father an engineer. Ruslan's father, whom he describes as an amateur player, taught him chess at the age of seven, and sent him to a chess group for young children.

When Boris started coaching Ruslan, the future grandmaster hadn't won a major event yet. He was what the Ukrainians call a first category player, which is almost equivalent to a FIDE master. He only came sixth in the Under-10s Ukrainian Championship, "but his ability was obvious," Boris told me. Ruslan achieved his first big success in 1994, third place in the Under-12s World Championship at the age of 10. The following year, he won the Under-12s world title.

There is one serious disadvantage to becoming a grandmaster at age 14: you can't celebrate properly. "There was a banquet at the tournament and then a party at home that lasted for three days," said Boris. "It was very tiring because in Ukraine we drink vodka, not wine, so after two days I'd had enough. But Ruslan only drank juice."

Personality has played an important role in Ruslan's high-speed chess improvement. "Ruslan has a very tough character," said Boris. "I don't know whether you would describe what he has as talent, but he's very strong-willed and a logical thinker. If he didn't play chess, he would do extremely well at something else, he's very intellectual. I think that chess is a test of intelligence and if you devote all your brain power to chess, you become good at it."

Boris coaches Ruslan full time, so he doesn't play in tournaments. "You should play or not play. I wouldn't enjoy playing here because I would be worrying about Ruslan's game. It's very important for me to watch him playing, that way it's easier for me to spot things that are wrong. We have been together for so long, we are like husband and wife. We argue and swear at each other, but these are mainly creative arguments."

Neither the "husband" nor the "wife" thought it worth mentioning that Ruslan went to live with Boris and his family in Kramatorsk (about 50 km from Gorlovka) when he was nine years old. "Ruslan wanted to concentrate on chess, and this made it easier," explained Ukrainian player Peter Marusenko. Boris did say that Ruslan's picture is on the first page of a book celebrating the 130th anniversary of Kramatorsk. "Everyone there recognises him, but I think he's less popular in the West," he added.

"Until I was 10 I liked Anderssen and Morphy, but now I don't have any particular chess heroes," Ruslan told me. Handsome and smartly dressed in a light blue blazer with a FIDE badge pinned onto it (in contrast to the well-worn T-shirt and sandals of his opponent Jonathan Speelman), he looked like a blond Capablanca. And like the "chess machine," he claims never to have felt any fear, even when he was a little boy sitting opposite a grandmaster.

"What should I have been afraid of? It's not boxing!" he said. Ruslan certainly didn't seem overawed in analysis with Speelman, calmly sitting back as the English grandmaster chattered away in Russian, fingers flying across the board, interrupted only when Ruslan picked up a bishop and placed it on an unexpected square. "That's quite a move," said Speelman.

Ruslan prepares using Chess Assistant, the Russian database, and he is unfazed by the rapid development of computer chess programs – after all, he has never known a time when they didn't exist. "You can get information from computers quickly," he said. "But you can still create your own ideas, computers only help humans to do that." The telephone system in Ukraine is not very advanced and Ruslan has little opportunity to use the Internet. "I don't have direct access to the Internet," he said. "I hardly ever play chess on it, I just use it for reference."

Life on the professional chess circuit has apparently not affected Ruslan's exam results – Boris assured me that he always gets a four or a five, the top marks. But he is only at home for about six months out of 12 and for the past couple of years he has been having lessons on his own. "It's not that interesting to make friends with people of my own age," he said. "We have different interests. I get to know people at tournaments, the players, the organisers... I was friendly with [GM] Mikhail Gurevich at Belfort, for instance. I would describe some of these people as colleagues, rather than friends. There is a difference." Doesn't Ruslan find chess players slightly odd – mad, even? "I don't think chess players are particularly crazy. Certainly not the ones in this tournament," he added diplomatically. "You get ordinary people who are crazy, too."

Few teenagers would be able to cope with the day-to-day routine Ruslan has followed to reach his level of chess. He studies chess for six or seven hours a day, five days a week, and according to Boris, he regularly runs 10 km and swims 2 km. "I don't go with him," said Boris. "I'm lazy – I would die! Chess players tend to lead an unhealthy life, so the fit ones have an advantage."

At weekends Ruslan said he tidies up and goes shopping. For relaxation he reads adventure stories and listens to classical music, but not rock music, which he doesn't like. He is learning English, but hasn't got very far because he has so little spare time. On rest days during tournaments he usually stays in his hotel room and watches television.

"I like being in Ukraine because there are no problems with the language," Ruslan said. "It's interesting to see other countries, but sometimes I get fed up and I want to go home. The time differences make it hard as well. After I've been home for a while I get bored and want to travel again. I was in France before Hastings, so I'm ready to go home again now."

Ruslan's debut in the Hastings Premier didn't start too spectacularly. He and Boris got lost on the way back from a trip to buy fruit in the town, which made them late for the first round and the mayor's opening move. Boris blamed Ruslan, who wanted to take a short cut back to the hotel. "He was like Susanin, who led the Poles through a bog," said Boris. Later in the tournament Ruslan was involved in another incident, when he stopped writing down moves in his opponent's time trouble. The arbiter wanted to give him a time penalty, but the digital game timers were too difficult to reset. Instead, they had to be stopped and then started again a few minutes later.

In general, Ruslan avoids controversy; he would make an excellent diplomat if he ever decided to switch careers. He has no criticisms of FIDE or Kirsan Ilyumzhinov. "Ilyumzhinov has promoted chess, he organised the Karpov-Kamsky match and the knockout World Championship. I know there is some unrest in Kalmykia, but that doesn't affect chess. There's no proof that Ilyumzhinov has anything to do with the mafia – people seem to think that all Russians are in the mafia. When I arrived in France, the taxi driver asked me where I had come from, and I told him Kiev. He said, 'Oh, you must be in the mafia!'"

Ruslan played in the Olympiad as second reserve on the Ukrainian team, scoring 7/9, and he followed this by winning the Donetsk Zonal ahead of 19 other grandmasters, which he considers to be his greatest success to date. He won about $1,500 and the right to play in the next knockout World Championship, which is scheduled to start on June 19. Ponomariov was also the source of enormous local pride: "There are no grandmasters from the Donetsk Oblast, but people love chess very much. About 500 people were watching the tournament on some days. The conditions were excellent, there were several sponsors."

Ruslan is convinced that the FIDE World Championship will take place, despite the cancellation last December. He has no objections to Ilyumzhinov's new system. "More chess players take part because it's a knockout, so there's more interest. If I have to play blitz then I have to, but that's far away – there are two serious games first, and two rapidplay games. The World Championship will show who is the world champion; at the moment it's hard to say. It will still be the World Championship, even without Kasparov. If he doesn't want to play, he doesn't have to. Fischer also didn't want to play Karpov."

Boris is more sceptical about the knockout system: "It's a lottery. You could fall into your opponent's opening preparation and lose – and you lose the whole match. Two games aren't very much." Boris believes that Ruslan already stands shoulder-to-shoulder with the greatest chess players in history. "There's inflation, so you can't compare the world's youngest grandmaster record with Fischer's record. But Ruslan was also the youngest ever under-18 European champion, at 12, and the youngest ever under-18 world champion, at 14. Those events have existed for a long time.

"It's difficult to say whether Ruslan will be better than Kasparov and Fischer, but he could be FIDE world champion at 16 or 18. In Kasparov's system maybe more than a year is needed, because Kasparov works with top grandmasters, he has a whole brigade, he can afford to pay them with his big prizes. In football the players don't have to pay coaches out of their own money – in chess they do."

On the perilous road to the World Championship, Ruslan has no intention of revealing any of his chess secrets. He won't say what his weak points are, because he doesn't want his opponents to know them. Boris describes him as "a very cautious player," which is confirmed by the number of lengthy draws he grinds out. "I try to play as well as I can – I want to be world champion, but I will have to do a lot of work," Ruslan said. "I have no time to write a book at the moment, maybe I will when I'm older. It's not so easy to publish a book in Ukraine, we have economic problems." However, he does write occasionally in the Ukrainian chess magazine *Vertikal*.

Ruslan's main rival hasn't yet fallen by the wayside, of course. A few years ago he drew a game with Etienne Bacrot, the French boy who held the youngest grandmaster record until Ruslan broke it, and they will face each other again at a tournament this spring. "Bacrot is about the same strength as Ruslan," said Boris. "Luke McShane is further behind."

There is always someone lurking in the bushes, ready to ambush the weary traveller, and it is not clear for how long these young players can put up with the kind of pressure they are under, or maintain their thirst for victory. "Maybe Ruslan will do something else when he's older," said Boris. "I think Kamsky was right to give up chess – he'd already earned enough money and played in a World Championship. He had achieved enough."

Ruslan Ponomariov won the FIDE knockout World Championship in 2002, at the age of 18. He was rated 2743 on the 2002 FIDE list, No. 7 in the world (behind the inactive Bobby Fischer at No. 3). Ponomariov's former rival Etienne Bacrot was rated 2653.

Amy Spurling, who had accompanied me to Kalmykia, was living in the Georgian capital, Tbilisi, in spring 1999. I'd always wanted to see Georgia, a holy land of women's chess, and with Amy there I had more of an incentive. Also, I was still working for the magazine *CIS Today*, and by promising to write a number of travel articles, I obtained a complimentary return ticket from an airline. A Georgian advertising salesman in our London office said I could stay with his mother and sister (for a not unsubstantial fee). During my visit I sought out the woman who had become world champion at the tender age of 17, Maya Chiburdanidze.

The Pride of Georgia
(*New in Chess*, mid-1999)

Sitting on an uncomfortable wooden chair in the corridor outside Zurab Azmaiparashvili's office, staring at an Elista Olympiad 1998 poster, I felt horribly nervous. The problem was this: I had wanted to arrange an interview with Maya Chiburdanidze, but the young woman I was staying with in Tbilisi insisted on calling the Georgian Chess Federation herself. As my knowledge of Georgian was limited to "Gamarjobat" ("Hello") and "Garcharad!" ("Stop!"), used when travelling on minibuses, I didn't object. But the result was a few crossed wires.

To make contact with Chiburdanidze, my hostess – also called Maya – rang the federation and was eventually put through to the president, Azmaiparashvili. Maya told him that I was writing for a business magazine called *CIS Today*, as I was doing some other articles for it and I hadn't mentioned *New in Chess*. Azmaiparashvili said there was a funeral on at the chess federation headquarters and no one there could possibly consider organising interviews because they were all too distressed.

After that rejection, I belatedly explained to Maya that it was essential to tell Azmaiparashvili about *New in Chess*. She spoke to him again, and this time his attitude was completely different. In an instant, an appointment was made for me to see him. Actually, all I'd wanted was Chiburdanidze's number, but that isn't the way things work in Georgia. It appeared that I'd thrown myself into the lions' den, because Azmaiparashvili was bound to be a crony of my old enemy Kirsan Ilyumzhinov.

When Maya and I were at last ushered into Azmaiparashvili's office, my fears were not allayed. He looked more like a heavyweight boxer than a chess player. "Why did you come and see me in Tbilisi, if you're from *New in Chess*?" he asked in Russian. "Geuzendam could talk to me anywhere." Now I had to find a tactful way of saying that I was more interested in Chiburdanidze.

I stammered something about not wanting to take up much of his valuable time and that my main purpose was to discuss women's chess in Georgia. I suggested that I could ask a couple of general questions for background. In fact, Azmaiparashvili had plenty to say and we were soon in the midst of a full-length interview.

"There is no women's chess in Georgia now, it's a different generation," Azmaiparashvili said. "Chess used to be a privileged activity in the USSR, especially in Georgia. The emergence of world-famous players like [Nona] Gaprindashvili was particularly important for Georgia. The USSR was trying to prove its intellectual superiority to the world, so a lot of money was invested in chess players. They had a free flat, a car for almost nothing and free all-year-round training. In Georgia, when Gaprindashvili became world champion [in 1962], that put the accent on women." The republic's players held on to the women's world title until Xie Jun wrested it from Chiburdanidze in 1991.

The population of Georgia is just 5.1 million, and in a fiercely proud, chess-mad nation, the impact of producing their first world champion must have been enormous. Gaprindashvili was probably the most famous Georgian since Stalin. In Kalmykia last year she was still being treated like a celebrity, signing autographs for spectators at a blitz tournament.

Did Gaprindashvili's success go against the grain, I wondered, having seen so many women in the former Soviet Union who are prisoners of the kitchen stove and the laundry basket? Not at all, Azmaiparashvili assured me. "It's genetic – women in Georgia have a special position," he said. Some are elevated to extraordinary heights. The revered Queen Tamar, who reigned over the 12th-century "Georgian renaissance", is also known as "King Tamar" because she had all the qualities of a heroic male. Tbilisi itself is watched over by the Mother Georgia statue on a hilltop, holding a wine bowl in one hand and a sword in the other.

The truth behind the myth is that most Georgian women are expected to earn their bread and bake it, too. In other words, they have jobs and are also expected to do all the domestic chores. There isn't any time left for fun or relaxation. "Women pay little attention to entertainment," Azmaiparashvili said. "Chess is work, it's serious. You have to study for at least six hours a day if you are going to be world champion. Women can do this. Southern men need more leisure time. Chess was invented for women. But the world champions didn't do housework," he claimed.

"All the male chess strength in Georgia was directed towards serving the women," Azmaiparashvili said. Indeed, he was surrounded by their faces, staring impassively down on him from framed black-and-white photographs on the wall. In a corner of the room stood the huge gold cup won by the Georgian women in the 1997 European Team Championships.

"The state didn't want to lose its superiority," Azmaiparashvili continued. "All the men, including grandmasters like Gurgenidze and Gufeld, worked for the women. It was a strategy, and it resulted in Maya Chiburdanidze becoming world champion at the age of 17." Eduard Gufeld, who was born in Kiev, trained Chiburdanidze and co-authored a book about her, *Maya's 17 Springs*.

Azmaiparashvili, who is 39, couldn't tell me if it is a galling experience having to devote all your energies to the successes of women chess players, because he managed to escape that. "I helped the women for a bit, Chiburdanidze and [Nana] Ioseliani, then I got together with Kasparov in 1980 and I was lucky – I was in a different orbit." These days, though, Azmaiparashvili and Chiburdanidze do prepare together. They were both injured in a car crash on the way to Elista in May 1998, and this year they went to the Georgian town of Borzhomi together to prepare for the FIDE knockout World Championship in Las Vegas.

Chiburdanidze is one of Azmaiparashvili's few supporters in the messy arena of Georgian chess politics. Gaprindashvili, Ioseliani, [Nino] Gurieli and [Nana] Alexandria are all opposed to Azmaiparashvili's presidency of the federation, he says. "The people who are against me are my age and older. The younger generation supports me. The ones against me are used to their leader being a non-chess player, a member of the Central Committee or something like that. Also, there is the financial crisis. My credo is that we have to respect the history of chess, protect what we have, but I have to stop chess from dying out, support the young chess players."

According to Azmaiparashvili, Georgian President Eduard Shevardnadze (formerly Soviet foreign minister under Gorbachev) signed a decree in 1996 giving 50 percent of the shares in the Chess Federation building to the country's most famous women chess players. The building itself is a two-storey concrete structure in one of Tbilisi's main parks, next to the Philharmonia.

"I said this building is for chess, not for individuals," Azmaiparashvili explained. "The government should give this building to the chess federation so that we can rent out half of it. It's important for us to win the Olympiad, but we shouldn't give so much to six women. This decree was written without consulting a lot of people. The building is named after Gaprindashvili, but that doesn't mean she has to be the owner. Chiburdanidze refused her shares."

Some of Georgia's top women players are living abroad or turning to new professions to make ends meet. Gaprindashvili recently finished a long spell as the head of Georgia's Olympic Committee. Ioseliani lives in Prague and Azmaiparashvili thinks that she may have her own business. Alexandria is a city councillor in Tbilisi, and chairs the committee for sport and culture. Both Ketino Kachiani and Ketevan Arakhamia now live in Western Europe. "We've lost Kachiani, but Arakhamia still plays for Georgia," Azmaiparashvili said.

The Georgian women's team took the bronze medal at the Elista Olympiad, behind Russia and China. "We had a friendly team," Azmaiparashvili said. "But afterwards they started to argue again and to propose a new president. I was elected for four years. If I've committed a crime, they can get rid of me, but if it's personal ambition, they should wait. I won the bid for the European Team Championships, competing against 12 countries. I organised the Women's Zonal. We should be together for the European Team Championships, we should show that we're together, then I agreed to have a congress in December where they could elect a new president if they weren't satisfied with me, even though I've only been in office for two years. The federation's executive committee voted against this proposal. But if they don't want me, I'll go. I just have to finish everything that I've planned to do this year."

The Georgian Chess Federation persuaded FIDE to hold this year's European Team Championships in the Black Sea resort town of Batumi when the British Chess Federation's previously accepted bid was deemed too expensive. The BCF issued a press release blaming the August 1998 rouble crash. Azmaiparashvili says this was not the problem. "The BCF was charging too much. I think lots of countries will come to Georgia. We'll have a charter flight from Germany because it's the centre of Europe and we have good contacts there. We'll have another flight from a centre in Eastern Europe. The price of a ticket won't be more than $350. Hotel rooms will cost between $30 and $35."

At the time of the interview, a venue for the event had not been decided upon, although the local Intourist hotel was a possibility. One thing was certain, however: Azmaiparashvili had no intention of building another Elista-style City Chess. To my enormous relief, he was quite critical of Ilyumzhinov. "They were wrong to build City Chess. What is happening there now? Nothing. And we don't know how they got the money to build it. Ilyumzhinov didn't go back on his word – he said he'd show us, and he did. If you build a tennis court it's better because it brings in income, but chess can't bring in income in Georgia. Wealthy Georgians want their children to play tennis, they think it's prestigious. You get talented people playing chess, but there's no money. Playing on the Internet brings in money, but you don't have to build a chess palace for that."

At the end of the interview, Azmaiparashvili offered to invite Chiburdanidze to his office the next day. I had been under the impression that she was about to leave for Borzhomi. "She won't go until I say we're going," Azmaiparashvili said. We duly reconvened the next day in the same place, with the addition of "Georgia's pride", as one young man described her.

Rumours that Chiburdanidze had retreated into a nunnery were greatly exaggerated, apparently, although she was wearing a black scarf around her head. "I've always been religious, since my childhood," she said. "Someone wrote that I was in a nunnery, but it wasn't true. I've never had any intention of doing that!"

Certainly, Chiburdanidze did not give the impression of being unworldly or distant. Devout, perhaps. Compassionate – yes. She was relaxed and friendly, but quickly steered the conversation away from the subject of religion. "I'm also very interested in homeopathy and folk medicine," she said. "I don't think that conventional medicine brings any more benefit than alternative forms. I have a very close friend who practises homeopathy and I study with him. It's not developed in Georgia, but I think it has a future. It can't do any harm. If it doesn't cure, it won't kill, either."

Chiburdanidze was born in Kutaisi, western Georgia. Her father was an agronomist and her mother a teacher. She has two sisters, who are engineers. Chiburdanidze herself studied in a medical institute and qualified as a doctor, "but chess always took first place," she said. She learnt chess at the age of eight and started having lessons at the Tbilisi Palace of Pioneers shortly afterwards, when it was clear that she had talent. When she was 10 years old she became Georgian girls' champion. "From then on I can say that I was professional. I had very quick successes."

When Chiburdanidze won the World Championship in 1978, Gaprindashvili had already brought interest in women's chess to its peak. "There was an unbelievable atmosphere of chess in Georgia 20 years ago," Chiburdanidze said. "I remember when they had just built this place, for the Soviet Championships: the whole top floor was full of people, the park was full, people were following the games on demonstration boards. I don't know, maybe they got used to it and the interest gradually declined."

Like Gaprindashvili, Chiburdanidze was a national hero. "Everyone knew me. Sometimes it was unpleasant being recognised on the street and I wished I was a normal person, incognito. It's the same now." However, Chiburdanidze said that the top Georgian women players never had a particularly high standard of living. "Nothing changed when I became world champion, we had no material benefits. Only later FIDE started to have a better attitude towards women's chess, bigger prizes."

Chiburdanidze at least received a free flat in the Soviet era. "The government then took culture and sport more seriously," she said. Her status helped her to become a deputy in the Georgian Supreme Soviet for eight years and a delegate to many congresses of the Komsomol (the Communist youth organisation) between 1978 and 1990. "There was a commission for youth, I was on that," she said. "I did all I could using my title. I opened a museum of sport, I helped people when I could. I've left politics now, but chess players still have a significant voice in Georgian society, we have respect."

Women's chess in Georgia was "a phenomenon", Chiburdanidze said. "I think it's unrepeatable, it can't be explained. Nowadays, everything is suffering, not just chess, but we didn't attain such high standards in fields other than chess. I don't want us to lose what we have achieved in chess, because it is easy to lose, but very difficult to get back. I think that this rift with the chess federation is temporary and I hope that people will forget their personal ambitions. I don't like conflicts."

Chiburdanidze scoffed at Azmaiparashvili's theory that southern women succeed at chess because the men are so lazy. "If that's true, then why didn't the same thing happen in Armenia?" she said. But she confirmed the claim that women have a special place in Georgian society. "Women here have equal rights, maybe even more rights than men," she said.

In chess, though, Chiburdanidze sees a considerable difference between women and men. "It's very difficult for women to play against men. There are mental, physical, psychological and even social factors. Women's chess should continue. To abolish it would be like having mixed football or boxing. If chess wasn't a sport, but an art or a science, it would be understandable."

Chiburdanidze added that she gets on well with the Polgar sisters and was sad that Zsuzsa had not been playing recently. "It would be very difficult for Judit to start playing in women's tournaments," she said. "I don't know if she has achieved anything politically by avoiding them, you would have to ask her."

It remains to be seen how Chiburdanidze will fare in the Las Vegas World Championship, where she is paired in the first round against Akopian. She is quietly optimistic about her chances in the next women's World Championship, which as we spoke was still supposed to take place in Moldova, in September. Could she regain the World Championship for Georgia? "Anything is possible," she said, and smiled. By the way, Chiburdanidze's FIDE rating was 2551 in January, while Xie Jun's was 2532.

The eight years that Chiburdanidze has spent as an ex-world champion have actually strengthened her will to return to the top. "I don't have ambitions, I have desires," she said. "At one time I lost my enthusiasm for chess, but it has come back, and I think I'll continue for a bit longer. Strange as it may seem, the enthusiasm came back when I lost the world title. When you're on the throne, you feel a bit inert. It was never easy to keep the title, even against a weak opponent. There was a huge amount of nerves and psychological stress. All the matches were very hard."

Chiburdanidze won 8½-6½ against Gaprindashvili in 1978; then retained the title in 1981 with a score of 8-8 against Alexandria; in 1984 she defeated Levitina 8½-5½; in 1986 she beat Akhmylovskaya by the same score; in 1988 she beat Ioseliani by 8½-7½; and in 1991 she lost to Xie Jun 8½-6½.

The match with Xie took place immediately after the August 1991 attempted communist coup against Mikhail Gorbachev. Tanks had invaded the streets of Moscow and for a while it seemed that the darkest days of the Soviet era might return. After three days the coup failed and the USSR began to break up, with Georgia heading for independence. Understandably, Chiburdanidze was distracted. "I was in a political mood during my match with Xie Jun," she said. "I didn't prepare. It's more accurate to say that I lost the match than that she won it."

Remarkably, Chiburdanidze has never used a computer for preparation. "I'm one of the most conservative players, but I probably will use a computer in the future," she said. "Computers can rule people and you have to control this. The computer disease has had a very damaging effect on chess. Computers can't give you classical ideas – they reduce creativity and make chess mechanical, technocratic. There is far too much information now, I can't imagine what chess will be like in 10 years' time. Maybe it will die, maybe computers will play each other. Maybe people will play Fischer random chess."

Chiburdanidze has been keeping in form recently by playing regularly in events such as the Women vs. Veterans tournaments and for a women's team in Belgrade. When we spoke, the NATO bombing campaign against Serbia had just begun. "I really love Yugoslavia, I've been going there for 20 years," Chiburdanidze said. "It's a genuine chess country, there isn't anywhere else in the world where they love chess as much as in Yugoslavia, not even Georgia. I am very upset about the war, I want peace soon, but only God knows who is in the right."

Italy, Spain and Greece are some of Chiburdanidze's other favourite countries out of the 40 or 50 she has visited. She also likes England, partly because of the help she received in an emergency. Just before playing in the Lloyds Bank tournament in the mid-'80s, she had a tooth out in Moscow. When she got to the tournament, her mouth wouldn't open. Stewart Reuben, the organiser, took her to a doctor, who told her that she would have died if she hadn't come to see him.

Chiburdanidze again narrowly avoided death in the car crash in Kalmykia last year. She described the accident vividly: "It was very hot and we had been driving for four hours. We were 10 kilometres from Elista and we all fell asleep. Kiril Georgiev was in the car, too. I saw a big lorry ahead of us, we were going too fast. The driver had his eyes open and I thought he'd seen it, so I closed my eyes. When I opened them again, I saw that we were 10 metres away from the lorry, I shouted out – if I hadn't, we would have been killed. I didn't know a person could sleep with their eyes open. The driver reacted quickly. Then I don't remember anything, I lost consciousness.

"When I woke up, I had a broken rib and my head hurt. It was a miracle that we weren't killed. I was in a fog when Ilyumzhinov came to the hospital, but I heard his voice. I spent a month in hospital. But I really like Kalmykia, the people are very warm. I have very good memories of the Olympiad. I don't like to get involved in chess politics."

After the interview, Chiburdanidze posed outside in the park for several photographs. In that same spot the next day, a large group of chess players dressed in black gathered for the funeral of a keen amateur who had died of a heart attack caused by an excess of partying over the Easter holidays. To make matters worse, Georgian GM Tamaz Georgadze's wife had also been killed in a car crash at around the same time. A community was in mourning.

As for their dominance on the world chess stage – that, too, is gone. But the enthusiasm for chess still exists in Georgia, and it would not be wise to rule out the possibility of a champion rising from the ashes, even a very familiar one.

In 2002 Maya Chiburdanidze was the No. 4 woman chess player in the world, rated 2516 behind Judit Polgar (2677), the inactive Zsuzsa Polgar (2565) and Xie Jun (2562). Zurab Azmaiparashvili's rating was 2676, the highest in Georgia. He was sharing the presidency of the Georgian Chess Federation with Nino Gurieli.

Chiburdanidze lost to Vladimir Akopian in the first round of the Las Vegas World Championship. The Georgian women's team won the silver medal, behind China, at the Istanbul Olympiad in 2000. Chiburdanidze lost to eventual winner Zhu Chen in Round 5 of the women's World Championship in 2001.

Although I never succeeded in persuading Batsford to publish a book on the history of Soviet chess, I did eventually sign a contract with them for quite a different book. GM Nigel Davies had replaced chess editor David Cummings. My friend IM Gary Lane, a prolific Batsford author, introduced me to Nigel at a Chinese restaurant in London. Nigel had come up with the idea of a book called *Chess on the Web*, and Gary suggested that I should write it. Gary knew that I had some Internet expertise, having co-edited a book for Haymarket, *Winning Business Strategies on the Internet.*

In my excitement about *Chess on the Web* I ignored all the rumours that Batsford was in its death throes. I wrote the book and was paid a few hundred pounds for it. The book came out late and was shoddily produced, with some mistakes on the cover. Batsford was bankrupt. The bigger company Chrysalis bought it up and later commissioned me to write a second edition, which I did, with the help of two very able co-authors, Richard Palliser and Graham Brown.

The second edition was a vast improvement. Batsford didn't take up my suggestion that it should be updated annually, which was a shame because chess websites are changing continually, and *Chess on the Web* ought to have been a kind of guidebook. To promote the first edition I wrote the following lighthearted article for *Kingpin*. It includes some nonsensical word-for-word quotes (typos and all) from the Internet, to illustrate the nature of the medium.

My friend Gary Lane, a prolific chess author, helped get me the contract for
Chess on the Web.

A Tangled Web
(*Kingpin*, spring 1999)

One fine Sunday afternoon, when the sun was blazing down on the lush green
grass of the English countryside and most intelligent people were lying semi-naked
on their balconies or heading for the nearest outdoor swimming pool, MateMe
was sitting in front of the computer as usual, idly toying with her mouse. "I want to
play chess!" she was thinking. "I am desperate to learn everything I can about this
wonderful game which has been in all the newspapers because of the Cathy Forbes
buttock-slapping incident and government minister Tony Banks wanting to make
it a sport, but no one will help me. They're all boring!"

In truth, MateMe had a rather hazy notion of chess. She thought it must be really
exciting. This view had been confirmed that morning, when she logged on to the
Internet Chess Club for the first time. It was full of people with names like Porno,
SlugBucket, BostonStrangler, Severed and ParalyseCabbage. "Enter your handle",
she was instructed, cryptically. She knew only one rule of chess – that the aim of
the game was to checkmate – so she decided to call herself MateMe, without
considering the implications.

The atmosphere at the Internet Chess Club was somewhat confusing. TriviaBot
said: "The notorious 'cold fusion' episode had several examples of 'the dog that

didn't bark' – phenomena whose *absence* should have raised suspicions. All of the following are examples but one; name it. 1. Experimenters dying of radiation sickness, 2. Neutron emission, 3. Dendrite formation on the electrodes, 4. Gamma-ray emission, 5. Buildup of helium-3."

MateMe realised she had completely underestimated the amount of work she would have to do to learn chess. The BCF Yearbook hadn't warned her about particle physics! While she was pondering this, ROBOadmin s-shouted: "A hush fills the room as GRANDMASTER Ariela walks in! :)" Then BrownSugar wrote: "how do you see your tournementstatistics og t-rating?" and JFernandez replied: "tell tomato finger". Now MateMe was completely mystified. She logged off just as Olenin (1287) was seeking bullet 1 0 rated and sumo was shouting: "KILLER ccccccccmmmmwwwwwwww COWKILLER KILERKILERKILERcccccccmmmmwwwwwwww". It was all a bit much. MateMe hadn't felt ready to digest MrSpock's lecture on Complex Endings, Part 2, as she didn't even know how the pieces moved yet.

After lunch, staring glumly at a site called Yahoo!, MateMe was wondering where on Earth to start. "Quick, get me chess!" she typed into the search engine. Seconds later, she was presented with a suggestion: QuickChess. That sounded good, and MateMe cheered up a little. Clicking on the site address, she was immediately assailed by the question, "Challenged by Chess?" Yes, MateMe thought. "You can still be a 'rook'-ie and play. You can even learn in just one 'knight'", the new site promised. Joe Miccio, a New York City firefighter, was the man with the plan. Apparently he invented QuickChess shortly after having a repetitive dream of a rook moving in circles, even though he had no previous business experience of this nature and minimal knowledge of chess.

MateMe was enthralled. A handsome, heroic guy with a brilliant idea – were all chess players like this? She read on. QuickChess was played on a board with 30 squares, and each player had 10 pieces. No need to double those rooks, as you only have one of them! And the instructions came as a comic book, in which the pieces had fanciful and memorable names like Bubba the Bishop and Robok the Rook.

Coloured in bright blue and white, splash-proof, and with smash-proof pieces, too, QuickChess was clearly perfect for beginners who couldn't cope with the enormous, drab, 64-square board. MateMe was about to order a set, when she realised that she didn't have $10 – she had exceeded her overdraft limit when she joined the Internet Chess Club. Bitterly disappointed, she clicked back to Yahoo! in search of a free way to learn.

"Maybe a grandmaster will help me," MateMe thought. "I know, why don't I ask the women's world champion? I am a woman and I like chess, we'll bond instantly." So MateMe connected to the site belonging to Susan Polgar.

In the photograph, Susan was smiling warmly, but all she seemed to want were MateMe's credit card details. "Private Lessons as low as $100," Susan offered. Well, perhaps not, thought MateMe. "I ought to aim lower. I'll go for someone who isn't quite as famous." Somehow she found her way to the site of WGM Anjelina Belakovskaia, chairperson of the Women's Committee of the USCF and leader of the U.S. Women's Olympic Chess Team.

Anjelina came to New York from Moscow with $100 in her pocket – enough for one lesson with Susan Polgar. But she didn't spend it on that. She already understood a few things about the market economy, and soon she got a job in an investment company as a currency trader. Afterwards she became a Professional Chess Player and Chess Teacher. Anjelina still wanted to make money, however, so she decided to charge $75 for an hour's lesson in person or $60 by phone or Internet. MateMe's thirst for chess remained unquenched.

The male grandmasters weren't much cheaper than the women. Cheeky little Gabriel Schwartzman, who boasted that he was very active in teaching chess, including a TV show he produced and hosted for Romanian National Television which aired for eight seasons, wanted $10 per month for membership of his Internet Chess Academy. He does seem to be very clever, thought MateMe. He graduated from Buchholz High School with a 3.95/4.0 Grade Point Average and was now a senior with a 4.0 GPA at the University of Florida, majoring in finance and minoring in telecommunications and economics. He could speak Romanian, English, German and French fluently (and Russian, and Spanish pretty well).

Surfing across the Atlantic to the British Isles, MateMe found herself confronted by a cool, slick-looking young man in dark glasses. Wow, these chess players are something else! MateMe swooned. Nigel Davies implored her to let him turn her into a lean, mean chess machine. "In many cases I have helped players who thought they'd never get much better to improve beyond their wildest dreams," said Nigel. But the Checkerwise PowerChess Program would cost £17.50 per month. I'll save up and buy the book from Batsford instead, MateMe told herself.

Just as she was about to give up hope and resort to doing something healthy outside in the open air, MateMe's deepest desires were unexpectedly fulfilled. It turned out that the slim and photogenic Jon Levitt had published some of his games, problems, studies and extracts from his books, as well as several pictures of himself, all for free! "Are You a Chess Genius?" he asked. "Now is the time to discover your chess talent!" It transpired that MateMe almost certainly was a chess genius, because she quickly deduced the Laws of Chess from looking at Jon's games, and within an hour or so she was solving serieshelpmates with ease. MateMe knew she had an IQ of 150, so it was inevitable that her Elo would be very high, as Jon pointed out.

MateMe felt exhilarated by the knowledge that she was a chess genius, but she realised that being a genius would be useless in this day and age without a deep study of opening theory. It was time to knuckle down and do some hard graft. I like taking risks, thought MateMe. I should learn about gambits.

The place to go for gambits was none other than GambitSite, devised by Thomas Stock, M.D., of Berlin. Thomas was working as a physician at the Bundesinstitut für Arzneimittel und Medizinprodukte (Federal Institute for Drugs and Medical Devices), where he was head of two clinical sub-departments, Oncology and Immunology. He was also keen on Correspondence Chess, Swimming and Snorkeling, Tropical Fresh Water Fishes, Stamps and Computing. MateMe was impressed.

Thomas was an expert in all gambits, including the Elephant, the Blackmar-Diemer, the Belgrade, the Falkbeer Counter-, the King's, the Smith-Morra, the Sicilian Wing, the Latvian, the Icelandic, the Budapest, the Evans, From's, Cochrane's and Steinitz's, but his favourite was the Muzio, which he was writing a book about, called *The Enigma of Signor Muzio*.

MateMe was soon au fait with all the nuances of the Muzio Gambit. However, she felt that Thomas had somewhat neglected the Diemer-Duhm Gambit, so she clicked on the link with the Diemer-Duhm Gambit site, where Jyrki Heikkinen from Finland presented a vast array of opening analysis, texts and games.

"The fun of chess lies more and more with these openings where like mountaineers climbing new peaks you can discover unknown, unbelievable positions at the board," a quote on the Diemer-Duhm Gambit site proclaimed. MateMe was utterly hooked. Chess was as thrilling as she had expected it to be. She felt almost ready to pit her wits against a real opponent, except that she hadn't yet mastered all the chess variants that existed in the world. Fortunately, The Chess Variant Pages provided a swift and easily digestible remedy to this problem.

MateMe was mildly interested in the Oriental chess variants such as Xiangqi and Shogi, unmoved by the small chess variants (they were just poor imitations of QuickChess), bored by chess variants with unequal armies, and less than satisfied by chess with cards and chess with dice. But she was absolutely fascinated by the chess variants with unusual equipment. Playing against herself on her pocket set, she quickly got the hang of atomic chess, in which the pieces explode when taken, and she was riveted by cornersquare chess, in which taking is only allowed when your king is on a cornersquare. Goliath chess, where pieces can shoot after they have captured, was fun, and selfeliminator pieces, where you are allowed to take your own pieces, was a riot.

At last, MateMe had the necessary armoury to make her a worthy member of a chess club. She was hesitant about returning to the Internet Chess Club after her previous unnerving experience, so she decided to look for somewhere with a more peaceful and reflective atmosphere. The Greater Grace Christian Academy chess club in Baltimore sounded like the ideal place.

The site informed her that St. Teresa of Avila was an outstanding chess player who authored a famous treatise on spirituality titled *The Way of Perfection*. She devoted a chapter on how to develop one's ability to receive God's love, and used chess-piece development as an analogy. Momentarily, MateMe was in seventh heaven, until she noticed that all the club's members were kids who lived in Baltimore, a social category that MateMe didn't fit into.

By now it was after midnight and MateMe was getting tired. Her eyelids were heavy and her stomach was rumbling. Still, she was unable to drag herself away from chess, which in the course of a single day had become the centre of her life, a black hole from which she could not escape. For a few seconds she must have nodded off, and a slip of the mouse connected her to an entirely unwished-for destination. Horrifyingly, she had fallen into Dante's Inferno and was surrounded by other tormented chess-playing souls, all trying to grasp at her and pull her down further into the depths of hell.

Virgil, the infernal webmaster, told MateMe that she was in Limbo and would find herself amongst the Lustful, the Gluttonous or the Frauds if she succumbed to the wicked allures of hell's vile inhabitants and managed to defeat them in battle on the e-mail chessboard. Virgil advised MateMe to write to her opponent with the words: "Dear Black. Hi, this is White. I will crush you! My minions will overwhelm your petty forces, dispatching them all quickly to their God in heaven while I continue my headlong plunge into the hideous torments of the Inferno! Here is my first move."

Lashed by flames, shaking with terror, MateMe fled from the Inferno to the friendliest chess club she could find. She relaxed when she landed in Kilkenny, where she could win a prize for composing a limerick or admire a picture of the Heidenfeld Heroes. This could be the club for me, MateMe thought. But it was rather disorganised, and MateMe liked things to run smoothly. A subcommittee formed in 1970 to examine the running of committees in general, in the hope that from the results of its findings a better than average club committee could be formed, reported back in 1980. It found:

"...that solicitors, self-employed businessmen, book collectors, archaeologists and the like became club secretaries. This always leads to conflicts in that the solicitor will always insist that club reports be written in clear and unambiguous language, whereas the businessman will insist on the opposite in case the tax man ever reads them (and sometimes the other way round depending on the honesty/dishonesty of the solicitor/businessman involved!) All the while the book collector and archaeologist insist that no living person be allowed to see a club report as this will enhance its value in the future, as well as insisting that the running of a club is no business of an ordinary club member anyway. The result is usually another 40-page document wherein the second part of the report usually contradicts everything written in the first part!"

Suddenly, MateMe had a staggering thought that illuminated the whole of chess for her in a blinding flash: I'll see if there's a chess club near where I live! By a bizarre coincidence, MateMe lived in Barnet, north London, and Barnet Chess Club just happened to have one of the biggest websites of any club in the world. It had a special historical report on the 2nd world champion Emanuel Lasker, a page linked from the Barnet member section in recognition of Barnet's honorary life member IM Neil Bradbury, an interactive trivia quiz, a Steinitz page, a Barnet Congress pictorial report and much, much more.

Seeing all the happy players laughing and chatting with each other in their cosy clubhouse caused a wave of emotion to surge through MateMe's body. I must be mad, she thought. What have I been doing on the Internet? I'm going to sell my computer tomorrow and join Barnet Chess Club. And she did.

This article also appeared on the GMChess website, run by GM Alexander Khalifman.

My boyfriend Tim Wall had applied for the job of Batsford editor when David Cummings left, but Nigel Davies got it. Tim was unemployed. GM Murray Chandler, the proprietor of *British Chess Magazine*, had promoted him from deputy editor to editor, then Chandler sold the magazine to a group that included chess webmaster John Saunders. Tim's services were no longer required, as Saunders wanted to take over as editor.

My freelance career was also on the rocks: I couldn't squeeze a pay rise out of *CHESS* magazine and Arena, the company that published *CIS Today*, was going bankrupt. It was one of my main employers. I'd invested some of my own money into the Georgia trip, expecting to earn much more back from all the articles I'd written and photographs I'd taken. The magazine published the articles and photographs, but I never got paid. A letter from the official receivers informed me that there was no point turning up to a creditors' meeting, as all the company's assets would go straight to the bank.

Amy Spurling also lost money from this. I'd persuaded her to go from Georgia to Kyrgyzstan via Moscow to interview the Kyrgyz president for *CIS Today*. She achieved this, remarkably, with only a few days' notice. She spent several hundred dollars on the trip and got nothing back, although her article was published in the magazine.

Due to my dire financial straits, when I saw the job of chief sub-editor in Baku for BBC Monitoring advertised in the *Guardian*, I applied for it. The headquarters of BBC Monitoring were in Caversham, just outside Reading, a few miles from Goring-on-Thames, where I grew up and my parents still lived. I was invited for an interview and editing test. Thanks to *CIS Today* I had a fairly in-depth knowledge of current affairs in the Caucasus region. I got the job and was ecstatic, briefly.

Tim and I moved out of our house in London and went to stay with my parents while I trained for six weeks in Caversham. The landlord in London refused to give our deposit back, and also stole the washing machine before we could return it to the rental company, so we had to fend off their demands for money. Then I found out that the chief sub-editor position wasn't a regular BBC expatriate job – I would be treated as a local Azeri employee with none of the benefits that other editors got, like free accommodation.

This was very upsetting news, as the package was much less enticing that it had seemed when I signed the contract. It emerged that I would be liable for 40 percent Azeri tax, while the other editors only had to pay tax at the much lower British rate. I considered quitting, but I didn't feel that I had any other options, other than remaining at my parents' house, broke, indefinitely. I decided to go to Baku, see how the job went, and perhaps look for another job from there.

We flew to Azerbaijan in June 1999. The plan was for Tim to write a book on the opening 1. b3, for which he had signed a contract with a publisher, and he would also try to find work locally. He did get a job with an English-language paper, *The Azeri Times*, which brought in a few hundred dollars a month. My job was rather routine, editing translations of Azeri, Armenian and Chechen media reports.

Azerbaijan was a miserable country, crippled by the war with Armenia over Nagorno-Karabakh and the endemic corruption. I didn't want to stay long. However, there was some interesting activity on the chess front. Michael Greengard, a chess columnist known as "Mig", contacted me asking for help with an Internet

Outdoor chess on the seafront in Baku.

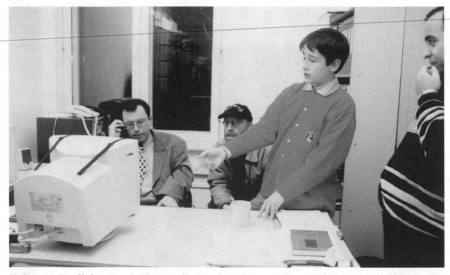

Teimour Radjabov and Tim Wall (on the phone to Israel) dispute a ruling in the KasparovChess Cadet Grand Prix, played via the Internet. This was at the offices of AzEuro Tel in Baku.

tournament, the Cadet Grand Prix, that was being organised by the KasparovChess website in Israel.

The tournament would be the first of its kind, with some of the world's strongest kids competing live from their various countries, including Britain, China and Azerbaijan. Mig needed someone to supervise 12-year-old Teimour Radjabov, the Azeri player, to give him technical assistance and ensure that he followed the rules. I said I'd help, but Tim would do most of the work as he was the experienced chess player.

Teimour attempted to play from the computer at his flat, but the Internet connection wouldn't work properly, so we moved over to the office of Azerbaijan's leading telecommunications provider. After long delays, Teimour got online and eventually won the tournament. Tim continually talked on the phone with the KasparovChess representatives in Israel, and passed on information to Teimour and his family; I sent photographs and an article to the KasparovChess website.

To celebrate Teimour's victory, Tim and I went to a bar and had a couple of drinks. When we got home, he told me that he was in love with a young Azeri woman I'd introduced him to a few weeks previously. I was stunned. He wanted to move out immediately, but I pleaded with him to stay and think things over. He stayed for another month, during which time he interviewed Teimour for *New in Chess* and I took photographs to accompany the article.

After I'd paid for a Valentine's weekend in a hotel, Tim said he was definitely leaving me. It was precisely two years to the day since our first date. The thought of being abandoned in Azerbaijan doing a job I disliked plunged me into depression. I told Tim he had to go back to England for three months, my notice period with the BBC, because I didn't want to see him around Baku. He agreed, and flew home. But without any warning he came back a month later, using the return portion of his ticket that he'd promised to throw away.

Now I was furious and made Tim pay me back some of the money I'd spent on him when we were living together in Baku. He got the money from his parents. Eventually he also had to ask his parents to repay the advance he'd received for the book he was supposed to write, because he'd accumulated piles of research notes, but never managed to write it.

From Baku I applied for a job in China, editing an English-language entertainment magazine called *Beijing Journal*. The publisher in Hong Kong interviewed me briskly on the phone and offered me the job at the end of the conversation. She wasn't concerned that I didn't speak a word of Chinese. In the midst of bitter legal wrangling with the BBC over money that they owed me and I owed them, I finished the job after about a year and went back to England for a few weeks. There I worked on the second edition of *Chess on the Web* and completed it when I arrived in Beijing in July 2000.

Tim stayed in Azerbaijan, became the editor of another English-language paper, the *Baku Sun*, and, as far as I know, still lives there. I heard he married an Azeri woman, but not the one he was originally "in love with". Teimour Radjabov's rise

Thanks to my team-mate, I played for the Democratic Republic of Congo in a tournament at the Slovak Embassy in Beijing. Our opponents in this game were Mongolian diplomats.

in chess was meteoric. He became a grandmaster at the age of 14. In 2002 he was already in the world's top 100 players, rated 2610.

I stayed in China for a year. It was a fantastic experience. I travelled around the country and even learnt a few sentences of Mandarin, which came in handy with taxi drivers. During that time I wrote a couple of chess book reviews for *Kingpin*, and I also started a small chess club in an English pub. A bunch of people from various countries played friendly games over beer and coffee. Some of us also competed in an inter-embassy tournament. As I wasn't a diplomat, I couldn't get permission to represent the British Embassy, so I formed a team with a guy from the Republic of Congo, whose embassy didn't have such rigid rules. Up against chess-hardened Czechs, Slovaks, Romanians and Mongolians, we made a poor showing – but we had fun. I wrote a short report that was published on the Internet.

Beijing Journal wasn't a particularly reliable employer. Editors had an average shelf life of six months, and I was no exception. I was under severe pressure to write content that the advertisers (mainly luxury hotels) would approve of, and we had two virus-ridden computers between seven people. When I became too outspoken about the problems, my employer simply stopped paying my salary. I left the company, but stayed in China for a while longer to work on a satirical novel called *Tofu Tigers*.

Meanwhile, in response to the dearth of available, English-speaking men in Beijing, I had taken up a new hobby: Internet dating. By sheer luck I very quickly found a kindred spirit in a part of America that had close ties with Russia – Alaska. I have dual British and U.S. nationality thanks to my mother being American, so there was no problem with planning a move to the States. After all my travels, going back to England would have been boring. My friends were scattered around the world. Amy was still in Georgia, and Gary Lane had got married in Australia.

After three months of correspondence, live Internet chats and phone calls with Jon Savage, an Alaskan with absolutely no interest in chess, I flew from Beijing to Anchorage. Our rapport in real life was as strong as it had been in cyberspace. We have been living together since we met in June 2001. I now work in the marketing department of the University of Alaska Anchorage. I finished *Tofu Tigers*, and a literary agent in London is seeking a publisher for it.

From my northern perspective, the chess world seems distant. I miss the friends that I made through chess, but I don't miss chess itself. I've seen chess players at their best and their worst. I'm cured of the infection. I only hope that one day I'll be as passionate about something else as I was about chess.

Index